DATE DUE			

9595

The Catholic Tradition:
Sacred Scriptures, Vol. 2

The Catholic Tradition

REV. CHARLES J. DOLLEN
DR. JAMES K. McGOWAN
DR. JAMES J. MEGIVERN
EDITORS

The Catholic Tradition

Sacred Scripture

Volume 2

A Consortium Book

Library of Congress Card Catalog Number: 79-1977
ISBN: 0-8434-0735-2
ISBN: 0-8434-0725-5 series

The publisher gratefully acknowledges permission to quote from the following copyrighted sources. In cases where those properties contain scholarly apparatus such as footnotes, such footnotes have been omitted in the interest of the general reader.

HARRY N. ABRAMS, INC.
Chapter 6 from *Biblical Inspiration* by Bruce Vawter. Copyright ©1972 Bruce Vawter. Reprinted by permission of Harry N. Abrams, Inc.

CAMBRIDGE UNIVERSITY PRESS
Chapter 6 reprinted from *Catholic Theories of Biblical Inspiration Since 1810* by James T. Burtchaell by permission of Cambridge University Press, 1969.

DESCLEE COMPANY
"Formation of the Old Testament" by Pierre Grelot from *Introduction to the Old Testament* by A. Robert & A. Feuillet, 1968.

GEOFFREY CHAPMAN LTD.
Selection from *The Bible, Word of God in Words of Men* by Jean Levie, S.J. © Geoffrey Chapman, a division of Cassel Ltd. Reprinted by permission of Geoffrey Chapman, Ltd.

HARPER & ROW, PUBLISHERS, INC.
Chapter 1 from *A Study of the Synoptic Gospels* by Augustin Cardinal Bea, S.J., edited by Joseph A. Fitzmyer, S.J. © translation, 1965, Augustin Cardinal Bea. Reprinted by permission of Harper & Row, Publishers, Inc.

VERLAG HERDER KG
Selection from *The Relevance of the New Testament* by Heinrich Schlier. © 1967 Herder & Co. GMBH. Reprinted by permission of Verlag Herder KG.

Table of Contents

THE CATHOLIC TRADITION: Sacred Scripture

Ceslaus Spicq
1901-

Spicq was born in Saint Mihiel, France, in 1901. After his ordination as a Dominican priest he did further studies at the Ecole Biblique in Jerusalem before becoming Professor of New Testament at Le Saulchoir in 1928. He held that position until 1953 when he joined the faculty of the University of Fribourg, Switzerland. In his more than half a century of teaching the New Testament, he has demonstrated an extraordinary capacity for work and unusual powers of synthesis.

Père Spicq first came to the attention of the English-speaking clergy when his work on priestly spirituality according to St. Paul appeared in English translation in 1954 as The Mystery of Godliness. *The warmth and simplicity of that work hardly conveyed the exhaustive scholarship that characterized his commentaries on the Pastoral Epistles (1947) and on the Epistle to the Hebrews (1952/1953). Understandably after his monumental two-volume analysis he was asked to prepare the translation and commentary on Hebrews for the* Jerusalem Bible.

Père Spicq belongs to that impressive "second wave" of French Dominican scholars who were inspired by Père Lagrange and made such an extraordinary contribution to the Catholic Biblical renewal, of which the Jerusalem Bible *is only the most visible result. One of his most exemplary traits is his unwilling-*

ness to remain fixed in a position as long as all avenues to fuller understanding have not been explored. Thus, for instance, the fourth edition of his commentary on the Pastorals, appearing 22 years after the first, was completely reworked and earlier positions modified in light of the progress that had been made due to the Dead Sea Scrolls and other factors that came to light during the interim.

Typical of Père Spicq's comprehensive, synthesizing approach is the work sampled here, his exhaustive examination of the key New Testament word for "love," "agape." In the introductory volume brought out in 1955 he explained that his hope was "to understand not only the morality taught by our Lord but also the whole religion of love revealed and founded by Him." His assumption was that a chronological development had taken place that could be traced by careful analysis of the New Testament texts. "Between the Sermon on the Mount and the Apocalypse, "charity" evolved, the notion becoming richer and more precise while remaining homogeneous, since the apostles' teaching was an explanation of the charity revealed by Jesus. A study of the history of the word AGAPE will reveal the evolution of the concept and make it possible to penetrate its profundity."

The three volumes of the English translation divide the material somewhat differently than the original three volumes in French. The first traces the word through the Synoptic Gospels, the second deals with Acts and all the epistles except John's, and the third treats its usage in the Johannine corpus: epistles, Gospel, and Apocalypse. The selection is thus the "grand finale," chapter five of volume three, where he presents a comprehensive conclusion of his investigation of what "love" is in St. John. One may quarrel with certain aspects of such a method, but the results largely speak for themselves. Père Spicq has helped a generation of Christians to find a depth of meaning in the New Testament which few others have been able to match.

AGAPE IN THE NEW TESTAMENT

T he doctrinal content of the texts have been brought out. It is now necessary to compare and harmonize their many teachings and to disengage the principal themes of St. John's thought on *agape*. His writing is far removed from the Jerusalem *kerygma,* which was more or less eschatological, yet "the beloved disciple" is not only the theologian of charity; he is also and above all the witness of love. For him, as for St. Paul and the other apostles, Christ is the gift which God has made to humanity. St. John expresses the evangelical message in his own vocabulary. As his theology became more profound and his personal experience more intense, he summarized the entire mystery of salvation in the divine *agape.* The idea was not an innovation, for the revealed religion had always been presented as God's gratuitous gift and condescendence to men, but in Christ the meaning of his initiative and generous outpouring became clear. No one but the only-begotten Son was able to disclose the nature and secrets of his Father (Jn. 1:18). Only his confidants (15:15) can know that God is love or know what his love means. Everything is clear now that he has come, and the believer is defined as a person who both knows what love is and clings to it (1 Jn. 4:16).

1. God and Jesus

According to the Synoptics, God revealed his love for Christ, a love of sovereign respect and delight, and Christ referred to his Father's signal love for him. The declarations from heaven heard at the Jordan and Tabor are not mentioned by St. John. On the other hand, Jesus' awareness of God's love for him is constantly being represented, and the best expression of their reciprocal relation and union is *agape.*

When Jesus speaks of the divine love for him, he always presents it as the love of a Father for his Son—"the Father loves the Son"—even when God's charity is addressed to the Christ-man. In these cases, the Savior proclaims that the Father is greater than he, and the elements of the Father's love which are emphasized are kindness, intimacy, and the generosity of his gift. "The Father loves the Son and has put all things at his disposal." God manifests his charity by confiding his secrets to his ambassador and giving all power to him. *Agapan,* "to love," and *didonai,* "to give," are almost synonymous, because the generosity of the Father's gift is the expression of his love for his Son. The Father "honors" the Son: he holds him in special esteem; he respects him greatly; and his gifts are his way of giving authenticity to his message—"God the Father has set his seal of approval on him" (6:27; cf. 10:36)—and of proving his *agape* for his Son.

On Jesus' part, his charity for his Father is no less active or generous. It is expressed by a constant fidelity to the Father's will. In Christ's soul there is an exact equivalence between love for God and observance of God's commands "I treasure my Father's commandments and thus secure his love" (Jn. 15:10). His filial love manifests itself in obedience (*tērein tas entolas*). It inspires all his actions (17:6), especially his acceptance of the sacrifice of the cross. "The world must come to know that I love the Father and am acting strictly according to the Father's instructions" (14:31). Jesus' love reveals itself not only in a more or less passive, even though exact, fidelity, but also in a deep accord of wills and a sovereign spontaneity that extends even to total self-sacrifice. It is not so much that the Savior's deeds and actions correspond to the divine orders as it is that his soul thinks and loves as the Father himself thinks and loves. The precise point of their union is the salvation of men by the sacrifice on Calvary.

Christ is like a good shepherd who gives his life for the sheep God has entrusted to him. His obedience is so courageous and so completely inspired by his love for the Father that the Father in his turn manifests even more openly the bond of love

4

that unites him to the Son: "The Father loves me because I lay down my life" (Jn. 10:17). The Father's *agape* includes gratitude for Jesus' love of him, and their love for one another is seen to be permanent, active, and reciprocal. Christ and God never cease loving one another, telling their love to one another, and proving it to one another. Each initiative of one is met by a response of the other. Their relationship is an exchange in which total love is expressed in every sort of way. The Father loves Jesus and lavishes gifts upon him. Jesus loves the Father and glorifies him. The Father is again thankful for what his Son does for him (12:28; 13:31). Jesus, aware of his Father's love, takes pleasure and rejoices in it (15:11; 17:25-26). His joy springs from his knowledge of the Father's delight. It supremely honors the Father. In all truth, Jesus can summarize his spiritual life in these words: "I remain in his *agape*" (Jn. 15:10).

This degree of love cannot be God's love for one of his creatures, even the one chosen above all (Lk. 9:35); it must be the unchanging love which unites two divine Persons in a beatifying delight. Jesus relates the love his Father bears him now to the charity with which he has surrounded him from all eternity, before the incarnation and even before the creation. "You loved me before the world was founded" (17:24; cf. v. 26). In this context, the Father's *agape* is presented as a source of beatitude, since closeness and communion between two persons who love one another bring beatitude, especially if their union is not only a bond but also a mutual indwelling. "The Father and I are one" (10:30). "You in me . . . as you love me" (17:23).

2. Jesus and his disciples

The Master's tender, deep friendship for Martha, Mary, and Lazarus was the admiration of the Jews. He made no attempt to hide his predilection for St. John, a predilection which was at the same time both human tenderness and supernatural attachment. The twelve were especially singled out (15:16), and the Master seemed to have a special affection for Peter (21:15-17). In other words, the *agape* of the incarnate Word took on a thousand different shades which St. John was given the grace to discover and reveal to the world. The "beloved disciple," who rested his head on Jesus' breast during the Last Supper, shows himself uniquely informed of the secrets of the heart which he had heard beat, and he came to understand that Christ is divine love incarnate. More exactly, the only Son came to make the love of the Father present in the world. He incarnated the charity of God which rests on him for all eternity, and he died in order to transmit it to us (17:26). His mission and sacrifice were commanded by the manifestation and communication of the divine *agape*.

St. Paul considered the Savior's whole life an epiphany of God's kindness and "philanthropy" (Tit. 3:4). St. John summarizes it as a deployment of *agape*. "The feast of the Passover was approaching, and Jesus knew that his time for passing from this world to his Father had arrived. He had always loved his own who were in the world, and he loved them to the end" (13:1), that is, he loved them totally. Having shown his love for his disciples all his life long, Jesus gave them the greatest proof of his love during his last hours when he made his supreme confidences to them, entrusting the eucharist to them and, especially, sacrificing himself for them. St. John's description is singularly suggestive of the dimensions of the Savior's charity. He defined Jesus' soul by his charity for the Father and then went on to say that his charity extends to the disciples at the same time. Jesus' love for his disciples has several principal characteristics. It is

a) *A declared love,* affirmed and reaffirmed and always proved. The Lord wants to convince the disciples of his love for them—"I love you"—and he associates his love with the Father's love for him and for men.

b) *A love of respect,* for the Savior's whole mission is ordained to those whom the Father confides to him (Jn. 17: 6, 9) and whom the Father draws to his Son (6:44). This accounts for the value we have in Christ's eyes and for the attention with which he receives us (6:37; 10:29).

c) *A delicate, extremely solicitous love,* which wants to exclude all anxiety and fear from the hearts of those he loves (14:1). It communicates his peace and joy to them and exhorts them to absolute trust.

6

d) *A love of predilection,* because he chose his disciples with a first and gratuitous choice. "I have chosen you" (15:16) as a shepherd who knows his sheep and calls each one by name (10:3, 14).

e) *An intimate love.* "His own" are his familiars, *tous idious,* or even his friends, *hymeis philoi mou este,* whom he initiates into the mystery of the life of the Trinity (15:14-15). Knowing what a trial isolation is, he wants to shield his disciples from experiencing it and he brings about an intimate, mutual presence in spite of physical separation. The presence will be their "abode in love" (15:4-9) as they await the final reunion in the house of the Father. This communion is the supreme wish of Christ's charity. "I in them!"

f) *A merciful and generous love.* Jesus did not come to judge; his entire mission was to save man from darkness, sin, and death. When he offered living water to those who thirst (6:35; 7:37), he wanted to communicate to them a super-abundance of the divine life (10:10; 17:2) and a participation in his glory and his beatitude (17:23-24). Mediator of the divine charity, the Son transmits what he has received from the Father, all that fills him interiorly, his plērōma (1:16). Further-more, he is the way, the truth, the life, the resurrection, and the light (14:6). His gifts are identical with his Person (6:35) so that when he gives himself, he gives all things (1 Jn. 5:11). Can it be said that Christ transmits even greater riches, *meizona toutōn* (14:12)? He will send you "another advocate to be with you for all time to come" (14:15).

g) *A gift-giving love.* "He loved them to the end." Christ manifested his charity to his own from the moment of his first call of them by the lake. He loved them all through the life they lived together intimately like nomads sharing the same tent, and his love culminated in his immolation on Calvary. His sacrifice is a decisive proof of his love and a gesture which shows how great a love it is. Having always loved his own, the Savior ended his life by sacrificing himself for them. This is supreme charity. "No one can give a greater proof of his love than by laying down his life for his friends" (15:13).

The apostles could not help understanding the meaning of such declarations and especially of such actions. They saw the

Master's whole ministry as a manifestation of charity and his death as the decisive revelation of his love. "We know what love is from the fact that Jesus Christ laid down his life for us" (1 Jn. 3:16). According to the Lord's own declaration, his *agape* is identical with his Father's. Jesus loves his own with the same absoluteness and the same delicacy with which God loves his Son. "Just as the Father loves me, so I love you" (15:9). In revealing his own charity, Christ especially wants to make his Father's love known. "I have made known to them your name, and will continue to make it known, so that the love with which you love me may dwell in them." In and through Christ, men can see what God's *agape* is. This is St. John's Gospel.

3. God and the world

It cannot be too often repeated that the essence of the faith of the primitive Church lay in its seeing the life and death of Jesus as a signal manifestation of God's love for men. The incarnation and death on the cross are an epiphany of the Father's *agape*. The captivity Epistles and especially the Pastorals had already taught this lesson, but St. John makes it explicit and repeats it frequently. "So marked, indeed, has been God's love for the world that he gave his only-begotten Son; everyone who believes in him is not to perish, but to have eternal life" (Jn. 3:16). "God's love was made manifest among us by the fact that God sent his only-begotten Son into the world that we might have life through him" (1 Jn. 4:9). This is the summit of "revelation" and the center of the Christian religion. The coming of Christ to earth, his life, and his death on the cross are historical facts, and believers discover a mystery in these particular events. They contemplate the "glory" of the Son-made-flesh, who reflects his Father's divine nature (1:14), and they understand that Christ's gift begins in the divine charity and is ordained to procure them eternal life, participation in God's own life. In the Sermon on the Mount Jesus had proposed his Father's kindness as an example to his disciples. Because he loves all men, even thankless ones, God generously gives them all they need for the life of the body. The angels had praised the heavenly *eudokia* which proposed salvation for men and reconciliation of sinners with God (Lk. 2:14). The Virgin Mary

8

and Zachary sang the mercy of the Almighty. After Christ returned to his Father, the apostles meditated upon his teachings and his stay among them. They concluded that the Savior had been sent because of the divine mercy, and they also understood the nature and extent of his *agape*. Their knowledge of charity grew as their faith in the person of Christ grew.

Christ is more than an ambassador, more than a revealer full of grace and truth, more than the Messiah, more even than a Savior who sacrifices himself personally. He is God's only Son. "Everyone who believes that Jesus is the Christ is born of God" (1 Jn. 5:1). His only-begotten Son is the person whom God honors and cherishes above all others. That the Father has turned him over to sinners in order to bring them to a part in his own life is proof of an infinite love which no human imagination could ever have conceived. The price of the gift reveals the depth of his *agape*. It is almost unthinkable that God would love creatures so much, especially creatures who had offended him. "The world must come to acknowledge that I am your ambassador, and that you love them as you love me" (17:23). Faith enlightens us on precisely this point: "God's love was made manifest among us by this fact" (1 Jn. 4:9). Such love can scarcely be imagined, let alone put into words, so each Christian is invited to meditate on it. "See what kind of love the Father has bestowed on us" (1 Jn. 3:1). "*Thus* has God loved us" (4:11), with this prodigious generosity. The beloved Son, crucified for us, reveals how much God loves us and what his love, *agape,* is. "This love consists not in our having loved God but in his having loved us and having sent his Son as a propitiation for our sins."

4. God is love

For St. John, what distinguishes believers from other men is their understanding of the mystery of Jesus. It is not only a matter of proclaiming the authenticity of the Messiah and the lordship of the Son of God, of adhering to the efficacy of his death, of awaiting his return in glory, but also of relating all these saving deeds to the love which conceived and directed them, of reading in the person and life of Jesus the divine charity they express. God, who is pure spirit (Jn. 4:24), is by his very nature invisible. No one has ever seen him (1 Jn. 4:12), but he becomes present in Christ, and we can see the Father through the Son (Jn. 14:9). In the charity which Jesus manifested for us, we reach the love of God himself. The strong conviction the apostles felt about Jesus' manifestation is expressed with the force of a clear discovery. "We ourselves know and believe in God's enduring love at work among us. God is love" (1 Jn. 4:16). In the religion of Jesus Christ, to know God is not simply to perceive his omnipotence, holiness, or justice, but to grasp that he is love (v. 8).

Deus charitas est! The import of the assertion in St. John's first Epistle must be understood in terms of its genesis. It is not a statement made by the Lord or a dogmatic declaration unrelated to history, but the outcome of St. John's contemplation of the life and death of Christ and of Jesus' relations with God. The more the Christian meditates on what the Savior did and on his teachings about charity, the more he discovers that Christ is first and foremost the revealer of God, not like the prophets who proclaimed what the Spirit suggested to them, but as the only Son who rests permanently on the Father's bosom and explains and makes known the mysteries of his intimate life with God (Jn. 1:18). Whether we consider God's relations with Jesus and men or the relations of the Son of God with his Father and "his own," *agape* is the summary and exhaustive explanation of everything.

First of all, *agape* is a gift—"See what kind of love the Father has given us" (1 Jn. 3:1)—and it can come only from God. "Love takes its origin in God" (1 Jn. 4:7). However, this charity as virtue is only an infinitesimal part of the divine attribute. Faith discovers an adequate object in the love God possesses in his own right in the person of his incarnate Son, "God's love among us" (1 Jn. 4:16). Jesus appears as love personified, and through him the Christian can truly know what love in God is. If Christ is all love, then his Father is all love too. The following two verses must be juxtaposed. "We know what love is from the fact that Jesus Christ laid down his life for us" (1 Jn. 3:16) and "God's love was made manifest among us by the fact that God sent his only-begotten Son into the world" (1 Jn. 4:9). There is so complete an identity between Christ's love and the Father's love that we can conclude from one to the other. It is more than a matter of manifestations and marks of love, as if God and Jesus were acting with one and the same heart. The relationship between the Father and his only Son springs from a reciprocal, permanent, and eternal charity (Jn. 17:23-24). Everything that Christ has revealed about the intimate life of God is summarized in its being an exchange made within the mutual relationship of knowledge and love between God and his Son. The union of the two persons seems to be accomplished in *agape*. Thus one arrives at conceiving of a substantial charity which is God (1 Jn. 4:10). Love is of the same nature as God.

These remarks indicate that when St. John wrote "God is love," he intended first of all to furnish the explicative principle of the economy of salvation—in this he agrees with St. Paul—and to take into account the personal relations which unite the Father to the Son within a single glory. Their *agape* is primarily the active manifestation of love. This is no definition of the God of philosophers, specified by aseity, but a valid designation of the essence of the living God. Love is more than an attribute of God; according to the supreme revelation of the New Covenant, it is his own name. Love expresses God's nature and consequently all his other attributes—justice, patience, strength, etc. Above all else, God is love. *Agape* is not something *of* God. It is God himself, his substance; God is incapable of not loving.

Here we are face to face with a great mystery. Biblical theology cannot make it any more explicit, but the declaration, "God is love," says what is most proper to God and what he desires us to know about him. He has shown that he is love, and he wants to be recognized as he is. If we may dare to say so, charity is the property of his nature which means the most to him. St. John saw it as his most specific quality, as Jesus had implied in his teaching on "the Father who is in heaven." The Holy Spirit made St. John understand that charity is an active love; it is a fullness overflowing in kindness, whose movements are their own determination and justification, like a spring that overflows into the stream which it feeds. God is life, so his immanent love is completely spontaneous and communicative

He is light (1 Jn. 1:5) because his love is spiritual and clear. *Agape* expresses all of this. Like a sun that illuminates and radiates, like a spring that flows and fecundates, God is pure charity which loves by expressing and giving itself. His communication and sharing of himself are his nature and, therefore, the law of his life.

5. Divine sonship, the work and gift of the Father's *agape*

God loves men so much that he sacrificed his Son for them, and his charity does not remain external in the form of helpful providence which would first surround men with good things and finally assure their happiness. Instead it gives them eternal life (Jn. 3:16), which must be understood as the life of God himself rather than as a life that death cannot reach. In the depths of his being, the Christian possesses the life with which God himself lives. More profoundly still, out of love God begets believers by communicating his own nature to them. Of sinners, he makes children capable of entering into intimacy with him. "See what kind of love the Father has bestowed on us that we should be called his children, for that is what we are." The words, "for that is what we are," *kai esmen,* exclude any watered-down or softened interpretation of the expression "children of God." It is not a metaphor, honorific title or affectionate name, as if God had for us a love like a father's love for his sons or as if only he treated us like sons. God actually is our father just as truly as our human fathers are, who begot us and transmitted their own lives to us. This is so true that according to St. John, the Christian is called "he who has been begotten by God." Indeed, according to the mode of begetting of living things, "the life-germ implanted by God abides in him" (1 Jn. 3:9).

Anyone who is surprised or doubtful about this should reread St. Paul's teaching on the new birth (Tit. 3:5) and Jesus' conversation with Nicodemus in which the Master used the analogy of human birth to explain birth according to the spirit (Jn. 3:3-9). The new or divine begetting is just as real as the first begetting in the mother's womb, and Christians can truly consider themselves "of the race of God" (Acts

17:28). In fact, strictly speaking, begetting by the spirit is more true and authentic than human begetting. For one thing, human fathers are intermediaries who can only transmit a life that is not their own property (Eph. 3:14-15); for another, a human child is autonomous from the moment he comes into the world. Once the umbilical cord is cut, his dependence on his parents becomes only moral. The child of God, on the contrary, is forever being born. He is permanently being begotten, as the perfect tense of the verb *gennan* shows. He is always being born; he is always receiving direct participation in God's nature and life. For St. Paul, the Christian is a person who "is from God" or "is from the Father" (1 Jn. 2:16).

Theologians identify the truly divine nature communicated to believers with sanctifying grace. Jesus called it "glory." "The glory you have bestowed on me I have bestowed on them, that they may be one as we are one—I in them and you in me. Thus their oneness will be perfected. The world must come to acknowledge . . . that you love them as you love me" (Jn. 17:22-23). Since the basic nature of the heavenly Father is *agape* and since, strictly speaking, a begetter transmits his own nature in begetting, God's children will clearly be persons who are essentially loving. The divine glory or the divine nature in which we participate, thanks to Christ, includes, first and foremost, entitative possession of the Father's love which also belongs to all his sons. "May the love with which you love me dwell in them as I dwell in them myself" (Jn. 17:26). This explains why and how the children of the God who is love can be recognized by their capacity to love. For St. John, the words *ek tou theou*, "to be (born) of God," mean to belong to God and to resemble, him, as well as to take one's origin from him (1 Jn. 2:16). Someone who is especially patient, consoling, or easily angered is sometimes referred to as "a son of" patience, consolation, or anger. In the same way, the description "son of God" suggests not only that a person is born of God but also that he depends on the heavenly Father and possesses the same qualities that his Father has. If God is love, "those who are of God" are also love, and not accidentally, but by nature. Furthermore, the child acts like his father. At birth he is furnished with both his nature and his faculties, which exercise themselves in activities. Authentic children of God can be recognized by the charitable quality of their activities.

This doctrine must be kept in mind for an understanding of the Johannine definition: "Everyone that loves is a child of God" (1 Jn. 4:7), which follows the assertion, "Love takes its origin in God." Charity is the criterion of sonship, and, consequently, of the disciple. There is no more basic teaching in the New Testament. Like St. Paul, St. John does call the Christian "one who believes," *ho pisteuōn,* but he conceives of him principally as "one who loves," *ho agapōn.* The present participle indicates both incessant activity and a condition of stability—sometimes very much emphasized, as "he who abides in love," *ho memōn en tēi agapēi* (1 Jn. 4:16). The child of God is, as it were, always in the act of loving, like his heavenly Father. At least, he has a permanent disposition to love, and he is prompt to manifest his charity. Love is his life, because love is his being. Just as it can be stated categorically that "he who does not love abides in death" (1 Jn. 3:14b), so it is equally true to say that he who loves has passed from death to life (3:14a) and lives in the light (2:10), in participation in the divine life.

6. What is *agape*?

Having seen that for St. John a disciple is one who possesses divine love and lives from it, it is possible to examine the nature of the divine love and determine its characteristics. According to the Synoptics, God was the model for a love which is respectful, kind and tender in its manifestations toward neighbor. St. Paul is faithful to this meaning, but the central place he gives to *agape,* the bond of perfection, in his development of Christian theology forces him to enrich its content. He says that the love of God conceived and accomplished the whole economy of salvation. Along with the crucified Christ, God is "he who has loved us" (Rom. 8:37; Gal. 2:20). Charity inseparably unites the Father and the Son in their relationship with redeemed men (2 Cor. 13:13). St. Paul's words in Rom. 8:39, "God's love for us, which is in Christ Jesus our Lord," can be considered the point of departure for St. John's speculation on Christ, the redeemer and giver of the divine charity to believers. Furthermore, St. Paul had the merit of exalting *agape* as the essence of the Christian life. To have charity is everything; not to have it is to be reduced to nothing (1 Cor. 13). All morality is summed up in charity (Rom. 13:10). This, too, prepares for St. John's repeated assertions of the unrivaled importance of fraternal love.

Moreover, St. Paul prays unceasingly to God to make *agape* increase and abound in the disciples' hearts, and he writes that *agape* is constantly diffused in them by the Holy Spirit (Rom. 5:5). St. John insists on this point even more, and makes *agape* more than a simple gift of God, even if the greatest one, and more than a grace; it is participation in the divine nature. For St. Paul, the Christian is an adopted son of God, *huios tou theou,* whose soul is endowed with the qualities and titles appropriate to his new state, particularly with the right to his inheritance. For St. John, the Christian is a child, *teknon,* begotten by the heavenly Father. The Father is charity. When he communicates his nature and life to his child, he transmits something of the *agape* which is proper to him. The supernatural, divine character of Christian love could not be more clearly stated. Taken literally, many Pauline texts might seem to indicate that charity is a moral virtue, because the emphasis in them is on *agape*'s practical efficiency, "the labor of love," *ho kopos tēs agapēs* (1 Thess. 1:3). In St. John, however, the theological character of *agape* is always evident. Because of its origin *agape* is different from all human attachments. "Love is from God" (1 Jn. 4:7). Its origin is its specific character. God alone has charity. He alone loves in his way. On this earth, only those whom he begets possess this love and only they can love as God loves.

Pauline *agape* is a force, an extremely active *dynamis;* Johannine *agape* is above all a nature, considered sometimes as transcendent, sometimes as immanent, precisely because it is both divine and incarnate. It can be said that the Christian (*ho agapōn*) is in a stable condition because he possesses charity. He remains in a state which testifies to his spiritual authenticity. In a way, the love he has received surpasses him. It is greater than his own heart, and he is bound to *agape* and must plunge himself into it. At any rate, charity is the bond which unites the believer to God. It is the child of God's permanent participation in the nature and life of his Father.

This conception takes into account the expressions proper to St. John. He says that the charity of God or of the Father remains in the Christian (1 Jn. 3:17; cf. 2:15) and is rooted in him (Jn. 5:42). He defines the disciple as a man who abides in the love (1 Jn. 4:16) which God or Christ have for him (Jn. 15:9-10). Charity is a mutual attachment, therefore, between perfectly real and living persons; it is the love proper to God and revealed by Christ. It is divine and is given first, taking the initiative in every communication and gift (1 Jn. 4:10, 19). The disciple welcomes its declarations and manifestations. He believes in love (4:16), and his firm, stable adherence makes him live and remain in charity, live and remain in God. "He who abides in love abides in God and God in him" (1 Jn. 4:16; cf. v. 12). This way of expressing the link between God and the believer is original with St. John, and it is noteworthy that he already insisted on it so strongly when he had only just discovered it. Nevertheless, the indwelling was self-evident once it was realized that *agape* is a nature common to God and to his children. Charity is characterized, therefore, by the depth of its attachment. The whole person loves and is directed toward the beloved.

Charity is more than a simple relationship of delight. It draws together persons who love one another to the point of realizing a presence. The immediacy of the nearness is spiritual, of course, since it is a question of God and the soul, but it is also in a certain sense local, since St. John calls it a mutual indwelling and even an existence of one within the other. It is the common psychology of love that the beloved haunts the spirit and heart of the lover, and *vice versa*. *Ubi thesaurus tuus, ibi et cor tuum.* . . . However, the presence of a memory or an affection is purely psychological, whereas charity brings God, Christ, and the believer together, uniting them in their very being rather than by extrinsic relation. *Agape* is the place, the home, where the Father, the Son, and all believers meet (1 Jn. 5:1, 2, 18) because they all possess the same nature. It is not enough, then, to say that charity assures the mutual intimacy of the lover and the beloved, or even that it makes them present to one another. There is more than contact; there is communication of being and life, and it is on this level that we must understand the reciprocal indwelling which *agape* causes.

St. John's first epistle emphasizes so strongly the relationship between Christian charity and the new birth (1 Jn. 3:1; 4:7; 5:1) that we are led to conceive charity as a family love. God loves as Father. Christians love him as his children, and they love one another as brothers (1 Jn. 3:16). We are bound to love Christ and Christians because "everyone who loves the parent loves his child also" (1 Jn. 5:1). If we have God for a Father, we cannot help loving his Son (Jn. 8:42). In other words, God's *agape* for his only-begotten Son and for his children is of the same nature and founded on a fundamental similarity. "You love them as you love me." The glory proper to the Father is received by Jesus and communicated to the disciples (Jn. 17:22, 24). The counterproof, "He who does not love his brother is no child of God" (1 Jn. 3:10), is as absolute as the proof, "We know by this sign that we love the children of God; when we love God." *Agape* is a familial affection, an immense kindness which can contain a great deal of tenderness. This helps us to understand better why it has an innate tendency to unity (Jn. 17:23). Father, Son, and brothers are to form only one; the whole economy of salvation is ordained to this ideal (Jn. 12:52), precisely because it is governed by the Father's charity.

Progress in the Christian life is progress in love, and it is marked by an ever closer union. No matter how strong the assimilation of his new child to him is at baptism, it can always be intensified, since it is conditioned by an increased awareness of God's love for us. The more the Christian knows the Father's *agape,* the more he becomes attached to Christ who manifests it to him, and the more the Father and Son draw near, uniting themselves more closely to him. "He who accepts my commandments and keeps them—he is the one that loves me. And he that loves me will, in turn, be loved by my Father; and I will love him, and will manifest myself to him. . . . My Father will love him, and we shall visit him and make our home with him" (Jn. 14:21, 23). The love which at first seemed so static appears here as singularly active. The highest faculties have come into

17

play. For spiritual beings, to be is to live and to act. Therefore, to live in love is not an ideal of repose; it is rather to know God, direct the affection of the heart to him, and to prove one's fidelity. For his part, Christ manifests himself, *emphanisò,* and comes with the Father, *eleusometha;* together they bring about an active presence, *monēn poiesomētha.* The disciple cannot be unaware of their coming and permanent dwelling within him, because he lives in the light. Since *agape* is a lucid love, it is very much aware of God and of all its relations with him. One of St. John's most original contributions to the theology of charity is his reiterated affirmation of the new vision. "Everyone that loves . . . knows God" (1 Jn. 4:7); "we ourselves know and believe in God's enduring love at work among us" (v. 16); "we know . . . because we love" (3:14); "by this we shall know" (v. 19); "by this we know . . . when we love God" (1 Jn. 5:2).

The knowledge intrinsically linked to charity comes from experience, from an intimate grasping based on the communion of nature and life established with God. The Christian is converted when he sees God's charity revealed. In the beginning, he sees a proof of God's love in the person of Christ, and as he grows, he acquires a clearer awareness of the Father's love. His supreme wish is not so much the Parousia or entrance into heaven as it is the consummation in unity (Jn. 17:22-23) and finally, the sight of the glory, *doxa,* and love, *agape,* that the Father has given the Son before the creation of the world (v. 24). The union and presence which he experiences will be completed in the contemplation of the Trinitarian life he shares. *Agape* will have become perfect when the manifestation is total (cf. 1 Jn. 3:2).

This doctrine is apparent in the texts only if *agapan-agapē* keeps its classical and biblical nuance of manifestation of love. More than any other New Testament writer, St. John shows charity as a love which reveals and proves itself. We have seen how enlightening this meaning was for an understanding of the divine "nature." "God is love," *ho theos agapē estin,* must be understood primarily in terms of the fact of Christ and of the economy of salvation, the epiphany of the *agape* of God. God is manifest and generous love. He makes no secret of his love for his Son and for men. St. Paul traced everything to

18

God's paternity (Eph. 3:14), but for St. John, God is an over-flowing and communicative love, a fullness poured out—*Bonum diffusivum sui*—and consequently the source of all love and all good. Thus the "greater love," *meizona agapēn,* of Jn. 15:13 is the most convincing proof of love and its decisive manifes-tation. Jesus' death is the most expressive act of his charity (cf. 13:1).

Furthermore, the Savior multiplies his declarations of love; he requires the apostles' declarations in turn (Jn. 21:15-17), and he wants the proclamations to be confirmed by deeds. Just as the incarnation is for believers a manifestation of the Father's charity (1 Jn. 4:9), so they will recognize one another as God's authentic children through the exercise of fraternal charity (3:10). The activity of this love will be an unmistakable sign by which even unbelievers can always identify Christ's disciples (Jn. 13:35). Charity is spiritual, yet it draws attention to itself; it is invisible, yet it is radiant; it is intimate affection, yet it acts openly; it is recognizable in its works (1 Jn. 3:16). In definitions, *agape* must be understood in its traditional sense of manifest love. For example, *en toutōi estin hē agapē* is usually translated, "Love consists in this" (1 Jn. 4:10, 16), but the correct sense is, "The manifestation of love consists in this: God sends his Son as a propitiation for our sins."

Just as God proves his love and just as charity is neces-sarily efficient and effective, so St. John "defines" the Chris-tian's *agape* (1 Jn. 5:3; 2 Jn. 6) by the proof of his love for God: the manifestation of charity is the observance of the precepts. Like St. Paul, he insists as much on the efficiency of the divine charity as on the disciples' works as characteristic of their love. To have charity is to keep the word of God (1 Jn. 2:5). To love God is to put his commandments into practice (5:2); the proof of *agape* is the keeping of the commandments (v. 3). "To walk in truth," "to walk according to his precepts," "to walk in love" (2 Jn. 4-6; cf. v. 3) all mean the same thing. The entire moral life, which is fidelity to the divine will, is the blossoming of charity. A person shows his attachment to God by obeying him, and the activities of *agape* constitute perfect obedience because the divine precept *par excellence* prescribes love. "His commandment is this, that we should believe in the name of his Son, Jesus Christ, and love one another, as he commanded us" (1 Jn. 3:23).

St. John did not invent this notion of charity. He learned it from the Master and then declared it in his own words: "We know what love is from the fact that Jesus Christ laid down his life for us. We, too, ought to lay down our lives for our brothers" (1 Jn. 3:16). Christ's example reveals how extremely active and efficient *agape* is. Jesus had commanded several times, "Love one another, as I have loved you" (Jn. 13:34, 15:12). He himself is the model of total devotion, carried even to the sacrifice of the cross. More clearly still, the Lord had defined, "Anyone who loves me with charity will keep my word. . . . Anyone who does not love me does not keep my word" (Jn. 14:23). This is the same as saying, "He who has my commandments and keeps them—he is the one that loves me with charity" (v. 21), and "If you love me, you will keep my commandments" (v. 15).

Charity and fidelity are one and the same thing, as the Old Testament consistently taught. Given the emphasis placed on the values of delight and union in Johannine *agape*, however, fidelity is no longer so much a matter of obedience pure and simple or of strictly material submission as it is of accepted dependence and agreement of wills. The disciple fulfills the prescriptions of God and Christ out of love; more exactly, he adopts their will and conforms to it. "We keep his commandments and do what is pleasing in his sight" (1 Jn. 3:22). *Agape,* authentic love, is exact in fidelity and prompt and fervent in welcoming the Father's will, which it takes so completely to itself that God's will actually becomes the believer's own will. That is why *agape* never feels that its precepts are heavy (5:3). Jesus was referring to the depth of this spontaneous adherence and conformity when he said, "If you observe my commandments you will remain in my love, just as I have observed my Father's commandments and I remain in his love" (Jn. 15:10). St. John echoes, "He who keeps his commandments abides in God and God in him" (1 Jn. 3:23), and, "To love God means to keep his commandments" (1 Jn. 5:3).

Our piety should be essentially filial, and Jesus is its perfect model. "As he is, so we are" (14:17; cf. 2:6). The children of God love not only because God has commanded them to and because his Son has given them the example of love, but also because as children of the Father and sharers in his loving nature, they are incapable of having feelings and desires different from his. When they love with infused *agape,* their love has the essentially effective quality of divine love. It manifests itself, dedicates itself, sacrifices itself and proves itself in every way. For a Christian, loving is never anything other than manifesting what he really is (1 Jn. 3:10), just as God's *agape* manifests him in himself.

It is now possible to understand the strength of the exhortation, "Little children, let us love not merely in word or with the tongue but in deed and in truth" (3:18). It would be monstrous for God's children to pretend to love if their actions were to belie the sincerity of their words (cf. 4:20). In any case, it would be contradictory to the nature of effective, convincing *agape.* True charity conforms to the effectively beneficent, generous, divine model (4:11), as St. John emphasizes in the stereotyped expression, "In this is love."

In conclusion, we must sum up St. John's very complex notion of *agape. Agape* is an overflowing fullness which springs from the very being of the lover and expresses him adequately. Completely spontaneous and gratuitous, it is a love of holiness and beauty which expresses itself in esteem and sovereign respect, in delight and kindness. Sometimes it vibrates with compassion at the sight of another's misery (1 Jn. 3:17); sometimes it rejoices in the happiness of its beloved (Jn. 14:28). It is so closely united with its beloved that it remains always in his presence. Its communion is the most intimate possible because it is reciprocal indwelling. We possess within ourselves the person whom we love and he exists in us. Mutual indwelling is possible because *agape* is God himself. His children remain in him (1 Jn. 4:16), and the loving and beloved brothers are united in the Father's charity which they share (Jn. 15:9). On this level, St. John explains, there is no true charity unless one loves God. "We know by this sign that we love the children of God: when we love God" (1 Jn. 5:2). In other words, charity is something completely different from tender *storgē* or the most perfect *philia,* although it includes the highest values of both these loves (cf. Jn. 11:3, 5, 11, 36), particularly the confiding of secrets to a friend (15:14-15) and the gentle, generous welcome reserved to guests (3 Jn. 6). As in the Septuagint, the Synoptics, and St. Paul, *agape* in St. John is extremely active, powerful, and generous. It communicates the most precious thing it has; it gives of its best (1 Jn. 4:10). It tends to sacrifice itself for the beloved (Jn. 15:13). Charity is belonging to another (1 Jn. 2:15), and it demands unchanging fidelity. When it is a matter of man's love for God or Christ, charity is equivalent to consecration (Jn. 21:15-17). At least, that is its ideal, for St. John's expressions, like our Lord's in the Sermon on the Mount, show that man, magnificently endowed with divine charity as he is (Jn. 17:26), tries to love his best but can never fully realize the infinite delight and gift that such a love includes by its very nature. "Whoever keeps God's word, truly that man's love for God is perfect" (1 Jn. 2:5).

7. Fraternal love

From the very beginning God had asked his people to love one another (Lev. 19:18). In the Sermon on the Mount Jesus extended charity even to enemies (Mt. 5:44-48), and in his Farewell Discourse he made fraternal *agape* his own precept: "This is my commandment: love one another" (Jn. 15:12). He called it a new precept: "A new commandment I give you: love one another" (13:34). He was referring to the love which his own must actively bear one another and which characterizes them as his disciples: "You are my friends, provided you do what I command you" (15:14). They are to love as Christ has loved them, as Jn. 13:34 and 15:12 emphasize. These texts show how the precept can be called completely new and absolutely proper to Christ. "As I love you, so I want you, too, to love one another" (Jn. 13:34). Thus, simple philanthropy, tenderness, and the kind of devotion which people ordinarily feel and practice are not what he was referring to. The Master was consciously introducing into this world an original love which was unknown until he himself lived it.

He immediately explained how he understands and manifests his love: "No one can give a greater proof of his love than by laying down his life for his friends" (15:13). Love is therefore gift of self and desire for the happiness of one's friends which is so profound that one is even willing to sacrifice oneself for them. Examples of this kind of generosity exist outside Christianity (Rom. 5:7), however, and the Lord goes even further. "Just as the Father loves me, so I love you" (Jn. 15:9). Consequently, there can no longer be a question of human attachment alone; Christ's love is also divine love. To love as Christ loves is to love both religiously and humanly, to share in God's own love and to extend it to others. That is what makes Christian *agape* specific and new. Its origin and nature are heavenly, and it has the power to unite all God's children within the Church. Clearly, then, *agape* has something of the infinite about it and, clearly, it tends to immolation. Because it is divine, it is without measure. Christ alone has shown its perfect realization.

To love as Christ loves is not a more or less optional counsel or simply one precept among many. It is the last testament and supreme will of the Lord and Master who was actively fulfilling what he ordained for others (13:13-14). Love is the spirit of his Church and the soul of the new covenant which he sealed with his blood. Therefore Christ kept only fraternal love, as he defined it, as the criterion of authentic discipleship; he identified love with the Christian life itself. Jesus practiced all the virtues and prescribed them for his own, but only *agape* is specific because *agape* makes Christianity what it is. "By this token all the world must know that you are my disciples—if you have the love of charity for one another" (Jn. 13:35). Love that is a token must be active and manifest, able to play the role of witness and proof. It must be love so special that it cannot possibly be confused with any counterfeit. It must be an attachment so broad, constant and patient that even strangers can see in it the fulfillment of the command of Christ. They must see Christ's way of loving and even his presence and the presence of his Father in the disciples' community and communion. "I in them and you in me, that their unity may be perfect, so that the world will recognize that you sent me and that you love them as you love me" (17:23). *Agape* is the "mark" of the visible church, because no one can possess this love unless he has been chosen and loved by God, who transmits it to him in his beloved Son present with his Father, by love, in the midst of his own (Jn. 14:23).

St. John had meditated for a long time on the testament of the Lord, and the essence of his Epistles seems to comment: "This is all I command you: love one another" (Jn. 15:17). Referring to the very first catechesis which each convert received, he wrote: "This is precisely the message which you have heard from the beginning—that we should love one another" (1 Jn. 3:11). His reference to the early stages of initiation into Christianity seems to imply that the convert's commitment was made first of all to the reciprocal love within the Church. In any case, St. John does not consider love simply a wish or precept of Christ, but rather the will of God himself: "This is his (God's) commandment" (1 Jn. 3:23). The Christian life is summed up in faith in Christ and fraternal love, *en alētheiai kai agapēi* (2 Jn. 3). It would be impossible to give greater fullness to *agape* or to associate it more happily with the Witness-Revealer who prescribed it.

This is not just a general juxtaposition of dogma and morality in which the faithful are characterized by their confession of the incarnate Son of God and by their loving conduct. For St. John, the proper object of faith is the divine charity: "to believe in the love that God has manifested among us" (1 Jn. 4:16; cf. v. 10) in the person of his Son. He is the epiphany of the Father's *agape,* so that fraternal love finds its model in the love Christ has for his own. Fraternal love is verified in him: "the truth is in him" (2:8). Jesus had said: "Love one another as I love you. No one can give a greater proof of his love than by laying down his life for his friends" (Jn. 15:12-13), and the disciple comments: "We know what love is from the fact that Jesus Christ laid down his life for us. We, too, ought to lay down our lives for our brothers" (1 Jn. 3:16; cf. 4:11). "We ought," *opheilomen,* implies more than the necessity of conforming to a model; it refers to the obligation of the debt of gratitude. Having received so great a gift of love, how could we in our turn not love and surround our brothers with the same kind of generosity?

On the human plane, it is fitting that a superior person be able to rise to difficult circumstances. An honorable and noble-hearted person tries to share with others any benefits he has received. The Lord, who was severe to the slave who had been acquitted of his debts and then was intransigent toward his own debtors (Mt. 18:23-34), went on to say, "In the same way my heavenly Father will treat you if you do not each forgive your brother from your heart" (v. 35). St. John was not taking his position on the plane of human decency, however. He was intrinsically linking charity received from God with charity toward neighbor, and this connection is his most personal contribution to the theology of *agape.*

Jesus had associated the two commandments as making up a single supreme class of precepts (Mt. 22:36-40). St. Paul had summed up Christian morality in fraternal charity (Rom. 13:8-10). St. John teaches that it is impossible to love God without loving one's brother. To pretend to have charity for God without extending it to one's neighbor would be a lie (1 Jn. 4:20). Worse still, the divine *agape* cannot live in a heart that closes itself to compassion for a brother in need (1 Jn. 3:17). *A priori,* when the objects of the two loves are so diverse, it is difficult to see why they cannot be dissociated. But the apostle declares that this is the divine ordinance: "We have received this command from God: He who loves God must love his brother also" (1 Jn. 4:21).

The command does not actually appear in the Gospel, so it must be understood that St. John, by his apostolic authority, was interpreting and clarifying the Lord's will in a sort of theological conclusion to which he gave the force of law. In any case, it is easy to retrace the evolution of his thought. *Agape* is a very particular kind of love, which bespeaks absolute initiative and anteriority, not reciprocity. God has revealed his charity under this mode (4:11, 19). How then can Christians possess and exercise *agape* without themselves taking the first steps? *Vis-à-vis* God, their *agape* is necessarily response; only toward neighbor can it manifest authentic spontaneity. Perhaps it is in this sense that 1 Jn. 4:19 and 1 Jn. 4:12 should be understood: "We must take the initiative in loving our brothers since he first loved us"; and "No one has ever seen God, yet if we love one another, God abides in us and our love for him reaches its perfection," its full *ratio* of *agape.*

Another, more profound consideration is added to this one. The love which the believer possesses is infused (4:7). It is the charity with which God loves himself and all Christians. It keeps the same objects in our hearts, therefore, as it has in God, as 1 Jn. 5:2 suggests: "We know by this sign that we love the children of God, when we love God." What does this mean if not that the possession of the divine reality which is *agape* is enough to unite us *ipso facto* with God and his children? Charity accomplishes this communion because it is its nature to do so, and that is why it is unthinkable that anyone could be attached to God and exclude his neighbor, or *vice versa*. This dichotomy, which could be valid in human affections or in certain mystiques, is contrary to the very notion of charity, which is a love that is proper only to God and to his own.

We arrive, then, at St. John's ultimate reflection, one already made by Peter and Paul. According to St. John, the proper fruit of faith is not justification or even obtaining eternal life, but, first of all, becoming the child and sharer of the divine life. "Everyone who believes that Jesus is the Christ is born of God" (1 Jn. 5:1; Jn. 1:12). God is love, the manifestation and gift of love (1 Jn. 4:8, 16). When he begets children, he gives them the *agape* which characterizes his nature. From the gift, it is easy to deduce the consequence: the child of God is "naturally" loving; charity is the rightful possession of every disciple who is reborn of God. "Everyone that loves is a child of God" (1 Jn. 4:7).

This is certainly the supreme motive of fraternal love. Christians are exhorted to love their neighbor because of the loving nature they received at baptism. "Beloved, let us love one another, *because* love is from God" (1 Jn. 4:7). St. John tells us that this love is a family love. God is the Father; he loves his children; and each of them must consider the others also children of their common Father and must love them as their brothers. "Everyone who loves the parent loves his child also" (1 Jn. 5:1). This notion makes everything clear, and we can understand why St. John united charity for God so intimately with charity for neighbor, or rather for other Christians. Fraternal *agape* is much less a love prescribed for the sake of resembling God and conforming to Christ's example than it is a sharing and application of God's love of predilection for all the disciples of Jesus.

That is why our fraternal charity is a proof that God lives in us (1 Jn. 4:12). To distinguish between the children of God and the children of the devil, it is only necessary to observe who loves his neighbor and who does not (1 Jn. 3:19). Only those who do are sure of "being born of the truth" (3:10) and of having passed from death to life. "We know that we have passed from death to life, because we love our brothers. He who does not love abides in death" (3:14). The charitable person is truly alive (v. 15); he possesses God's own life in him and he walks in the light (1 Jn. 2:10).

Although St. John multiplies statements about the duty of manifesting love of neighbor and about the reasons love is necessary, he is silent about the acts and modes of its being carried out. He emphasizes only that it must be effective, because effectiveness is the characteristic of charity which God and Christ have revealed to him. Since true love consists in the Father's giving the Son and the Son's giving his life (4:10; 3:16), the essential sign of fraternal love is that it does not love "in word or tongue, but in deed and truth" (3:18). It dedicates itself to the kind of humble and fervent service of which our Lord gave a very concrete example when he washed his disciples' feet (Jn. 13:15; cf. Lk. 22:26). A good spirit is not enough; we must really give ourselves to others in a union of heartfelt love and self-sacrifice—"happy are you if you do these things" (Jn. 13:17). Consequently, just as God sacrificed his only Son out of mercy for us, so the disciple will feel himself full of pity for those in need and will share everything he has with them. He must even be ready to give his life, following the Savior's example (1 Jn. 3:16) and the law of infused charity.

Furthermore, when Jesus was told that his friend Lazarus was sick, he let him die—"Jesus loved . . . Lazarus" (Jn. 11:5)— and he even rejoiced because he had not helped him sooner (Jn. 11:15, *chairō*), because Lazarus' sickness and death were to manifest God's glory (v. 4). Attachment to neighbor is subordinate to the demands of divine love. If it is a matter of God's honor (cf. 9:3-4), we must agree to the most painful trials for those we love—"your dear friend is ill" (v. 3). Then, however, we will taste the joy of being in full accord with the Father's will (*echarēte;* 14:28), in direct contrast to the Jews who, not having charity within themselves (5:42), "cared more for the approval of men than for the approval of God" (12:43).

8. The progress and fruits of *agape*

Because *agape* is God's nature in us, nothing is more stable than our love. Whether it is charity for God, Christ, or neighbor, the person who possesses it is assured of being forever established in God or in Christ, in life eternal and heavenly light. "He who abides in love abides in God and God in him." The moral life is seen as a walking under the inspiration of charity (2 Jn. 6), and the Christian is sure that he will never stumble (1 Jn. 2:10). Where there is *agape,* there is also security.

But stability, permanence, or even fixedness are not synonymous with inertia. Johannine charity, like Pauline, is extremely active, proving itself above all in the practice of the commandments. Diligent fidelity arouses the delight of the three divine Persons and wins new gifts, first of all the coming and indwelling of the Holy Spirit: "If you love me you will keep my commandments. And I will ask the Father, and he will give you another Advocate to be with you for all times to come" (Jn. 14:15-16). The believer's first reaction before the divine ambassador is to "receive" him (Jn. 1:11-12). Only those who love God "welcome Jesus." The person who gives himself and attaches himself to Christ has the assurance that both the Father and Christ will return his love. Just as the faithful person's charity expresses itself in works, so Jesus' charity is shown in his gifts: "He who has my commandments and keeps them—he is the one that loves me. And he that loves me will, in turn, be loved by my Father; and I will love him, and will manifest myself to him" (14:21; cf. vv. 19-20). The disciple's loving obedience brings him deeper into the divine intimacy. As the charitable person proves the sincerity and force of his *agape,* the Father and the Son draw nearer and their indwelling in the soul becomes more profound. "Anyone who loves me will keep my word, and my Father will love him, and we shall come to him and make our home with him" (14:23).

In these three texts (14:15-16, 21, 23) the fervor of *agape* is proved by fidelity. Everything depends on "keeping the commandments" or "the word." John 14:21 accentuates even more the notion of practical realization and perseverance: "he who has my commandments and keeps them." The disciple receives, keeps, and accomplishes the will of Jesus. As he does so, his charity not only proves itself but also is strengthened by use; consequently, his divine participation becomes even fuller. Christ shows him still more love (Jn. 14:21). With his Father, he establishes himself permanently in the soul (1 Jn. 14:23), and, if we may dare to say so, the stay of the Holy Spirit becomes even more active (Jn. 14:16).

Since the coming and abiding of the Trinity are presented as something new with respect to the first divine indwelling within the convert (1 Jn. 4:16), the whole Christian life may be considered an incessant, always-increasing manifestation and reciprocity of love between the disciple and God. On God's side, this is self-evident, since he is charity and charity is pure gift and communication. God never stops loving, manifesting his love, and lavishing his gifts upon his children. On the Christians' side, however, since their charity is received from God—"the love of the Father in him" (1 Jn. 2:15; cf. 4:7)—the problem is to increase love by a more generous sharing in the divine *agape*. St. John calls this God's *agape* among us (4:17) or in us (v. 12) or in this person (2:5). Charity itself cannot grow, since it is already all fullness, but it can make progress in the soul that assimilates it. It occupies or inhabits the soul with greater sovereignty. Its mastery increases until it becomes "finished" or consummated, until it is "perfect love," *he teleia agapē* (1 Jn. 4:18).

St. John writes several times that God's *agape* reaches perfection in us (1 Jn. 4:12, 17; 2:5). This amounts to saying that we grow and become perfect in *agape* (4:18). We should understand that the disciple of Jesus Christ assimilates more and more profoundly the entity which is "the *agape* that comes from God." He gives it full place in his soul. He "realizes" it better and better in himself, so that he exists integrally in *agape* and, like God himself, arrives at identifying himself with love. Certainly that is his ideal and the direction of his progress.

Thus the participation in the divine nature that the child of God received at his engendering in baptism is intended to grow. The essence of its nature is love; its acts are manifestations of love: observance of the commandments and fraternal love. Its progress, linked to its concrete activity, is progress in charity. Its perfection is the perfection of love itself, and finally it is consummated in the unity, which will be complete only in heaven, of all those who participate in *agape*—of God, Christ, and the children of God (Jn. 17:23, 26). Heaven and earth could not be brought closer to each other. *Agape* is at once link and place of meeting. This is true only because *agape* is God himself.

As *agape* grows and acts, the psychology of the Christian changes; he no longer fears God. If we really understood the content of this revelation, we would have to call it a miracle. After all, God is the holy one, the transcendent one, and before him every creature is seized with fear (Lk. 4:36). Furthermore, ever since the flight of the first guilty man before God (Gen. 3:8-10), every man feels himself a sinner (Lk. 5:8-9). His instinctive reaction is to see God as a judge whose punishments he fears. He is afraid. But the immense manifestation of God's love in the merciful coming of the Savior teaches man that God is a father and that he does not want to lose any of his creatures (Jn. 3:16-17) but on the contrary wants to associate them with his own life and make them share his intimacy (1 Jn. 1:3).

The realization of the immensity of God's love ought to dissolve all apprehension and "reassure our heart" (3:19). Even when he is conscious of his sins, the Christian still dares to approach God, because he knows that God is "greater than our heart" (v. 20), that he is magnificent in his pardon, and that he does not treat us according to our iniquities (1:8-2:2).

However, this conviction given by faith does not seem to be enough to eliminate the instinctive terror of the human heart before the divine majesty and holiness. There can be no question of establishing a *koinōnia* between the Father and his children until fear has first been dissipated. St. John attributes the psychological victory of confidence over fear to *agape*. He declares, "There is no fear in love" (1 Jn. 4:18). He understands clearly that the two feelings can coexist only in souls that are not sufficiently evolved. When *agape* succeeds in establishing its reign profoundly and the disciple understands what God's manifestations of love for us mean (4:16), then he attains to authentic, perfect charity, *hē teleia agapē,* which casts out fear. For St. John, the triumph of divine love in the human heart is the criterion of perfection. "In this has *agape* become perfect in us: that we have full assurance, *parrēsia,* against the day of judgment. . . . He who fears has not yet reached the perfection of love" (1 Jn. 4:17-18; cf. 3:21). *Paresia* is not only the daring confidence of the innocent who appear before the tribunal with their heads held high, but also the liberty, clarity and intimacy of the relationships which have been established in an atmosphere of joy between the Father and his children. When *agape* raises the children to the level of their Father, it allows them a true "society" and a perfect intimacy.

The contrast between the Church and the synagogue can be summarized in the substitution of loving assurance for fear and of filial piety for servility. It is not that life in the Church is easier or obedience to precepts any less constraining. On the contrary, in the Church it is necessary to sacrifice one's life totally and to be strictly faithful to the commandments. But Christ took Moses' place as mediator (Jn. 1:17), and *agape* replaces the Law; consequently, "his commandments are not burdensome" (1 Jn. 5:3).

According to St. John, not only is *agape* the first reality and the foundation on which everything else rests, as it is for St. Paul, but also it is the very essence of the Gospel, stated in Jn. 3:16 and repeated in 1 Jn. 4:9. The relationship between God and man, which is what religion is, has been revealed and established by the mediator Jesus Christ. "No one comes to the Father except through me" (Jn. 14:6-9). Christ's love for his disciples desires that God's love for him should extend to his own, and he accomplishes his desire by making his disciples dependent on the divine paternity (1:12), by making them begotten of the Father (17:26). The teaching and life of Jesus are summed up in his manifestation of God's true name— Father. His religion is a loving relationship between father and children, between God and the Word, between the Word and his adopted brothers, and between the Father and children.

St. John knows only one love, *agape,* unlike St. Paul and St. Peter, who also mention *philanthrōpia, chrēstotēs, philadelphia* and *philoxenia. Agape* is the love which God alone possesses and, consequently, with which he loves himself and in which he envelops his incarnate Son and all his children. He communicates his charity to them, so that Christ's disciples love God, Christ, and their brothers by a law of nature and not because they have been commanded to. Consequently, it is correct to say that *agape* is a reciprocal love. However, the reciprocity is first of all the relation of effect to cause, since it is God's charity in the Christian that returns to God and extends to neighbor. Besides, reciprocity or mutual exchange are not strong enough to express the intimacy of the *koinōnia* or, especially, the unity among the persons who love and are loved. Johannine *agape* is more than a link. *Agape* is God himself in whom the Christian is and lives. By love, the Christian participates in God and in his nature; consequently, it is he and his Son who love in the Christian. That is why to live in charity is the same thing as to live in Christ, as Christ lives in the Father and the Father in him.

The "theonomic" moral life, according to St. John, depends on this essential conviction. Since to live is to act, it reconciles in a marvelous harmony the double fundamental requirement of "living in God" and "acting in God." The Christian's activity is in the line of the structure of his being. "We are born of God and his need is in us" (1 Jn. 3:9). By faith the disciple of Jesus Christ is removed from the kingdom of darkness and admitted to the light of life (Jn. 17:3). Clinging to the word made flesh, he has become a child of God (1:12) or a child of the light (12:36). The Christian life will be perseverance in this attitude of soul which is oriented toward Christ—or, rather, united with Christ, who is the way, *hodos* (14:6)—and faithful to the light, *en tōi phōti peripatōmen.*

Practically speaking, walking in the Savior's footsteps according to his example consists in fulfilling God's will and observing his commandment. It is called "walking in truth," *peripatein en agapēi* (1 Jn. 6) or *en aletheiai kai agapēi* (2 Jn.

3). Just as to hate is to be the son of the devil and walk in the darkness (1 Jn. 2:11; cf. 3:10-11), so to love is to behave as a son of God and walk in the light.

In short, St. John knows only two virtues which can animate the Christian life. More exactly, since faith is primarily the initial condition and fundamental decision, all the dynamism and fidelity of the Christian's action are attributed to *agape*. Faith itself consists of "believing in love" (1 Jn. 4:16), and its conviction first arouses adherence to the divine will and then inspires conformity to it. Thus the precept or law is inherent in faith and not superimposed upon it. The unique normative principle is truly the love of God manifest in Jesus Christ. The Christian is confronted less with the task of determining his duties than with the necessity of understanding better and better the meaning amd implications of *agape*. Johannine charity is life, overflowing richness, and fecundity (Jn. 15:4-11). All the disciple's "fruits" as well as his permanent "living in Christ" must be attributed to *agape*'s intensive nature. Unlike St. James, St. John tells very little about the details of Christian works. His panoply of virtues—*agathopoiein* (Jn. 5:29); *poien tēn dikaiosynēn* (1 Jn. 2:29; 3:7, 10)—is considerably poorer than that of the Synoptics, of Peter, and especially of Paul. Except for Apoc. 2:19, he has no "catalogue of virtues," no *Haustafeln,* and no traditional *topoi.*

This is not to say that for St. John the disciple is a pure contemplative or a mystic who is disinterested in morality. No one insisted more than St. John on the connection between the theological virtues and practical conduct. He is the specialist of observance. He knows no love except in "deed and truth" (1 Jn. 3:18), and he is the one who consecrated the meaning of *agape* as the manifestation and effective proof of love. However, St. John is more interested in the basic inspiration, the fundamental principles, and the main axes of the new morality than in the details of practical applications. No one had a greater sense of the hierarchy of values or of their synthesis. His great merit is to have organized the Christian ethic as a function of *agape* conceived as total gift of self. "We know what love is from the fact that Jesus Christ laid down his life for us. We, too, ought to lay down our lives for our brothers" (1 Jn. 3:16).

Everything is in this statement. To love is to forget oneself, to give oneself without reserve, to sacrifice oneself.

This kind of heroism or sanctity, carried out in the variety of everyday circumstances, can come only from God. Therefore, just as St. Paul prayed without ceasing that divine charity might grow in the souls of the faithful, so St. John has only one desire, that we may share perfectly in God's *agape* and that his *agape* may act without impediment "in us and with us." All the rest follows of itself. There is no real danger on the way (*skandalon;* 1 Jn. 2:10-12). His commandments seem light (1 Jn. 5:3). Untouched by fear, our hearts are filled with the confidence and assurance (*parrēsia, tharsein*) of one who triumphs (1 Jn. 5:4). Our joy is complete (Jn. 15:11; 16:24); it is the very joy of the glorified Lord (14:28). The disciple in St. John has nothing taut or strained about him; he is calm and radiant and all on fire.

Such a psychology is understandable if "this love is a vital movement, a form of existence, an actualisation of God in this world." It is understandable if God is charity and if he inspires the person who loves him and in whom he dwells. Truly, *agape* is everything. To know means to experience and to possess, and "everyone that loves is born of God and knows God" (1 Jn. 4:7).

Jean Levie
1885-1966

Jean Levie was born in Charleroi, Belgium. He studied classical philology in Namur and joined the Jesuits in 1902. After completing his doctorate in philology at Louvain, He was ordained a priest in 1917 and appointed to teach New Testament at Louvain. He went to Paris for two years of special preparation for this task, then started his fruitful teaching career at Louvain that was to last for more than forty years. In the spring of 1922 he visited the Holy Land and took courses at the Ecole Biblique, thus coming into contact with Pères Lagrange, Vincent, Abel, and Dhorme, whom he came to admire greatly for the pioneer work they were doing in bringing Catholic Biblical studies to a status of respectability.

From 1926 to 1951 Levie was director of the Louvain periodical, La Nouvelle Revue Théologique, *and contributed to it regularly. Under his guidance its quality improved greatly and it became an important instrument of biblical and theological renewal.*

The Bible, Word of God in Words of Men *was the end-product prompted by* Divino Afflante Spiritu *of Pius XII in 1943. Levie ran a series of articles analyzing that liberating document, exploring the conditions required for a fully Christian interpretation of the Bible, and probing the relationship between exegesis and theology. In gathering these articles together, he saw fit to introduce them with a lengthy survey of relevant events over the previous century. In speaking of this arrangement in the foreword he says: "(The second) more doctrinal part remains independent of the first; although it is shorter it seems to me more important than the first and emphasizes aspects of Catholic exegesis that I believe to be essential." It is from this second part that the following selection is taken.*

The book appeared the year that Pius XII died and John XXIII was elected. That made it coincide with the orchestrated attempt of the ultraconservative group to reverse the trend toward acceptance of modern Biblical studies in the Church. Levie was an obvious target since he admitted openly "how much I regret that narrow conservatism which has lasted too long and on occasion showed itself suspicious and aggressive." The same article in a Roman journal that attacked Professors Zerwick and Lyonnet of the Biblical Institute also unleashed a vicious, unjust, salvo against Levie's book. The momentary pain which this caused him was more than compensated for a few years later when the Vatican II Constitution on Revelation *totally vindicated him and his colleagues.*

When Levie died at the age of 81 the summer after the Council completed its work, he had the consolation of having seen his life's work fructify. In 1962, when the English translation of his book appeared, Leonard Bushinski in the Catholic Biblical Quarterly *said of it: "It still remains the only work known to this reviewer which attempts a history of biblical exegesis and ancillary studies, for the past 100 years, and gives suggestion for further progress in things Biblical . . . It is an excellent aid in acquainting people with the true nature of the modern Biblical Movement."*

THE BIBLE, WORD OF GOD IN WORDS OF MEN

*In what respect and in what way does the divine message
transcend the understanding and the intention of the
human author?*

The Fundamental Principle

As was stated from the outset, the fundamental principle
governing the part played by God in holy Scripture is
the realization and the revelation of the mystery of
God. God works through the facts of Scripture and tells us in
Scripture his own divine plan for the Kingdom of God, for the
raising of man to the supernatural order and for his eternal
salvation through the Incarnation of the Word, the centre of the
whole divine economy—the preparation of this plan in Israel in
the Old Testament, its realization at a given point of time
through Jesus Christ, and its reception in a new Israel, the
Church, Christ's mystical Body.

God as the master of history, as the master of all human
psychology, while respecting man's freedom, makes events and
the religious and literary powers of men serve to establish and
to reveal his plan. God alone can see this plan as a whole, he
alone can comprehend the interdependence of its various parts
and understand to the full all their moral and religious value in
terms of the mentality of the men of each century. Our act of
faith in the truth of Scripture is above all an act of faith in this
divine unity of Scripture, in God's control of the events and the
words of Scripture in the interests of an overall plan whose
centre is Jesus Christ and whose consummation is the ultimate
share that men will receive in the eternal love of the Son for the
Father in the Spirit.

The inspired authors most certainly were granted a great share in the understanding of this mystery. God has a supreme respect for the mind which transmits and the minds which are to receive his messages. But is this understanding complete and adequate? What exactly did Abraham understand when God told him how great his posterity was to be? What did Isaias understand when he prophesied the transcendence of Emmanuel, or Micheas when he caught a glimpse of salvation from Bethlehem? And if the prophets were unable to penetrate the full meaning of their own message, how much less must they have been able to have a complete view of the place and scope of their individual message in the totality of the whole divine plan, in the doctrinal synthesis foreseen by God!

If God willed that the Old Testament should be a kind of progressive ascent towards the fullness of the light, we draw near to the divine understanding (which alone is fully objective) of the Scriptures when we try to discover this progressive movement without falling into any hasty form of concordism but with complete exegetic and theological honesty and insight. If God willed that the Old Testament should announce, predict and in some measure prefigure the New, we are entitled, with the inspired authors of the New Testament, to find in the Old Testament anticipations, symbols, 'types' of Christian realities. If God willed that the whole of Scripture, the New and the Old Testaments, should accompany the human race in its intellectual progress until the end of time and should be relevant and alive in every era from generation to generation, we should expect that the Christian message itself, while remaining fundamentally one and the same, will constantly adapt itself to developing thought and developing civilization, will ceaselessly explain itself in such a way that it remains in perfect communion with living humanity and so links it ever more closely to the living God.

If we are to interpret Scripture in this way and in the fullness of its divine value, it is not enough to be first class historians or literary critics; we must enter into a close religious communion with the divine spirit of Scripture. All Scripture must be read in the same spirit in which it was written, that is, under the active impulse of the Holy Spirit. This communion must be individual and emerge from a deep Christian awareness and from a personal dedication in answer to God's call. It must be a communion within the fellowship of the Church through faith in the vision of the divine message which the Church possesses. It is in union with the Holy Spirit, the same Spirit which enlightens and guides the Church, it is in union with the Church enlightened and guided by the Holy Spirit, that every Catholic reads holy Scripture. And the nearer he is to Christ in the Church through his whole supernatural life, through his enlightened faith and his effort towards holiness, the better is he able to perceive the profound religious riches of Scripture. Of course this does not dispense anyone from keeping in touch with current progress in the human, literal interpretation of the inspired writings. A twentieth century adult does not testify to the glory of the plenitude of divine inspiration if he reads Scripture with the mind of a medieval child. Yet it would be worse still if he read it without that spirit of faith in the transcendence of the mystery of God which, in every era, is the essential principle underlying a Christian reading of the Bible.

Two applications of this fundamental principle

I shall now attempt to clarify this fundamental principle by discussing two traditional theses which apply it and indicate its full scope. The first of these is shared by the majority of believing Christian exegetes, Protestants and Orthodox not in communion with Rome, as well as Catholics. The second in its absolute form is characteristic of the Catholic Faith. Yet it seems, even though only partially and unconsciously, to be still active in some aspects in the method used by several contemporary non-Catholic exegetes.

First Thesis. The unity of the divine plan presented to us in Scripture

If holy Scripture in its entirety is centred on the fundamental fact of our faith, the Incarnation of the Word of God; if this 'mystery', foreseen by God from all eternity and prepared from the first beginnings of the human race, is the essential object of Scripture in the unity and continuity of its realization in history, then the highest point of Christian exegesis is that at which we understand as a whole, as far as this is possible, the unity, internal cohesion and profoundly religious value of this divine 'mystery' in its successive stages throughout the passage of time: its preparation in the Old Testament; its historical realization in the person and the works of Jesus as narrated in our Gospels; the development of its religious, dogmatic and moral significance in the New Testament and, in these same books of the New Testament, the foreseeing of the forward movement of Christianity's future in Christ until the end of time, until the consummation in heaven of the Kingdom of God. But only God knows the full details of this divine plan as a whole. Only he fully perceives the interdependence of its parts from the beginning to the final goal. He alone foresees its effective development from age to age until the end. This unity of the divine plan manifested in Scripture has at every epoch been beyond the understanding of the narrators of and the actors in this divine historical drama. Holy Scripture, since it is the Word of God, has never been limited by what the inspired writers, used by God to utter it, have consciously perceived and been aware of within it. At its highest point, it rises above their thoughts and their will as God's interpreters.

Hence this is tantamount to saying that a purely human though literal exegesis may and does actually discover in our time, at the present stage of the realization of God's plan, a large number of partial aspects of this divine plan, yet it will only reach the final synthesis through and in faith. This 'total biblical theology' which is the supreme goal of exegesis is fully revealed only to the believer.

An exegetical task of this kind is immense and all-embracing. In the present chapter I intend to treat briefly its characteristic aspects in connection with one specific point: the way in which the Old Testament prepares for the New and, as a corollary, the close union of the two Covenants in the unity of the divine plan.

Second thesis (essentially Catholic). For Catholics holy Scripture is not self-sufficient. It is entrusted to a society, the Church, which is the continuation of Christ himself and throughout the centuries lives by his thought and his teaching. In her Christ's doctrine, thus 'lived', unfolds its meaning and adapts itself to the development of the Church's life and thought, since the Church herself is involved in the general progress of mankind.

Scripture is certainly an essential factor in the life of this Church and a sacred, indestructible norm in her thought and her action. But, according to Catholics, Christ the Church's founder intended that Scripture should be given to us within the structure of the Church's life. It is to be ever more intensively 'lived' by the Church, ever more deeply probed by the mind of the Church as her inner life progresses towards the full stature of Christ. Through her inner life under the influence of the Holy Spirit, in the light of her dogma which develops and deepens in the minds of Christians, the Church is led to a better understanding of Scripture and, through her efforts to form a synthesis of the various texts of Scripture in relation to the present state of her dogma and her devotion, to the discovery of deeper, richer, more luminously Christian interpretations.

This concept of the part played by the Church is not a theory that has come into existence recently, it is clearly active from the beginnings of Christianity. Whoever studies, on the basis of the scriptural texts of the New Testament, the progressive formulation of our most ancient dogmas during the first Councils—the dogma of the Trinity, the Christological dogmas— is forced to note that no private exegete, reasoning according to a purely human logic, could arrive by strict deduction at all our most ancient dogmatic formulas by using scriptural texts alone. He may show that these formulas are perfectly in harmony with these texts in their literal sense and that Christian life under the direction of these formulas continues to be the same, and gives an increasingly deeper understanding of Christian life in earlier times as it was directed by these scriptural texts. But he will be obliged to note that certain of these formulas and the scriptural texts fully correspond only through and in the Christian life of the Church. The experience of those early centuries continues to be the same in the many succeeding generations of Christians.

We must not be afraid to deduce, from the fact that in the history of Christianity our faith had been formulated in this way, the following essential principle: God, who alone sees the ultimate connection between the doctrinal passages scattered throughout Scripture, gives to his Church, enlightened by the continual presence of the Spirit, the privilege of progressively gaining a deeper insight into the dogmatic synthesis he intended and willed from the beginning, and this as a result of the moral endeavours of the saints, the religious needs of the mass of the faithful, the scientific work of the exegetes, theologians and doctors, and the directives of the Magisterium. Once more, this dogmatic synthesis must be perfectly at one with the faith of the early Church, with the scriptural texts that reveal that faith and with the Christian message which was complete in its essentials at the end of the apostolic era. But we cannot deny the part played by the Church, if we are to make any objective study of the real evolution of our faith. It is clear that this part played by the Church is something far wider and deeper than her function as the controller of the interpretation of Scripture, as the eventual and final judge of that meaning of its texts which is binding on our faith, for this function is only one part of the Church's total rôle.

It must not be objected that I am mixing up and unduly confusing two different aspects of Catholic theological life, namely scriptural exegesis properly so called and the development of dogma. I am not confusing them, I am stating that they are closely related to each other. As thinking believers, we cannot justify from a theological standpoint the genuine, authentic development of dogma by comparison with the sometimes still rudimentary and, in a sense, still incomplete character of some of our scriptural texts, unless we admit that these texts, lived in the Christian life of the Church, and clarified by the whole of Catholic dogma as it has developed, have revealed to the Church guided by the Spirit, a richer, deeper, more complete meaning than that which can be logically deduced from the actual words by a strict critical exegesis. It is this more complete meaning which has been rightly called the plenary sense of Scripture.

I. *Interpretation of the Old Testament in the Light of the New*

The first Thesis applied

By his whole attitude and his explicit teaching Christ told us that he came to perfect the morality of the Old Testament which was one of preparation (Matt. 5). He told us on many occasion that, from the beginning, all the expectation of all the prophets and of the people of the Old Testament was directed towards him, and that in him all the ancient promises were fulfilled.

St Paul has explicitly clarified the historical meaning of the Old Testament. The centre of gravity of the history of Israel was the promise made to Abraham (and renewed to the other patriarchs), and the object of this promise was Jesus the Christ (this theme is frequent in his great epistles: Galatians, Romans, etc.); it was by his faith in Christ that Abraham was justified (St Paul continually makes this assertion). By the promise, Christ was from the beginning with the children of Israel, playing his part in all the events of their history, accompanying them in their journey as the miraculous rock of the Jewish legend: 'and the rock was Christ' (1 Cor. 10.4). The Jews were those who had hoped in Christ before his coming (Ephes. 1.12). Through the severe discipline of the Law and its observances, they were kept on the path that led to Christ, just as the child is led to school by the slave, the *paedagogos* (Gal. 3.24). Their life was transformed by the gift from on high, the promise of the Messias, and their whole history was directed towards its accomplishment.

The people of Israel prepared the way for the Church, the Israel of God. In the divine plan, the Church was to be the heir to the faith of the patriarchs, the religion of the prophets, the sacrifices of the priests, the generosity of the 'poor' of Israel; or rather, the Church was the perfection, the consummation of what had been a long and intricate preparation. Israel had been the shadow in the past of the Church which is the divine reality manifest in this world.

Slowly down the ages, from Abraham to Moses, from Moses to David, from David to the exile, from the exile to Christ, the Jewish soul gradually made ready for the Christian soul, the Jewish people made ready for the Church, the mystical body of Christ. God had chosen this people, not through any merit on its part, 'thy father was an Amorrhite, and thy mother a Cethite, and when thou wast born . . . thou wast cast out upon the face of the earth' (Ezech. 16.5); and he formed in this people, by his revelations, his graces and his punishments also, a 'remnant', living by the thought of the prophets and destined one day to become the Israel of God.

A few examples of this interpretation of the Old Testament in the light of the New

(a) The development of the exalted idea of God in Israel. To begin with Moses, we see Yahweh presented at that time under aspects which were destined increasingly to free Israel from every false and narrow concept of its God. Freely and by an act of grace, Yahweh chose Israel. This God of the little nation of Israel gradually appears to his people as he who, far from being the peculiar property of the nation he protected, as were the Semitic gods, would manifest his power over the other nations and over nature and reveal himself as the master of all natural forces. This God whom it was forbidden to represent by images or symbols, appears more and more clearly as a being superior by nature to everything visible and tangible, and so even the simplest souls will realize something of God's spirituality and transcendence. This God does not seem concerned primarily with worship and sacrifices but with obedience to his moral precepts, to the Decalogue. Thus there grew up in Israel that moral monotheism which was unique in the ancient world.

The prophets were never to cease raising the soul of Israel to an increasingly profound understanding of the divine attributes. Amos drew attention to his justice. Osee to his tender but jealous love, Isaias to his grandeur and transcendence. Jeremias taught the Israelites a more inward religion, Ezechiel called their attention to the demands of God's holiness, deutero-Isaias, in the period of the exile, enlarged the universal scope of Yahweh's religion and the place of suffering in the service of God. The Psalms, Israel's book of prayer, taught Israel increasingly to be constantly searching for God, and to have that confidence in him, which is the soul of true religion.

In the course of her journey through the centuries, Israel received from God these exquisite texts which are of eternal value and were to be repeated by our Lord: 'Though shalt love the Lord thy God, with thy whole heart, and with thy whole soul, and with thy whole strength' (Deut. 6.5) and 'Be ye holy, because I the Lord your God am holy' (Lev. 19.2).

Of course any historian can find historical evidence of this increasingly clear progress of Israel in moral monotheism and will reach this conclusion on the basis of the literal sense alone of the scriptural texts. But where he will only see an interesting historical fact which clearly created a climate favourable to the birth of Christianity, the exegete who is also a believer will discover, in the light of the New Testament, a plan willed by God and God's positive intervention through the agency of Moses and the prophets in the history of Israel.

(b) The Covenant between God and Israel leading to the Church, Christ's mystical body. Christ linked the society he founded to the society or people of Israel whose history is seen as a preparation for Christianity, introducing gradually into the Israelite community the religious attitudes which were to find in the religion of Christ their fulfilment and their consummation.

Jesus understood his work as a supreme fulfilment of Israel's expectation ('I am not come to destroy but to fulfil', Matt. 5.17); he chose twelve apostles who 'shall sit on twelve thrones, judging the twelve tribes of Israel' (Matt. 19.28). St Paul considers the Christians as the true sons of Abraham (Gal. 3.29; 4.31) and the Christian community as the Israel of God (Gal. 6.16). One point must be emphasized: Paul expressly taught that the whole outlook of the Old Testament was centred not on the Law but on the *promise,* God's free and gratuitous choice of Abraham's posterity.

Now this covenant manifested increasingly clearly in the course of the ages the fundamental characteristics of the choice God was to make of his Church. There is a gratuitous covenant on God's part, a divine gift (hence the way is prepared for the Christian doctrine of grace); a covenant whose final goal will only become fully clear during the last centuries before Christ.

The ultimate goal of this covenant was the establishment of the reign of Yahweh over the world (in the early days Christianity was preached as the coming of the Kingdom); the covenant was characterized by the promise of an astonishing posterity for Abraham (a posterity whose meaning would only be revealed in its final outcome, in Jesus Christ). The covenant, which God always kept, was constantly violated by acts of infidelity on Israel's part and so implanted in men's souls an acute sense of sin (and this sense of sin is the foundation of the Christian doctrine of Redemption). The idea of the covenant became spiritualized as a result of the nation's misfortunes, at least in the noblest souls of Israel, and these were to constitute the 'remnant' announced by the prophets (and this 'remnant' was to become the nucleus of the Christian Church). The covenant in the last centuries before Christ was destined, as men realized, to be fulfilled in the future, in the prospect of 'better times', and this prospect, which became increasingly eschatological in character, was directed towards the end of time (and so Christian thought would be helped to turn easily towards the world of the future, towards eternity). In this evolution of the idea of the Covenant, ideas that are even specifically Christian are seen to come temporarily to the surface of Israel's consciousness at certain periods: the idea of redemptive suffering in the second part of Isaias, the idea of universalism in the same book and in Jonas.

Here again a strict historical exegesis, divorced from faith, can note these essential characteristics of Israel's religion. It can observe these ideological links between Israel's religion and that of Christ; but only intellectual understanding based on belief in the divine and human value of the Incarnation will permit us to see in these characteristics of the religion of Israel a gradual ascent towards a higher truth and so, *pro modulo nostro,* to grasp the true meaning of Israel's evolution in the mind of God.

(c) The expectation of the Messias in Israel. We cannot attempt to sketch here, even in its main outlines, the complex and intricate history of the messianic hope in Israel. Such a subject requires a whole volume. Every exegete is aware of the manifold problems regarding dating and interpretation which this branch of study presents and the numerous points that remain obscure. It is certain however that, if the evolution of the messianic hope still remains difficult to follow from period to period, the fact of this hope, such as it was on the eve of Christ's coming, cannot be contested. For the precise purposes of this chapter what is important is to emphasize how this messianic hope was always closely united to and incorporated

Jean Levie

in the events and the persons of Israel's history. It is because David was the national sovereign *par excellence* (in whom the whole ideal of the nation's mind was fulfilled) that the Messias to come was thought of as a son of David. It was with David in mind, a native of Bethlehem, that the prophet Micheas saw salvation emerging from a birth at Bethlehem. It was on account of the great role of the prophets in Israel that the prophecy of Deuteronomy promising Israel a line of prophets for as long as her history should last (Deut. 18.15 seq.) was interpreted as referring to him whom Israel awaited as the prophet *par excellence,* the Messias. And so the examples continue. The need for this 'saviour' was experienced in times of national disaster and his characteristics were determined on the basis of the concrete realities of the nation's life. In a word, we are not to imagine the messianic expectation and its expression in our inspired texts as heavenly phenomena appearing from on high from beyond space and time. It is through a more intimate understanding of Israel's history with all its vicissitudes, its trials and its revivals, that we shall reach a better understanding of the messianic hope. Here, too, faith penetrating to the total meaning of the Incarnation must be linked with a very accurate historical interpretation if we are to have a true appreciation of Israel's messianic hope.

(d) The Old Testament development of the terms in which Christian dogma was to be expressed. Jesus was born into the Jewish environment at a given moment in history. It is from the thought processes of this environment that he himself chose the terms in which to express his own mission, his own doctrine, and by choosing them, conferred on them a definitive Christian value. He declared that it was he who would establish the reign of God on earth and, although he gave a unique height and depth to this idea, he maintained intact the foundations it had acquired in Israel in the course of the centuries. He gradually led his disciples to recognize that he was the 'Christ', the 'Messias' of Israel's expectation (the confession of Peter: Mark 8.29; Matt. 16.16) and, though he infinitely enlarged the scope of the word by the implicit inclusion of the attributes of his own personality, he preserved its ancient and fundamental meaning of 'anointing' by God.

47

He presented his teaching in the religious terms common in Israel: 'justification' in the sight of God; the antithesis of 'the just' and 'the sinners'; the 'poor' are blessed, (and the word 'poor', *ébiônim* had a more complex meaning in Israel than among us today) and a host of other expressions which are being carefully studied in our times, as they evolved from the earliest period down to that of Jesus and on his lips acquired a deeper meaning in the Christian synthesis while remaining in line with the past. It is in the context of the ancient commandments—ἐντολαί—(the greatest of the commandments (Matt. 22.37); the duty to keep the commandments of the Decalogue (Matt. 19.17 seq.); the second commandment like unto the first (Matt. 21.39); that he inculcates the obligations of the new Law. But he extends to all men with exception the precept of brotherly charity (parable of the good Samaritan, which excludes all racial distinctions: Luke 10.29-37) and admits no limits to the duty to forgive (Matt. 18.21-2). He returns to the ancient Decalogue but gives it a far deeper significance (Matt. 5.21 seq.).

For his hearers Christ's preaching was vibrant with the religious past of the Old Testament. They found in it many a familiar image—God the shepherd of Israel (Jesus, the good shepherd); Israel, Yahweh's vineyard ('I am the vine, you are the branches'), etc.; literary devices their piety cherished (parables; Semitic metres) etc. But this past looks towards new and hitherto unheard-of prospects ('Never did man speak like this man', John 7.46).

What was true of Christ during his life on earth was equally true after his death. For his disciples and for the first Christian converts from Judaism, the cross of Christ became intelligible because it stood out against the background of the sacrifices of the Old Law (cf. among other texts the Epistle to the Hebrews) and because it appeared interpreted beforehand by Isaias, chapters 52, 53 (cf. for example, Acts 8.32-5). In this way, they were ready to understand and to express its redemptive value. When the early Church desired to express to herself and to tell others all that Christ was, as he had revealed himself to her, it was in the texts of the Old Testament devoted to the

Wisdom of Yahweh that she first found a vocabulary most suited to her purpose.

These few examples—chosen from many—are sufficient to give us an understanding of this remote preparation for the Christian revelation through the vocabulary of the Old Testament. Any historian can take note of this fact without departing from the literal exegesis of the texts. It seems natural enough to him that Jesus and his disciples should draw upon their times and their religious environment. The Jewish contemporaries of Jesus were happy to rely on the whole of their religious past in order to understand him. But for us Christians, the point of view is the exact opposite: it is in the light of Christ that the meaning of the Old Testament as a whole becomes clear, it is through and in Christ that we reach a better understanding of all that prepared the way for him.

(e) Facts, events, persons and formulas in the Old Testament: symbols and types that prefigure and prophesy the facts, the events, the persons and the truths of the New Testament.

As we have seen, the Old Testament, in the total evolution of its history, and above all through the evolution of its religious thought, forms a progressive ascent (in spite of temporary recessions, checks and deviations) towards Christ and Christianity. Through its prophets (often obscurely and in an involved kind of way) it announces Christ and Christianity. These aspects of the Old Testament are clearly manifest to anyone who studies them; he need not set aside the literal meaning of the inspired texts, but he acquires a deeper understanding of this literal meaning.

Can we go further and discover in certain particular facts and in certain persons in the Old Testament a prophetic meaning, a foretaste of the realities of the New Testament? Can we even discover occasionally in certain formulas of the Old Testament an almost prophetic capacity for expressing realities belonging to the New? If so, this would be a (limited) extension of prophecy properly so-called, but with this difference that it would be not a conscious and willed prophecy on the part of the human author, but intended and uttered by God alone as the principal author of Scripture.

Now we find that from the first days of Christianity, from the times of Jesus, his apostles and evangelists, the Old Testament was looked on in this light. Christ saw in Elias a type of John the Baptist and he considered that the Jewish expectation concerning Elias's literal return had been fulfilled in John the Baptist (Matt. 11.14; 17.12-3). When Christ instituted the Eucharist, he did so in terms which called, in relation to his own blood of the New Testament, the blood of the Old Covenant with which Moses sprinkled the people (Exod. 24.8) as a former 'type' of the New Covenant.

St Paul (Rom. 5.14) pointed to Adam as the type of the Christ to come (τύπος τοῦ μέλλοντος) and, in the celebrated passage in Rome. 5.12-19, emphasized that this comparison was possible because both Adam and Christ were the sources of things to come, were initial causes; on the other hand, St Paul underlines the essential differences that separated them (vv. 15-9). This word τύπος is the root of the expression 'typological sense' which we tend to prefer nowadays to the other terms (spiritual sense, allegorical sense, etc.). St Paul uses the same word again (1 Cor. 10.1-11) when he compares the Israelites at the time of the Exodus with certain Christians at Corinth and their apparent tendencies. All these Israelites 'in Moses were baptized, in the cloud and in the sea' (the crossing of the Red Sea), all 'did eat of the same spiritual food' (the miraculous manna) and 'all drank the same spiritual drink' (the water from the miraculous rock), like these Corinthian Christians who had been baptized and had received the Eucharist; and yet what happened to the Israelites might happen also to them: 'but with the most of them God was not well pleased'. Paul further stressed this parallel by seeing in the 'miraculous rock' a presence (in some sense) of Christ in the midst of the Israelites in the desert: 'and the rock was Christ'. He concluded with these words: 'Now these things were done in a figure of us': ταῦτα δὲ τύποι ἡμῶν ἐγενήθησαν (v. 6), and further on (v. 11): 'Now all these things happened to them in figure; and they are written for our correction, upon whom the ends of the world are come': εἰς οὓς τὰ τέλη τῶν αἰώνων κατήντηκεν. This seems to suggest that it is the privilege of Christians who are people 'upon whom the ends of the world

50

are come', to be able to be prefigured in this way. In Gal. 4.21-9, he makes a very detailed parallel between Sara and Agar, as prefiguring respectively the Jerusalem from on high, the mother of Christians, and the earthly Jerusalem, the mother of the Jews. He uses this expression: 'Which things are said by an allegory': ἅτινά ἐστιν ἀλληγορούμενα, (4.24). But from this point of view, what is of far greater importance is the constant insistence in St Paul's letters (for instance, Gal. 3.7-9, 14, 16-8, 29; Rom. 4.1-5, 9-13, 16-25, etc.) upon Abraham as the father of all believers and justified by his faith: 'Now it is not written only for him, that it was reputed to him unto justice, but also for us, to whom it shall be reputed, if we believe . . .' (Rom. 4.23-4). Cf. other examples: Rom. 9.6-13; 11.4-5 (Christians form the 'remnant' chosen by grace and prefigured in the 7,000 men saved in 3 Kings 19.18), etc.

The evangelist St Matthew offers a fair number of cases of typological application, for instance, Matt. 3.1: the desert through which the Israelites returned from exile (Matt. 1-3) to their native land so long desired, is seen as the symbol of the desert in which John the Baptist announced that the Kingdom of God had begun. The preaching of Jonas, which Jesus treated as a symbol of his own (Luke 11.29-30), is given the exact sense in Matt. 12.39-41 of a figurative prophecy of the resurrection of Jesus. Matthew likes to form his own sentences with words from the Old Testament used formerly in similar situations; for instance, the angel's words to Joseph in Egypt telling him to return to his own country, are an exact reproduction of those used in Exod. 4.19 instructing Moses to go back to Egypt. Cf. also Matt. 2.15 and Osee 11.1; Matt. 2.19 and Jer. 31.15; Matt. 26.31 and Zach. 13.7 (it should be added that these cases are often closer to 'accommodation' than to the typological sense).

The first Epistle of St Peter compares salvation through Christian baptism with the rescuing of the eight persons saved from the Flood in Noe's ark (3.20-1) and expressly says: 'Whereunto baptism being of the like form, now saveth you also'.

The Epistle to the Hebrews contains a good deal of typology, especially in its comparison between the supreme priesthood of Christ and the priesthood of Melchisedech (6.20-7.28), and in the antithesis of the sacrifice of Christ, the sovereign priest, by which he entered once and for all into the heavenly Holy of Holies, and the annual sacrifice of the Old Covenant by the High Priest in Israel (8.1-10.18).

On the strength of similar examples and under various other influences (Philo, for example, and the secular exegesis of Alexandria), Christian exegesis in the early centuries acquired in certain circles, in particular among the Christians of Alexandria, a very pronounced and often excessive allegorical character. It is not part of our task here to give an account of of the various movements that make up the history of exegesis. On the chief and best representative of allegorical exegesis, Origen, the recent books of Fr Daniélou and Fr de Lubac may be consulted with profit.

St Thomas introduced a distinction that has become universally accepted, between the words of the inspired author which establish the literal sense, and the things signified by these words, which establish the spiritual sense (which we now prefer to call the typological sense, since the literal sense is often eminently spiritual). *Ipsae res significatae per voces etiam significant aliquid . . . Significatio qua voces significant res, pertinet ad . . . sensum litteralem. Illa vero significatio qua res significatae per voces iterum res alias significant dicitur sensus spiritualis, qui super litteralem fundatur et eum supponit.* It is then easy to see that the literal meaning expressed by the phrase as the inspired author thought it, must be consciously grasped by him, while the typological sense which is expressed by the things to which he refers depends on God alone who alone creates and disposes according to his own plan the things, the events and the persons in this world. Yet it must be added that this 'type' must be studied as the sacred author presents it with the characteristics he high-lights and which normally provided the foundation for the typological interpretation.

The typological sense of Scripture (and this is true also of its plenary sense) has aroused keen interest among Catholic exegetes—as well as among a certain number of Protestants—during the past twenty years, and has given rise to a fairly copious literature (both books and articles). The subject has even given rise to polemics between two opposing tendencies in modern minds; there was, for example, the fairly strong opposition (*Dieu vivant,* No. 14, 1949, pp. 75-94) of Paul Claudel, Louis Massignon and Fr Jean Daniélou, against an article by Fr Steinmann (*La Vie intellectuelle,* March 1949). This is not the place to write the history of these controversies.

The principles and the scriptural examples brought forward above make it possible for us to arrive at the following conclusions:

I. Typological (or spiritual) exegesis, to be found in Christian thought from the earliest times and constantly continuing with various alternatives down to our own time, is to be considered legitimate and justified from the supernatural standpoint both theologically and historically, and spiritually fruitful.

II. This typological exegesis has found its surest, deepest expression in those inspired texts of the New Testament which are the foundation of dogmatic or theological conclusions of immense importance: Christ the second Adam; Abraham the father of all believers; the Christian Church as Israel according to the Spirit by contrast with Israel according to the flesh, etc.

III. In so far as it proceeds on the analogy of these fundamental examples and of others to be found in the Fathers or the liturgy, and which have become part of the treasury of Christian devotion: for instance the traditional 'types' of the sacrifice of Calvary—the sacrifice of Isaac, the trials of Jeremias, Isaias's Suffering Servant, etc.; the traditional symbols for Mary—the new Eve, the Ark of the Covenant, etc., in so far then, as it proceeds on these lines, typological exegesis will prove uplifting and enriching for Christian souls, and will avoid degenerating into mere human virtuosity and ingenuity, brilliant rather than solid or constructive.

IV. Typological exegesis will prove justified to the extent that it fits naturally into the general evolution of Israel's history and thought as they move towards Christ and Christianity, as I have shown in the previous pages. In his fine book *La lecture chrétienne de la Bible* (quoted above), Fr Charlier has underlined the following principle governing typological interpretation: 'the typological value of an Old Testament fact is only certain if on the plane of historical evolution and by internal continuity it is linked with the fulfilment in Christianity of the prototype we read into it' (p. 325).

Our Christian understanding of the Old Testament will be all the more accurate and a greater inspiration to our devotion in proportion as it refuses to attach itself to isolated and incidental superficial resemblances, and remains ever attentive to the overall movement of Israel's gradual progress towards Christ. Any priest, as he recites the Psalms in his breviary, knows that God loved Israel, for her own sake doubtless, but still more as preparing the way for the Church of Christ. He knows that the kings of David's line are called blessed in the Psalms for their own sakes no doubt, but still more because they were signs and figures of the supreme Anointed One, Jesus the Christ. In a sense then, in his present-day devotion, *a fortiori* he can think of Christ in the passages where the king is exalted, of the Church as the community of the faithful in the passages where Israel is praised, and so on. If God's plan is essentially centred on the mystery of the Incarnation, we enter into it when we pray in this way.

Explanatory note. In principle I have vindicated typological exegesis of the Old Testament in the light of the New. May I go further and admit a typological exegesis of the New Testament (and so by implication of the Old Testament) in the light of the consummation of God's kingdom in the blessedness of heaven? Such an exegesis would be in line with the fundamental logic of Christian typology. If God's reign is merely in a state of preparation in this world and is only fully realized in its consummation in heaven, if the Church militant only reaches its full stature in the Church triumphant, if grace is essentially an *initium gloriae* (a beginning of glory), if faith prepares us for vision, and so forth, must we not conclude that religious realities in this world, as they prepare the way for the ultimate realities of heaven, must be capable of prefiguring and proclaiming their future accomplishment, and so of directing souls towards them?

Jean Levie

II. *Sacred Scripture in the Light of Dogma as a living reality in the Church*

The second Thesis applied.

(a) God alone can contemplate from the beginning the total synthesis of Christian doctrine, essentially communicated in the apostolic era and growing more explicit and more highly developed until the end of time in Christ's Church. God alone can contemplate from the beginning and in terms of this synthesis, the ultimate connection between the doctrinal texts scattered throughout Scripture. So that the full Christian doctrine and the continual light of Scripture might always be present, indefectible and unerring at every period, God has willed to found a Church composed of pastors and of the faithful, which lives ever more intimately Christ's own life throughout the centuries and discovers ever more clearly this same Christ in inspired Scripture. Scripture has been given to us as something that must be lived, penetrated, interpreted in and by the Church of Christ and in the light of this same Church's doctrinal, moral and mystical progress. The part the Church is called upon to play is by no means limited to guidance and control of scriptural interpretation by the Magisterium. It is brought into action also in the collective Christian thought, in the common religious life of the Church's children, both pastors and faithful, under the influence of the Spirit. It is not just a matter of projecting artificially into the scriptural formulas a conceptual explanation that has been acquired after five, ten or twenty centuries of Christian faith. It is rather to draw the logical consequences of the dogma which teaches that Christ infallibly guides his Church by discovering in the light of doctrine already explicit or in the process of becoming so, what announced and prepared it in the inspired texts. This is what has been rightly called the plenary sense of Scripture, that is, in accordance with the definition which has been admirably formulated by several writers over the past twenty years, that deeper sense, willed by God, obscurely glimpsed, grasped implicitly but not explicitly elucidated by the human author, which becomes explicit through the instrumentality of the whole of revelation as it is lived at any given moment in the Church and so clarifies more completely the inspired texts in the eyes of the believer.

An attempt must now be made to clarify these principles by applying them.

i. Christ, the God-Man, involved in the concrete environment of his time and in the mentality of the period, clearly spoke in language directly suited to his hearers, corresponding to their religious formation and their noblest aspirations which he had shared since his childhood. But transcending his environment and his time by his superior knowledge as Man-God, he alone was able to create a theandric language contemporary with every epoch.

In this world, a man, even if he is a genius, is rarely fully master of his own thought, whose fundamental principles may remain below the level of his consciousness. He is never master of the future of his teaching, for the latter escapes his control as soon as it is formulated. Does he even know what history will have done a century later with his most cherished ideas? Since Jesus is God-Man, he is complete master of his teaching both in the realm of its inherent values and in that of its active power over men. As men's Creator and able to penetrate to the most secret places of human nature, he knows the power over our life and thought possessed by the least idea, the least emotion introduced by him into the souls of his disciples. As master of the future, he knows under what form— thought, action, rite, prayer or precept—he should communicate a given truth to men so that, progressing in accordance with man's nature, it may develop without ceasing to be itself, and become more explicit without losing its identity. Jesus does not leave his doctrine to the hazards of history which would inevitably do away with or deform certain parts of it. He does not deliver it over to the whims of individual interpretation which, even when forced to acknowledge the weight of evidence, still keeps its privilege of turning the blind eye. Jesus knows that a Church, his

Bride, is the continuation of himself, and that she understands him by word or action. He knows his Church in advance both in the state in which she now is and in the process of her evolution, and in her he will continue to live until the end of time. This is why the revelation Jesus left to his Church, a revelation in the strictest sense complete and perfect, was not to be and could not be perfected in any human fashion, as would be the case with a philosophical doctrine passed on to his disciples by some thinker, but in a far deeper, far more living fashion, at once divine and human. The thinker is in fact only one point in history and he is doomed to disappear. Jesus commands the future and himself controls the destiny of the words he has entrusted to it.

He alone is able to cast into the soil of humanity a doctrine so perfectly adapted to man's psychology and human evolution, that it will grow, develop with mankind without ceasing to be itself, and this is because he alone knows the secret of life, he alone can see the tree in its seed. Such a type of teaching is doubtless unprecedented, unique, but is not Christianity the only divine religion, and is not the soul of Christ unique in history?

All Catholic theologians agree, I think, as to this plenary sense of Christ's words in the Gospel. But several may object that in the Gospel we are dealing with the words of Christ, Man-God and supreme source of revelation, and not with the words of inspired apostles. The plenary sense of the supreme word of revelation is not absolutely identical with the plenary sense of inspired writing as such. Agreed. But this transcendent and unique case is fundamentally the essential principle underlying all the other examples of the plenary sense, and gives the reason for and throws its light on them all.

2. I now pass from Christ's teaching in the Gospels to the teaching of the apostles in their Epistles. I said at the beginning that all exegetes have an essential duty to aim at understanding as intimately and as deeply as possible each of the inspired writers (Paul, John, etc.) not only from the standpoint of human

psychology, but above all in line with the whole living and lived synthesis of their religious and theological ideas. This study must be as objective as possible, strictly faithful to the texts and during this primary work of literal interpretation must scrupulously avoid any unconscious introduction of our present thought as twentieth century Christians into that of Paul.

But this effort at strictly literal interpretation will sometimes note in Paul's thought ideas that are adumbrated but left incomplete, tendencies which do not yet reach their full development, various aspects of his thought which are not yet completely reconciled, and so this attempt at a strictly literal interpretation of the man himself must be continued by an effort—through the analogy of faith and the flowering of Paul's thought in the Church—to reach the thought of God speaking through Paul. The living synthesis of Paul's thought, which is the final aim of Pauline exegesis, is not for us Christian interpreters merely the thought of a man, as in the case of the thought of a philosopher or a secular moralist; it is the expression of God's thought, it is a message from God. It can only be fully understood in its deepest and ultimate sense by God. True it is, in Paul, something personal, something intimately lived, closely incorporated into the aspirations and experiences of the man. Yet at the same time it is, and much more profoundly, God's possession and he alone knows the secret of the most central truths of his revelation.

Paul therefore in his own thought is transcended by a greater than himself, by the very Master of all thought who has only expressed himself completely in the human thought of Christ. Of course the sincere exegete may nowhere put in a 'finishing touch', so as to make Paul say what the Church says today, but he must be able to note Paul's 'unfinished work', Paul's 'limitations' and in this he is guided by the more complete answers offered by the Church as a result of the progressive explicit definition of divine revelation.

In any case, Paul's 'unfinished' work is not merely something negative. 'Unfinished' implies 'beginning', and how often, in a short section of a sentence, in the logical convergence of two lines of thought, the exegete will acknowledge how astonishingly up-to-date St Paul can be!

God who has made man, like society, capable of evolution and progress, wills that divine truth which is always substantially identical with itself, should grow in the minds and hearts of men and be constantly adapted to the forward movement of man's life on earth. Hence in the present-day dogmatic synthesis which has issued from the inspired writing of the Epistles of Paul, there will be explicitations, developments which existed only in germ, only virtually in the considered thought of St Paul and appeared there under a quite different aspect, in spite of the fundamental identity between them. All this was part of God's original plan, for he is the one and only Master of time and its epochs, of past, present and future.

The Church alone is kept in being by God as 'magistra veritatis', mistress of truth, it is in her alone that the Christian synthesis is fashioned as God wills, in her alone that we can find it and live it more and more perfectly as the centuries go by. This is why the fundamental interpretation of holy Scripture by the Church is not merely a matter of correcting the individual errors of the exegetes, of simply remedying the 'obscurities' of Scripture; it is essentially deduced from the very nature of holy Scripture as God has conceived it; Scripture has been given to us, destined to be continually interpreted by the Church.

How often as he considers more closely the conclusions drawn by the Church from the texts of St. Paul in our Catholic dogma, the exegete notes that, on the one hand, these conclusions make explicit and complete what only appears in outline in St Paul and, on the other, that they are perfectly homogeneous with St Paul's thought and carefully follow all its trends. A given contribution to Christian thought from Paul's pen in a given text only acquires its genuine value for Christian life as a whole in the precise terms the Church uses to complete it and to make it explicit. And surely this is precisely what is meant by the plenary sense?

3. In the divine plan, the theological synthesis of each inspired New Testament author's thought is only part of a greater doctrinal synthesis, whose centre God alone knows and whose manifold ramifications he alone can see. Paul's thought has to take its place beside that of John, Peter and James, so that all their thoughts may together constitute the Christian synthesis.

An exegete interpreting secular authors is never allowed to elucidate, to clarify or to make explicit the thought of one writer by using the thought of another of the same or a previous period, unless he is able to discover and prove by historical facts that one influenced the other or that there was at least some common influence exercised by their environment upon both. But if, on the contrary, we are dealing with inspired writers who are witnesses to the climate of thought in the infant Church—and on the Christian hypothesis this climate of thought is guided by God towards his total divine synthesis just as they themselves also are—the Catholic exegete will have to take into account this divine factor in his interpretation. This will certainly not give him the right as an exegete to read rash concordances into the writings of different inspired authors, but it will often help him in cases where the thought of Paul, John or Luke seems to come to a halt, to gain a better insight, in the light of the total revelation as it grows increasingly explicit, into the radical agreement between the various individual inspired thoughts. It will help him to discern more clearly the general direction of each particular movement of thought towards the doctrinal synthesis in its present stage of development, it will help him to a better understanding and a better vindication, before the demands of his conscience as a historian, of the progress of dogma as it has evolved in the Church, on the basis of the convergence of various inspired writings whose implications have been 'lived' in Christian thought. Here again, this whole process is only seen to be coherent and intelligible in the light of the concept of the plenary sense of certain inspired texts.

4. It seems logical to extend still further the fundamental principles in this field by considering, in its entirety, the Church's task. The doctrinal synthesis of the mystery of Christ, founded as it is upon primitive tradition and Sacred Scripture, becomes explicit throughout the centuries in the Church. The Church's understanding of divine revelation is called upon to grow ever deeper 'unto the measure of the age of the fullness of Christ' (Ephes. 4.13). At each stage in this development, the thought of the inspired writers shows itself rich in new inferences and applications which were not explicitly stated in previous cen-

turies, but which now are seen to be in line with this thought. If the exegete, using the correct method, always adheres to his duty to note as precisely as is humanly possible the degree to which the conscious teaching of the inspired writers was explicit, in the light of the information provided by the environment and the period in which these writers lived, then he should also be able, as a theologian, to recognize and bring to light the homogeneous nature, the fundamental continuity clearly existing between the doctrinal synthesis of the first century and the Catholic synthesis of the twentieth. At this point, the great Christian criteria are relevant: the analogy of faith, the rôle of tradition, the interpretation of the Magisterium. What is relevant above all is that fundamental sense, which the exegete must preserve, of the divine thought adapting to each era our understanding of the mystery of Christ in and through the Church. The divine thought causes the understanding of Jesus Christ to grow increasingly explicit throughout the centuries in our Christian minds guided by the Magisterium.

In the great edifice whose builder is God, in the temple whose corner-stone is Christ (Ephes. 3.20-2), each of the apostles had his part and God himself determined his place in the building as a whole. The foundations, laid by each one independently of the others, met and joined at the precise spots foreseen by the divine Architect. Each man's style of architecture is predestined to harmonize with that of the others in the interests of the beauty of the whole. The Temple is faithfully built on the foundations that have been laid, under the guidance of the same Spirit who inspired the apostles and the prophets and who enlightens God's Church until the end of time.

Pierre Grelot
1917-

In 1959 the second edition of a comprehensive two-volume work called Introduction à la Bible *appeared in France. Edited by A. Robert (who died before it came out) and A. Feuillet, it bore a laudatory preface by the Bishop of Strasbourg, Jean Julien Weber. It represented the cream of French Catholic scholarship and was widely acclaimed as solid testimony to the marvelous progress made since Pius XII's 1943 encyclical promoting Biblical studies. No one was therefore really surprised that this work should have been singled out for special attack by the ultraconservative group that was making its last-ditch effort to prevent the acceptance of modern studies in the Church. When the work appeared in English translation in 1968, that battle was long over, thanks to Pope John XXIII and Vatican II.*

Pierre Grelot, eminent Professor for long years at the Institut Catholique in Paris, authored the final chapter of the first volume of that work, a broad overview of how the Old Testament came into being. It is that chapter which appears as the following selection. It is a model of clarity, showing how an awareness of the various developments of the six different periods in the life of Israel is essential for a proper grasp of the literature found in the Old Testament. It is in summarizing a wealth of detail in such a way as to bring out the contour of the evolving community that Grelot is at his best. In 1962, before Vatican II got under way, he demonstrated this same ability again with the publication of a wide-ranging study of the problems of "a Christian interpretation" of the Old Testament, grappling with the thorny issue of the various senses of Scripture and the whole problem of how the Old Testament ought to be used in Christian theology. Whether one was persuaded by his arguments or not, it was impossible not to admire his vast historical knowledge, his keen sense for the theological, and the responsible manner in which he approached the entire question.

To admit some of the difficulties associated with formulating a "theology of the Old Testament," however, should not be construed as any kind of questioning of the importance of the Old Testament. On the contrary, it is precisely the Christian conviction of the irreplaceable position of the Old as the key to the New Testament that prompts the concern for clarification. Ever since the second century, when Gnostics like Marcion wanted to jettison the Old Testament, the Church has doggedly insisted that both Testaments be printed under one cover as parts of one "Book," phases of one story. Even in the darkest days of Biblical neglect, fundamentalism, and fear, the Catholic tradition never let loose of that conviction. But a new day has clearly dawned when work of the caliber of Grelot's begins to characterize Catholic handling of the Old Testament.

INTRODUCTION TO
THE OLD TESTAMENT

PRELIMINARY REMARKS

1. The Genesis of the Bible

The various parts of the Old Testament have been studied in the preceding chapters. After having traced as a whole the history of Israel from the patriarchal period to the threshold of the New Testament, each of the biblical books was analyzed in the framework of the broader category in which it is now present: Torah, prophets, hagiographers and deuterocanonical books. It will be profitable now to take up again from a new angle the results of these analyses, in order to present as a whole the development of the Old Testament from an essentially *literary* point of view. It is not as though this were the principal aspect of the Bible; its doctrinal value is infinitely more important. But in order to realize what was, in its concrete reality, the progress of divine revelation linked to the spiritual education of Israel, it is necessary to follow first of all step by step the genesis of the collection of books, which, in each period, testify to it. The historical framework of its formation henceforth is known and each book or book fragment has been the object of a critical and doctrinal exposition; it is fitting to show groupings, linkings, influences, and subordinations which could not be the object of the preceding studies since they separated for practical reasons works deriving from the same time or the same milieu. If, in this perspective, it sometimes happens that a side-glance is cast upon some works foreign to the Bible, it does not follow that they are being put on the same footing as the Bible. What we are trying to retrace here is not a history of Hebraic and Jewish literature, but only the gradual formation of the inspired books.

Thus conceived, the literary history of the Old Testament affords a solid point of departure for biblical theology, in order for the latter to be something else than a repertory of themes, presented independently from the historical development which, from the faith of Abraham, leads to the Judaism contemporaneous with Christ. That is to say that this development itself will constantly be sketched on the background of our study. We will avoid, however, attempting on the sole plan of the Old Testament a doctrinal synthesis which could seem desirable to more than one reader. It is because, first of all, the Christian study of the Bible cannot separate the two Covenants; the theological meaning of the Old Testament, which we must uphold, reveals itself only in light of the New Testament. The first constitutes an ascent toward Christ; but it still carries with it, on the level of institutions as well as of ideas, provisional materials which must either be surpassed or rethought. Christ, in His person, His acts and His words, clarifies, in retrospect, all that precedes Him; He is, by that very fact, a principle of interpretation and a criterion for choice. We will therefore reserve the synthesis of biblical theology for the time when the New Testament will allow us to define the meaning of the Old Testament, since in its original novelty, it will be a fulfilment of the Sacred Scriptures.

Furthermore, it seems useful to us not to confuse two aspects of the Old Testament which despite the fact that they are closely united, are yet quite distinct: the books where biblical revelation was crystallized and the complex of institutions where these books were born. God, by various means, spoke to a people whom He was calling to the faith. The people not only preserved His Word in the form of a written collection which grew with time, but also in its living tradition, much more elusive, even though the writings which it left us find their roots in it. In order to be complete, a history of revelation should evoke this living tradition which is the echo of the Divine Word in the history of a human community. One would then have to go beyond the framework of the Bible and give a place, for instance, to the literary productions of Judaism during the last centuries before Christ and during the time of the New Testament: is it not in relation to this concrete milieu, broader than the canon of the Scriptures shows it to be, that Jesus preached and lived, that the Gospel was announced, and the Church founded, in short that the New Covenant relieved the Old? So be it; but our present intention is more restricted; we are studying the Sacred Scriptures and them alone; we are trying to realize how their collection was made. This undoubtedly requires close attention to the life of the Chosen People, in all the meanderings of a complicated history, but only as a term of reference without which the genesis of the Bible could not at all be understood.

2. Limits and Divisions of this Sketch

Useful as a genetic study of the Bible is, it nonetheless entails a measure of uncertainty. Not only because our information on Israelite and Jewish literature is sparse: it is understood that we are limiting our study only to the preserved works which appear in the canon. But, even for these, how many precise details are lacking! The localities, the authors and even the periods cause problems. Next to assured critical conclusions, there are times when we can only count upon probable or possible solutions. A tableau like the one we are undertaking here can only be presented therefore as a provisional plan. If it allows a better view of the organic unity of the Bible, it is certain that the future will bring corrections, and more precise and perfect details to it. It is important to understand it with this reservation of principle, which from the outset establishes its limitations.

As to the great literary periods of the Old Testament, they coincide in a way with that of the history of Israel. The period of preparation which precedes the reign of David is very important from the historical and religious point of view, since it sees revelation born with Abraham, become more precise with Moses, and implanted in Chanaan after the conquest and at the time of the Judges. But on the literary level, it is much more difficult to capture because, in a certain measure, its productions were incorporated into vaster syntheses, done during the royal period. With David and Solomon, Israelite literature soars under its written form, when Jerusalem becomes an important cultural center (10th-9th centuries). After the schism, this literature develops in a parallel fashion in the two kingdoms of Juda and of Israel; but primarily, the two traditions meet when the "remnant" of Israel takes refuge in Juda after the ruin of Samaria (9th-8th centuries). The humiliation of Juda during the apogee of Assyria coincides with an apparently slack literary period; then, during the last fifty years of the Judean State, there is a renewal which continues at the time of the Babylonian captivity, while the theocratic organization of Judaism little by little replaces the former political institutions of the royal period (7th-6th centuries). The Persian period sees Judaism becoming established; at the same time, collections of the ancient books become a body and new literary currents are developed (6th-4th centuries). Finally, the conquests of Alexander place Judaism opposite the Hellenistic civilization, and its literature suffers the shocks of this confrontation (4th-1st centuries). We will thus distinguish six successive periods, while recognizing that such a schema comprises its share of artificality.

CHAPTER 1

AT THE ORIGINS OF THE BIBLE: MOSES

1. From the Age of the Oral Tradition to the Written Civilization

If revelation occurs at a time when the Near East has for a long time already reached a written civilization, the human community which receives it accedes to it only little by little. The fact is elucidated by the Bible itself. The Hebrew patriarchs which Genesis describes to us still belong to the nomadic or semi-nomadic age where oral traditions reign. Subsequently, Exodus evokes the use of writing at the time of Moses (Ex 17, 14; 34, 28). But one must surely not exaggerate its extension for if at the time of the Judges, the art of writing seems spread even to the common people, it is only with precise and defined ends of an altogether practical order (Jgs 8, 14). Finally, one enters fully into the domain of the written civilization when Israel becomes master of the urban centers and especially when David establishes his monarchy in Jerusalem.

It is therefore normal to place oneself first of all in the perspective of this historical framework when one wants to study the birth of sacred literature in the people of God, and from that point of view, to cast a glance on the preceding centuries to draw a balance sheet on them, without trying to trace their literary history in detail. The point of view of the royal scribes is then seen; these latter were interested in collecting all the inheritance of the past and transmitted it to us in their books.

It must also be noted that the oral tradition did not end at the moment when written literature was in full sway. It was born first and had served as a cradle for the archaic works established before the royal period. It then continued subsequently to feed literature from century to century, thanks to its partially autonomous development. For example, with respect to the Pentateuch, the priestly narrators drew materials that had been previously unexploited. Likewise, one must not represent the oral tradition and written literature as two domains foreign to one another from the point of view of the means of expression used. Solomon's contemporaries must not have seen any appreciable difference between the narratives spread orally (as had been the immemorial custom) and the narrations put into form by the court scribes, for the art of the latter proceeded from that of the ancient story-tellers and the transition from the one to the other was effected rather imperceptibly. However, an important turn of events took place at the moment when there was fixed in writing what up to then had been entrusted to the living memory of men.

2. The Traditions of Israel

Israelite traditions, at the time of the monarchy, appear under extremely varied aspects as to their origin, their aim, their form and their atmosphere. The internal unity of the nation is already an established fact, but from social groups which, though conscious of a certain original relationship, yet have had various historical experiences. Each of these groups (clans, tribes and groups of tribes) has its own traditions. Thus, Gn 38 is peculiar to Juda, while the wars of Josue apparently refer to the battles of the Benjaminites and in Gn 4 a Kenite origin is discerned. Other traditions are bound up with places: burial places or battlegrounds, former tribal resting places (such as Cades) or venerated shrines (such as Sichem). Each institution, finally, has its own traditions, especially the shrine of the Ark of the Covenant, which since Exodus has a whole history, and the Aaronite clergy, guardian of a tradition of worship formed at Cades.

It would be a mistake to look in these traditions only for memories of history. Their aims differ profoundly according to each case. Often, it is actually a question of preserving the memory of ancestors and of their accomplishments: military leaders, such as the Judges and most recently Saul; religious leaders, such as Samuel; Moses, founder of the nation and its legislator; the fathers of the race, Abraham, Isaac, Jacob whose tradition subsists in the places where they have lived. But it happens also that the adventures of the groups are hidden behind the exploits of eponymous heroes (Gn 34) or that the religious causality is brought out in preference to secondary details (as in the Exodus from Egypt). Furthermore, with the help of hindsight, history has become schematized. The most important elements still emerge next to a large number that are forgotten; they center around a few very living figures which animate an anonymous mass: it is thus that popular memory can narrate the past. However, many traditions have a purpose of an entirely different order: they explain the how and the why of present customs (cf. the rite of the paschal lamb), names of places (Jgs 2, 1-5), the states of the tribes (Gn 49); they tell the origin of groups, institutions and tribes, frequently resorting to the procedure of eponyms, organizing them into genealogies, which is a popular way of explaining with simplicity the origin of things. It also happens that these traditions tend to give rules of conduct, either by conveying juridical or ritual material which is imposed to be practiced by the Israelites (Gn 32, 33; Ex 12, 21-22), or by introducing moral or religious lessons about the history of former heroes (the story of Joseph): this is a feature of popular wisdom known in all countries. It is constantly this Jewish conception of God, of the world, of man and of history which is thus concretely expressed in order to be transmitted from one age to the next. The traditions contain practically all the baggage of national culture before the creation of a written literature.

As to the forms in which they are presented, some are already fixed (we will come back to them later), but most are still fluctuating. They are canvasses in prose, more or less precise in their details. Their genres vary, from the very short etiological narrative to the more developed episode which tends to be transformed into a "short story." On this point, it is difficult to distinguish what belongs properly to the traditional sources used by the chroniclers of the royal period and what was actually done by them. It is possible, however, to hold as probable that as a whole they respected the manner of the materials they had at hand.

Let us add that the atmosphere of the narratives differs considerably from one to the other. The story is realistic and down to earth in the miserable adventure of Abimelek; but the story is treated as a religious epic in the exodus from Egypt. The harsh enthusiasm of the war of conquest contrasts with the rustic calm brought about by the memory of Abraham and Isaac. The pilgrimage to Sinai is very closely linked to notions of worship, while the stories of Joseph and Samson, each in its way, serve to inculcate a lesson wisdom. There is no doubt that these variations already existed in the ancient traditions when they were still being transmitted orally. It would be wrong therefore to consider the traditions as formless, pre-literary or infra-literary materials. At the time when they are going to be collected, they already constitute a true literature whose genres are a prelude to those of written literature.

It is even likely that, from the time of the Judges, they tended to group themselves into *cycles.* Either according to their historical origin: cycles of conquest and of Judges, cycle of Saul . . . Or, according to their geographical roots: cycles of Bersabee, of Sichem, of Cades, of Bethel (of shrines, most of the time). Or finally according to the institutions that preserve them: traditions of the Aaronite clergy, traditions around the Ark of the Covenant, tribal traditions . . . Better still, as national unity becomes a reality, not only in fact but in the consciousness of men, particular groups of memories and customs also tended to become interpenetrated to become the common good of all Israel. Thus, the state in which the royal scribes find them is the result of a more or less long, more or less complicated evolution. On the whole, they make up a rich treasure, both cultural and religious.

3. The Most Ancient Written Texts: Moses

In the framework of the oral traditions, Israel also possesses the first elements of a written tradition. In fact, the specimens of archaic texts that the Bible has preserved are perhaps only the remnants of a much more extensive literary production, for the poetic texts allow us to see, starting with the 12th century, the existence of an art which far surpasses its first stammerings. In this regard a remarkable difference is observed between the refrains of the nomadic times, brief and short-winded, and the war-chants of the conquest, like those of Josue (fragmentary) and of Debora: Israel had quickly assimilated the culture of the conquered lands. Let us notice again, in the order of worship, the refrains of the Ark, in the prophetic "genre," the oracles of Jacob, Balaam and Moses; with the sapiential literature, there are the apology of Jotham and the parable of Nathan; finally, the two elegies of David, prior to his reign in Jerusalem. We even know the title of two collections of works of this type used by Hebrew historians: the book of *Jashar* and that of "The Wars of Yahweh"; but it is difficult to say if they are ancient or if the initiative is that of the Solomonian scribes. These first manifestations of the Israelite literary genius make it rather probable that certain traditions had been put into written prose relatively early, although on this point the texts do not bear up under scrutiny. It is known, however, that several pages attributed by critics to the Elohist or to the Yahwist traditions contain a very definite archaic flavor; moreover, it is likely that certain prayer formulae in more recent recensions existed before in some way in the Israelite shrines from the time of the Judges.

But it is especially in the matter of law that the existence of ancient written texts is solidly attested by the Bible. Moses' activity in this field is too strongly affirmed by Hebrew tradition for us to deny him any literary activity, even if it is difficult to circumscribe it. There is agreement on the earliness of the Book of the Covenant (Ex 20, 22-23, 33), despite the trace of certain refinements, and of the ethical *Decalogue* (Ex 20 and Dt 5), probably enlarged by its later revisors, and there is no stringent reason which could oblige us to deny to

Moses what remains the core of the Mosaic Law. But one would unduly restrict Moses' part in the Torah, if one attributed to him only these few writings: around them is centered the common law which largely overflows its limits and which is Mosaic just as they are. Finally, one can say that with Moses the Bible, as an *inspired book,* was born at the same time as the people of Israel was itself born by contracting a covenant with Yahweh. At the time when Hebrew literature begins to develop in a more tangible way, thanks to a concurrence of providential circumstances, the personality of the founder of the nation already dominates it, not only by the texts which derive from him, but by his religious message which will entirely impregnate it.

CHAPTER II

JERUSALEM, CULTURAL CENTER

1. Hebrew Culture at the Beginning of the Monarchy

Saul's monarchy prolonged in many ways the period of the Judges; David's finally transformed the nation. It created the Israelite State by superimposing upon the former framework of the tribes, a specificially Chanaanite institution: centralized urban kingship. At the same time that Israel is peacefully absorbing independent populations, it takes on structures that are mostly inspired from contemporary monarchies: those of Phenicia and even, all things being equal, of Egypt. In keeping with this social and political development, the religion of Israel finds a new balance. Victoriously overcoming the crisis of the time of the Judges, it finally incorporates what could be assimilated from the Chanaanite cults in matters of rite, concepts and phraseology.

Two facts mark this change. First of all, kingship is henceforth part and parcel of the religious charter of the nation: the monarch, the anointed of Yahweh, becomes a part of theocracy and the promises of the Covenant are personally renewed to him, for himself and for his race (2 Sm 7). In the second place, with the transfer of the Ark to Jerusalem, the old confederational shrine of the tribes, formerly located in Sichem and Silo, is now located in the royal capital, which becomes the holy place par excellence, the one where "Yahweh makes His name dwell." In the preceding ages, a first form of hope had developed; that of living happily in a land "flowing with milk and honey," and of ruling over the peoples "who do not know Yahweh." To these fundamental elements are added henceforth those that have been introduced by a most recent history; the king and the holy city and soon the Temple enrich the tableau of the marvelous future which Israel expects from its God. Let us add that in Jerusalem there is realized a sort of synthesis between two currents of cults which both issued from Hebrew origins: that of the North, linked to the shrine of the Ark, which thus reflects in a very direct way the tradition of Moses and of Josue; and that of the South, coming also from the tradition of Cades, which had already been able to open to independent worship elements by assimilating them. This duality is found, it seems, in the two priests attached to the person of David: Ebiathar, a descendant of Eli, who will be dismissed under Solomon; Sadoq, whose genealogy ties him to the lineage of Aaron and who finally will prevail alone.

Such is the framework in which Israelite culture is affirmed. Once the urban kingship is created, a whole people of scribes tends to the affairs of the palace: it is charged with keeping the annals of the reign, preserving the archives, writing the correspondence, administering the goods of the royal house, collecting the taxes. Schools furnish the training for this personnel; along with the sons of functionaries, the royal princes and the members of the aristocratic families receive there a more perfect education; naturally the clergy of the royal shrine profit from this movement. These institutions take on unequaled scope under Solomon; thus, everything is ready for the flourishing of a literature of learned men, still rooted in popular tradition, but wearing the stamp of the literate caste whence it emanates.

To create this cultural foyer, the Hebrew state does not start from scratch. On the one hand, the preceding periods (Moses and the Judges) have left to it institutions where the first elements of the national culture have already been developed in an embryonic manner. On the other hand, while absorbing Jerusalem and the other Chanaanite cities, David incorporated into his state and transferred to the religion of Yahweh the indigenous institutions of a much more ancient origin: scribes, cantors, etc. . . . Finally, as the political and economic horizon of Israel becomes wider, especially under the reign of Solomon, the country is introduced into an international traffic of ideas and of artistic tastes which is favorable to the flourishing of letters. It is not astonishing in these conditions to see Hebrew literature reach its classical period in the 10th century, without always being able to distinguish the origin, national or foreign, of the elements which are narrowly fused in it.

2. The Vestiges of an Administration

The archives and the administrative and juridical documents do not properly speaking belong to literature; however, they constitute for historians a source of information of the first order. The Books of Samuel and of Kings have preserved a certain number of them which come either from the royal chancery or from the archives of the Temple. This is sufficient to allow us to see an essential aspect of the activity of the royal scribes.

Given the profound evolution of the institutions which marks this period, one would expect to find also in the texts the trace of a juridical activity directed toward a legislative reformulation. But on this point investigations prove to be rather disappointing. The Book of the Covenant presupposes a more archaic economic and social state, and the Yahwist Decalogue (Ex 34) deals essentially with worship. It seems therefore that, in the time of David and Solomon, royal law is exercised only in the framework of ancient customs, partially codified, without yet attaining a reformulation of Mosaic law. The adaptation to new circumstances of the texts and customs of yesteryear is thus left to the appreciation of those who fill the positions of judges, and this flexibility guarantees a living law always dominated by the authority of Moses.

3. Around the Worship

We would like to know in detail the transformation and the development of the rituals, which took place after the removal of the Ark to Jerusalem and especially after the building of the Temple of Solomon. The state of the evidence does not allow us to satisfy our curiosity: this is because the rites and religious customs are much more easily transmitted from one generation to the next by the simple operation of the existing institutions than by dead documents. Texts such as Ex 13, 3-10 and 34, 10-26 (except for Deuteronomist additions) can preserve in a succinct form old Yahwist rituals brought from Cades by the Aaronite clergy. But to these archaic rites, the Yahwist Decalogue (Ex 34) adds others which are more easily understood as adaptations to Yahwism of agrarian rites long since implanted in Chanaan (especially the three agricultural feasts of the annual cycle). One could therefore think here of a composition during the royal period, which would also have left traces in some places in the Book of the Covenant (Ex 22, 28-29; 23, 14-19). Finally, one must look for the collections of customs done during the periods of David and Solomon in the late priestly compilations made in "Sadoqite" milieus. The conservative spirit of the religious centers assures us that these texts substantially reflect the ancient tradition; but one should not overlook the part played by more recent adaptations: ritual conservatism is not necessarily fixed. From the point of view in which we place ourselves here, these compilations are therefore utilizable only with some difficulty.

In Chanaanite and Aramean centers, prophetism was linked with worship, such as, it seems, Hebrew prophetism at the time of the Judges. Thus, in David's service one finds two accredited seers, Gad and Nathan, and the texts give us some idea of the oracles performed by these religious counselors of the king in the exercise of their official capacities. Furthermore, their personality already breaks through the framework of professional prophetism, both by the authentic inspiration which is manifested in them and by their freedom of speech with regard to the king: they thus announce the grand-style prophets of the following centuries. The oracle of Nathan preserved in 2 Sm 7 (with Deuteronomist glosses) is of first-rate importance: it is at the origin of dynastic Messianism. The question of the two "royal psalms" is more difficult: these are Ps 2 and 110 which contain prophetic oracles. The first apparently alludes to 2 Sm 7; but some authors see in it rather a late literary imitation. On the other hand, the archaic origin of Ps 110 is often retained, because there are rather strong arguments in favor of it. Some even see here a Hebrew adaptation of a royal enthronement psalm of Jebusean origin; whence would come the mention of royal priesthood, actually by David (2 Sm 6, 17-18) and by Solomon (3 Kgs 3, 15) and of Melchisedech, king-priest of Salem, whose inheritance would have been received by David. The hypothesis cannot be considered as demonstrated.

These two texts introduce the problem of the psalms. One should not be surprised that a large number of them are attributed to David. He was a poet and musician himself as is shown in his two elegies on the death of Saul and of Abner. The king surely must have played an important role in the development of worship lyricism. The genre existed before him, both with the Hebrews and with the Chanaanites, and especially in the city of Jerusalem whose personnel he incorporated into his service. The transfer of the Ark could have given him the opportunity of organizing a guild of cantors which must have become increasingly important after the building of the Temple. It is hardly doubtful that originally Chanaanite hymns were then adapted to the liturgy of Yahweh; in any case, the style of the native poetry did not fail to influence the new compositions. Unfortunately, in the present state of the problem, it is difficult to say what part of the psalter dates from this period. For example, the following are generally placed among the ancient psalms: 18 (royal *Te Deum*), 20 and 21 (prayers for the king), 24, 7-10 (processional of the Ark), 29 (with heavy Chanaanite coloring), 72 (retouched later on) . . . But in fact there are as many questions as there are psalms. One can admit that from the very beginning of the royal period, most of the genres and literary canons now present in the psalter were already fixed and their place in the liturgy was determined by usage. However, a literary current such as that one is bound to be developed normally with time; there should be no hurry in wanting to reconstitute a whole "royal liturgy" on the basis of the internal criticism of the psalter and the analogies offered by the other Semitic religions. There are certainly relations, but they are not easy to pinpoint and in particular the existence in Israel of a "New Year's day" similar to that of neighboring religions remains problematic.

4. Wisdom Literature

With the schools for scribes Wisdom literature also takes hold in Israel. The Bible honors Solomon with it, and attributes to him considerable literary activity (3 Kgs 5, 9-14). One must take hyperbole into consideration, but there is no reason for doubting this testimony. In fact, Wisdom is at that time an international fact, and traces of it are found from Egypt to Mesopotamia; if the Chanaanite documents are lacking on this point, the fact is probably accidental (cf. 3 Kgs 5, 11; Ez 27, 8-9 and 28, 3-4).

Wisdom is first of all the concern of the king: the art of governing well and of succeeding in temporal matters. But this art concerns also many people in the royal administration: every scribe must be a wise man; that is why the education he receives strives to impart this knowledge to him. Doubtless a practical wisdom; but from the knowledge of man and of the world, full of refined psychology, is easily developed a reflection which, altogether empirical at its origins, rapidly tends toward speculation, especially when it blends in the data of religious thought. With respect to this, one can say, for example, that the ancient oriental myths which were vivid expressions of a conception of the human world in its relations to the gods, bordered on the sapiential genre.

In Israel, this literary current crosses immediately on its way a religious tradition solidly anchored in the minds. Surely it is first of all receptive to maxims of all kinds, similar to those collected in the Book of Proverbs (10, 1-22, 16; 25-29). A large portion of these, especially those which appear to be the "mirror of the king's people" (Duesberg), can date back to Solomon, but the later development of the genre must be reckoned with. But from the very outset, wisdom, knowledge, and discernment are considered as a privilege of Yahweh who alone can give them to men (2 Sm 14, 17 and 20; 3 Kgs 3, 9; cf. Gn 3). Thereby, all the moral ideal of Yahwism, its conception of the world and of man seem to be one of the areas of the sapiential field; there is no frontier between it and religious reflection. We will not be astonished to find trace of the sapiential current in a good number of writings which theoretically depend on altogether different literary genres.

5. Memorialists and Historians

Such are the intellectual components of the milieu in which a very important historiography is going to develop by leaps and bounds; in Jerusalem from the reign of David and especially from that of Solomon, a well-organized clergy, a caste of scribes and an already ancient prophetism are so side-by-side that their fields overlap. Born at their crossroads historiography will reflect in variable proportions their respective preoccupations. The work of the annalists precedes historiography properly speaking and opens the way for it. We no longer have the official chronicles of the kings; but in their dryness, certain indications give us some idea of them (2 Sm 8). As to the work of the memorialists and the historians, this directly outclasses all that oriental antiquity has left us in this genre. In Assyria, the royal annals are dithyrambs in praise of the monarch; in Egypt one particular event of the reign is recounted, but without yet creating a continuous historiography; with the Hittites, religious causality in history is not ignored, but one does not rise to broad views embracing whole reigns or even longer periods. It is difficult to say in what measure the knowledge of the former stimulates the genius of Israelite scribes; they nonetheless draw from their faith a concept of man and of history which allows them to catch a broader glimpse of the events. With them, all the actors of history, even the greatest, remain subject to a divine law which surpasses them, judges them, commands their destinies because, consciously or not, they are the artisans of Yahweh's design. Whence come both breadth of outlook and remarkable impartiality.

From the reign of David, it seems that a long narrative retraces already the origins of the Israelite monarchy, from the anointing of Saul to the capture of Jerusalem (that is, during the whole duration of the wars of independence). A history of the Ark of the Covenant perhaps has to date from the same period; it traces its history from its capture by the Philistines to its transferral into the royal city. The masterpiece of this genre, probably written under Solomon, is the history of David's succession (2 Sm 10-20 and 3 Kgs 1-2). Then there is a history of Solomon (where the author of Kings drew the matter of 3 Kgs 3-11); without counting the remarks devoted the particular episodes or to the exploits of David's paladins (2 Sm 21-24), but their date is more doubtful. All these pieces treat of contemporary events, whose actors or witnesses are often still living. Recourse to oral tradition is discernible in some places (David's youth); and this is normal for the matter treated. As for the style, it prolongs and brings to its perfection the art of ancient storytellers: all the popular vim and vigor passed into these productions of literate men.

6. A Synthesis of Sacred History

But the traditions of Israel allow us to go much further back into the past; by drawing abundantly from this trove, the Israelite scribes are going to achieve a large work of religious history. These traditions, as has been seen, were already becoming interpenetrated and were beginning to take form from the time of the Judges. Now, after the establishment of the monarchy and the foundation of the empire, their total meaning becomes more evident, in a broader perspective. The Israelite historians discover the profound unity, underlying both their expansion and their diversity: the unity of a *sacred history* directed by God; of a history whose point of departure is the promise made to Abraham, whose heart is the Covenant and whose justification and purpose is the glory of Yahweh present in His Temple and triumphant by the victories of the Anointed One. This is not merely a simple human reconstruction, but a view of faith which becomes explicit under divine inspiration.

Since all the traditions preserved in the various parts of the nation are thus convergent, it is the duty of historians to stress the link which united them around memories of the Exodus and of Sinai, which are as it were their center of gravity. On the other hand, they underline, from the earliest centuries, the cohesion of all the Hebrew groups called to live in fateful solidarity inside the people of Yahweh: these groups are members of the same family. Whence the importance of the genealogies around which will be centered the sacred history; more than extracts of civil-status, they will be a concrete translation of the profound idea which polarizes all of history: that of the divine choice which singled out men called to make up the people of God.

That is why, contrary to the ancient traditions of India for example, which dealt essentially with worship and were independent of time, those of Israel are fixed in the framework of a history. It is a real history but told with the help of the most diverse of materials; it is a very human history, but its religious significance is much more important than the precision of the details. It is this history which drains all the other components of the national tradition (law, customs, worship, folklore) and establishes them in the perspective where they derive their profound meaning. Furthermore, this history will go back beyond the patriarchal period, beyond even the oriental empires and the faraway neolithic age, the rather imprecise memory of which hovers in chapters 4-11 of Genesis. It will even incorporate sacred cosmogony which Israelite monotheism contrasts to the pagan myths, whose images it does not fear to use again for its own doctrine. Moreover, creation is the point of departure of the divine design which was little by little revealed with the call of the patriarchs, the deliverance from Egypt, the Covenant at Sinai, the gift of the "promised land," the installation of the monarchy, the promises made to David and the choice of the Temple at Jerusalem as the residence of Yahweh among men . . . And if Yahweh had thus painfully and gradually to form this people called to serve Him and to procure His glory from a barbarian human mass by giving to it little by little the rules of conduct capable of making of it a wise people, is it not because at the beginning, at the origins, a mysterious catastrophe had disturbed the order of a world that had issued from His hands in perfect condition? By explaining on the one hand the present condition of man and on the other the meaning of the historical work of God, the inspired book thus introduces into the picture of the origins the fact of human sin which right from this period interferes with divine will and from century to century continues to place obstacles before the unfolding of Yahweh's design.

Such is the grandiose plan of this work which, for lack of knowing exactly its author or authors, we call the holy Yahwist history (J). It is of little importance if it was realized in one stroke or by one author; if it contained or not in a continuous story all of past history up to the period of David and of Solomon; if it used, next to pieces drawn from the oral tradition, certain bits of more ancient writings (J[1] or L of the critics); if certain pieces, where theology is more closely allied, were added after the event to the primitive collection. It is sufficient to notice that it existed at least virtually in a whole collection of accounts related by doctrine and by the editorial procedures used. Just as diverse as the materials that serve as its base, it sometimes borders on religious lyricism (the flight from Egypt), sometimes on sapiential teaching (Gn 3; the story of Joseph); sometimes on historiography (the story of Gideon) and sometimes on juridical teaching (Mosaic Torah and certain etiological accounts). On the whole, it is a literary monument without parallel in the history of religions, because it condenses in it what is specific and irreducible in Yahwism: a theology of history based on the theology of the Promise. As to its composition, it is difficult to suggest precise dates: we would ascribe the whole work to the reign of Solomon; but, for many authors, the work would have spread itself over the following century in the cultured centers of the court and of the Temple. There is no doubt that it then played a role in the training of the elite just as did in Egypt sapiential literature or with the priests of Mesopotamia the Sumero-Akkadian myths; but what a difference in intellectual and religious climate!

Thus, at the cultural and political climax which marks the first century of the Israelite monarchy, in a certain sense the Bible can be said to have a literary structure. Around this nucleus of sacred texts dating back to the Mosaic period, the traditions of God's people were crystallized in written form. They nonetheless continued to be transmitted orally; so, other crystallizations will subsequently appear analogous to the first. But the fundamental ideas of the Yahwist writer—or school—first synthesis of a revelation started long ago, will continue to assert itself to similar syntheses attempted in slightly different perspectives. The New Testament itself, by fulfilling the revelation of the secrets of the mysterious plan of God, will show in Christ the crowning and the completion of this age-long work, the first outlines of which were being shown by the Yahwist.

CHAPTER III

THE PARALLEL KINGDOMS

1. The Tradition of Israel and that of Juda

From this schism which follows the reign of Solomon on, the kingdoms of Juda and of Israel find themselves in rather different situations. In Jerusalem, the continuity of the Davidic dynasty assures a certain internal stability; but, on the religious level, the kingdom experiences alternately rises of Chanaanite paganism and Yahwist renewal, according to the attitudes of its kings. Nonetheless, the Temple remains a stronghold for the religious traditions of the nation; it is the place where "Yahweh roars" (Am 1, 2), and from this place will be prepared the revolution that will overthrow Athalia; Isaias also receives his vocation here. In its shadow, the literature inaugurated during the reigns of David and of Solomon continues to develop (worship .lyricism, rituals, common law, wisdom, religious historiography, archives and annals); it is not possible to follow this development closely. The permanent armor of this intellectual activity is made up of three fundamental institutions: scribes (or wise men), priests and prophets (Jer 18, 18; cf. 2, 8).

In Israel on the contrary, if the secession is upheld by the country populations tired of tributes that are too heavy, by the clergy of the provincial shrines, whom Jerusalem risks offending, and by the prophetic bodies hostile to innovations in the name of ancient tradition, it is virtually the merchant class and the landowners who take the gain of it to their profit. Thus the monarchy leaning on this class will withdraw from primitive Yahwism more than the Judean monarchy. Following the schism and especially after the founding of Samaria, a second center of culture, emulator and rival of Jerusalem, grows in the court of the kings of Israel; its light falls on rich classes, on the clergy of royal sanctuaries created in order to compete with Solomon's Temple, on the caste of the officials. But the kingdom of the North is too open to foreign influences, especially those of Tyre, causing the nation's religious tradition to suffer. One may notice it in particular when Omri marries his son Achab to the Tyrenian Jezabel: the political fortune of the "house of Omri" and the relative cultural expansion which accompanies it then are tied to the renewal of Chanaanite paganism. The cult of a national God, in the measure to which it subsists, tends to be no longer anything but a syncretized Yahwism; from the reign of Jeroboam I, the sign of the golden calf was an unequivocal indication of this falling away. Thus it is not surprising that the literary productions of the time left only a few traces in the Bible: the fervent Yahwists to whom we owe the holy books had no choice but to let them fall into oblivion. The happy exception of Psalm 45, if one were to interpret it as a royal epithalamium, would be due to an allegorical re-interpretation which would define its biblical sense. However, the archeological documentation hints at a certain administrative (ostraca) and artistic (the ivories of Samaria) activity, which was fairly intense during the 9th and the 8th centuries.

In Israel during the 9th century, the attachment to authentic Yahwist tradition is, with exceptions, true more of strangers to the cultural movement: the "sons of prophets" who gravitate around Elias and Eliseus give no evidence of preoccupations of a cultural nature, not considering the Rekabites or an old soldier like Jehu. The literary consequence: the speeches of Elias and Eliseus have not come down to us in original MS, though the oracle of Micheas, son of Yimla, (3 Kgs 22, 1-28) is an exception to this. The religious consequence: the Yahwism of the North, reacting against a syncretism which seems tied to modern institutions, remains more archaic, and closer to what it had been at the time of the Judges in the shrines of the country. The Mosaic tradition is present there, it would seem, though less well developed than at Jerusalem, or rather, it develops along another line, more conservative regarding the ideas and the rites of Chanaan, and in more direct relation with the form it had assumed in the ancient shrine of the Ark. It is symptomatic to see Elias pilgrimaging to Horeb to renew his faith or to rebuild the altar of Carmel in the ancient manner (cf. Ex 20, 24-25). It is true that at the same time local shrines of the same kind also exist in the Judean countryside; but the Temple of Jerusalem already initiates a centralization which is soon realized.

2. The Prophetic Influence in Israel

The revolution of Jehu (841), however, allows the prophetic influence to gain ground in cultivated circles; even kings seek the counsel of Eliseus. Thus one may glimpse the formation of fervent circles whose members also belong to state institutions: priestly colleges and scribes of the administration. United by a common attachment to the spirit of Elias and Eliseus, they end the current of reform in literary works, quite similar in their form to those which appeared in Jerusalem in the 10th century when the same spirit of religious fervor moved the scribes of the court and the Temple. There is first of all the collating and the fixing in writing of traditions relative to Elias and Eliseus. The cycle of Elias may have been edited toward the end of the 9th century; that of Eliseus at present mixed with a history of Aramean wars, around 750. Next to popular tales which bear the mark of their origins, one may find beautiful pages worthy of the best historians, such as the story of the revolution of Jehu (4 Kgs 9, 1-10, 27).

There is much evidence supporting a relation of the Elohist material of the Pentateuch (E) to the same milieu, as well as several narratives found in the "early prophets," from the wars of Josue to the history of Saul. This recension of ancient traditions is comparable to Yahwist sacred history, to which it is often related in matter and sometimes even in literary expression. It may have included written documents edited much earlier: probably certain tales waxing an archaic flavor (E[1] of the critics); certainly the Decalogue of Ex 20 and the Book of the Covenant. But on the whole, one would surmise rather the shaping of an oral tradition which was still alive, with the added influence of the work edited in Yahwist circles. But whereas for the historians of Jerusalem sacred history culminated in the establishment of the Davidic monarchy and the Solomonian Temple, those of Israel show a greater reserve with regard to modern institutions. Their more conservative point of view, which is explained as a reaction against the abuses of the time, prolong the tradition of the shrine of the Ark into the time of the Judges. The Yahwism which they dream of seeing revived is less that of the Davidic epoch than that of the Exodus, of the desert, of the conquest: here is their ideal. With them this is not an archaism of poor quality but rather a desire to remain faithful to the most essential values of the national religion. Besides, they feel the needs of their time; proof is that in retracing past history they bring it up to date to find in it rules of conduct to be used by their contemporaries. Hence an emphasis on the "prophetic" side of the ancestors (Abraham, Joseph, Moses, or Samuel); from this also come certain polemical jabs against the worship of the golden calf (Ex 32) or of the Chanaanite Baal (Jgs 6, 25-32) and against the institution of monarchy itself (I Sm 8 and 12).

Certain of these traits may be more easily understood if one admits that the Elohist collection was made in the course of the 8th century, under the brilliant and prosperous rule of Jeroboam II, as a salutary reaction against the social and religious disorders which were only too apparent. In fact, a similar spirit, sometimes even identical themes, are found in the preaching of Amos and especially of Osee. The first of these two "writer prophets" (a very poor expression) has no ties with the fervent circles of the North: he is a Judean, whose hard and vigorous poetry bursts directly from popular sap. Putting these oracles into writing seems to have been in part his personal work (cf. 7, 1-4; 8, 1; 9, 1), in part that of disciples spontaneously grouped about him; but it is with the Judeans, Isaias and Micheas, that one will afterwards have to look to find the trace of his influence. On the other hand, the work of Osee, deeply rooted in the religious tradition of the North, noticeably enriches the current of thought in which it buries itself. Though it takes certain characteristic themes from it (moral decalogue, attachment to the Covenant and to the ideal time in the desert, memories of the ancestor Jacob, the preponderance of Ephraim, and the hostility to the golden calf and even to the institution of royalty), it introduces into it other themes which reappear later (love of Yahweh for His people, affective religion, comparison of the Covenant to an espousal, announcement of a new Covenant after the purification of guilty Israel). With Osee, the sacred history, from now on prolonged until new times yet to come, assumes the appearance of a drama of love in which Yahweh and Israel are partners: an original interpretation which is a direct prelude to the revelation of the love of God in the New Testament.

In the atmosphere of the prophetic movement, a juridic reform is preparing itself, parallel to the historico-religious work of which we have just spoken. When Osee alludes to "articles of law" (8, 2), he is thinking, undoubtedly, of the ancient legislative compilations (Moral Decalogue and Book of the Covenant). But in the 8th century, this written law no longer corresponds exactly to the practical needs of an evolved society: its rule is surpassed by the facts. It must be adapted to the circumstances, completed, and on certain points, remade, so that it may present an effective barrier to the abuses of power of the royal administration, to the extortions of the rich, the venality of the judges, the moral and religious laxity, which, from Elias to Osee, were unceasingly denounced by the prophets. Such a work presupposes first an evolution of customary law before becoming crystallized into a code. The prophetic preaching, completely in the service of the authentic tradition, indicates in what sense the reform must be directed. Now fervent circles influenced by this reform include levite-priests, guardians of customs and laws, called on more than once to practice law in trials (Dt 17, 18-20). Such is the jurisprudence which, by completing existing texts, prepares the constitution of a new code. This will come in its time, probably after the ruin of Samaria, when the rooting of a foreign aristocracy in the country makes spiritual resistance an urgency if one wishes to save the threatened tradition. Further, the fall of the kingdom of the North will then invite reflection: it will show the necessity of the reform to which the prophets have been vainly exhorting the nation for a century and a half. But on what basis could it be wrought except on the Mosaic Torah itself, enriched by a recent prophetic contribution and readapted to the needs of the time? This is, it would seem, the state of mind which will preside over the edition of the Deuteronomist Code (Dt 12, 2-26, 15), which we would prefer to relate to the tradition of the North rather than to Judean circles, though it may have been written down in the South (see *below*).

3. The Prophetic Influence in Juda

While this work is being done in original priestly circles of Israel, the kingdom of Juda is won over, in turn, by the influence of prophetism. Amos, the Judean, preached in the North in about 750; his preoccupations and several of his themes reappear in the following decades in Isaias and Micheas, although one cannot clearly define the relation of the latter with the group of disciples which preserved the oracles of the shepherd of Teqoa. The connection is probably closer with Micheas, a man of the country, apparently without culture. But we know that at the time of Ezechias, this preacher, in his crude syntax, deeply impressed minds and hastened the religious reform of the country (Jer 26, 17-19).

The personality of Isaias is more typical of the tradition of Jerusalem. No doubt his supernatural inspiration and his native genius enjoy a profound originality. But he does not stand out in his century as an erratic fragment; rather his work can be situated at the juncture of various literary and doctrinal currents which we have noted in the Judean capital. He is connected with the Sadoqite ministry by his knowledge of its technical vocabulary and by his echoing of certain aspects of its theology: the glory of Yahweh, the holy God in His royal majesty; the essential role of the Temple, His abode. On the other hand, some of his major ideas recover themes dear to "Yahwist" historians: the doctrine of the "remnant," directly related to the Yahwist interpretation of the Deluge; attachment to the Davidic dynasty, which is supported by the oracle of Nathan. Finally, the prophet did not misuse a literate education: he practices the *mashal,* a sapiential genre *par excellence,* and when he denounces a false wisdom impregnated with pride, it is to contrast it to a true wisdom, pierced by a religious spirit, a gift of the divine Spirit. Although a messenger of punishment, as were Amos and Osee, Isaias is no less attached to the national hope; but, like Osee, he carries it forward to a "second time." The comparison of this eschatology with that of Osee is instructive, however. The latter sought the golden age of Israel at the time of Exodus and the desert; Isaias finds it in the Davidic and Solomonian epoch, the purified image of which he projects into the future in order to evoke the reign of the future "son of David." On both sides, the concept of the end of the world takes on the air of a Paradise regained, but the historical experience associated with this wondrous evocation does not exactly cover the same period: for Osee tied himself again to the tradition of the North, which reappears also in Deuteronomy, whereas Isaias endorses the doctrinal development peculiar to the sanctuary of Jerusalem. The fundamental dualism of the nation will thus be found even in the prophetic milieu; but it would be useless, however, to oppose two complementary currents each attentive to different aspects of the divine work: the unique revelation progresses on both sides, along lines which will, in the end, be united.

There is yet another point on which the Book of Isaias gives us a valuable piece of information. It shows us the prophet surrounded by a circle of disciples. In their "hearts," that is, in their living memories, he "binds his testimony and seals his teaching" (8, 16). Thus the prophet appears with the unexpected traits of a master of wisdom who concentrates his care on the formation of a restricted group. One grasps in the raw the existence of one of those faithful groups which gather the words of every inspired man and prolong his activity. Such is the distant origin of pietist groups called to play such a great role in the formation of Judaism. The Isaian circle preserves the oracles of the master, which have already been set down in writing under his dictation; it also preserves the memory of a few important facts of his life (cf. 7; 36-39). One will be indebted to it for the making of his collection, a compilation which through the care of new inspired men allied with the same school, will increase in time.

4. After the Fall of Samaria

After the fall of Samaria, the remaining devout Israelites in a country decimated by deportation, seek support in the South. At the same time, Jerusalem is reforming itself. From this a double literary activity results. On the one hand, Ezechias tries to gather the cultural and moral if not the political heritage of the North, in order to rebuild around Jerusalem a sort of national unity. His scribes make a collation of Solomonian proverbs (Prv 25, 1). Above all, they revise and complete the collections of ancient traditions formed during the course of preceding centuries in the Judean capital (a Yahwist collection) with the help of materials which Israelite refugees have brought with them (Elohist collection). Such at least is the hypothesis which, in the actual state of our knowledge, would best explain the origin of the J-E compilation (sometimes called Jehovist compilation) used in the Pentateuch. The Book of Judges could have received in the same manner its almost definitive form (except for additions due to later revisions). It is interesting to thus see the traditions of the North and South converge once again, as at the time of the conquest and at the beginning of the monarchy, to form a wholly Israelite *Tradition:* the people of the Covenant remains attached to its internal unity in the midst of historical troubles in which it is steeped despite itself.

An autonomous survival of Elohist traditions in circles of Israelite origin, in refuge in Jerusalem, must not however be excluded: the Deuteronomist literature will constitute its direct prolonging. It is exactly in these circles that the Deuteronomist code seems to us to have been edited, probably during the very reign of Ezechias, on the basis of ancient material of which we have spoken. If finally the levite-priests, to whom it is due, deposit it in the Temple at Jerusalem, where it will be rediscovered a century later, it is because the Ark of the Covenant is located there. Behind the royal Temple, they see the ancient federal shrine of the tribes, the same one which an ancient tradition, mentioned in Deuteronomy and the Book of Josue placed at Sichem and at Garizim (Dt 11, 29-30; 27, 4-8 and 11-26; Jos 8, 30-35; 24, 1 and 25-26). In order to cut short the liturgical deviations of the high places, they dream of making it the only legitimate sanctuary of Yahweh in Israel. But for the time being, Sichem is occupied by the semi-pagan Samaritans and the Ark is in Jerusalem; because of this fact, it is Jerusalem which will finally inherit the traditions of the North. One more century will have to pass before the code which synthesizes its religious and social requirements will receive official sanction and will start to become a reality.

In fact, the reign of Ezechias was only the beginning of a reforming movement which does not survive his death. The campaigns of Sennacherib spell the end of the political fall of Juda. Under Manasses, the double influence of ancient Chanaanite paganism (the eternal temptation of Israel) and of Assyrian forms of worship provoke the gradual degradation of official Yahwism, which has become more and more syncretized (4 Kgs 21, 1-9). The resistance to national apostasy remains the work of fervent circles resulting on the one hand from milieus where Deuteronomy was born, and on the other hand from the disciples of Isaias. These groupings which are without a defined status, and are the distant ancestors of Jewish pietism, struggle against the meddlings of the powers, but we cannot exactly determine the extent of their influence. However, in order to feed their religious faithfulness, they preserve as a treasure the books willed to them by previous centuries and use them as spiritual sustenance. The Mosaic Torah, written and oral, is their rule of life; sacred history is the object of their meditations; the oracles of the prophets teach them at the same time the fear of Yahweh, the need for a conversion of the heart and for an unfailing hope. Divine revelation which is the basis for their faith is thus present to them under the form of books which they become used to considering as sacred because they find in them the Word of God.

CHAPTER IV

THE ORIGINS OF JUDAISM

1. The Deuteronomist Movement

The weakness of Assyria allows the kingdom of Juda to enjoy a certain amount of glory from the time Josias takes over the reins of power (*ca.* 630). From that time the progressive elimination of Assyrian cults, the first manifestation of nationalism, prepares from afar a much deeper reform. This was provoked in 622 by the discovery in the Temple of the Deuteronomic Code, which had been left there 100 years before. Converging witnesses showed that a profound renovation was about to take place. For Josias, in order to restore his kingdom on the basis of the Covenant and of the Mosaic Torah, immediately applied the Law at the cost of radical measures (4 Kgs 22-23).

This religious policy marks a date in literary history. In fact, with the recognition of Deuteronomy as the law of the state, the northern tradition is fully sown in Jerusalem. At the same time, the work of synthesis undertaken by the scribes of Ezechias is resumed and completed, resulting in a theological and historical literature of great depth. On the one hand, the code that was adopted during the renewal of the Covenant (cf. 4 Kgs 23, 1-3) is completed by parenetic discourses which structure it and sharpen its impact; the doctrine and the spirituality of the pietist circles of the North flourished there in long periods charged with religious emotion. On the other hand, all the historical material accumulated during the preceding centuries is methodically assembled and organized at the cost of glosses and revisions which are easily recognizable by their style. On the whole, the work covers our canonical books, from Genesis to Kings, but not in their present state because the passages of priestly origin are added later. The Deuteronomist additions are rare in Genesis, Exodus, and Numbers; whereas the end of Moses' story (E) is linked up with Deuteronomy; the Book of Josue is given rather important amplifications, while the Book of Judges takes on its profound meaning by the addition of chapter 2 which clarifies its general thesis; finally the Books of Samuel and Kings, composed of various materials, retrace all the events from the Philistine wars to the renewal of the Covenant by Josias. The method of Deuteronomist historians has already been explained. Usually in their works, the sources are juxtaposed rather than blended, and they are respected not only in their essential meaning but also to the letter; thus, they are still discernible through analysis. This manner of compiling documents did not prevent great theological theses from underlying these books of religious history: the doctrine of the Covenant is verified in all its facts. The teaching which comes from it is related to that of the parenetic discourses of Deuteronomy; it is like a concrete teaching which seeks to awaken in hearts the desire to love

Yahweh, to keep His Covenant, and to obey His law in order to live in peace in His holy land. There is something else to note. In adapting itself to Jerusalem, the Deuteronomist tradition becomes enriched. Its concept of national hope, surpassing what it had been in the 8th century with Osee, entails from then on a profound attachment to the Davidic dynasty (cf. 2 Sm 7) and to the Solomonian Temple (3 Kgs 8).

Unfortunately, the reforming activity of Josias ended with his tragic death. Though the code sanctioned by him still kept its official value, its application left much to be desired. The Deuteronomist movement subsisted, nevertheless, in the circles which had previously supported it. As keepers of its writings, they perpetuated its spirit; and much more, they completed them and brought them to light to make of them, in the midst of the national disaster culminated by the destruction of Jerusalem, the charter for future restorations. Thus Deuteronomy and the Book of Kings were enriched in their new editions, with pieces which assumed the death of Josias, Jerusalem destroyed and the people dispersed. It is generally estimated that a work of this kind was carried out during the restoration of the 6th century. In the meantime, the legislation of Josias, which had remained the official law in the country conquered by the Babylonians and connected by them to the province of Samaria, was introduced under this title even to the Samaritans, for whom Jerusalem had become the only possible place for the worship of Yahweh since Josias had destroyed the high places in the North. This situation was to have important consequences later on: God leads history through unexpected detours.

2. Rebirth of Prophetism

It would be impossible to affirm with certitude that the prophetic spirit ever completely ceased to be manifest, even under the reign of Manasses; but it was at least dormant. When it reappeared in full bloom under Josias it reestablished ties with the two pietist currents noted above: the one grouped around the disciples of Isaias, ends with Sophonias; the other, which depends on the tradition of Osee and the North, reappears in Jeremias. It is not known to which of the two should be related

Nahum, the announcer of the ruin of Ninive (shortly before 612), and Habacuc who, toward the end of the 6th century, sketched on an evocation of the Chaldean invasion his sorrowful reflections, his curses on the aggressor, his song of faith. The two works have some affinity to liturgical poetry; but this does not suffice to make of their authors "cultic prophets," a corporate body which Jeremias has shown us in a very poor light; no doubt they imitated its literary genre as Jeremias himself does on occasion.

The long ministry of Jeremias was concerned not only in having us relive in spirit the last decades of Judean history. It informs us rather fully on the religious personality of the prophet himself. Not only do we see him struggling against a crowd of enemies who have vowed to destroy him: nationalist politicians, priests and official prophets; but we also know what echoes the events of his painful mission awakened in his soul. The same affective spirituality, which in his discourses caused him to present Yahweh as a father and a spouse, colors the passages in which he reveals the dark rooms of his soul: this is the intimacy of an incessant dialogue with Him who called him and who continues to give him an extraordinary strength of soul during a ministry full of disappointments.

Although a diffident man, Jeremias maintained a surprising prestige among his diverse listeners; but he hardly had disciples. A faithful friend remained close to him: Baruch, who seemed to belong to Deuteronomist circles, if one can judge by his style, was his secretary; he collected his sayings and read them publicly at the risk of his life. When after the destruction of Jerusalem and the murder of Godolias the governor, the old prophet was dragged to Egypt by fanatic Jews, Baruch followed him there. After his death he gathered the scattered pieces of his work and added biographical chapters which are the apology of a persecuted man of God: had not Jeremias been right in the face of everyone, as evidenced by the recent catastrophe? But Jeremias also left a message of hope to his dispersed compatriots. He explained it in terms which recall somewhat the Messianism of Isaias (23, 5-6) but, in a stronger way, that of Osee. Like the Deuteronomist scribes, he constantly had in mind the thought of the Covenant at Sinai and the entry into the holy land. Through Israel's fault, this plan of divine love sketched in the past ended in failure. But after purifying His people, Yahweh will begin again, this will then be a new Covenant inscribed in all hearts (31, 31-34) and a return to the holy land under the guidance of the Shepherd of Israel (23, 1-4; 31, 1-22). By this updating of ancient history, Jeremias managed to stress its religious significance, which had been exploited in another manner, more moralizing, by Deuteronomist historians: without Israel's knowing it, the events through which it had lived since the Exodus bore prophetic weight.

Probably framed in Egypt, Jeremias' collection must have been brought to Palestine fairly early during the Exile (after 570). It was apparently edited there in Deuteronomist circles. When it was communicated to the Eastern Diaspora, it was enriched by new additions (notably chaps. 50-51), so that toward 520 it had taken the shape it was to preserve in the Hebrew Bible; still the Greek Bible has it in a slightly different form. Isolated and misunderstood during his lifetime, the prophet thus exercised a profound influence in Judea as well as in Babylonia after his death.

3. The Priestly Tradition

The name "priestly" is given to the tradition which is proper to the clergy of Jerusalem. This expression consecrated by the use of exegetes is useful but a little ambiguous, for the Deuteronomist code is also probably of priestly origin; but it is our opinion that it comes from the shrines in the North. We have already seen how, after the royal period, this tradition of the Temple of Jerusalem is linked also to the very origins of Israel in many ways.

The introduction of the Deuteronomist tradition in Jerusalem as the law of the Temple was not accomplished without provoking some struggles. Certainly the exclusive privilege recognized in the sanctuary, whose task it is theirs to guard satisfied the Sadoqite priests; but they intended to maintain their privileges. That is why 4 Kgs 23, 9 remarks that Dt 18, 7 remained a dead issue. The levitical priests of the provinces did not receive the right to officiate in the national shrine. However, the event also provoked, as a counter-stroke, an original development of priestly customs and doctrine. The result of this work was crystallized in a little collection which, however recent its writing, no less expressed very ancient concepts: the "code of holiness" (Lev 17-26, with the exception of later additions). Undoubtedly all the critics do not agree in assigning this date to the work in question; however, it seems to us to be situated between Deuteronomy and Ezechiel. Throughout this booklet there appears a sensitively different spirituality from that of Deuteronomy, all centered around divine greatness and sanctity. What is most profound in the liturgical service, the spirit of religion, appears in it as the supreme motive of all human action. All obedience to the Law of Yahweh is assimilated to a sort of liturgical service: in all circumstances the "holy" people works to the glory of its God just as the priests do in the Temple. Such is the core of the doctrine of the milieu out of which, towards the same period, issues forth a very original prophetic figure: Ezechiel.

Even once seized by the prophetic spirit, Ezechiel remained profoundly affected by his original association with the priesthood of Jerusalem. There is discussion as to when he was deported to Babylon: 597 or 586; the question is of secondary importance. It is more important to notice his dependence on the code of holiness, his contact with Osee, the Deuteronomist and perhaps Jeremias; this shows what his readings were. For Ezechiel is clearly a "man of the book." When he first saw his vocation, the Word of God was present to him not in the form of an oral message (cf. Is 6, 6-7; Jer 1, 9) but of a written volume (Ez 2, 9-3, 2). It is a sign of the times. Furthermore, his work shows him to be erudite: he is not ignorant either of the data of Phoenician mythology (Ez 28), nor of certain characteristics of Mesopotamian art (Ez 1); especially he displays a deep knowledge of the laws and rituals used in the Temple.

His message of conversion, prior to the ruin of Jerusalem, no doubt echoes the preoccupations of the Deuteronomist circles, but he reinterprets them in a way in keeping with the Sadoqite theology. The doctrine of individual retribution is affirmed in it, but as a datum rather badly coordinated to the whole of the system; this could be a development of the doctrine of the "remnant" (cf. 9, 1-4) which recalls the message of

Isaias. As for the plans for the future which the prophet draws up after 586, by mixing eschatological evocations and practical data, once again we can trace there the priestly tradition: the purification of hearts in the new Israel has a ritual aspect about it (36, 16 ff.); the holy city and the Temple, the priests, sons of Sadoq, to whom are joined the other levitical priests, and the fulfilment of the ceremonies according to the prescribed calendar occupy stage-front; on the contrary the prince of Israel (*naśi*) is reduced to a subordinate position, subordinate to the priesthood. Ezechiel thus sketches the picture of a new theocracy which introduces in its own manner the state-like organization of the royal period. In fact, the Judaism which will issue from the test of Israel will resemble this picture rather closely, with the exception that no prince will be able to maintain himself next to the high priests, who have become the undisputed leaders of the nation.

The manner in which the Book of Ezechiel at present appears, allows us somewhat to see extensive editorial reworking produced after the death of the prophet, in the schools of priestly scribes which had inherited his written work and his spirit. These schools must be looked for in the Eastern Diaspora, and it is this same milieu and in this same atmosphere that the priestly traditions give birth to a vast historico-judaic *corpus* where Mosaic legislation is readopted in a more specifically ritualistic manner. The circumstances of the priests exiled far from their Temple obliged them to accurately collate the customaries and the rituals, with an eye toward the day when they will return home; furthermore, they must outline for the deported Jews rules of conduct to protect them against the contagion of paganism. The fundamental writing called the Priestly Code seems to answer this double purpose. But, as always in Israel, the Torah thus edited on the basis of the ancestral tradition is presented in a living manner in the framework of a holy history. Taking up again the plan of the Yahwist and systematizing it even more, the priestly scribes show how the plan of the Covenant of Yahweh was realized during the course of the ages in four stages: creation, the covenant with Noah, the patriarchal covenant and the Mosaic Covenant. In each stage, God gave His laws to men until He founded, through

Moses, the Israelite theocracy centered around the liturgical service to Yahweh in the Sanctuary of the Ark. At the top of the hierarchy of the holy people thus set apart from the other nations, Yahweh placed at the same time Aaron, Moses' brother, the ancestor to the line of high priests. This is not profane history written with the preoccupations of modern critics; it is a theology of the Chosen People presented in an elaborate doctrinal synthesis. In the concrete framework of the sojourn in the desert, the authors draw up the ideal prototype of the institutions about which they dream. Archaic in certain respects, their work assimilates everything acquired during the previous centuries to present a program for the future. It thus prolongs the sketch of Ezechiel and gives to Judaism its charter.

4. The Consolation of the Exiles

Thus once the institutions created by the Davidic monarchy are ruined, the people of God finds the means to survive in a form that is both very new and very old: after the royal period it reestablishes ties with the sacral community born on Sinai. However, it preserves an important inheritance from the royal period. First of all there are the sacred books: the Mosaic Torah represented by several collections, from the Book of the Covenant to the Sacerdotal Code, to say nothing of a customary law which will not be late in becoming established; history books re-edited several times: at the beginning of the monarchy, under Ezechias, under Josias, and since the destruction of Jerusalem; psalms, the number of which is impossible to judge; and finally the wisdom maxims preserved by the royal scribes. This collection of works gives witness to a revelation profoundly united in its essential principles, but varied, however, in its expression as much as in the currents which are manifested therein. Israel not only possesses a religious wisdom which sets it apart from its neighboring peoples; the national hope which arose from the Sinaitic Covenant took on at this time an unequaled breadth thanks to the contribution of prophetic eschatology. The dispersed people draws from it a reason for living in the midst of difficult conditions imposed upon it. The whole experience of its past is now projected into the future and it thus continues to feed its hopes.

During the Exile, the Jews regroup in local communities and thus escape assimilation. Each community has its natural functionaries: the heads of families and the elders, the levitic and priestly caste which is hereditary, and finally the literate laymen, former civil servants who will find new markets for their talents as scribes. Schools are little by little founded, as the Jews become adjusted to their new ways of life and find the means to improve their material condition. The heirs to the former pietist groups, disciples of the prophets, members of the Deuteronomist or priestly circles, are the soul of this nascent Judaism. If Judaism finds in its natural functionaries a support to *last,* it is thanks to its most fervent members that God causes it to become conscious of itself. In the "remnant of the just" which escaped the disaster, the people finds spiritual guides capable of orienting it in a manner consonant with the wishes of Yahweh.

In Palestine there remains a restricted worship, for which the Temple of Jerusalem continues to be the center despite its shabby condition; it is likely that the Lamentations were composed in this framework, on the occasion of a solemn mourning celebrated on the anniversary of the ruin of the Temple. It is probable that some psalms were also born in similar circumstances. In Babylonia and in other lands of exile, the religious practices must be adapted to the new living circumstances. Certain exterior rites take on then an increased importance: the Sabbath, prohibitions, circumcision, and fasts on the traditional dates. Furthermore, the local communities habitually meet on determined days to pray together: this is a distant origin of synagogal worship. From the ancient worship of the shrines, all possible elements were preserved: recitations or readings of the Torah and of sacred history (written or only confided to traditional schemata), exhortation, prayer and the signing of hymns and the blessing of the assembly.

These meetings undoubtedly play an important role in the constitution of the sacred books. Already established texts are used—and thus is explained in part the preservation of ancient works. In second place, the synagogal liturgy can be considered as the *Sitz im Leben* of a certain number of new works. For example, the same meditation on Exodus, which allows one to suppose a previous reading, is found again in the penitential liturgy of Is 63, 7-64, 11, the exhortations to confidence of Is 43, 16-21, the meditation of Ps 78, 105 or 106. In the second case would not this look like a sermon for Easter time, in which the past would have been updated in order to draw from it the hope of a new deliverance? It is in this manner that *midrash* was born, from a reflection on the Scriptures which are now the consolation of Israel in its time of trial. Naturally the schools of priests, of cantors or of scribes are narrowly linked to the communities of the exile as to their places of worship meetings. The ancient books are collected there, copied, edited and enriched with glosses which complete them and apply them to the needs of the times. The young scribes learn there their trade at the same time as their hearts and minds are trained. Therefore, in the works which flow from their pens, there are multiple allusions to and a systematic re-use of expressions consecrated by usage (what is called the anthological style).

Such is the milieu in which can be best explained, in our opinion, the composition of the great prophetic work which reached us through the Book of Isaias. In a circle where is perpetuated the tradition of the disciples of the prophet, an author who has remained anonymous addresses to the exiles between 547 (the first victory of Cyrus and 538 (decree of emancipation of the Jews), a message of consolation wherein can be distinguished, despite the very pronounced literary personality of the author, numerous references to the preexilian books: Isaias, Nehum (cf. Is 52, 7-10), Sophonias (Is 49, 13), Jeremias, Deuteronomy, the ancient traditions of Israel and certain aspects of the priestly tradition, without considering a certain affinity with the style of the wisdom writings. The author is truly literate, as well as a very capable poet; his message especially constitutes one of the peaks of the Old Testament. Not only the eschatology with which his book is completely impregnated is purified of its political elements in order to be centered on the reign of Yahweh in Jerusalem, His holy city, in a perspective of complete universalism; not only the people of this kingdom, beneficiaries of eschatological salvation, is represented in the image of the *'anawim:* a people seeking justice, which has the Law of Yahweh in its heart;

but to the royal Messias, either peaceful or warlike, is substituted the high figure of the Servant, mediator of a new covenant and spiritual saviour of the multitudes by his suffering, which is a new sacrifice of expiation. This *Gospel* surpasses by far the doctrinal import of several anonymous works almost contemporary to it such as Is 13-14 or Jer 50-51.

Did the prophet of the captivity come back from the exile with the first repatriates and did he then pursue his ministry, so that the last poems of the Servant would take place in the bitter context of the year following 538? There is discussion on this point. In any case, his collection, composed through his own care or that of his disciples, exercised a profound influence in Jerusalem in the first quarter of the 6th century, in a parallel manner to the Deuteronomist, to the books of Jeremias and, perhaps to a lesser degree, of Ezechiel. But with this quarter century there begins the period of the second Temple. Once the shrine is rebuilt, Judaism refinds its center. In the midst of new political difficulties, it will acquire its definitive equilibrium.

CHAPTER V
JUDAISM DURING THE PERSIAN PERIOD

1. Prophetism at the Time of the Second Temple

During the Persian period, it becomes more difficult to follow the chronological order of the formation of the collection of sacred books. On the one hand, data to retrace the history of Judaism are lacking more than once, especially between the years 515 and 445 and from 398 to Alexander. On the other hand, the biblical works themselves do not date themselves very easily, witness to the diversity of opinions shared by the exegetes. However what appears more clearly is the development of the different currents which give expression to the Revelation. They will therefore serve as guidelines.

Around the reconstruction of the Temple, we notice first of all a certain prophetic activity. But while Aggeus, Isaias 34-35 and 56-66 (whose unity of authorship is problematic) extend especially the line of the message of consolation, the visions of Zacharias 1-8 follow rather the footsteps of Ezechiel by their recourses to all sorts of complicated symbols. In a general way, the prophetic genre moreover manifests a tendency to evolve. It is less spontaneous, closer to the written style than to the spoken word. The new authors have attended the schools for scribes; they are aware of the works of their predecessors and sometimes point them out (cf. Is 35). The various preoccupations of an ill-known period conflict in juxtaposed pages whose exact historical framework is often unknown to us (especially for Is 56-66); whence, next to one another, there appear fires of religious nationalism (Is 63, 1-6) and proclamations of universalism (Is 56, 1-8). The repatriates are re-established in their country at the cost of a thousand difficulties; the South is invaded by the Edomites, upon whom the Jews call down the divine wrath (Is 34; 1-6; Abd). Their hope is exalted however at the sight of their reconstructed city (Is 60-62).

As time goes on, a sort of disassociation of prophetism takes place. On the one hand, the role of the prophet as preacher and guide to consciences is being assumed by the wisdom master; on the other hand, eschatological oracles undergo an autonomous development, often at the hands of anonymous authors, in a style where conventional clichés and obscure expressions abound. We cannot, for example, exclude the fact that Ez 38-39 was added to the book of the prophets at about this time in the circles where it was being preserved. According to other critics, Is 24-27 would be ascribed the date of 485 at the time when Babylon was laid to ruin by the armies of Xerxes. But these are only hypotheses, for the works of this type are difficult to date. If the collection of Malachias (only slightly affected by this development of prophetism) can be placed rather accurately around the time when Nehemias came to Juda (middle of the 5th century), Joel escapes the grasp of the historians. Finally, the second part of Zacharias (9-14), contemporaneous with the conquests of Alexander, presents an enigmatic aspect despite the frequent re-use of images drawn from the ancient prophetic works. It is a work for the initiated rather than the echo of a public action. Furthermore, the book foresees the extinction of a decried prophetism (Za 13, 2-6). Soon the combination of the former eschatological oracle and of the prophetic vision (already frequent in Ezechiel and Zacharias) will give birth to a new genre: the apocalypse, a revelation of the divine secrets manifested in dreams or in symbolic visions. The anguishes of fervent souls, who desire to understand the meaning of a deceitful present, and to be enlightened on the future realization of the plan of God, will all pass into this strange literary form, which during the next period will undergo a growing development.

2. The Development of the Wisdom Current

The Wisdom current does not date from the Persian period. We have seen it take root in Israel at the time of Solomon. Imbued even at this time by the Yahwist ferment which, in the biblical framework, already gave a peculiar twist to the wisdom of nations, it developed all during the royal period in the circles of the scribes, ending in collections of maxims and exercising its influence on certain other sectors of literature, such as historiography. With the captivity its former literary creations took their place in the treasure of national traditions. As for the scribe, he will no longer be only a functionary who edits acts or annals, but rather a pious man who will enrich the sacred books by meditating upon the ancient texts.

Henceforth, the Wisdom current will experience a great development, at the same time as the religious influence of Yahwism presents itself in a clearer and more direct fashion. It overflows even into the prophetic collections (Is 40, 12-26) as it did in some of the most recent Deuteronomic chapters. But, in general, it preserves the same exterior appearance, affecting a language accessible to every upright man; however, in this apparently neutral expression, it systematically transposes the data of Mosaic and prophetic revelation. Its very method allows it to do its deed with everything, retaining the assimilable elements which foreign literatures can offer (these include Edomite, Phoenician, Egyptian and Assyrian literatures); but, in the final analysis, its essential sources show up: the sacred books, with which the anonymous scribes nourish their thought to the point that they impregnate their vocabulary with the expressions that they find in them. Under this sapiential form, the doctrine of the Covenant takes on a less specifically national character, and this effort at adjustment corresponds to one of the tendencies which, from the Exile onwards, are manifested inside Judaism: next to a strict nationalism, a current affirms itself, one that is more universalistic and more missionary. Wisdom literature will be for it an instrument of penetration even in the pagan circles where it will recruit proselytes, for, in its framework, there is elaborated a doctrine on human life parallel to that reflection which in Greece towards the same period gives birth to philosophy.

At the chronological point of departure of this literature there is the collection of Proverbs. Comprising several ancient collections, it is furnished with a substantial introduction by its editor (Prv 1-9) whose theological scope is much larger. The dates assigned to the work by critics vary from the beginning of the 5th century to the end of the 4th; the time around 480 can be held if we admit that the work precedes Job (Robert). Treating the problems of the righteous and happy life and of divine retribution, the Proverbs serenely repeat a resolutely optimistic traditional thesis: the way of justice is that of life, that of sin leads to death. To this thesis the poet of Job (*ca.* 450: Dhorme) offers a contrary factual argument. The suffering of the just is a painful problem! Mesopotamian thought had not ignored this problem and we can admit at least an indirect literary influence on Job from the works that this literature had produced on the subject. But finally it is by virtue of specifically Yahwist data that the dialogue of Job and of his friends is elaborated; if it ends with no firm conclusion on the level of theoretical reflection, it is at least noticeable that biblical revelation does not grow in a rectilinear fashion, but through a process of *sic et non:* divine light will not be manifested to man except at the end of a painful experiment where he will have fathomed the mystery of his condition. The timeliness of the problems treated by Proverbs and Job appears even more when we relate these books to a certain number of apparently contemporary psalms, which treat the same problems.

3. The Development of Religious Lyricism

It is known that the problem of the psalter is resolved by critics in radically different ways, whatever be their sectarian allegiances. Some tend to appeal to the royal period for almost all the psalms; others place a large number of them (if not the majority) after the Exile. In fact it would be very strange if the religious lyricism of the preexilian period left only a few traces in the Bible, when it is known what care the scribes used to collect the other literary works prior to the destruction of Jerusalem. However, account must be taken of two facts: the readaptation of ancient psalms to new perspectives of Jewish life and thought, when they are reconsidered after the Exile, and the natural development of genres from the past in the corporations of cantors created around the second Temple. The result is that the solution of the problem of the psalms can only be complex. If it is evident that some are ancient (those who clearly speak of the king or come from the Israel of the North), it is possible to hesitate for a number of others. Practically speaking it is their literary and doctrinal situation with respect to the prophetic texts which, very often, constitutes the principal element for their dates.

Critics gladly relate to the postexilian period several categories of works whose dependence upon the prophets seems assured: wisdom psalms such as Pss 1, 34, 37, or legalistic psalms, such as Pss 19, 8 ff and 119; the suffering psalms, born in the circle of the "poor" which prolong certain themes of Jeremias, even though the genre of individual or collective lamentation is ancient; the psalms of the kingdom of Yahweh, at least when after Second-Isaias they present the kingdom in an eschatological perspective; the "historical" psalms; and the psalms into which pass the spiritual deceptions which are accumulated in the Jewish soul during the Persian period. These general indications leave intact the question raised by each individual psalm; they want only to show how the study of the psalter allows us to penetrate further into the interior drama lived by Judaism after the great dream of the returning years (538-515) is dissipated. At the same time, it is possible to discover how the Scriptures are then for the believers the only reliable source of hope; their prayers feed on them so much so that the theology of the Prophets, of Deuteronomy or of the priestly current passes entirely into its inspired expression.

The Canticle of Canticles can be linked to religious lyricism, and a good number of interpreters give the end of the

Persian period as its date. But this is as far as their agreement goes. We have read that some see in it a collection of human love songs with the marriage ceremonies being their framework (*Sitz im Leben*); others consider them as symbolic poems, more or less allegorized, which would sing the spiritual marriage of Yahweh and Israel. Perhaps these theses are not as removed as they first appear, if one realizes that the introduction of the Canticle among the sacred books read publicly in the synagogal liturgy could not have been done without this book being jointly interpreted in relation to the prophetic texts where the Covenant was compared to a marriage (Osee, Jeremias, Ezechiel and 2nd and 3rd Isaias). It could be an allegorical reinterpretation of ancient marriage poems or a lyrical composition hiding a secret meaning behind the sumptuous images of a refined art: in either case, the Canticle testifies to the ingeniousness of the Jewish scribes, skilled at exploiting the prophetic writings and at using an apparently hermetic language to translate the revealed doctrine.

4. From History to Midrash

Ancient Israel was not unaware of the historical genre under, however, extremely varied forms. Nonetheless, it has been seen that the literary form of *narrative* was not always used for the purpose of historical teaching, even without taking into account the diversity which could affect it in itself (epic narrative, etiological narrative, popular tradition, historiographical narration, etc. . . . .). All sorts of teachings could be translated in them in a concrete manner: juridical, moral or theological. Generally reflection on the historical traditions of Israel or the texts which testify to the past led even to a higher plane than history: that of doctrine and spirituality as in the works of the Deuteronomist school. In the priestly current, the genre tended to become even more stylized; it did not fear to reconstruct the past in a systematic manner by inextricably mixing the data of tradition and the theological concepts of the narrators. This method of developing history with an essentially didactic purpose, with a view to seeking in it a religious significance capable of teaching and edifying souls, is nothing other than one of the forms of midrash. The priestly holy history already obeys the fundamental laws of the genre. After the Exile, it will experience a greater and greater development, without sacrificing a parallel persistence of historiography.

For example, the sources used by the Chronicler in the Books of Esdras-Nehemias are clearly situated on the historical side of the narrative genre: memories of the return, anti-Samaritan dossier, and remembrances of both Nehemias and Esdras. On the other hand, it is the essentially didactic narrative which is developed in the Book of Jonas, and the delightful "novella" of Ruth, even if in fact this latter rests on a valid historical tradition (the genealogy of David).

Midrash, however, does not always take on a narrative form. Thus, the so-called "historical" psalms (78, 105, 106) are also *midrashim,* which flourish in meditation and prayer instead of only ending in stylized narratives of the past. So also, when later eschatological texts, which are generally anonymous, repeat, while developing them, themes and expressions drawn from the prophetic writings, this systematic reinterpretation of ancient material is still in a way midrash: the texts were carefully studied and their meaning was clarified in the light of other passages; finally their explanation gives birth to a new Scripture. Since the discoveries of Qumran, the name *pesher* is given to the exegesis of prophetic texts which tend to bring them up to date in order to clarify the meaning of present events and of "what will happen later on." The Jewish tradition itself has called *halakha* the exploitation of the Scriptures to find in them rules of conduct and *haggada* the free development grafted upon the Scriptures with a view only to edification, especially when it includes narrative materials drawn from the popular tradition or from the imagination of the interpreters. It would be wrong to see in these, literary genres foreign to the Bible: they are the natural result of its reading by the Jewish people. We believe that the first traces of those genres can already be found in the inspired books of the Persian period.

5. The Fixing of the Torah

The center of Jewish thought is neither the Wisdom current nor religious lyricism, or even the prophetic teaching: it is the Torah. In the Persian period, it is fixed in its definitive form. It has been seen how, as early as the Mosaic period, it was the charter of the Covenant; then, in the royal period, it tended to become crystallized into two parallel currents: that of the North, represented by the moral Decalogue and by the Book of the Covenant; and that of the South, attested especially by the cultic Decalogue (Ex 34). At the end, these two currents, while intercrossing several times, experienced their own development, the first giving rise to Deuteronomy, the second to the code of holiness, to the Torah of Ezechiel and to the fundamental writing of the priestly code. Next to these written recensions there remained furthermore a customary law and rituals whose transmission could be accomplished orally without injuring their faithful preservation. During the captivity, it seems that the spirit of the Deuteronomist current dominated the intellectual and religious center that Judaism preserved in Palestine, while that of the priestly current was perpetuated in the Babylonian schools imbued with the influence of Ezechiel. Upon their return from the exile, the Sadoqite priests who came back with Josue brought back with them not only oral traditions, but written works which, for them, enjoyed an authority equal to the books already legally sanctioned in the prior period: ancient juridical compilations and Deuteronomy. Furthermore, from the return onwards, the ancient customaries of the Temple are put back into force, now that the worship service is started anew. It seems that it is in these circumstances that several codes drawn at this time from the Pentateuch are edited, on the basis of preexilian traditions readapted to the needs of the times: code of sacrifices, code of purity, various tariffs.

Whatever be the solution to these very controverted problems, when Nehemias accomplishes in Judea his mission so important for the future of Judaism, the situation of the Torah is complicated. On the one hand, a certain number of texts are probably already recognized by the Persian authorities as the *law of the state* in Israel: these are the archaic codes and Deuteronomy. Undoubtedly there must be added local customs, but it is impossible to say what is their official status. It is rather likely that the priestly compilations are an object of dispute between the repatriated Jews from Babylonia and the "people of the country," especially the Samaritans. In fact, these latter also claim the worship of the "God of heaven" and Jerusalem became their center of worship since the time when Josias had destroyed all the high places of the former Northern Kingdom. It seems that it was to avoid this opposition of two groups that the Persian authorities undertook at this time to fix once and for all their laws and their status. Such seems to have been the mission of Esdras, which could preferably be placed in 398 (some propose the 5th century). To prepare the unification of Jewish laws into a *corpus* officially sanctioned by the state, jurists, belonging to the "priestly" schools (of Babylon such as Esdras himself, or of Palestine) would then have added to the prior texts supplementary articles destined to make them harmonious among themselves and to adapt them to the needs of the times. Finally the historico-juridical entirely of the Pentateuch seems to have come from this work, by blending the two great currents which inherit all the Israelite past: the Deuteronomist and the priestly.

In the present state of our knowledge, this presentation of things seems the most satisfactory *salvo meliore judicio*. On the one hand, it assigns to the fixation of the Torah a set of circumstances which allow us to understand its motive and its importance; on the other hand, it shows how the work accomplished at the time of Esdras did not have as its object to create anew nor to sanction the result of a juridical evolution completely ordered by factors external to the religion of Israel, but on the contrary to collect in a reasoned compilation the proliferation of texts issued from Israelite tradition, such as it had been developed throughout the ages.

Even if there enters into the hypothesis a share of disputable conjectures, it is certain that, well before the Persian period, the Torah is fixed. Samaritans and Jews will preserve it under the same form after their separation (which is preferably placed toward the beginning of the Greek period, even if the prodromes date back to preceding decades). Inside Judaism, the divergences will henceforth bear only on its practical interpretation: harmonization of apparently contradictory passages, proper value of the non-written customs, and of the solutions proposed by the private doctors. On this point, the various tendencies will continue to be confronted, opposing especially the priestly circles with the lay doctors; but this no longer concerns the formation of the holy books.

CHAPTER VI

JUDAISM IN THE HELLENISTIC PERIOD

1. The Development of Genres in Palestinian Judaism

Documents are almost completely lacking to retrace the history of Judaism during the 4th and 3rd centuries. However, it is at this time that the Jewish institutions find their definitive equilibrium after the fixing of the Torah. Fixed through the cares of the priestly legists, the Torah is confided first of all to the clergy, divided into 24 classes followed by the levitical orders, among which the cantors have henceforth taken their place. In order to interpret it, the priests intend to hold only to the letter; on the contrary, the literate laymen, the Wise Men, who attribute in their study and in their teaching a large place to other ancient writings, give equal attention to the written Torah and to customs (called "oral Torah"). The gap between the two tendencies will widen with time to end in the sects of the Asmonean period.

With the conquests of Alexander, the Hellenist civilization invades the East, but Judaism does not immediately conflict with it. The most noticeable repercussion of the political changes which took place around 330 seems to be, for Palestinian Judaism, the definitive schism of the Samaritan community which was already virtually realized during the preceding decades but was consummated only with the construction of the temple of Garizim (at an uncertain date). Various institutions compete at this time for the preservation and explanation of the ancient books, as well as for the composition of new ones: priestly circles of the temple and the corporation of cantors, schools for scribes, and the synagogal liturgy. The communities of the Diaspora also have their schools and their synagogues, but we have very little information on their operation and on their real influence in the constitution of the biblical collection. We can only suspect the Eastern origin of the traditions which are at the basis of Daniel, of Tobias and of

Esther; but the transmission of these materials until their actual writing remains out of reach.

The fixing of the Torah leads as a counterstroke to that of the prophetic collections. But here, it becomes difficult to assign dates. The last pages of the Book of Isaias seem to be chapters 24-27; certain critics place them around 485, while others place them around the Greek period. The content and the order of Jeremias are considerably different in the Hebrew and the Greek: it is possible to see in this a rather late final draft. For Ezechiel, a certain affinity to the supplementary laws of the Pentateuch is noticed in some passages; while also the date of chapters 38-39 remains under discussion, certain critics place them during the Greek period. In the group of the *Prophetae priores* the priestly rewritings seem more numerous for Josue than for the other books; but it may not be necessary to suppose an editorial work later than the fixing of the Torah. Finally, in the collection of the twelve minor prophets only one characteristic ensemble brings us back to the Greek period, toward the last quarter of the 4th century: Za 9-14. But even these chapters are added as a supplement to the already formed book, just as Is 24-27 is added to the Book of Isaias; it is possible to envisage in these two cases an insertion later than the formation of these collections, as though these were enlarged editions. All this allows one to see a rather large work of collating and editing, realized in these schools for scribes in the 5th and 4th centuries. The collection of the Ketubim then includes several important works: the Proverbs and Job, the most ancient of the Megillot (Lamentations, Ruth, and the Canticle of Canticles which can be brought into this period), but the canonical grouping of the five books does not as yet appear achieved. As for the psalter, it is not known to exactly what date its cloture is to be assigned. Perhaps we must go as late as the beginning of the Hellenistic period, but the existence of Machabean psalms is very problematical.

It is in this group of Ketubim that we must look for the few works composed after Alexander. The great work of the Chronicler (1 and 2 Par, Esd and Neh), seems to have as its framework the reaction of orthodox Judaism to the schismatic Samaritans; in this perspective, it would be easy to explain its insistence upon the legitimacy of the unique sanctuary of Jerusalem and of the unique Davidic dynasty, from which will come the Messias. Using ancient materials, the book (at present divided into four volumes) could well have been born towards the end of the 4th century or during the 3rd). As it has for its purpose to justify through history a theological thesis, it resorts more often to midrash techniques than, for example, to works of history resulting from the Deuteronomist current; but already, on this point, the priestly sacred history has already opened the way. With the Book of Esther whose date is unfortunately not clear, we are fully into haggadic midrash, even if the story told has its point of departure in facts. Linked to the feast of the *Purim,* the work has, furthermore, an orientation to worship.

In the category of the Wisdom writings, Ecclesiastes manifests a certain knowledge of Greek thought, but this contact is without depth; his literary activity can be placed in the 3rd century. Tobias (toward the same time) could rather be tied to Eastern origins (especially in what concerns its angelology), but the place of its composition is a subject of discussion. In any case, this book is distinguished by the way in which it narrowly unites wisdom teaching, the narrative techniques of the *haggada* and the recourse to lyricism: in the lower Jewish literature, the ancient literary currents are thus readily joined. The same mixture reappears in the collection of Baruch, whose most ancient sections could go back to the 3rd century and be of Palestinian origin. Finally, toward the beginning of the 2nd century, Ecclesiasticus (Ben Sira), master of a school at Jerusalem, in his composite collection makes the inventory of Wisdom in his time: the data from the Torah, from the prophetic teachings and from the more ancient wisdom writings appear in it as closely united. Less creative than in the past, Judaism thus feeds upon what it has acquired, waiting for the Day when the prophetic oracles will be realized, when Yahweh will reign and where the Messias will be at the head of His people.

2. The Confrontation between Judaism and Hellenism

The first contacts between Judaism and Hellenism, at the time of the domination of the Ptolemies over Palestine, did not lead to any crisis. On the contrary, the creation of a large Jewish community in Alexandria led little by little to the translation of the essentials of Jewish ideas into the Greek language; during the course of the 3rd century, the Torah was translated, then other sacred books, at dates more difficult to establish.

The conflict breaks out in Palestinian Judaism, under Antiochus Epiphanes. The Machabean crisis is located at the outset of a rather abundant non-canonical literature, which we cannot deal with here. It is necessary to note only the development at this time of the apocalyptic genre; the oldest sections of the Book of Enoch could be assigned a date around 170. These are the circumstances when the traditions of Daniel perhaps already edited in part, start to take shape, serving as a framework for the only apocalypse properly so-called which appears in the canon of the Old Testament. The book seems to reflect the thought of the *hasidim,* who had been rallied to Judas Machabee toward the beginning of the holy way. A similar spirit, although more nationalistic, is found again in the *haggada* of Judith, which seems to echo the climate of the Machabean wars. Under the Asmonean dynasty the history of the way of independence finds a good narrator (I Machabees) whose work intimately joins to the traditional techniques of Hebrew historiography a recourse to those of Greek historiography. As for the work of Jason the Cyrene, who related the same events, we only have a Greek summary of it, composed in Alexandria; there again, Hebrew historiography readily mingled with *haggada* evolved toward the genre of pathetic history, similar to the one practiced by contemporary Hellenism.

Finally, it is in the framework of Alexandrine Judaism that the confrontation of Judaism and Hellenism is resolved, not by a conflict or an absorption of the first by the second, but by a victory of biblical Revelation, which had become capable of assimilating certain elements of Hellenism. The fact is not yet very felt in the recent parts of the Book of Baruch; chapters 4, 5-5, 9 which give the appearance of a sermon delivered in a synagogue and which perhaps were written in Greek, only echo the prophetic Scriptures. The "Letter of Jeremias" is a diatribe against idolatry, which gives us some idea of Jewish apologetics. The deuterocanonical additions to Esther and Daniel contain nothing specifically Greek. We must wait for the Wisdom of Solomon (during the 1st century) to see the inspired literature express itself in a Greek terminology. Still we must remark that this terminology is put into the service of a perfectly traditional doctrine. We know that since the 5th century, the Wisdom current agitated the problem of individual retribution. At the time of Antiochus' persecution, the Book of Daniel had, in our opinion, shed light on this problem in revealing the resurrection of the just, called to share the kingdom of God at the end of time. This is this participation of the just in beatific immortality that the Wisdom book explicitly teaches, transposing an essential datum of Jewish apocalyptic into sapiential language.

Judaism continues therefore to enrich its inspired literature at a time when its non-canonical productions start to become more and more numerous. But very often these productions represent less the great traditional current than the spirit of the sects which, as early as the Machabean period, are more and more opposed to one another. Without talking about the Samaritans, three principal sects are distinguished at the end of the 2nd century: the Sadducees, who support the Asmonean dynasty; the Pharisees, who refuse to recognize the legitimacy of the non-Davidic royalty; and the "Sadoqites," whose exact origin remains still a problem and who lead to Essenism. This tableau of a divided Judaism is instructive. It shows how difficult it is at this time to define Jewish orthodoxy on the sole basis of Scripture and oral tradition. On both sides, there are currents and tendencies whose definitive synthesis has not been made. Even in the Torah, the harmonizing of the different lines of development, represented by pieces more juxtaposed than blended, give rise to discussion. The concept of individual retribution, and of Messianism is not the same in the sects we have just mentioned, no more than is the list of books considered as sacred. Finally, the recourse to Scripture cannot always be sufficient to resolve the controversies, since they crystallize divine revelation in its successive stages: whence there are apparent contradictions between equally inspired passages, but born at different periods and in different places, answering very different needs and resolving them in a more or less complete manner. The reason for this state of fact only appears in the light of the New Testament. In fact, Judaism is only a provisory and preparatory economy which tends towards a "fulfilment." Christ, in His person, His work and His teaching, "will fulfill the Scriptures," finally making explicit their meaning and their import, by reason of the divine plan which, from the very beginning, led toward it.

Thus, we will finish this rapid synthesis. The reader will not forget that in sketching it, we have incorporated into it more than one hypothetical element, when critical problems were raised that have not been definitively solved. Not that the value of the Bible as historical document would thereby be questioned. But today it is not sufficient to affirm this value as a whole without going into detail in order to determine the exact dates of the events, the dates of the inspired books and their places of origin. It is from this point of view that questions are still being asked. To make a choice in these debates, to propose probable points of view founded on serious arguments, was the only possible attitude in matters where research is not complete. It is then legitimate to hope that after these approximations there will come firmer certitudes and that our knowledge of the Old Testament will grow in accuracy even in its minute details. Discussions of this nature moreover leave intact the properly doctrinal value of the Sacred Books: whoever be their human authors and whatever be their dates, God speaks to us through them, and what is essential is to grasp His message. But if, furthermore, it is possible to reconstitute in a sure way the steps of divine pedagogy which led our Fathers in the faith (cf. Gal 3, 24) to Christ, then the relation of the Old Testament to Christ only becomes clearer, and faith finds in this an additional benefit. This is why the critical study of the Old Testament is worthwhile attempting: far from leading to skepticism, its only aim is to penetrate further into the knowledge of Revelation.

Roland de Vaux
1903-1971

Roland Marie Etienne Guérin de Vaux was born and grew up in Paris. After studies at the Sorbonne he entered the seminary and was ordained for the diocese of Paris in 1929. He then joined the Dominican Fathers in Amiens and was professed in 1930. In 1933 he went to the Ecole Biblique *in Jerusalem and spent the rest of his life there. He was its director from 1945 to 1965.*

Between 1946 and 1960 de Vaux directed nine archeological campaigns at Tell el Far'ah, probably the biblical town of Tirzah that served as the capital of the Israelite King Omri before he moved to Samaria. When the Dead Sea Scrolls were discovered in the area of Qumran, de Vaux led the excavation of the community center and the surrounding region, and played a major role in the entire operation. From 1953 until his death he was chief editor in charge of the international project to get the scrolls published. And from 1961 to 1963 he shared with Kathleen Kenyon the direction of the excavations in Jerusalem.

Père de Vaux was Stillman Professor of Roman Catholic Studies at Harvard Divinity School for the year 1964-1965. Deeply involved in the production of the Jerusalem Bible, *he was responsible for the Books of Genesis, Samuel and Kings. He wrote the section on Palestine for the* New Cambridge Ancient History. *He planned a monumental three-volume work on the entire history of Israel, but had only completed the first volume, which came out the year he died.*

Ancient Israel *originally appeared in two volumes in French, called "The Institutions of the Old Testament." (1958/1960). It is a work of vast erudition, filled with a bewildering amount of minute detail about every aspect of Old Testament life. Dr. William F. Albright described it as "without a peer in its field."*

Père de Vaux organized his two volumes into four parts, each dealing with a different class of institutions. Part I has six chapters about family institutions, part II has 13 chapters about civil institutions, part III has five chapters about military institutions, and part IV has 18 chapters about religious institutions. As is obvious, there is no way in the world in which such a massive work could be usefully summarized. But what we have chosen to include here are the last two chapters of the entire work, dealing with the liturgical feasts of Israel. They provide fascinating background for the Gospels as well as for the Christian Liturgy, and also throw light on much in modern Judaism.

The reason for including this sample of Père de Vaux's work is not hard to find. Reference is often made to the great advances that have taken place in modern Biblical studies, to the "knowledge explosion" that has already and that will continue to throw new light on virtually every page of the Bible. The situation for the contemporary Christian is obviously unparalleled. Even with the best of intentions in the past, limits on available insight were quickly reached. But such is no longer the case. As the results of scholarly research mount, the responsibilities also mount, requiring all to make greater efforts to plumb the depths of God's Word. Few have shown the way more deftly than Père de Vaux.

ANCIENT ISRAEL

CHAPTER SEVENTEEN

THE ANCIENT FEASTS OF ISRAEL

I n ancient Israel, the great annual feasts were the three
feasts of pilgrimage (*hag*), *i.e.* the feasts of Unleavened
Bread, of Weeks and of Tents, and the feast of the
Passover, which was eventually combined with the feast of
Unleavened Bread.

1. The feasts of the Passover and of Unleavened Bread

In New Testament times, the Passover was the principal
feast in the Jewish year, and it has remained so ever since; but
it was not always the main feast, and several points in its long
history are still obscure. It is not our intention to discuss here
the form which the feast has taken in post-biblical Judaism (this
is the subject of the treatise in the Mishnah entitled *Pesahim*),
nor the feast which the Samaritans still keep to-day, in accordance
with their own ancient rites; we shall restrict ourselves to what
we learn from the Old Testament. The information it contains
is not very plentiful, and it is sometimes difficult to interpret.
First we have liturgical texts: the ritual for the Passover contained
in the story of the Exodus from Egypt (Ex 12); the religious
calendars in Ex 23:15; 34:18 and 25; Dt 16:1-8; Lv 23:5-8;
the rituals in Nb 28:16-25 and Ez 45:21-24; and the story in
Nb 9:1-14, which provides a justification for keeping the Passover in the second month. Secondly, certain historical texts
mention or describe the celebration of a particular Passover:
the first Passover, at the Exodus (Ex 12); the first Passover in
Canaan (Jos 5:10-12); the one celebrated by Josias (2 K 23:
21-23=2 Ch 35:1-18); that celebrated after the Return from
the Exile (Esd 6:19-22); to these we should add the Passover
under Ezechias, which is described at length in 2 Ch 30, though
it has no parallel in the Books of Kings. Lastly, we must take

into account three important non-biblical documents, a papyrus and two ostraka, from the Jewish colony at Elephantine.

(a) *The historical development.* The legislative texts (apart from the one in Ezechiel) all come from the Pentateuch, and they belong to different traditions. Hence they enable us to trace the historical development of the feast; this development is confirmed by the more laconic information in the historical books and in the documents from Elephantine. Since the latest texts are the most detailed and the clearest, the best approach is to start with them and then to trace the history of the feast further back, to see if we can decide anything about its origin.

1. *The Priestly tradition.* This tradition is contained in Lv 23:5-8; Nb 28:16-25, cf. Nb 9:1-14 and, in Ex 12, by vv. 1-20 and 40-51. In fact, these texts speak of two successive feasts, the feast of the Passover and the feast of the Unleavened Bread. The Passover was to be celebrated at the full moon in the first month of a year beginning in spring. According to this account, on the 10th day of the month, every family chose a one-year old lamb, a male and one without blemish; this lamb was killed at twilight on the 14th, and its blood was sprinkled over the lintel and the stiles of the door of the house. This was a *zebah* sacrifice, the meat of which had to be roasted and eaten on this same night of the full moon; not a bone of the victim was to be broken, and the remains of this religious meal were to be burnt. Unleavened bread and bitter herbs were eaten at the meal, and all who took part in the ceremony were in travelling dress. If the family was too small to eat a whole lamb, it joined with some neighbouring family. Slaves and *gerim* (resident aliens) could share in the meal, provided they were circumcised.

On the following day, the 15th, the feast of Unleavened Bread (*massoth*) began. All the old, leavened, bread was destroyed, and for seven days, from the 15th to the 21st, only unleavened bread was eaten; the first and the seventh day were days of rest from work, and a religious meeting was held.

This ritual is in harmony with the brief injunction in Ez 45:21, with the description of the Passover celebrated upon the Return (Esd 6:19-22), and with the information supplied by the 'Passover Papyrus' from Elephantine. This last document, dating from 419 B.C., lays great stress on the dates to be followed for the Passover and the feast of Unleavened Bread; and the reason for this insistence is that the prescription was new to this Jewish colony.

2. *Deuteronomy.* At first reading, the passage in Dt 16:1-8 seems to combine the Passover and the feast of Unleavened Bread even more closely than the Priestly texts do. The passage, however, is not a literary unity. Verses 1, 2, 4*b*-7 refer to the Passover: it was to be celebrated in the month of Abib, but the day was not fixed. (In the ancient calendar, where the year began in autumn, the month of Abib corresponded to what was, in the later calendar, the first month of the year, in the spring.) The text then says that the victim could be a head of cattle or a sheep or a goat; it was to be killed at sundown, not wherever a man lived, but 'in the place chosen by Yahweh for his name to dwell there', *i.e.* in Jerusalem. The victim was to be cooked, and eaten during the night, at this sanctuary; in the morning everyone was to return home.

Verses 3, 4*a*, and 8, however, refer to the feast of Unleavened Bread: for seven days, the Israelites were to eat (*massoth, i.e.* 'bread of misery'. On the seventh day, no work was to be done, but a religious meeting was to be held. The connection of the two feasts is clearly artificial, for if the people went home on the morning after the Passover, they did not stay until the final meeting on the seventh day to eat unleavened bread.

The Passover under Josias (2 K 23:21-23) was celebrated according to this Deuteronomic ritual, and this text makes no mention of any feast of Unleavened Bread. On the other hand, the novelty of this feast is strongly underlined: 'No Passover like this had ever been celebrated since the days of the Judges who ruled Israel, or during all the time of the kings of Israel and of Judah.' There is a much longer account of this Passover in 2 Ch 35:1-18 but it tells us nothing more about the customs followed in the time of Josias: the additional information is inspired by practices in vogue during the Chronicler's day: the feast of Unleavened Bread is mentioned (v. 17) and the contradiction between the rules for the Passover and for the feast of Unleavened Bread (cf. Dt 16:7-8) is suppressed. The Chronicler, too, insists that this feast was of quite a new kind: no Passover like that had ever been celebrated since the time of Samuel (2 Ch 35:18).

In order to discover precisely how this was a new kind of feast, we must compare it with more ancient customs.

3. *The ancient religious calendars.* Of the religious calendars listed on pp. 471-473, the two most ancient ones speak of the feast of Unleavened Bread (Ex 23:15; 34:18), but not of the Passover. *Massoth* were to be eaten for seven days in the month of Abib, and this was one of the three feasts of pilgrimage, *hag* (cf. Ex 23:14, 17; 34:23). These were the three feasts on which Solomon officiated in person at the Temple (according to 1 K 9:25), and they are mentioned by name (Unleavened Bread, Weeks, Tents) in the parallel passage in 2 Ch 8:13; cf. Dt 16:16.

The Passover is mentioned in Ex 34:25, but this is not part of a calendar for pilgrimage feasts; the parallel cited in this verse would suggest that we ought to see a reference to the Passover in Ex 23:18 as well; but the context of this verse, too, is not concerned with the three pilgrimages. However, since the word *hag* occurs in both verses, both must have been edited after Deuteronomy, when the Passover had become a pilgrimage (*hag*).

And this is precisely where the innovation of Deuteronomy and of Josias lay: they made the Passover a pilgrimage, for which men came to the one central sanctuary. It was a consequence of the centralization of worship. The Passover had previously been a family feast kept in each town and in each home (cf. Ex 12:21-23 and Dt 16:5); it was quite distinct from the pilgrimage of the *massoth*. The two feasts, however, fell at the same time and had (as we shall see) several features in common: hence they were eventually combined. But they were not combined in the time of Josias, and the first mention of them as one feast is to be found in Ez 45:21 and in the Priests' traditions.

Yet, according to another test of Chronicles, Josias' feast was not so very novel an idea. A similar Passover had been held under Ezechias; under him, however, the time needed for the purification of the priests and for gathering all the faithful from the former Northern kingdom led to the postponement of the feast, and it was celebrated, by way of exception, on the 14th of the second month. It was, says 2 Ch 30:26, a feast such as had not been seen in Israel since the time of Solomon. Attempts have recently been made to defend the historicity even of the details in this story, and the observance of the feast in the second month has been attributed to a discrepancy between the calendars followed in Ephraim and in Judah. It seems, however, that the reform of Ezechias is a product of the Chronicler's imagination: the Books of Kings make only a passing allusion to this reform, but the Chronicler has described it on the pattern of Josias' reform. He has even stated that it ended with a solemn Passover; his description of this feast, however, follows the rules laid down by the Priests' Code rather than those of Deuteronomy, for the feast of Unleavened Bread is unhesitatingly connected with the Passover. The idea of a Passover in the second month is also taken from the Priests' Code; it is inspired by Nb 9:1-14, which mentions the two excusing causes advanced by the Chronicler (lack of purity, and a long journey). This rule in Nb 9:1-14 is to be explained by the conditions in which the Jews found themselves after the Exile, and in particular by the relations between the community in Palestine and those who had stayed in Babylonia, or who were living in the Diaspora.

It must be granted, then, that the Passover celebrated under Josias according to the prescriptions of Deuteronomy was something new; but had it never been heard of before? Certain texts in the Bible would indicate rather that it was a return to an older custom which had long been neglected: 'since the time of the Judges' says 2 K 23:22; 'since the time of Samuel', says 2 Ch 35:18 (which comes to the same thing). But we must distinguish two questions, namely, the combination of the Passover with the feast of Unleavened Bread, and the obligation to celebrate the Passover (alone) at Jerusalem.

The test of Jos 5:10-12 has been used to prove that these two feasts were already combined in ancient times: when the Israelites pitched their first camp in the Promised Land, at Gilgal, they celebrated the Passover on the evening of the 14th of the month; on 'this same day', 'the day after the Passover', they ate produce of the land, *massoth* and parched corn, and then the manna ceased to fall. This story, it is claimed, represents a tradition of the sanctuary at Gilgal, and both the Passover and the *massoth* commemorated the end of the Exodus and the

123

entry into the Promised Land. To this, other writers object that since the feast of Unleavened Bread is placed on the day after the Passover, the narrative must depend on the Priestly tradition, and must therefore be a late account. This objection, however, is not valid, for the words 'the day after the Passover' are missing from the best witnesses of the Greek version, and they contradict the phrase next to them, 'this same day'; in all probability, they are a gloss. On the other hand, it is by no means certain that the text is referring to that feast of *massoth* which is described by the liturgical texts: the oldest liturgical texts say that the feast lasted seven days, and they do not mention parched corn. Rather, the general impression is that Jos 5:10-12 represents an independent tradition which reflects a custom of the sanctuary at Gilgal; but this does not prove that, from the moment the Israelites settled in Canaan, the Passover and a feast of Unleavened Bread like that described in the other texts were combined. The earliest religious calendars mention the feast of Unleavened Bread, but not the Passover; the two feasts had not been combined when Deuteronomy was first made known; and the story of Josias' reform mentions only the Passover.

The other question concerns the obligation of keeping the Passover at Jerusalem, and here Deuteronomy does introduce something new. Before the institution of the monarchy, the Passover may well have been a common feast celebrated at the central sanctuary of the tribal federation, as 2 K 23:22 and 2 Ch 35:18 assert; it certainly had been a tribal feast before the settlement. But the settlement led to a loosening of tribal bonds, and to a decentralization of cultic worship; and so the Passover became a family feast. This would explain why it is not mentioned in the calendars of Ex 23 and 34, and it would also explain why such stress is placed on the details by the old Yahwistic ritual in Ex 12:21-23. The feast of Unleavened Bread, on the other hand, would be one of the annual pilgrimages to the local sanctuaries. Deuteronomy, and Josias' Reform, made Jerusalem the centre for both feasts, and in the end they were combined.

Whatever one may think of the details of this history, the two feasts were certainly of different character and of different origin.

(b) *The origin of the Passover.* The Hebrew word for the Passover is *pesah.* It seems impossible to draw any conclusions from the meaning of the word, for its etymology is warmly debated. The Bible connects it with the root *psh,* meaning 'to limp' (2 S 4:4), 'to limp, to hobble, to jump' (1 K 18:21); in the last plague of Egypt, Yahweh 'jumped over, left out' the houses where the Passover was being observed (Ex 12:13, 23, 27); this is not the primary meaning, but an explanation added in later times. Others have compared it with the Akkadian word *pashahu,* meaning 'to appease'; but the Israelite Passover never had any expiatory purpose. According to a more modern theory, it is to be explained by the Egyptian: it is said to be a transcription of an Egyptian word meaning 'a stroke, a blow': the Passover would then be the 'blow' of the tenth plague (Ex 11:1), in which Yahweh 'struck' the first-born of Egypt (Ex 12:12, 13, 23, 27, 29). This too is not convincing: it is easy to allow that the Israelites gave an Egyptian name to a custom borrowed from Egypt, but it is hard to admit that they gave an Egyptian name to a custom which was strictly their own and which was actually instituted against the Egyptians. In addition, this explanation looks for the origin and the meaning of the Passover in the plague of the first-born of Egypt, and this is a secondary feature of the feast.

If we leave etymology aside, the Passover is seen to be a rite practised by shepherds. It is the kind of sacrifice which nomads or semi-nomads offer, and no other sacrifice in all Israelite ritual is more like the sacrifices of the ancient Arabs: there is no priest, no altar, and the use of the blood is most important. The Passover was the spring-time sacrifice of a young animal in order to secure fecundity and prosperity for the flock. The purpose of putting blood upon the stiles of the door (originally, on the tent-poles) was to drive away evil powers, the *mashhit* or Exterminator, who is mentioned in the Yahwistic tradition (Ex 12:23), and also perhaps, in a disfigured text, in the Priestly tradition (Ex 12:13). As we have suggested, it may have been a feast celebrated when the tribe struck camp before setting out for the spring pastures, but this is not the whole explanation: it was, in a more general way, an offering for the welfare of the flock, like the old Arab feast which fell in the month of Rajab, the first month of spring. The other details of the Passover stress still more that it was essentially a feast for nomads: the victim was roasted over a fire without any kitchen utensils; it was eaten with unleavened bread (which is still the normal bread of Bedouin to-day), and with bitter herbs (which does not mean vegetables grown in the garden, but the desert plants which Bedouin pick to season their food). The ritual prescribed that those eating it should have their belts already fastened, sandals on their feet (as if they were going to make a long journey on foot), and a shepherd's stick in one hand.

This pastoral feast was not an offering of the 'first-born' of the flock; this is nowhere stated, even in the most detailed texts about the choice of the victim or about the rites to be followed at the feast. Nevertheless, Ex 34:19-20 has put the law about the first-born in between the regulation for the feast of Unleavened Bread and its natural conclusion in 20*b* (as a comparison with Ex 23:15 shows): and Ex 13:1-2, 11-16 connects the law about the first-born with the law about the Passover and Unleavened Bread. It is an artificial connection, to establish which the tenth plague is used; during the night of the Passover, God struck the first-born of Egypt and spared the houses marked with the blood of the Passover victim; and, says Ex 13:15, that is why the first-born of animals are killed, and the first-born of men are redeemed. This connection, however, is not mentioned in the basic account: there is no reference to it in the Passover ritual, and the law about the first-born is given separately in the old Code of the Covenant (Ex 22:28-29).

The only texts which fix the date of the Passover are the Priestly texts and Ez 45:21: they fix it for the 14th-15th of the first month, *i.e.* at the full moon. This must have been the date of the Passover from the very beginning. Since it was kept in the night-time, and in the desert, it would be observed at the full moon, not necessarily because it was connected with the cult of the stars, but simply because it was the brightest night of the month. This common-sense explanation is itself sufficient to refute the suggestion that the Passover was at first celebrated on the night of the new moon. Since *hodesh* meant the 'new moon' before it came to mean 'a month', the following rendering of Dt 16:1 has recently been suggested: 'Take care to observe the new moon (*hodesh*) of Abib, and to celebrate then a Passover for Yahweh thy God'; the rest of the verse, in which *hodesh* occurs again (this time certainly with the meaning 'month') would be an addition by the Priests. There is, however, a more serious objection against the idea that from ancient times the Passover was kept at the full moon: an ostrakon found at Elephantine has on it a letter which, it is suggested, should read: 'Let me know when you celebrate the Passover.' If this is the correct interpretation of the text (and it is a most attractive rendering), and if this document is earlier than the Passover Papyrus mentioned above (which is probable), it still does not necessarily mean that the Passover was not previously kept at the full moon in the Jewish colonies of Egypt: the writer might be in doubt as to the month in which the feast was to be held, if the year could have had an intercalary month.

One fact, however, is certain: the Passover was a most ancient feast. It dated back to the time when the Israelites were still semi-nomads. It dated back even before the Exodus, if the feast which the Israelites wanted to celebrate in the desert (Ex 5:1) was itself a Passover. It was the Israelite version of the spring-time feast which all the Semitic nomads kept, but in Israel it acquired a particular meaning, which we shall explain in a moment.

(c) *The origin of the feast of Unleavened Bread.* The word *massoth* means 'unleavened, or unfermented, bread'. The feast of the *massoth* marked the beginning of the barley harvest, which was the first crop to be gathered. The seven weeks to the Harvest feast (or 'the feast of Weeks') were counted 'from the moment when the sickle begins to cut the grain' (Dt 16:9). For the first seven days of the barley harvest, only bread made with the new grain was eaten: it was eaten 'without leaven', *i.e,* without anything from the harvest of the previous year in it. It represented, therefore, a new beginning. Further, it was wrong to present oneself before Yahweh with empty hands (Ex 23:15 and 34:20, where this rule is separated from the rule about Unleavened Bread by the insertion of the law about the first-born). The characteristic feature of this feast lay, therefore, in a first offering of the first-fruits, and this trait was accentuated in the later ritual giving details for the offering of the first sheaf (Lv 23:9-14). But the real feast to celebrate the first-fruits of the harvest was the feast of Weeks, which marked the end of the cereal harvests; the feast of Unleavened Bread was merely a preparation for this second feast, and the two together marked the beginning and the end of harvest-time.

The feast of Unleavened Bread was, therefore, an agricultural feast, and was not observed until the Israelites had settled in Canaan (Lv 23:10 states this explicitly when referring to the first sheaf). It is quite possible, then, that the Israelites adopted this feast from the Canaanites. In this context, we may recall the execution of Saul's descendants at the high place near Gibeon (2 S 21:9-11): it took place 'at the beginning of the barley harvest', and the Gibeonites took their revenge in the form of a fertility rite (as a passage in the poems of Ras Shamra shows). The two rituals have nothing in common, however, except the date, and, in Israel, the feast of Unleavened Bread was always bound up with the week: the feast lasted seven days (Ex 23:15; 34:18), from one sabbath to the next (Ex 12:16, Dt 16:8; Lv 23:6-8). This is the justification for the insertion of the law about the sabbath after that about the *massoth* in Ex 34:21, and for the added detail 'even at harvest-time' (which began with the feast of Unleavened Bread). This connection with the sabbath shows that the seven days consecrated to the feast were not reckoned haphazardly, though seven-days feasts are found outside Israel; in Israel, this feast was essentially tied up with the system of the week, and this is confirmed by the fact that the Harvest feast was fixed for seven weeks after the feast of Unleavened Bread (Lv 23:15; Dt 16:9). The feast of Unleavened Bread may have been adopted by the Israelites from the Canaanites; but since the week and the sabbath are not found outside Israel, this feast must have taken on, apparently from the moment of its adoption, a strictly Israelite character. Since it was an agricultural feast, it depended on the condition of the crops, and could not be dated more precisely than in 'the month of the ears of corn', *i.e.* the month of Abib; this is the only regulation in the calendars of Ex 23 and 34 and in Deuteronomy.

We have seen that the Passover was kept during this same month, and at the full moon. Deuteronomy and the reform of Josias made the Passover a pilgrimage feast, as the feast of

Unleavened Bread already was, and the obvious move was to combine the two feasts. The old rubric about eating unleavened bread at the Passover (a rubric which has nothing to do with the feast of Unleavened Bread) favoured the combination, and so perhaps did local usages, like that followed in the sanctuary at Gilgal (Jos 5:10-12). The date of the Passover was already fixed for the full moon, and this was left unchanged; the feast of Unleavened Bread was attached to it, and ordered to be kept during the following seven days. This is the rule laid down in Lv 23:5-8. Now, if the date we suggested for the Law of Holiness is correct, this took place after Josias' reform, but before the Exile; this would then explain why Ezechiel knew of and accepted these dates (Ez 45:21). Unfortunately, the Passover was reckoned by the phases of the moon, and the Unleavened Bread by the days of the week; this led to an insoluble problem, for the Passover would not necessarily fall on the day before a sabbath, and the feast of Unleavened Bread had to begin on a sabbath. In practice, the connection of the feast of Unleavened Bread with the week was abandoned, and both feasts were fixed by the moon, with the feast of Unleavened Bread following immediately after Passover, whether it was a sabbath day or not. But in later times, the Pharisees and the Boethuseans (a group of the Sadducees) argued, without reaching any conclusion, as to how one should interpret the sabbath of the *massoth* and the 'day after the sabbath' in Lv 23:11, 15. This was the day on which the first sheaf was to be offered, and from which the seven weeks were to be counted before the feast of Weeks; the Boethuseans said it was the sabbath which fell during the week of the *massoth*, whereas the Pharisees claimed that it was the very day of the Passover.

(d) *Their connection with the history of salvation.* All the traditions of the Pentateuch connect the feast of Unleavened Bread (Ex 23:15; 34:18; Dt 16:3), or the Passover (Dt 16:1 and 6), or both the Passover and the feast of Unleavened Bread (Ex 12:23-27 and 39 [Yahwistic tradition]; Ex 12:12-13 and 17 [Priestly tradition]), with the Exodus from Egypt. The text which connects them most closely is Ex 12, in which the rites for both feasts are incorporated into the story of the Exodus; and the theme of this chapter is that the two rites were instituted to help in setting Israel free, and to commemorate this deliverance.

Some scholars, who see in cult the actualization of myths, look upon the first sixteen chapters of Exodus (Ex 1-15) as the 'legend' of the Passover feast, and claim that it is useless to try to find historical events behind them: these chapters, they hold, are nothing more than the cultic expression of a myth about Yahweh's struggle with his enemies. The culminating point of the story is that night which is relived on the Passover night, on which men keep vigil as Yahweh himself 'kept vigil' (Ex 12:42). In the morning (Ex 14:24) the Egyptians are defeated: this is Yahweh's triumph, celebrated in a victory hymn; and this hymn ends with the glorification of the Temple at Jerusalem, in which the feast is held, and in which Yahweh dwells for evermore (Ex 15:17).

No one will deny that there are cultic elements in the story of Ex 12, for the text itself stresses them; and everyone admits that the rites for the Passover and for the feast of Unleavened Bread have influenced the presentation of history. But this does not mean that Ex 12 (much less Ex 1-15) is merely a sacred commentary on certain rites. There are other elements in these chapters besides ritual ones, and the entire section forms part of a larger whole, which claims to be an historical work. Once more we must insist that Israel's religion was an historical religion, and that the faith of Israel was based on God's interventions in the history of his people. There was a feast called the Passover, probably even before Israel became a people; there was also a feast of Unleavened Bread, adopted perhaps from the Canaanites, but adopted in the fullest sense by the Israelites; and these two feasts were celebrated in the spring-time. One spring-time there had been a startling intervention of God: he had brought Israel out of Egypt, and this divine intervention marked the beginning of Israel's history as a people, as God's Chosen People: this period of liberation reached its consummation when they settled in the Promised Land. The feasts of the Passover and of Unleavened Bread commemorated this event, which dominated the history of salvation. Both feasts soon took on this meaning, but in the older traditions there are two separate feasts which commemorate the event independently; their common feature, however, made it almost inevitable that they should one day be combined.

2. *The feast of Weeks*

The second great feast of the year is called, in Ex 23:16, the Harvest feast (*qasir*), or, more strictly, the feast of the wheat harvest (as in Ex 34:22). It was one of the main periods in the agricultural calendar of Palestine (Gn 30:14; Jg 15:1; 1 S 6:13; 12:17) and in the calendar of Gezer. In Ex 34:22, the feast is also called the feast of Weeks; the phrase is perhaps a gloss to underline the fact that it was the same feast as that mentioned in Dt 16:9-10 (the *hag* of the *shabu 'oth, i.e.* the 'pilgrimage' of the 'weeks'). This last text gives an explanation of the name, and fixes the date precisely: the feast was celebrated seven weeks after the first cereals had been cut, *i.e.* seven weeks after the feast of the *massoth*. In Nb 28:26 it is called both the 'feast of Weeks' and the 'feast of the first-fruits' (*bikkurim*). This was the real feast for the first-fruits of the harvest, and it was a joyful feast (cf. Dt 16:11; Is. 9:2).

The most detailed account of its ritual is found in Lv 23:15-21: starting from the day after the sabbath on which the first sheaf was presented to Yahweh, seven complete weeks were reckoned, which brings us to the day after the seventh sabbath, making fifty days in all. (Hence the Greek name for the feast: Πεντηκοστή, the 'fiftieth' day or Pentecost; it is first mentioned in 2 M 12:31-32 and Tb 2:1, along with the name 'feast of Weeks'.) These 'fifty' days between the beginning of the barley harvest and the end of the wheat harvest are probably connected with the periods given in an old system of reckoning for the use of farmers. The ceremony was marked by the offering of two loaves made out of the new flour, baked with leaven, and this is the only instance in which the use of yeast is ritually prescribed for an offering to Yahweh. The unusual nature of the offering underlines the fact that it was a farmers' feast, and closely connected with the feast of the *massoth:* at the beginning of the harvest, unleavened bread was eaten as a sign that here was a new beginning; at the end of the wheat harvest, leavened bread was offered in sacrifice, because it was the ordinary bread of a farming population. It meant that the harvest-time was over; with this offering, ordinary customs were again observed. This connection with the feast of Unleavened Bread (and later with the Passover) explains why the Rabbis called this feast the closing 'asereth (assembly) and even 'the 'asereth of the Passover'.

The feast of Weeks was a feast for farmers living a settled life; Israel adopted it only after its entry into Palestine, and must have taken it from the Canaanites. (The custom of presenting to a god the first-fruits of the harvest is very widespread.) At first the date of the feast was not fixed (Ex 23:16; 34:22); the earliest text which states anything with precision is Dt 16: 9-10, but the dating is only relative, for it is reckoned from the feast of Unleavened Bread; and this latter feast was, at that period, dependent on the condition of the crops. Hence the date of Pentecost was not fixed until the Priests connected the feast of Unleavened Bread with the Passover. We have seen, however, that the interpretation of this ruling gave rise to disputes. In the calendar followed by the Book of Jubilees and by the Qumran sect, in which the same feasts fall every year on the same days of the week, the first sheaf, which had to be offered 'on the day after the sabbath', was presented on the Sunday following the octave of the Passover, i.e. on the 26th of the first month; the feast of Weeks fell, consequently, on the 15th of the third month.

Like the Passover, the feast of Weeks was eventually related to the history of salvation, but this connection was made at a far later date. Ex 19:1 says that the Israelites reached Sinai in the third month after they had left Egypt: and since they had left Egypt in the middle of the first month, the feast of Weeks became the feast commemorating the Covenant at Sinai. 2 Ch 15:10 mentions that under Asa, a religious feast was held in the third month to renew the Covenant, but it does not expressly state that this was the feast of weeks. The first time the connection is openly mentioned is in the Book of Jubilees, which puts all the covenants it can discover in the Old Testament (from Noah to Sinai) on the day of the feast of Weeks. The Qumran sect, too, which called itself the community of the New Covenant, celebrated the renewal of the Covenant on the feast of Weeks, and this was the most important feast in its calendar.

Among orthodox Jews, however, the feast of Weeks always remained of secondary importance. It is omitted from the calendar of Ez 45:18-25, and (apart from liturgical texts) it is mentioned only in late books of the Old Testament, and only in connection with something else (2 M 12:31-32 and Tb 2:1). The Mishnah gives a complete treatise to all the annual feasts except this one, and the idea that it commemorated the day on which the Law was given on Sinai was not accepted by the Rabbis until the second century of our era.

The Christian feast of Pentecost had, from the first, a different meaning. According to Ac 2, it was marked by the gift of the Holy Spirit and by the calling of all nations into the new Church. The fact that it coincides with a Jewish feast shows that the old system of worship has passed away, and that the promises which that system foreshadowed are now fulfilled. But there is no connection between the Christian feast of Pentecost and the feast of Weeks as understood by the Qumran community or, in later days, by orthodox Judaism. The story in Acts contains no allusion to the Sinaitic Covenant nor to the New Covenant of which Christ is the mediator.

3. The feast of Tents

(a) *The names of the feast: its importance.* The third great feast of the year is called, in the English versions of the Bible, the feast of Tabernacles or Booths. 'Tabernacles' is a transliteration of the word used by the Vulgate, and means little to a modern reader. 'Booths' is just as meaningless, and it is not quite so familiar. 'Tents', which is a literal translation of the Latin *tabernacula,* tells the reader more, but it may also lead him into error: the feast never involved the erection of 'tents'. We shall, however, keep this term, for want of a more suitable word. In Hebrew, the feast is called *sukkoth,* and the correct translation of this is 'Huts'; but 'the feast of Huts' is not a very pretty phrase, and is just as likely to give a wrong impression as the rendering 'Tents', though for different reasons.

The name *sukkoth* first appears in the later religious calendars (Dt 16:13, 16; Lv 23:34) and in those later texts which depend on them (Esd 3:4; Za 14:16, 18, etc.); but the feast itself is certainly the same one as that referred to, in the two oldest calendars (Ex 23:16 and 34:22), as the 'feast of Ingathering' ('*asiph*).

It was the most important and the most crowded of the three annual pilgrimages to the sanctuary. Lv 23:39 calls it 'the feast of Yahweh' (cf. Nb 29:12). In Ez 45:25 it is *the* feast, without further qualification, *i.e.* the feast *par excellence,* as it is in 1 K 8:2, 65. It can be recognized too, in 'the feast of Yahweh which was held each year at Shiloh' (Jg 21:19), and this, no doubt, was the occasion of Elqanah's annual visit to Shiloh (1 S 1:3). Zacharias foretold that all the nations would come each year to worship Yahweh in Jerusalem, at the feast of Tents (Za 14:16). Even in Josephus' time, it was 'the holiest and the greatest of Hebrew feasts' (*Ant.* VIII, iv. 1), and a pagan, Plutarch, uses an almost identical formula (*Quaest. conv.* IV, 6).

(b) *Its historical development.* The older texts leave us in no doubt about the character of the feast: it was a farmers' feast, the feast of Ingathering, when all the produce of the fields (Ex 23:16), and all the produce of the threshing-floor and of the presses (Dt 16:13), had been gathered in. When all the fruits of the earth had been gathered, and the olives and the grapes had been pressed, the farmers assembled to give thanks to God. It was a joyful feast, and Eli's suspicion that Anna was tipsy (1 S 1:14-15) shows that heavy drinking of the new wine was not unknown.

Naturally, it was an occasion for popular rejoicing. Jg 21: 19-21 tells how the Benjamites, when they had been decimated, carried off young girls from Shiloh while they were dancing in the vineyards at the feast of Yahweh. A similar tradition is preserved in the Mishnah (*Taanith* IV, 8): on the 15th day of Ab (July-August), and on the Day of Atonement, the young girls of Jerusalem went out in white clothes, newly washed, to dance in the vineyards and to sing: 'Young man, raise your eyes and see whom you are going to choose. Do not look for beauty, but for good family.' We need not consider the dance in the month of Ab. The other could not possibly have taken place, as the text says, on the Day of Atonement, for this was the great day of penance. If (as it seems) the story records an ancient tradition, then it must refer to the feast of Tents, which was held a few days later. Dancing still took place at this feast even in New Testament times: good-living men, the leading figures in the community, would dance in the Temple court-yards, singing and brandishing lighted torches. It was a gala occasion, and the saying went: 'The man who has never seen the joy of the night of this feast has never seen real joy in all his life.'

Among the ancient liturgical texts, the first details about the ritual are to be found in Dt 16:13-15, where the feast is called the feast of 'Huts' (*sukkoth*) without further explanation; it is described as a pilgrimage to the one central sanctuary, Jerusalem, and it lasted seven days. If we leave aside the mention of huts, this is exactly how the dedication of Solomon's Temple is described (it coincided with the feast of Tents): the faithful, we are told, came from all over the kingdom, kept a feast for seven days, and on the eighth day, at the command of the king, returned home (1 K 8:65-66): the whole passage comes from the Deuteronomic editors.

The ritual outlined in Lv 23:33-43 is far more precise, but it also raises questions of literary criticism. Verses 34-36 repeat the prescriptions of Deuteronomy, but they mention an eighth day after the seven days of feasting; on this eighth day, a day of rest from work, the people were to assemble for worship and sacrifice. Nb 29:12-34 lays down what sacrifices were to be offered during the seven days (the number of the main victims, bulls, grows steadily less), and Nb 29:35-38 lays down the sacrifices for the eighth day, which were far less numerous. This eighth day is everywhere mentioned apart from the seven days of the feast, and is obviously a conclusion or appendix. In the later ritual contained in the Mishnah, there is no mention of living in huts or keeping a feast at night; the only rule is that the people are to remain in Jerusalem; the eighth day then, the day after the feast, was a day of transition before the return to normal life. It is wrong, therefore, to emphasize the silence of Ez 45:25, for this verse is a very concise text which is dealing only with the sacrifices offered by the prince during the seven days of the feast of Tents (just as the previous two verses deal with the sacrifices to be offered during the seven days of the Passover and the feast of Unleavened Bread, Ez 45:23-24).

This is how 2 Ch 7:8-10 presents the celebration of the feast in Solomon's day, but it puts the feast of Tents after the feast for the dedication of the Temple; the writer imagined that there had been seven days' celebration for the dedication of the Temple, followed by a further seven days for the feast of Tents. This way of looking at the dedication has been introduced into 1 K 8:65 by a gloss in the Hebrew text which is not found in the Greek version.

The account of the celebration of the feast under Esdras (Ne 8:13-18), in connection with the reading of the Law, is obviously inspired by the text of Lv 23; but this chapter was by then in a second (though not the final) stage of its redaction. Ne 8:14 refers to Lv 23:42-43: for seven days, men are to live in huts, in memory of the huts in which Israel dwelt after the Exodus from Egypt. When the people heard this text read out, they went off to cut branches and to erect huts for their families, either on the roof-tops or in the Temple courts or in the squares of Jerusalem: the text adds 'The Israelites had never done anything like this since the days of Josue (Ne 8:17). It is hard to say what was so new about this action. It cannot have been the building of the huts themselves, for this must have been a feature of the feast in ancient times, since the feast had this name before Deuteronomy; it seems rather that, for the first time, these huts were erected at Jerusalem itself (which Dt 16:15 does not mention).

Nor is this contradicted by Os 12:10: 'I shall make thee live under tents once again, as on the day of Meeting (mo 'ed)'. Mo 'ed can also mean 'a solemn feast' (so the argument runs). Osee, however, lived before the centralization of worship, and therefore he could only be referring to a feast celebrated at a local sanctuary. Yet even this is not the true interpretation for the text speaks of 'tents', not of 'huts', and it is referring to the golden age of the desert period, when Yahweh 'met' Israel.

Lv 23:40-41 represents a third, and last stage in the redaction of the passage: men are to take 'good fruit' and branches and to rejoice for seven days. There is no mention of fruit in Ne 8:13-18, and the fruit had nothing to do with the erection of the huts; rather it was carried round in a joyous procession. This we know from later historical texts: in 2 M 10:6-8, the renovation of the Temple is said to have been celebrated 'like the feast of Tents', and for eight days the Jews carried around thyrsus, green branches and palms; Josephus, too, tells a story about Alexander Jannaeus, that high priest and king who was so hated by the Pharisees and the people: at the feast of Tents, he was pelted with the citrons which the people had in their hands (Ant. XIII, xiv, 5). The ritual in the Mishnah says that a citron (*'etrog*) was carried in one hand, and a *lulab* (a supple palm) in the other; branches of myrtle and of willow were tied to the *lulab*.

(c) *Its dates.* If we take the literal sense of the terms used, the feast was celebrated at the beginning of the autumnal year (according to Ex 23:16), or at the end of this year (according to Ex 34:22). There is no need to see in these two texts either a contradiction or an evolution in the way the feast was fixed. They simply mean that the exact date was not fixed at the time when these two texts were written: it depended on how the crops were ripening, for it was the 'Feast of the Ingathering', and was therefore held when all the crops had been gathered in, just before, or just after, the beginning of the year. The old agricultural calendar from Gezer begins with two months of harvesting. Nor is this contradicted by Dt 31:10-11, which commands that the law be read out on the feast of Tents 'at the end (*miqqes*) of seven years', in the sabbatical year; the text should not be translated 'at the end of the seventh year', but 'every seven years', and the reference to the feast of Tents is of secondary importance: it merely indicates the occasion when this reading is to take place. In Dt 16:13, the date of the feast is determined only by the progress of work in the fields: it is to be held when the produce of the threshing-floor and of the presses has been gathered in.

Incidental references in the Books of Kings give more precise indications, but these same texts also raise difficult problems. The dedication of Solomon's Temple (which coincided with the feast of Tents) took place in the month of Ethanim, according to the Canaanite calendar: a later insertion has explained that this was the seventh month of the Babylonian calendar introduced by Josias (1 K 8:2). But, according to 1 K 6:38, the Temple was completed in the Canaanite month of

Bul; and another later insertion explains that this was the eighth month of the later Babylonian calendar. If we grant that these identifications are correct (and there is no reason to doubt it), then we must admit either that the dedication took place a month before work on the building was finished, or that it did not take place until eleven months afterwards. If the second alternative is correct, then the delay could be explained by the fact that all the bronze furnishings were still being cast: the story of how they were made is, in fact, contained in 1 K 7:13-51, *i.e.* between the time when the Temple building was finished (1 K 6:38) and the day of its dedication (1 K 8:2). A third possibility is that the feast of the dedication and of Tents fell in the last week of Ethanim, and that the eighth day was the 1st of the month Bul: this reconciles the two data, but it is scarcely convincing. It is essential to remember that in those days the date of the feast depended entirely on the condition of the crops: in that particular year, the harvest was gathered in before the work on the Temple was completely finished. Hence, the feast of Tents, and the dedication, were held in the month of Ethanim, but it was not until the following month, Bul, that the Temple was finished 'in all its plan and all its arrangement' (1 K 6:38).

The question becomes more complicated, however, if we take into account the short note in 1 K 12:32-33 about the inauguration of the new sanctuary at Bethel by Jeroboam I: 'Jeroboam celebrated a feast in the eighth month, on the fifteenth day of the month, like the feast they kept in Judah, and he went up to the altar . . . on the fifteenth day of the month, the month which he had arbitrarily chosen.' Two interpretations of this text have been put forward. One says that the feast was originally held in the eighth month, even in Jerusalem itself, and the arguments in its favour are these. First, Jeroboam celebrated a feast 'like the one they kept in Judah'; secondly, he must have held his feast at the same time, since his object was to prevent his subjects from going up to the Temple at Jerusalem (cf. 1 K 12:38); thirdly, this would harmonize with the statement of 1 K 6:38 that the Temple was finished (and dedicated) in the eighth month. The accusation that Jeroboam chose this date arbitrarily would be a tendentious note of a redactor, inserted after the time when the feast in Jerusalem had been put forward from the eighth to the seventh month; and this note of his would be in harmony with the date given (the seventh month) in 1 K 8:2. The other interpretation says that Jeroboam did in fact alter the liturgical calendar, or, more precisely, that he reintroduced an old North-Israelite calendar, in which the feasts were determined by the agricultural conditions in Ephraim, where the harvest was later than in Judah. His purpose was, of course, to introduce a rival calendar to the one followed in Jerusalem. To this we must object that there is no difference in the time of harvest between Bethel and Jerusalem, that there is no noticeable difference between Ephraim and Judah, and that, if there was any difference, Ephraim would be rather in advance of Judah: at the present day, the cereals, olives and grapes around Nablus ripen earlier than those around Bethlehem and Hebron.

The following remarks, however, tell against both interpretations. First, the passage was edited at a comparatively late date, and certainly after Deuteronomy, for the month is denoted by an ordinal number; indeed, it is later than Lv 23, for the feast is fixed for the 15th of the month. Secondly, the date of the feast would not be more precisely fixed under Jeroboam than it was under Solomon. Thirdly, if the feast really was held in the eighth month, this merely means that in that particular year the feast was celebrated in the eighth month, both at Bethel and at Jerusalem. Lastly, we may note that there is no evidence to show that this date was afterwards observed for the feast of Tents in the Northern kingdom.

The date was not fixed before Lv 23:34 (cf. Nb 29:12), which says that the feast is to begin on the 15th of the seventh month of a year beginning in spring, that it is to last seven days, and that it is to end on the eighth day. Ez 45:25 gives the same date. Attempts have been made, however, to show that this calendar was not yet observed in the time of Esdras. Ne 8: 13-18 does not state on which days of the month the feast was held, and from this some authors argue that the reference in v. 14 alludes to a law not contained in the Pentateuch. Some have even tried to calculate the date on which Esdras' feast was held: on the 1st of the seventh month, he read the Law before the whole people until midday (Ne 8:2); on the 2nd, the heads of families met to study the Law under Esdras' guidance (Ne 8:13); there they found a law telling them to live in huts during the feast of the seventh month, and this ruling was at once put into force (Ne 8:14f.). Therefore, it is said, the feast was observed from the 3rd to the 10th. This reasoning, however, is incorrect. The text states quite clearly that the people dispersed after the 1st of the month, and that only a limited number attended the meeting on the 2nd; it also states that they had to call together all the people of Jerusalem and of the other towns in order to prepare for the feast (Ne 8:15). Consequently, the feast could not possibly have begun on the 3rd. Moreover, since the references in vv. 14 and 18 correspond with Lv 23:36 and 42, they undoubtedly refer to these laws; therefore the feast must have been celebrated from the 15th to the 22nd, as Lv 23:34 prescribes.

(d) *The origin of the feast.* Plutarch (*Quaest. conv.* IV, 6) saw a similarity between the Jewish feast of Tents and the cult of Bacchus at vintage-time. This unhappy suggestion has from time to time been taken up by a few modern writers. Another writer has seen a connection with the feast of Adonis-Osiris; the *sukkoth* would then be the equivalent of the arbour erected over the bier of Adonis. There is, however, only one reference to the practice of this rite, and it comes from Alexandria, at the Greek period: Theocritus (*Idyll.* XV) is the source, and he says that the arbour was erected over the (dead) god, not over his devotees: there is, therefore, no possible connection.

An idea which has met with a more favourable welcome is based on the notion that at certain times, and especially at the turn of the year, evil powers are active, and attack homes: to cheat them, and to escape these attacks, the people would pass these days in temporary shelters. This would explain both the feast and the rites followed. In particular, nomads who had just begun to live as farmers would look upon their new way of life as fraught with all kinds of dangers. Hence, it is said, the feast must date from the early years of the settlement in Canaan, and must have been influenced by these primitive notions.

The texts in the Bible itself offer no support whatever to this hypothesis; on the contrary they provide all the elements of a far simpler and far more convincing solution. The ancient feast of Tents was an agricultural feast, as its other name (Ingathering) implies, and as the details added in Ex 23:16 and 34:22 show. Even when it had come to be known as the feast of Tents, it did not lose its agricultural character: the vague date in Dt 16:13 and the precise date in Lv 23:34 are both witnesses to this, and these features can be seen even in the most recent ritual, that ordering fruit to be carried in procession at the feast (Lv 23:40). The feast, then, could not have been instituted until after the settlement in Canaan, and the presumption is that it was adopted from the Canaanites. This presumption is confirmed by Jg 9:27: after the vintage, the people of Shechem held a joyful feast in the temple of their god. The story in Jg 21:19-21, which is of ancient origin, shows the connection between the two feasts.

It is by no means so certain that we ought to connect it (as some authors do) with the story in Nb 25:1-18: in the Plains of Moab, the Israelites took part in a licentious feast of Baal-Peor, and one of them was put to death for having taken a Midianite woman into his *qubbah*. The word means (a tent or an alcove' and it has been suggested that it is very like *sukkoth*. But this 'tent' was not a 'hut'; the word *qubbah* is found nowhere else in the Bible; and there is no proof that the feast in question was celebrated in the autumn, nor that it had any connection with the feast of Tents.

We can be certain that the feast of Tents was an agricultural feast: the rite about the *sukkoth* ought to find its explanation, then, in some present custom. Now from time immemorial until the present day, it has been the custom in Palestine to erect huts made out of tree-branches in the vineyards and orchards while the grapes and fruit are being gathered in: and this is still the most satisfactory explanation. Originally, the feast (or at least a part of it) was celebrated outside (cf. Jg 21:19-21), and the feast of Ingathering could also be called the feast of the huts (*sukkoth*). Deuteronomy retained the name, and allowed huts to be erected in the orchards, but prescribed that, for the sacrifices, men should go to the central sanctuary, not to the local sanctuaries (Dt 16:13-15). The last step (a consequence of the centralization of worship) was that similar shelters were eventually erected in Jerusalem itself, and so the 'huts' became an essential part of the feast (Lv 23:42; Ne 8:16).

Like the Passover before it, and the feast of Weeks in later times, the feast of Tents became connected with an event in the history of salvation: the Israelites are to live in huts, says the Bible, in memory of the 'huts' (*sukkoth*) in which Yahweh made their fathers live after the Exodus from Egypt (Lv 23:43). But this cannot be the primary meaning, for the Israelites lived in tents, not huts, during their days in the desert. Huts represent a custom followed among settled populations, and the first time the word is found in the Bible is when Jacob is settling in Canaan after his return from Mesopotamia: 'He built a house and made huts (*sukkoth*) for his cattle; that is how the place came to be called Sukkoth' (Gn 33:17).

Nevertheless, one recent writer has attempted to justify the connection of the feast of Tents with the desert. He does not deny that it was an agricultural feast, or that it is connected with Canaanite customs; he claims, however, that when the Israelites were living as semi-nomads, they still had a feast of Tents: the regulations in Nb 2, about the arrangement of the camp around the Tent of Re-union, refer, he says, to this. Secondly, Dt 31:9-13 prescribes that the Law be read out at the feast of Tents: therefore the feast must have been a feast for the renewal of the Covenant, celebrated, at first, at Shechem. It was later modified to correspond with the conditions of a settled life, and, under the influence of Canaanite cults, its connections with nature became the predominant feature; this is how it was celebrated at Shiloh. Once the monarchy was established, and the Temple built, there was no sense in recalling the wanderings in the desert: as Is 33:20 (a late text, however) says, 'Sion, city of our feasts' is 'a tent which is never moved'. The feast would, therefore, have taken on a new meaning: it commemorated the choice of Jerusalem as Yahweh's home, and the Covenant of Yahweh with the house of David. This argument is not convincing. The ancient texts (down to, and including, Deuteronomy) stress only the agricultural aspect of the feast, and the explanation given in Lv 23:43 is clearly not the primary one. There is no proof whatever that, in Old Testament times, the feast commemorated the Covenant, and Dt 31:9-13 connects the reading of the Law primarily with the sabbatical year, and only secondarily with the feast of Tents in that year. And when, in later ages, the Covenant was commemorated on a feast, the feast chosen was not the feast of Tents, but the feast of Weeks.

4. Was there a New Year feast?

Among the Jews, the New Year feast, the Rosh ha-Shanah, is one of the great feasts of the year. It was already so in New Testament times and the Mishnah devotes a special treatise to it. The feast was kept on the first of Tishri (the Babylonian name of the seventh month in a calendar beginning in spring); a horn (*shophar*) was sounded, and hymns of praise were sung.

Under this name, and with these rites, the feast never existed in Old Testament times. There is no mention of it in the liturgical texts, or in the pre-exilic historical texts. Ezechiel dates his vision of the future Temple at the *rosh hashshanah*, on the 10th of the month (Ez 40:1), and this is the only biblical text which uses the expression. In later Hebrew, it came to mean the New Year, but it cannot possibly have this meaning in Ezechiel; indeed it is surprising to find so many writers accepting, without the flicker of an eyelid, that New Year's Day was kept on the '10th day' of a month. In this verse, *rosh hashshanah* means 'the beginning of the year', and, in fact, of a year which commenced in the spring. This is the only kind of dating Ezechiel ever uses, and he must therefore be referring to the month of Nisan, not to the month of Tishri, in which the Rosh ha-Shanah was later observed. This reckoning of the year from the spring-time is emphasized by Ex 12:2, which refers to a change of calendar: 'This month shall come at the head of the others; you shall make it the first month of the year.' In this text, which comes from the Priestly editors, there is no mention of a New Year feast either; it merely tells us that the victim for the Passover was to be chosen on the 10th of this month' (Ex 12:3). It would be pointless to make the question still more complicated by comparing with the text of Ezechiel that of Lv 25:9-10 (a late text) fixing the 10th day of the seventh month as the Day of Atonement (cf. Lv 23:27) and the end of the Jubilee period.

143

Neither Ezechiel nor the Priests' Code knew of any New Year feast; nor did Esdras. On the 1st day of the seventh month, Esdras read out the Law until mid-day, and those listening wept as they heard him read. Esdras, however, told them rather to rejoice, and they did so (Ne 7:72—8:12); surely he would have mentioned the New Year feast, if it had been held on that same day?

This leaves only two texts, both of which belong to the last edition of the Pentateuch, after Esdras. Leviticus (Lv 23: 24-25) prescribes that the 1st day of the seventh month shall be kept as a day of rest, with sacrifices, a cultic assembly and acclamation (t'ru'ah). This ruling is given in a more extended form in Nb 29:1-6, which calls the feast 'The Day of Acclamation', and lays down what sacrifices are to be offered to it. But it is by no means clear that this feast on the 1st of the seventh month, Tishri, is there regarded as a New Year feast; in the calendar of Lv 23, and in the commentary on it in Nb 28-29, the religious year always begins at the Passover. The feast held on the 1st of the seventh month was simply an unusually solemn new moon, the first day of a month which, at that time, was full of feasts (the Day of Atonement on the 10th, and the feast of Tents, from the 15th to the 22nd); perhaps too, this feast perpetuated the memory of the old civil and religious year which used to begin in the autumn, about the time of the feast of Ingathering.

Those apocryphal books of the Old Testament which date from before the Christian era never mention any New Year feast; Josephus does not include it in his list of Jewish feasts; Philo, too (De special. legibus 11, 188), mentions ten Jewish feasts, among which we find the 1st Tishri, but he merely repeats what is said in Lv 23:24-25 and Nb 29:1-6: it is a 'feast of trumpets' at the beginning of the month of the great feasts, which he calls the sacred month (ἱερομηνία), using a Greek liturgical term. The Jewish feast of Rosh ha-Shanah adopted the rite of acclamation prescribed in the Priests' calendar for the new moon of the seventh month, but it is impossible to say at what time or under what influence this New Year feast was instituted. It is unlikely that it was due, as some have said, to the influence of the Syro-Macedonian calendar in which the year began in autumn, for, in their internal affairs, the Jews always kept to the Babylonian system of reckoning, which they had adopted shortly before the Exile.

5. Was there a feast of the Enthronement of Yahweh?

For all this, a considerable number of scholars hold that the New Year feast had its equivalent in ancient times, in the feast of Ingatherings or of Tents. This feast was kept, as we have said, at the turn of the year; it would have provided the framework for a 'New Year feast of Yahweh' or 'a feast of Yahweh's enthronement' or 'a feast of Yahweh's kingship', according to the different ways in which the thesis is proposed. The principal arguments put forward are these:

(1) In Babylon, a New Year feast (Akitu) was celebrated during the first twelve days of the month of Nisan (the beginning of the spring year). The feast commemorated the renewal of creation and the kingship of Marduk. The epic of creation, of Marduk's struggle against chaos, was recited and reenacted, and the god himself was acclaimed with the words 'Marduk is King!' The same elements, it is claimed, are found in Egypt; we may presume that they existed in Canaan, and we may therefore conclude that a similar drama was enacted at Jerusalem on the feast of Tents at the beginning (or the end) of the (autumnal) year.

(2) Traces of the same cultic customs are then sought for in the Old Testament, especially in the psalms about the reign of Yahweh (which include at least Pss 47, 93 and 96-99). The defenders of this thesis call them 'The Psalms of the Enthronement of Yahweh' and these psalms would have formed part of the liturgy for the feast of Tents.

(3) The two accounts of the transfer of the Ark (2 S 6: 1-23 and 1 K 8:1-13) would also have been used in worship, during an annual procession at which Yahweh was installed in his sanctuary; this procession is said to have taken place during the feast of Tents (on the basis of 1 K 8:2).

Working from this information, an ancient feast is reconstructed. It would have included (according to a relatively moderate partisan of this thesis): (a) the celebration of Yahweh's original triumph over the forces of chaos, his enthronement in the assembly of the gods, and the demonstration of his power, not only in the creation of the world, but also in the guidance of history; (b) a dramatic representation of the eschatological 'Day' when Yahweh would assert his power against the rebellious gods, and against the nations of the earth, when he would establish his kingship not only over nature, but also in the moral order; (c) a corresponding representation of the Messiah's (the earthly king's) descent into the lower world and of Yahweh's deliverance of him from darkness and death; (d) a triumphal procession, in which the Ark, the symbol of Yahweh's presence, and the king, the true Messiah, were led to the Temple for the final act of enthronement, which marked the beginning of a new era. Other scholars are still bolder, and use the Mesopotamian liturgies of Tammuz and the poems of Ras Shamra to add to this already rich ritual the death and resurrection of the god, and the sacred marriage between the god and his consort (the role of the god being played, in this liturgical drama, by the deified king).

In spite of the authority of the scholars who put forward these theories, and in spite of the erudition with which they defend them, one cannot help expressing very serious doubts as to whether the theories are true:

(1) The ritual for the New Year feast at Babylon dates from the Neo-Babylonian period. In all likelihood, its origins go back further into history, and Assyrian and Hittite texts from the end of the second millennium B.C. prove that a New Year feast was kept in Assyria and in Asia Minor; this feast included at least a procession of the god, and the fixing of destinies for the year. These texts, however, contain nothing similar to the mythological drama which is drawn out of the Babylonian ritual. If this mythical and cultic scheme is to be extended to the entire Near East, including Israel, further arguments are needed.

(2) In the psalms about the reign of Yahweh, the formula *yhwh malak* does not mean 'Yahweh has become king': it is not a formula of enthronement, for it is impossible to see who, according to Israel's religious concepts, could have enthroned Yahweh, since he himself possesses all power. Secondly, even in the Babylonian texts, and in those Egyptian texts which can be

compared with them, the words 'Marduk is King' are not a formula of enthronement either: they are an acclamation, a recognition of Marduk's power: he acts as king. The biblical formula has the same meaning; it too is an acclamation, like the cry 'Long live the king!', which was used at the crowning of kings in Israel; it did not make the man king; it merely acknowledged the royal character of the new Anointed of Yahweh.

These psalms, then, are not 'Enthronement Psalms', but psalms about the kingship of Yahweh. The idea of Yahweh as King certainly existed from early times in Israel, but the Psalms of his Kingship are so closely connected with second Isaias that they must be dependent upon him, and must therefore be post-exilic. They cannot possibly have been composed, or used, for a feast held under the monarchy.

(3) The accounts in 2 S 6 and 1 K 8 are concerned with two different transfers of the Ark: in the first, it is taken to the tent erected by David, and in the second, to the Temple built by Solomon. This entry (or these entries) of Yahweh into his sanctuary are commemorated in Pss 24 and 132, which certainly belong to the Temple liturgy, but we do not know on what occasion they were sung. There are no positive arguments for connecting them with the feast of Tents or with any 'enthronement' of Yahweh.

In addition, there are further objections of a more general kind. This feast of the enthronement of Yahweh is said to have been connected with the feast of Tents; why, then, is there no trace of it either in the liturgical or in the historical texts of the Old Testament? The only plausible argument is the late text of Za 14:16: 'All the survivors of all nations which have marched against Jerusalem will come, year by year, to bow in adoration before the King, Yahweh Sabaoth, and to celebrate the feast of Tents' (cf. vv. 17-18). The connection between the two terms, however, is merely accidental: the entire passage is devoted to the eschatological triumph, to that 'Day' when Yahweh will be king over the whole earth (v. 9), and the feast of Tents is mentioned only because it was the main feast for pilgrimage to Jerusalem. We have seen too, that the feast of Tents was from the very beginning, and always, remained, an agricultural feast; it is rather paradoxical to say (as some do) that this was not its primary feature, and that it had at first an 'historical' character, *i.e.* the celebration of creation, and of Yahweh's victory over chaos.

Moreover, when the Israelites decided to give an historical meaning to the feasts of Tents, late on in their history, they connected it not with a creation-myth, but with their days in the desert. Here we encounter once again a general characteristic of the Israelite cult; whatever may be said of neighbouring religious, the cult practised in Israel was not the outward expression of myths, but the homage paid by man to a personal God, who had made a Covenant with the people he had saved, and who remained faithful to that Covenant.

CHAPTER EIGHTEEN

THE LATER FEASTS

During the last centuries of Old Testament times, several new feasts were introduced into the liturgical calendar. We shall restrict ourselves here to those which are still observed: the Day of Atonement, the Hanukkah and Purim.

1. The Day of Atonement

The Yom Kippur is still one of the most solemn feasts of the Jews. In the New Testament times, the *yom hakkippurim* or 'Day of Expiations' was already important enough to be called 'The Day', without further qualification, and this is its name in the treatise (*Yomah*) which the Mishnah devotes to it. It has always been observed on the 10th Tishri (September-October).

Before the Babylonian names were adopted for the months of the year, the Day of Atonement was fixed for the same date, i.e. for the 10th of the seventh month (Lv 23:27-32; Nb 29: 7-11, both late Priestly texts). Details of the ritual are given in Lv 16, which is also a late text.

(a) *The ritual of expiation.* No work whatever was to be done on this day; instead, penance and fasting were enjoined, and there was to be a meeting in the Temple at which special sacrifices were to be offered, to make expiation for the sanctuary, the priests and the people. The ritual outlined in Lv 16 is evidently made up of various strata, for the text has been re-edited several times: there are a number of doublets (vv. 6 and 11, vv. 9*b* and 15, vv. 4 and 32); vv. 2 and 3 do not follow logically, and on the other hand, v. 4 should not come between vv. 3 and 5, etc.; there are two conclusions (vv. 29*a* and 24); and vv. 29*b*-34 are an addition commenting on the preceding rites which reminds us of Lv 23:27-32.

This ritual is a combination of two ceremonies which were different both in their spirit and in their origin. First, there is a Levitical ritual: the high priest offered a bull as a sacrifice for his own sinfulness and for that of his 'house', *i.e.* of the Aaronite priesthood; then he entered—the only occasion during the year—behind the veil which shut off the Holy of Holies, to incense the mercy-seat (*kapporeth*) and to sprinkle it with the bull's blood (vv. 11-14). Next he offered a goat for the sin of the people; he took the blood of the goat, too, behind the veil, where he sprinkled it over the mercy-seat, as he had sprinkled the bull's blood (v. 15). This expiation of the sins of the priesthood and of the people is linked, artificially, it seems with an expiation for the sanctuary, and more particulary for the altar, which also had blood rubbed and sprinkled upon it (vv. 16-19). The two ceremonies of expiation are combined in the final addition (v. 33), but the order is inverted. This ritual contains those ideas about purity and the expiatory value of blood which are a characteristic of the rulings in Leviticus.

(b) *The goat 'for Azazel'.* Into this ritual, however, another one has been inserted, which is based on other ideas. The community put forward two goats, and lots were cast: one was for Yahweh, and the other 'for Azazel'. The goat for Yahweh was used for the sacrifice for the sins of the people, which has just been described. When this ceremony was over the other goat, still alive, was set 'before Yahweh': the high priest placed his hands on the goat's head and transferred to it all the faults, deliberate and indeliberate, of the Israelites. A man then took this goat off into the desert, and it carried with it the sins of the people (vv. 8-10, 20-22). The man who took the goat away became impure by doing so, and could not rejoin the community until he had washed himself and his clothes (v. 26). Rabbinical tradition says that the goat was taken to Beth Hadudu, or Beth

Hadudun, the modern Khirbeth Khareidan, which overlooks the Kedron valley some three and a half miles away from Jerusalem.

It is interesting to compare with this a Babylonian rite which took place on the 5th day of the New Year feast, *i.e.* the 5th Nisan: a cantor, singing incantations, purified the sanctuaries of Bel and of Nabu with water, oil and perfumes; then someone else beheaded a sheep and rubbed the corpse against the temple of Nabu, to take away the impurities of the temple; the two men then carried the head and the body of the sheep to the Euphrates and threw them into the river; finally, they went off into the country and were not allowed to return to the town until the end of the feast, on the 12th Nisan. No one can deny that there is a marked similarity with the ritual of the 'scape-goat': the animal was taken away, loaded with impurity, and those who perform the ceremony become impure by contact with it. But in Babylon, the animal was killed and was used to purify the sanctuary; the Day of Atonement certainly included this rite, but the 'scapegoat' figured only in order to carry away the sins of the people (a feature which is not mentioned in the Babylonian ritual).

In their researches into primitive civilisation of folklore, scholars have collected evidence of many more or less similar rites about the transferring of guilt, stain or sickness to animals. But there is a very close analogy in the Bible itself: in the ritual for leprosy, a living bird was released in the country to carry the evil away, and the leper was declared clean.

In the ritual for the Day of Atonement, however, there is something more than this. The name 'scape-goat' is the common translation in our English Bible, but the Septuagint and Vulgate call it the 'goat sent out' (*caper emissarius*). In the Hebrew the goat is destined 'for '*aza'zel*'. One scholar has recently suggested that this is a common noun, as the Greek and Latin versions take it, but that it means 'the precipice' and is the name of the place to which the goat was taken. Whatever be the philological value of this suggestion, it does not really fit the text: the high priest drew lots between the goats, one 'for Yahweh' and the other 'for '*aza'zel*'. The translation 'for the Precipice' does not seem sufficient for a true parallelism, which demands that the second name, like the first, should be the name of a person. It is more probable, therefore, that Azazel is the name of a supernatural being, a devil, and this is how it is interpreted by the Syriac version, the Targum and even the Book of Henoch, which makes Azazel the prince of the devils, banished to the desert. (We may recall that the Israelites looked on desert places as the dwellings of devils: Is 13:21; 34:11-14; cf. Tb 8:3 and Mt 12:43.)

And yet it is important to remember that the transferring of sins and the expiation which results from it are said to be effective only because the goat is presented before Yahweh (v. 10): Yahweh brought about the transfer, and the expiation. The goat was not sacrificed to Azazel or to Yahweh because, once it had been charged with the sins of the people, it was impure, and therefore could not be used as a victim for sacrifice. The Levitical ritual has therefore incorporated an old custom of unknown origin into its liturgy, but it has at the same time exorcised it.

(c) *When was the feast instituted?* This does not mean, however, that the Day of Atonement and its ritual are of very ancient origin. On the contrary, the opposite would seem to be true, for we have already had occasion to note that the combination of Levitical customs with popular superstitions is a characteristic of the very latest rituals of purification. There is no mention of the feast in any pre-exilic text, either historical or prophetical. Ezechiel foretold that on the 1st and the 7th of the first month a bull would be offered in sacrifice: the blood of the first bull would be used for the purification of the Temple and of the altar, whereas the second would be offered for the indeliberate sins of the people; and the two together would constitute 'the expiation for the Temple' (Ez 45:18-20). Though the intention is undoubtedly the same, this is not yet the Day of Atonement, for the latter was fixed for the 10th day of the seventh month, and the ceremony of the goat 'for Azazel' is not mentioned.

There is no mention of it in the books of Esdras and of Nehemias, though this raises a further problem which is made still more complicated by difficulties of literary criticism. Esd 3:1-6 contains no mention of the Day of Atonement, but only of the feast of Tents, which was observed by the first groups to return from exile. Ne 8 (which is based on Esdras' memorandum, and is the sequel to Esd 8:36) says that the Law was read out, and then studied, on the 1st and the 2nd of the seventh month; it then goes on to describe the feast of Tents, which must have been held from the 15th to the 22nd; it makes no mention of a Day of Atonement, on the 10th of this month. One suggestion is that in this particular year, the preparation for the celebration of the feast of Tents in a new way (Ne 8: 14-15) led to the omission of the Day of Atonement; this explanation seems hardly satisfactory. On the other hand, Ne 9:1 (immediately after the account of the feast of Tents) says that on 'the 24th day of this month' there was a fast and a penitential ceremony. It is therefore suggested that this day was the Day of Atonement, and that it was either postponed, in this particular year, to the 24th, or that at this time it was celebrated on the 24th and later put forward to the 10th. Neither of these solutions is convincing, for Ne 9:1-2 does not form a sequel to the document in Ne 8: modern commentators connect Ne 9:1-2 either with Esd 10:17 (the mission of Esdras) or with Ne 10:1f. (the mission of Nehemias). The reference in Ne 9:1-2 is therefore useless, and so is the date which it gives: 'the 24th day of *this* month': we do not know to which year or to which month it is referring, and perhaps this feast had no connection at all with the Day of Atonement.

The argument from silence is not, of course, decisive, but it does furnish a presumption that the feast had not yet been instituted in the time of Esdras and Nehemias. We may add, too, that the ritual in Lv 23:26-32 begins with the words 'And Yahweh spoke', which would indicate an addition; we may also note that their ritual makes no mention of the goat for Azazel, which is a distinctive feature of the celebration of the feast in Lv 16. The only possible conclusion is that the feast was instituted at a late date, though we cannot say precisely either when it was instituted or when the ritual of Lv 16 was first put into practice. The connection in Lv 16:1 with an episode in the desert (the death of Nadab and Abihu) is quite artificial (cf. Lv 10:1-6).

2. *The feast of the Hanukkah*

Most modern translations call this feast the feast of the Dedication. Its Greek name, Τὰ 'Εγκαίνια, means the 'inauguration' or 'the renewal', and this is a more literal rendering of the Hebrew *hanukkah*, the name which was given to the feast by the Rabbis and by which it is still known among the Jews. Josephus calls it the feast of Lights, after the rite which was its principal feature.

(a) *The origin and history of the feast.* The story of its institution is told in 1 M 4:36-59. Antiochus Epiphanes, after desecrating the Temple of Jerusalem and its altar, erected, over the altar of holocausts, a pagan altar, the Abomination of Desolation (1 M 1:54; Dn 9:27; 11:31), and there offered the first sacrifice to Zeus Olympios, on the 25th Kisleu (December), 167. Three years later, Judas Maccabee, after his first victories, purified the sanctuary, built a new altar and inaugurated it on the 25th Kisleu, 164, the third anniversary of its profanation (2 M 10:5). It was then decided that the feast should be observed each year (1 M 4:59).

It is questionable whether the feast could have been regularly observed during the following years, for the Syrians occupied the Citadel and there was fighting in Jerusalem. The situation would have changed once religious freedom was regained, and once Jonathan was appointed high priest, in 152 B.C. The opening verses of the second book of Maccabees (2 M 1:1-9) contain a letter written to the Jews of Egypt in 124: in this letter, they are recommended to keep the Hanukkah, and reference is made to a previous letter sent in 143. This document bears all the marks of authenticity. It is followed, however, by another letter, for which the same claims cannot be made (2 M 1:10—2:18): this second letter is said to have been despatched at the first feast of the Dedication, in 164, and it already contains some legendary features. Like the first, it ends with an invitation to keep the Hanukkah. In the body of the book itself, all the first part (2 M 2:19—10:8) is an historical justification of the feast (cf. the author's preface, 2 M 2:19, and conclusion, 2 M 10:8). The second part of the book is parallel to the first, and gives the events leading up to the feast of Nicanor, which was held on the 13th Adar in memory of the defeat and death of this Syrian general (2 M 15:36). The feast of Nicanor was not observed for long, and we shall omit all further mention of it.

The feast of the Hanukkah, however, continued to be observed. It is mentioned in the New Testament (Jn 10:22), under its Greek name (Τὰ 'Εγκαίνια) and in Josephus (*Ant.* XII, vii, 7), under the name of the feast of the Lights. The Mishnah merely alludes to it here and there, but this can be explained by the hostility of orthodox circles to the Hasmoneans; the Rabbis had no desire to bestow their approval on a feast instituted by them. All the same, it remained a popular feast, and later rabbinical treatises give some casuistic solutions and some bizarre explanations of problems connected with it. The feast was originally in memory of the renovation of the Temple, but it survived the destruction of the Temple because the ritual of lights, as we shall see, made it independent of the sanctuary and allowed it to take on a new meaning. Even to-day, it is still one of the great Jewish feasts.

(b) *The rites: the Hanukkah and the feast of Tents.* The celebration of the feast lasted eight days from the 25th Kisleu (December), and it was a most joyful feast (1 M 4:56-59). Apart from the sacrifices offered in the Temple, thyrsus, green branches and palms were carried around, and hymns were sung (2 M 10: 6-8; cf. 1 M 4:54). The title of Ps 30 says it was to be sung at the Dedication of the Temple, and it must have been used on this occasion. But the principal psalms sung were the Hallel (Pss 113-118), and the addition of v. 27 in Ps 118 probably refers to a rite of this feast: it can be translated as 'Bring your procession (*or,* your dance, *hag*), palms in hand, close to the horns of the altar'.

Apart from this procession with palms and the singing of the Hallel, the feast was characterized by the use of lights (Josephus, as we have said, calls it 'The feast of Lights'). The Mishnah and rabbinical writings tell us that lamps were lit in front of each house, and that the number increased by one a day until the last day of the feast. The oldest texts do not mention this rite explicitly: the lighting of lamps in 1 M 4:50 refers to the reintroduction of the chandelier into the Temple, not to the inauguration of the altar. Nevertheless, there are allusions to the rite in the first letter of 2 M 1:8, which quotes a previous letter in the words 'We have lit lamps'; the second letter (2 M 1:18f.) connects the commemoration of the sacred fire, miraculously preserved, and found by Nehemias, with the feast of the Hanukkah; and Ps 118:27 has, just before the verse about the palms, 'Yahweh is God, he is our light'.

The second book of Maccabees stresses the similarity between the Hanukkah and the feast of Tents. It was celebrated on the first occasion, 'in the way they kept the feast of Tents' (2 M 10:6), and the letter of 124 B.C. calls it 'the feast of Tents in the month of Kisleu' (2 M 1:9). The first book of Maccabees does not make this connection, but the second deliberately underlines its relation to one of the great traditional feasts, in order to secure it a favourable reception in the Egyptian Diaspora. It is, of course, possible that Judas Maccabee himself wanted it to be the feast of Tents, for this was the date on which Solomon's Temple (1 K 8:2, 65) and the altar which was erected after the Exile (Esd 3:4) had been dedicated.

In fact, the two feasts both lasted eight days (if we include the closing day of the feast of Tents, Lv 23:34-36), and palms were carried both at the Hanukkah and at the feast of Tents (according to the ritual then in force, Lv 23:40-41). But this is where the resemblances end. Psalms were certainly sung at the feast of Tents, but there is no evidence that it was the Hallel; it seems rather that the Hallel was first sung at the Hanukkah and later extended to the feasts of the Passover, of Pentecost and of Tents. During the Hanukkah, no-one lived in huts, and the lights put out in front of the houses are only remotely connected with the illumination of the Temple on the nights of the feast of Tents. Josephus (*Ant.* XII, vii, 7) says the lights of the Hanukkah symbolized that freedom had 'shone' upon the Jews in a way that could never have been hoped for; in later times, they became the symbol of the Law, which, in Pr 6:23 and Ps 119:105, is called a light. We still have to explain, however, why one more lamp was lit on each succeeding day of the feast, and this brings us to the question of pagan influences on the festal rites.

(c) *Was there any pagan influence in the origin or the rites of the Hanukkah?* The Hanukkah is the only Jewish feast whose institution is recorded in a late text, and which is also connected with an undeniable historical event. For some scholars, this seems too simple, and they have tried to show that the feast originated outside Israel. They say it is the Jewish adaptation of a feast of the winter solstice, and that the 'Hanukkah' should be connected with Henoch, who lived 365 years (Gn 5:23), *i.e.* the number of days in a solar year. Other writers, leaving Henoch aside, have maintained with less improbability that the feast corresponds to that of the *Sol invictus,* which was celebrated at Rome on the 25th December. Others again recall that during the persecution of Antiochus Epiphanes, the Jews were ordered to wear crowns of ivy and to take part in a procession in honour of Bacchus (2 M 6:7), and that an old man from Athens (2 M 6:1) was sent by the king to instruct them in the new rites: they add that the assimilation of the Nabatean god Dusares and Bacchus could have made these rites less foreign to the Jews. But they forget to prove (and it cannot be proved) that the Dionysiac rites took place on the 25th Kisleu at Jerusalem: we shall see that the text of 2 M 6:7 implies rather that they fell at a different time. Lastly, other writers maintain that an extra light was lit each day to symbolize the lengthening of days after the winter solstice.

The objections which can be raised against these theories seems to be decisive. We cannot admit that this Jewish feast was of pagan origin, because all the information we possess about it shows that it was instituted, and thereafter observed, only to commemorate the purification of the Temple after it had been defiled by pagan customs, and the restoration of lawful worship. Further, even if this most unlikely possibility were accepted, it is impossible for a feast of the winter solstice, which is tied to the solar calendar, to be a feast fixed on a definite day of a lunar year, however many corrections one may introduce: the 25th Kisleu would fall on the day of the solstice only on rare occasions.

Nevertheless, there may have been a connection between the Hanukkah and certain pagan usages, but it is an indirect and an adverse connection. Judas Maccabee inaugurated the new altar on the precise anniversary of the profanation of the old one, the 25th Kisleu. Now Antiochus Epiphanes had deliberately chosen this date for the first sacrifice to Zeus Olympios. It has been suggested that in the year 167, the winter solstice fell on the 25th Kisleu, but attempts to prove this by calculation have not yielded any certain results. The texts themselves, however, indicate the answer: according to 2 M 6:7, the Jews were obliged to take part in the monthly sacrifice, on the king's birthday; according to 1 M 1:58-59, attacks were made every month on recalcitrant Jews, and on the 25th of each month, a sacrifice was offered on the pagan altar. In this last verse, both the grammar and the context show that the reference is not merely to the sacrifice of 25th Kisleu, 167, but to a sacrifice which was repeated on the 25th of each month, *i.e.* to a monthly sacrifice offered for the king's birthday, as 2 M 6:7 says. There is evidence of the custom in the Hellenistic East, and it continued in vogue in these same regions until after the establishment of the Roman Empire.

The feasts of Dionysus, in which the Jews were ordered to wear ivy crowns, are distinguished from this monthly sacrifice in 2 M 6:7 and this is yet another reason for denying that the branches carried at the Hanukkah were connected with the cult of Bacchus. Nevertheless, brandishing these branches in honour of the true God may have been intended to do away with the memory of the pagan rite which faithful Jews had been forced to follow, and which Hellenizing Jews had freely adopted: the custom followed on the feast of Tents would provide a justification. The lighting of lamps in front of the houses could be intended to replace the incense which, under Antiochus Epiphanes, had been burnt at the house-doors and on the squares (1 M 1:55). Why one more lamp should have been lit each day we do not know: there is no evidence of it in the earliest documents; but neither is there evidence to show that it was connected with the rising of the sun from its solstice. The rite may indicate merely the increasing solemnity of the feast, or it may merely mark its passing from day to day. Popular customs and liturgical rules love these gradations: to take one example in the Jewish ritual, the sacrificial code in Nb 29:13-32 prescribes that from the first to the seventh day of the feast of Tents, the number of bulls sacrificed should be one less each day, until, on the seventh day, seven victims were offered. If these secondary contacts with pagan customs are well-founded, and if our interpretation of them is valid, then the fundamental character of the Hanukkah is thereby confirmed: it was a feast for the purification of all the defilement contracted under the domination of the wicked (cf. 1 M 4:36). Hence 2 M 2:16 and 10:5 call it simply the day of 'the purification of the Temple'.

3. The feast of Purim

(a) *Its date and its rites.* Josephus (*Ant.* XI, vi, 13), writing in the first century of our era, says that the feast of Purim was held on the 14th and 15th Adar, to commemorate the revenge of the Jews of Persia upon their enemies. The ritual is described in rabbinical writings. The feast was preceded by a day's fasting, on the 13th Adar: in the evening, lamps were lit in all the houses, and everyone went to the synagogue. The 14th and 15th were days of rejoicing. Everyone went to the synagogue again, to listen to the reading of the book of Esther; while the story was being read, the congregation would interrupt with curses against Aman and the wicked in general, and the meeting closed with a solemn blessing of Mardochai, of Esther and of the Israelites. Apart from this reading, the feast was an occasion for the distribution of presents and of alms, and pious persons made these gifts with a religious intention; but otherwise, it was an utterly profane feast, taken up with banquets and amusements, and considerable liberty was allowed. The Rabbis allowed that anyone could go on drinking until he could no longer tell the difference between 'Cursed be Aman!' and 'Blessed be Mardochai!' Later, the custom of putting on disguises was introduced, and the feast of Purim became the Jewish carnival.

(b) *Purim and the Book of Esther.* Obviously, the Book of Esther had to be read, for the feast owed both its name and institution to this story. The final note in the Greek translation of the book calls it 'this letter about the Purim' (Est 10:3). Est 3:7 (completed with the aid of the Greek) and 9:24 tell us that these days are called 'Purim' because Aman had cast lots (*pur*) on the 14th of Adar to exterminate the Jews, and this wicked plot of his had turned against him, and he had been hanged. The word *pur* is not Hebrew, and in both cases needed to be glossed by the Hebrew *goral* (lot). Because of the background against which the story is told, attempts have been made to find a Persian etymology, but it is now certain that the word is Akkadian (*puru* means 'lot' or 'destiny'); we shall return to this point later.

It is curious that this casting of lots does not have a more prominent place in the story, and that there is no reference to it in the fast which bears its name. Moreover, Est 3:7 breaks the narrative, and the second mention of 'lots' is the section (Est 9:20-32) which tells how Mardochai wrote to the Jews of the Diaspora telling them to keep the feast; the same passage alludes to a previous letter of Mardochai on the same subject, and ends by saying that Esther herself issued an order confirming what Mardochai had written. It would seem that Est 3:7 and 9: 20-32 were inserted into the story to spread the feast and to fix its name as Purim.

The body of the book, however, is already a 'legend of a feast'. Everything in the story—Esther's elevation and the intervention of her uncle Mardochai, the hatred of Aman for the Jews, his punishment and the revenge of the Jews, thanks to the esteem in which Esther and Mardochai were held by the king—converges on the feast which took place on the day after the massacre, and the final verses are an attempt to explain why the feast lasted two days (the 14th and 15th Adar), 'amid joy and banquets, amid festivities and the exchange of presents' (Est 9:16-19). It is quite possible that the story has an historical foundation in some unexpected deliverance of the Jews of Susa from the threat of extermination, but we know nothing of the circumstances, and this historical basis would then have been freely adapted until it became the 'legend' of a feast.

(c) *The origin of the feast.* The origin of this feast is utterly different from that of the Hanukkah. The Book of Esther undertakes to justify the feast of Purim, but it is not an historical book, and the feast which it seeks to justify is quite unlike any of the feasts we have so far examined: it was not a religious feast; it was not held (at least directly) in honour of the God of Israel (whose name is not even mentioned in the Hebrew book of Esther); it was not connected with the ancient history of the

Chosen People; and it contained no cultic elements at all. It was a foreign feast, but its origins are obscure.

Attempts have been made to show that it came from Babylonia, and that it should be explained in terms of mythology: Mardochai-Esther would be the divine couple Marduk-Ishtar; Aman-Vashti would be the two Elamite divinities Uman-Mashti (though the present reading of this name is: Parti); and the story would be a symbol of the victory of the god of light over the god of darkness. Vashti's reign lasted one hundred and eighty days (*i.e.* throughout the winter) and Esther came to power with the coming of spring; the feast would then be connected with the New Year feast, in which 'lots' were cast. But there is nothing comparable to the feast of Purim in Babylonia, and to bring in the Persian and Babylonian feast of the Σακαῖα which was (or became) a popular feast in which masters changed place with their servants, and the king with a subject, is merely to add to the confusion: we do not know enough about the history or the meaning of the Σακαῖα to throw further light on the story of Esther.

There is a far more interesting connection with a story related at length by Herodotus (*Hist.* III, 68-79). After the death of Cambyses, the magus Gaumata usurped the throne by passing himself off as Smerdis, the brother of Cambyses, whom the latter had secretly put to death. The Pseudo-Smerdis was unmasked by a certain Otanes, assisted by his daughter, who was one of the royal harem. Gaumata was put to death, and the people turned against all the Magi, and massacred them. The Persians celebrated this event in a great feast called the Massacre of the Magi. The story is very similar to the story of Esther, and cuneiform texts prove that it has an historical basis, for they mention that this Gaumata did actually usurp the throne. But the cuneiform texts do not mention the feast itself. Nevertheless, other texts from Persia show that it had some connection with the New Year.

If we now return to the feast of Purim, the pronounced local colour in the Book of Esther and its correspondence with what we know of the ancient town of Susa and of the customs at the court of Xerxes (Assuerus) give us ground for thinking that the feast is of Persian origin. Nevertheless, there are certain

Babylonian features: the name Mardochai=Marduk, and Esther=Ishtar, and the Akkadian word *puru*, which gave the name to the feast (unless Esther is derived from the ancient Persian *star-*, meaning 'star'). We suggest, therefore, that the origin of the feast is not to be sought in one civilisation alone; but this reconstruction is largely hypothetical.

We can say for certain that the feast originated in the communitieis of the Easter Diaspora, perhaps at Susa itself. It probably commemorates a pogrom from which the Jews escaped in a way which seemed to them miraculous; this may have taken place in the fourth century B.C. It is clear, on the other hand, that the feast preserves certain characteristics of a foreign New Year feast (the amusements, the banquets, the New Year gifts, the notion of a change which brings a renovation); it is possible, therefore, that the Jewish feast was modelled on a Persian New Year feast. From Persia, the feast would have spread first to Mesopotamia, and would there have taken on its Babylonian character; in particular, it would have acquired its name (*purim*) from the casting of lots (*puru*); this would fit in with the Babylonian idea that at the beginning of each year men's destinies were fixed, and it might also be an attempt to explain the Persian name for the first month of the year (Farvadin) by the Akkadian. The feast did not reach Palestine until long afterwards; Ben Sirach, writing about 190 B.C., does not mention Mardochai or Esther in his praise of Israel's ancestors (Si 44-50). The first mention of the feast is in 2 M 15:36, where it is called the 'Day of Mardochai', and is fixed for the 14th Adar. The Hebrew text of Esther calls it 'the days of the Purim' (in the addition contained in Est 9:28, 31), and under this name, distorted into φρουραί ('watches' or 'guards') it was introduced into Egypt, from Jerusalem, in 114 B.C. (Est 10:3, Greek).

It is next mentioned in Josephus (*Ant.* XI, vi, 13), and so makes its definitive entry into history. It was a popular feast, of suspect origin, and we must ask the reader's pardon for so ending our study of the religious institutions of ancient Israel.

Jean Daniélou
1905-1974

Daniélou was born near Paris and received his degree in letters from the Sorbonne in 1927. He entered the Jesuits in 1929 and after studies in Jersey, Poitiers, and Lyon, was ordained in 1938. He defended his doctoral dissertation on the spiritual teaching of Gregory of Nyssa at the Institut Catholique in 1943, and taught there for the following quarter-century. Pope John XXIII appointed him a peritus to Vatican II in 1962 and Pope Paul VI named him cardinal in 1969.

Jean Daniélou holds a strange position in the story of Church renewal in post-World War II France. In the early days he was one of the leaders, inspired by his mentors in Lyon, Henri de Lubac and Hans Urs von Balthasar. His prolific work in patristics especially cleared the way for a dynamic recovery of elements of early Christianity that caught the imagination and satisfied the yearnings of an entire generation in search of a deeper spirituality. An article he wrote in 1946 brought him under suspicion and attack from ultraconservative quarters and provoked at least part of the repression of the "new theology" that followed. But 15 years later, in Scandaleuse Vérité *(1961) he sounded a cry of alarm at the direction things were taking. Many who previously had most admired his pioneering spirit were alienated by what they saw as a reactionary reversal of posture in his latter years. In 1970 he animated a movement in France to gather 100,000 signatures for a letter of "fidelity and obedience" that was then sent to the Pope.*

However one evaluates the latter phase of his career, there is no denying the great contribution of Daniélou to the scholarship of the important period from World War II to Vatican II. His work threw new light on the patristic era, rediscovering much of "Judaeo-Christianity," exploring the early mystical tradition and the spiritual exegesis beloved by so many of the Fathers. Throughout this period he was actively engaged in ecumenical endeavors of note on all fronts, and co-founded a community for young people interested in missionary work— Le Cercle Saint-Jean Baptiste. As chaplain he directed them toward an understanding that would meet non-Christian cultures in a positive way. The most lasting work of Daniélou will probably be the series of writings which he produced in his effort to provide this beloved circle with a thorough Christian education and spirituality.

In 1972 Cardinal Daniélou was named to the prestigious French Academy, assuming the position previously held by Cardinal Tisserant. In 1974, the year of his death, his autobiography appeared in French, called And Who Is My Neighbor?

The selection included here is from his 1961 volume in a series on the history of early Christian doctrine; it is entitled Gospel Message and Hellenistic Culture *and was first translated into English in 1973. Its 20 chapters have much to say about those early thinkers who first formulated the meaning of the Gospel in Hellenistic terms: Justin Martyr, Irenaeus, Melito of Sardis, Clement of Alexandria, and Hippolytus. But more space and attention is devoted to the giant in this process, Origen, than to anyone else. Due to his enormous influence on subsequent ages, especially in the interpretation of the Bible, our selection is chapter 12, "Origen's Exegetical Method."*

If all agree on the fact of Origen's subsequent influence, there is less agreement today on evaluating the merits and defects of that influence. But, no matter what view one ultimately takes of his method, there is no escape from the conclusion that, as Daniélou says, "his work marks a turning-point," and the rest of the journey through the ages was deeply marked by the direction in which Origen turned the tradition.

GOSPEL MESSAGE AND
HELLENISTIC CULTURE

CHAPTER TWELVE

ORIGEN'S EXEGETICAL METHOD

O rigen's exegetical writings represent a stage of primary
importance in the history of Christian interpretation
of Scripture in general and of the Old Testament in
particular. A considerable legacy of expository work was already
at his disposal, all of which, thanks to his immense learning, was
familiar to him. This consisted in part of Jewish exegesis, which
was in itself sufficiently complex, but principally of the work of
his Christian predecessors. He was acquainted with the typology
common to the Church as a whole, of which Justin and Irenaeus
had been the greatest exponents, in its christological, sacramental, ecclesiological, and eschatological aspects. Furthermore,
he had inherited the Gnostic exegesis of Clement of Alexandria,
in particular his interpretations of the Tabernacle and the High
Priest's vestments. Finally, Origen's frequent allusions to un-
named teachers who had preceded him suggest many other
sources which it is no longer possible to identify. Indeed, as he
explicitly states, he did not hesitate to draw inspiration from
heterodox Gnostic exegesis.

At the same time, however, his work marks a turning-
point. First, Scripture becomes for him the essential source of
revelation, and Tradition no longer plays anything more than a
secondary role. Origen is supremely a 'man of the Book', and
this Book he studies in its entirety; where Christian tradition
clung to its *testimonia* and its favourite sections, Origen knows
every nook and cranny of the Bible, and links up different
passages with dazzling virtuosity. Secondly, he studies Scripture
from every angle. He did an immense amount to establish a
correct text, and to lay the foundations of scientific exegesis,
though the present chapter must be concerned not with these
apsects of his work, but with the supreme purpose which they

served, namely the elucidation of the meaning—first of all, the literal sense, and then those meanings disclosed by the Church's traditional typology, by the moral allegorism of Philo, and by the Gnostic θεωρία of Clement of Alexandria.

To a greater extent even than Hippolytus he applies to the whole of Scripture the instruments of interpretation which he has inherited. He is convinced that every detail of the scriptural text, in addition to its literal sense, has other significations; and therefore he searches to the utmost of his power for the truth of which this detail is the type or the allegory. What is more, with his mighty genius for synthesis, he combines these diverse symbolisms in many different ways according to the particular readers or hearers he has in mind. Thus, in his *Homilies* the moral allegorism which he inherited from Philo predominates, while the character of other works is determined by christological and ecclesiological typology, in conjunction with traditional material. His personal preference, however, was for the Gnostic exegesis which he derived both from Clement of Alexandria, from Jewish gnosis, and from Gnosticism in the narrower sense of the word.

Nevertheless, everything that he took over from others Origen stamped with his own personal genius. This can best be seen in two particular contexts. First, Origen is a great speculative genius—the first thinker, indeed, to attempt a complete systematic account of the Christian deposit. This is not the place to analyse or evaluate this synthesis. It is, however, unquestionable that it involved a certain number of features which had no place in revelation; and since it formed the core of Origen's own thought, his exegesis became a highly disputable attempt to find the evidence for it in Scripture by means of allegory. Secondly, Origen is a man of deep spirituality; and since in his view the transition from the letter of Scripture to its spirit corresponded to the transformation in the reader from the carnal to the spiritual man, history, theology, and spirituality are all interwoven in his work in a striking unity.

The concern of the present work is not to provide an inventory of Origen's exegetical writings, but to show its continuity with the past and the new contributions which it contained, by studying first the forms which the traditional typology takes in his work, and then the underlying principles of his exegesis in terms of the problems which he employed it to solve. As it happens, Origen has in fact left an account of his methods in Chapter IV of the *De principiis;* and the criteria which he there expounds were to inspire all his exegetical works. They relate, it is true, primarily to the most original features of his thinking on the subject; and in his later years, restrained either by the audience to which his *Homilies* were addressed or by the prudence which the attacks of his critics had taught him, he tended rather to emphasis less idiosyncratic elements. But there is no reason to think that his basic theories ever changed, and therefore this chapter will be taken as the primary guide to his methods, qualified where necessary by reference to the later works.

The Organisation of Typology

In his writings Origen makes use of all the themes found in typology before his time, as the following examples will show. Jesus is our Noah, the spiritual Noah who gives rest to mankind (*Hom. Gen.* II, 3); the sacrifice of Isaac prefigures that of Christ (*Hom. Gen.* VIII, 8-9); the marriage of Isaac and Rebecca, and the marriage of Jacob and Rachel, together with the wells which figure in the two stories, are types of the marriage of Christ and the Church in baptism (*Hom. Gen.* X, 5); the words, 'and Joseph shall lay his hand upon thine eyes' (*Gn.* 46:4) signify that the true Joseph is Christ, who opens the eyes of the blind by touching them with his hand (*Mt.* 20:34) (*Hom. Gen.* XV, 7); the death of Joseph coincided with the multiplication of Israel, as the death of Christ ushered in the increase of the Church (*Hom. Exod.* I, 4); and Our Lord Jesus Christ is the true Moses (*Hom. Num.* VII, 2). Origen also gives his own special elaboration to the Joshua typology (*Hom. Num.* VII, 5; *Comm. Joh.* IV, 22).

The types of the Church are equally numerous. Origen, who regards the *Song of Songs* as the epithalamium of Christ and the Church, finds this mystery prefigured on almost every page of the Bible. Not only are Rebecca and Rachel interpreted in this sense, but Pharaoh's daughter even is expounded as a type of the Church who, on coming to the waters of baptism, finds there the Law, still a child, and takes it into her own house to bring it up to maturity (*Hom. Exod.* II, 3-4). The same applies to the Ethiopian woman whom Moses marries, and of whom his sister Miriam, prefiguring the synagogue, is jealous (*Hom. Num.* VI, 4; *Hom. Cant.* I, 6—'I am black but comely, O daughters of Jerusalem'), and to Rahab, the prostitute (*Hom. Josh.* III, 3-5), and to the Queen of Sheba (*Hom. Cant.* I, 6).

The events of the Old Testament are, however, very especially types of the sacraments. Just as Noah was saved in the Flood, so are the believers by baptism (*Comm. Rom.* III, 1); the well in the patriarchal stories, as mentioned above, also prefigures baptism. The crossing of the Red Sea is our deliverance in baptism, by which we are rescued from the pursuit of the Egyptians, who represent the demons (*Hom. Exod.* V, 5). But for Origen an even more important type of baptism is Joshua's crossing of the Jordan (*Comm. Joh.* VI, 43-45), with which he associates the healing of Naaman in the waters of Jordan (*Comm. Joh.* VI, 4; *Hom. Luc.* 33), and also the translation of Elijah, after he had crossed over Jordan (*Comm. Joh.* VI, 46).

Supremely, however, it is the religious institutions of the Old Testament which furnish Origen with types of the New. Thus, in the rite of circumcision he sees first a type of the redeeming blood (*Comm. Rom.* II, 13), and then of the sacrament of baptism (*ibid.*), while the eighth day after birth, the day on which the Jewish male child had to be circumcised, prefigures the day of the Resurrection, the day after the sabbath. The paschal lamb foreshadows future blessings, and is a type of the crucified Christ (*Hom. Num.* XI, 1; *Comm. Joh.* X, 88). Moreover, the various Old Testament sacrifices are all types of the sacrifice of Christ (*Hom. Lev.* II, 6; IV, 8), and the Tabernacle prefigures Christ and the Church (*Comm. Joh.* X, 229-306; *Hom. Num.* V, 1-3; *Comm. Rom.* III, 8).

Origen thus stands clearly in the authentic tradition of Saint Paul and Saint John, of Justin and Irenaeus. Like Hippolytus too he is able, thanks to his marvellous knowledge of the Bible, to trace particular themes through the various stages of the history of salvation. Thus he links the prostitute Rahab, who is a type of the Gentile Christian church, with the unfaithful wife of the prophet Hosea, who takes up the τύπος and turns it into a λόγος, and then with Mary Magdalene who is at one and the same time the reality (ἀλήθεια) prefigured by Rahab, and herself a type of the Gentile church (*Hom. Josh.* V, 6; *Comm. Matt.* XII, 4). There is in fact a typological relationship between Christ and the Church; the body of Christ, already prefigured by the Temple, is itself a type (τύπος) of the Church (*Comm. Joh.* X, 228). Similarly, there is a mutual correspondence between Rebecca by the well, the Samaritan woman at Jacob's well (*Jn.* 4), and the catechumen at the baptismal font (*Hom. Gen.* X, 3).

Furthermore, the history and the institutions of the Church are themselves an image of the future kingdom; typology unfolds in the successive phases of the Old Testament, Christ, the Church, and the eschaton. Origen's achievement is to have systematised the material which in his predecessors was still incoherent, and worked it out fully for all four phases. Thus he expounds the fall of Jericho as a type both of the destruction of the city of Satan by the coming of Christ in the flesh and also of the eschatological victory of Christ at his second coming at the end of time. This interpretation accords with the three stages of the 'shadow' (σκιά), the 'image' (εἰκών), and the 'reality' (ἀλήθεια), each stage being fulfilled in the next, and the whole process continuing through Christ and the times of the Church to the final consummation of all things (cf. *Comm. Joh.* I, 7; I, 39: *Comm. Cant.* 3).

In a curious passage Origen, commenting on the phrase 'the type of him that was to come' (τύπος μέλλοντος), applied by Saint Paul to Adam, explains that Adam may be considered as a type of Christ either in his earthly incarnation or in his eschatological reign. He then connects this phrase with the passage in which Paul says that 'food and drink or a . . . festival or a new moon or a sabbath' are only 'a shadow (σκιά) of what is to come' (*Col.* 2:16-17), and shows that these also may be interpreted in the same two senses. Thus, 'food and drink' may refer either to the Eucharist or to the heavenly banquet, the 'festival' may be the Pasch or the worship of the redeemed in eternity, the 'new moons' may signify the Apostles, who are the twelve months of the year that is Christ, or the eternal ages, the 'sabbath' our deliverance from sin by Christ or our rest in the life to come (*Comm. Rom.* V, 1).

Origen is here developing typological exegesis in a manner parallel to that of Hippolytus. Both are representatives of the same process by which the typology inherited from the first generations of Christians is extended to cover the whole of Scripture. The beneficiaries of this elaborated Origenist typology were to include, in the east, Cyril of Alexandria and Gregory Nazianzen, and in the west, Hilary and Jerome. It should, however, be noted that in one important respect Origen differs from Justin, Irenaeus, and Hippolytus; the eschatological typology of the latter was millenarian in character, looking for a kingdom of God on earth, whereas in Origen the expectation is entirely of a kingdom in heaven. For Origen, the ἰστορικά are not types of other ἰστορικά, but of πνευματικά (*Comm. Joh.* X, 18).

Origen is also an innovator in the extent to which he brings the New Testament into the typological process. Such a development presupposes that Christianity has become the religion of a book, that the New Testament is treated in the same way as the Old—something that could not possibly have come about before the end of the second century. The Gnostics were ahead of Origen here; nevertheless he was able, with that acute feeling for typology which was characteristic of him, and with his keen eye for biblical and ecclesiological analogies, to counter their distortions and to restore the true meaning to the correspondences between the New Testament, the sacraments of the Church, and eschatology. For this reason his commentaries on the New Testament—on the Fourth Gospel, on *Matthew,* and on *Romans*—or his *Homilies on Luke,* are the most irreplaceable of all his works. It is enough to read Hilary or Ambrose to see how creative their influence has been.

It is abundantly clear, therefore, that Origen's exegesis, as a result of his amazing knowledge both of Scripture and of the Church, contains a hard core of authentic typology, immune from infection by Gnostic speculation, which makes him a major figure in the history of typological exposition. But perhaps his greatest contribution was this: that as a result of his extension of the typological line from the common Christian interpretation of the Old Testament as a type of the New, through the New as a type of the Church, and the Church as a type of the eschaton, discerning, that is to say, the same characteristic divine plan in all the different stages of the history of salvation, he was able to find in the Scriptures adumbrations of Christian spirituality, of the interior life of the individual Christian.

Origen is himself an authentic master of the spiritual life; he reads Scripture in the light of his own spiritual experience, and there recognises the laws of Christian spirituality. It is he who first shows the way for all the great writers of the *lectio divina* who were to come afterwards—Gregory of Nyssa and Gregory the Great, Bernard of Clairvaux and John of the Cross; and to this day his work in this field provides substantial food for the soul. It is the product of a fusion of two types of material; first, the moralising interpretation of Scripture derived from Philo, and secondly, the extension of typology to the sphere of the individual, showing that God acts toward each soul in just the same kind of way as he operates on the larger scale of Israel, Christ, the Church, and the eschaton.

Some examples of this kind of teaching may be helpful. It was mentioned earlier that Origen interprets the rite of circumcision as a type both of the shedding of Christ's blood and of the sacrament of baptism: ' "And circumcision and my covenant shall be in your flesh," said God to Abraham. . . . But, I ask, how shall the covenant of Christ be in my flesh? If I "mortify my members which are upon the earth," (*Col.* 3:5), I have the covenant of Christ in my flesh. If I "ever bear about in my body the death of Jesus Christ" (*II Co.* 4:10), then the covenant of Christ is in my body, for "if we suffer with him, we shall also reign with him" (*II Tm.* 2:12). If I "have been planted together with him in the likeness of his death" (*Rm.* 6:5), I show forth his covenant in my flesh' (*Hom. Gen.* III, 6-7). There is no allegorism here, but simply the continuity of the two covenants, lived out spiritually in Christian existence.

It is the same with the sabbath as our ceasing from sin (*Hom. Num.* XXII, 4), with the Tabernacle as the centre of the soul, where the Trinity dwells (*Hom. Num.* X, 2), with unleavened bread as the purification of the heart (*Hom. Num.* XXIII, 7)—

all themes which can, in fact, be traced back to the New Testament. The transition from the external to the interior Law is one aspect of the transition from the Old to the New Covenant, which is actualised just as truly in the Person of Christ, in the sacraments of the Church, and in eschatology. The interior life of the Christian is one of these actualisations.

Even more than the institutions of the Old Testament the movement of sacred history, God's guidance of events, prefigures his dealings with the soul. The theme of the people of God leaving Egypt for the Holy Land, and crossing the desert, is a favourite with Origen, and inspires some of his finest pages: 'It is better to die in the desert than to be a slave in Egypt. It is better to die on the journey, on the quest for the perfect life, than never to undertake that quest' (*Hom. Ex.* V, 4). The *Homilies on Numbers* describe the stages of this spiritual pilgrimage. To the carnal man who puts behind him the dainties of Egypt the spiritual life at first seems bitter; but before long the soul begins to receive the consolations symbolised by the springs and palm-trees of Elim: 'You will never reach the palm-groves, if you have not first passed through the bitterness of temptation' (*Hom. Num.* XXVII, 11). The tents of the children of Israel are symbols of the perpetual onward movement of the spiritual life: 'For when the soul goes forward . . . and, "forgetting those things which are behind, and stretching forward to those which are before" (*Ph.* 3:13) grows and advances from its lower level to higher things, then from the increase of virtues . . . it is rightly said to live in tents' (*Hom. Num.* XVII, 4).

The *Homilies on the Song of Songs* go to the very heart of this mystery of the spiritual life, namely the love of Christ for the soul, and the response of the soul to that love. Hippolytus had understood the *Song* of the marriage of Christ and the Church; Cyril of Jerusalem and Ambrose were to see in it the union of the catechumen with Christ in baptism. Origen, while not unaware of these different interpretations, prefers to apply it to the spiritual life, thus uncovering a vein of exegesis which was to bear richly in succeeding generations. The themes of the wounds endured for love, of the eyes like doves, and of the cleft of the rock—all of which make their first appearance in Origen—were to become part of the stock-in-trade of many spiritual writers after him, from Gregory of Nyssa to Bernard of Clairvaux and John of the Cross.

If Origen's spiritual exegesis of the Old Testament is admirable, that of the New is perhaps even more so. In the visible actions of Jesus in the Gospel his contemplation discerns the invisible action of the Lord within the soul: 'All those who truly listen to Jesus first follow him, then discover where he lives, and are given permission to see him. Once arrived they not only see him but remain with him, all of them, naturally, for the day on which they come, but some, it may be, for several days longer. . . . So it is with us, if we desire to visit Jesus in his home in order to receive there some special gift' (*Comm. Matt.* X, 1). And there are some whom Jesus will even take up into a high mountain apart (*Comm. Matt.* XII, 36).

Allegorical Exegesis

Origen's writings are thus of primary importance because of the typology which they contain; but they are important also because of the theory of exegesis which he propounds, and which is to be found in Book IV of the *De principiis*. Origen begins by giving a traditional account of Christianity as the fulfilment of prophecy, and argues that the coming of Christ was bound to mean the end of independence for Israel. The disappearance of the sacrificial cultus, the altar, and the priesthood, now that the Temple had been destroyed, was a visible sign of the fact that the divine plan working through Israel had come to an end with the Incarnation, and that a new οἰκοκομία had begun, marked by the election of the Gentiles (*De princ.* IV, 1, 3).

Origen then cites certain major prophetic texts—*Ps.* 71:7-8 (EVV 72), *Is.* 7:14, and *Mi.* 5:2—which he uses as the basis of a brief argument for the divine origin of Christianity, stressing especially the remarkable fact that the Church extends throughout the world, whereas in other matters each nation has its own laws. He also urges that the conversion of the world by the Apostles is inexplicable, unless they were indeed aided by the power of God (*De princ.* IV, 1, 5). The argumentation here is similar to that at the beginning of the *Contra Celsum,* where the presence of this divine δύναμις is held up as the most striking evidence for the truth of Christianity; the Church is manifestly the work of God and not of Man. Conversely, the divine character of the Law and the Prophets is made plain by their fulfilment; until then it was open to doubt.

To return to the *De principiis*, Origen next comments on the inspiration of Scripture. Anyone who reads with care will recognise, he says, in the course of his reading 'the mark of inspiration (ἴχνος ἐνθουσιασμοῦ)', and will be persuaded that these are not the writings of men but the words of God (IV, 1, 6). Origen is here concerned to introduce a point of cardinal importance for his system; it is not merely the content, but also the form of Scripture which is divinely inspired, and therefore it is right to look for spiritual meaning in every single word.

Origen continues: 'The light that existed within the law of Moses was concealed by a veil, but with the coming of Jesus has shone forth, now that the veil has been taken away (cf. *II Co.* 3:15-16)', and it is now possible for men to achieve knowledge of those good things, 'of which the letter (sc, of the Law) had only the shadow' (*De princ.* IV, 1, 6). From this follow two conclusions of prime importance. First, that Moses knew all things as they truly were, but hid them under a veil in his writings (cf. *De princ.* IV, 2, 2); Origen explicitly makes this point on several occasions (cf. e.g., *Hom. Num.* V, 1). Secondly, progress consists in unveiling something originally hidden, not in discovering something new.

Origen now comes to an essential feature of his system. It often happens, especially to a simple believer, that the meaning of a passage of Scripture cannot be grasped; but this is due to the feebleness of our intelligence, which is 'not capable of discovering the thoughts hidden in each word.' 'Inspiration extends through the whole body of Scripture . . . but "we have this treasure in earthen vessels" (*II Co.* 4:7)' (*De princ.* IV, 1, 7). In this passage Origen's basic principle, the spiritual meaning of every verse of Scripture, is clearly stated; and he compares the relationship between the meaning and the words to that between an event and its providential significance, where again it often happens that the divine meaning escapes us.

Origen then states his position *vis-à-vis* his various opponents. The Jews understand the messianic prophecies in a literal sense; and therefore, because they do not see prisoners set free (*Is.* 61:1), or the wolf pasturing with the lamb (*Is.* 11:6) they conclude that the Christ has not yet come. For Justin, Irenaeus, and Hippolytus the answer to this difficulty was that these things would indeed come literally true in the earthly messianic kingdom; but for Origen with his Alexandrian spiritualising approach the problem hardly exists. Secondly, Origen denounces the Marcionites and Gnostics who, when they read in the Scripture of God being angry or repenting, conclude that the God of Israel cannot be the true God, and therefore reject the Old Testament as the work of an inferior Demiurge. Finally, there is a third group, that of the uninstructed Christians who take such phrases in a literal sense, and thus form an unworthy picture of God (*De princ.* IV, 2, 1).

For Origen all of these three deviations derive from the same fundamental mistake; their advocates take their stand on the letter of Scripture, and not on its spiritual meaning (πνευματικά). It should be noted, however, that this word 'spiritual' covers a great many different things. Thus, the spiritual interpretation of an anthropomorphic biblical description of God requires that the plain sense of the words should be taken figuratively; but the interpretation of the messianic promises means that the things promised should be understood not as material but as spiritual blessings.

Origen then turns to another aspect of this spiritual interpretation. Everyone, he says, is agreed that the sacred Scriptures are intended to indicate certain hidden (μυστικαί) designs (οἰκονομίαι) of God, as, for example, in the stories of the incest of the daughters of Lot, the two wives of Abraham, and the two sisters married to Jacob. 'These things cannot be understood by us as anything but mysteries (μυστήρια)' (*De princ.* IV, 2, 2). The examples cited are, of course, traditional; the first is found in Irenaeus, the second in St Paul (*Ga.* 4:24-27), the third in Irenaeus again; it will also be remembered that the theme of the patriarchal marriages bulks very large in both Justin and Irenaeus. There is nothing here, therefore, which does not derive from the common typology of the Church; and the same is true of his next example, the structure of the

Tabernacle, which is a standard type in exegesis from *Hebrews* to Clement of Alexandria.

Origen extends the same principle to the New Testament. Here too an exact understanding (ἀκριβὴς νοῦς) cannot be arrived at except as a gift of grace. This is supremely true in the case of the *Apocalypse,* in which ineffable mysteries are concealed, but applies also to the Epistles. Origen's material thus becomes more and more heterogeneous, with the symbolism of the *Apocalypse* and the theological profundities of St Paul now added to the messianic prophecies and types of the Old Testament; but the reason for this diversity is not his own arbitrary decision or desire for comprehensiveness regardless of consistency. All these parts of Scripture had already presented Christians with major problems of exegesis before his time; he is simply attempting to work out a common approach to a traditional list of difficulties.

That this is so is confirmed by his own statement in which he seeks to organise his varied material in terms of his philosophical system:

> The senses of Holy Scripture must therefore be given a threefold classification in accordance with the nature of one's own life. The simple man (ἀπλούστερος) has to be edified starting from what may be called the flesh (σάρξ) of Scripture, for such we term its obvious (πρόχειρος) meaning; the man who has made some progress may start from, so to speak, the soul (ψυχή); and the perfect man . . . from the spiritual (πνευματικός) law, 'which has a shadow of the good things to come' (*Heb.* 10:1). For just as Man is composed of body and soul and spirit, so is the Scripture, which was designed by God to be given for the salvation of mankind (*De princ.* IV, 2, 4).

This passage clearly displays Origen's liking for parallel classifications. The division of the believers into the three groups of beginners, intermediate, and advanced, is of Stoic provenance and comes to Origen through Philo. The trichotomous analysis of human nature he inherited from the psychology of the Apologists. But the co-ordination of the two is a piece of systematisation of his own, and even more so the tripartite division of the senses of Scripture which results. As mentioned earlier, the problems which he faced were in fact two: the first was that of the figurative use of language by the biblical writers with its concomitant danger of misunderstanding; the second was that of the relation between type (the literal or carnal sense) and reality (the mystical or spiritual). Now, however, Origen advances this new idea of three interpretations corresponding to three different spiritual levels of insight in the readers, which has little relevance to the two major problems, and which is in fact a piece of pure theorising, an attempt to construct a hierarchical framework for heterogeneous materials borrowed from disparate kinds of exegesis. Fortunately for himself Origen did not adhere to this artificial division in his other writings; but unfortunately for others it was to enjoy a considerable vogue among exegetes in general.

A passage from the *Homily on Numbers* will help to clarify the precise content of the three senses. Origen is using the image of the nut:

> In the school of Christ the teaching of the Law and the Prophets is clearly like this. On the outside it is bitter; it prescribes circumcision of the flesh, and sacrifices. Then comes the second covering, which is moral instruction in continence; these things are necessary, but they must vanish one day. Finally, enclosed and hidden within all the coverings, will be found the meaning of the mysteries of the Wisdom and Knowledge of God (*Rm.* 11:33), which nourishes and restores the souls of the saints (*Hom. Num.* IX, 7).

The hierarchy of stages in the spiritual life described here is a perfectly reasonable one; but its projection into a corresponding hierarchy of meanings of Scripture is quite gratuitous.

Origen further states that the bodily or carnal sense of Scripture, in the meaning which he gives to those terms, does not last for ever, but that the two other senses never fail. This assertion, at first sight utterly astonishing, nevertheless makes sense from the point of view just described. The literal meaning is taken as corresponding to a stage in the spiritual life; it is therefore of use only where the letter of the text is edifying in itself. On the other hand, wherever this literal meaning is shocking or merely disputed, it is necessary to have recourse to moral allegorism or Gnostic θεωρία, both of which, therefore, will always be in requisition. For Origen the practice of exegesis is marked by the quality of ὠφέλεια, utility.

Origen seeks to justify this threefold structure of meaning by appealing to the exegetical method of the biblical writers themselves. There is no difficulty in finding instances of literal interpretation. In support of the second, the 'psychic' sense, he cites *I Co.* 9:9-10, where Paul interprets *Dt.* 25:4—'You shall not muzzle an ox when it is treading out the grain'—as proving the right of the apostles to a wage for their work. This example gives a very clear idea of what Origen understands by the moral sense of Scripture; it is in fact the kind of interpretation common to all moral allegorism, whether in Palestine or Alexandria, and is extremely rare in the New Testament, being found only in St Paul, in whom it is a relic of rabbinic education and not a dogmatic principle.

Origen, as might be expected, places much more weight on the 'spiritual' sense, and collects in support of its Scriptural passages which recur constantly in his writings. Thus, the Jewish cultus is said to be the 'image and shadow of heavenly things' (*Heb.* 8:5); the Law 'contains the shadow (σκιά) of the good things to come' (*Heb.* 10:1); Saint Paul says of the Israelites in the wilderness, 'These things happened to them as a type (τυπικῶς); but they were written down for our instruction, on whom the ends of the ages have come' (*I Co.* 10:11), and includes among his examples the typology of the rock from which the children of Israel drank—'and that rock was Christ' (*I Co.* 10:4). Similarly, *Heb.* 8:5 refers to the pattern (τύπος) of the Tabernacle, shown to Moses on the mountain. Then comes the 'allegory' of the two sons of Abraham in *Ga.* 4:21-31, while in *Col.* 2:16-17, the festivals, new moons, and sabbaths are 'shadows (σκιαί) of what is to come.' Finally, after dealing with the types to be found in the Pentateuch, Origen adds an example from *Rm.* 11:4 of the typological exegesis of a verse from *I Kings* (19:10).

It is noteworthy that all the passages which Origen has here collected refer to typological exegesis. The first two (*Heb.* 8:5; 10:1) have in the past been held to have a different, for example a Platonist, sense, but it is now clear that they are in fact typolocial, and indicate a historical relation between the Jerusalem temple and the temple of the eschatological kingdom. Similarly, the verb ἀλληγορεῖν has been borrowed by Paul from the terminology of contemporary rhetoric, and in fact denotes a typological relation. The only possible exception in the list is the quotation from *Ex.* 25:40 in *Hebrews,* which speaks of the pattern (τύπος) seen by Moses during his forty days in the mount of God; this may refer either to a heavenly archetype or to an eschatological prophecy. Origen's authorities, therefore, justify nothing except a typological exegesis.

It is not, however, typology for which he is concerned to provide a theoretical basis. His view may rather be summed up as follows. The actions of God among men are 'mysteries', and the Holy Spirit has granted understanding of these mysteries to the prophets. The latter, therefore, while giving their straightforward account of the outward seeming of events or handing on the rules of particular observances, were in fact expounding these mysteries symbolically, in order that they might not fall into the hands of those who were not capable of understanding them, but that those only who had been made worthy to do so might be able to perceive the meaning hidden by the letter. This spiritual meaning is thus essentially Gnostic in character.

What then are these mysteries contained with the letter of Scripture? They concern first the triune nature of God, Father, Son, and Holy Spirit, secondly, the mysteries of the Incarnation, and then those 'of men and other rational creatures (λογικά), among whom some are holy and some fell from their beatitude; of the causes of the fall of the latter; of the differences between souls, and the reasons for these differences; of the nature of the universe and its origin; of evil, and of the extent of its dominion upon earth—and of its existence in other worlds' (*De princ.* IV, 2, 7). This is indeed the heart of the matter. The mysteries which Origen has in mind are the secrets of the beginning and end of all things, and of the heavenly and infernal worlds, in short, a gnosis in the strict sense.

Origen goes on to confirm this in the most explicit manner. The primary intention of the Holy Spirit is to reveal this gnosis of the mysteries to the saints. In order, however, to conceal it from the rest of mankind, he hides the mysteries in stories (λέξεις) which record the history of the visible creation, of the making of Man, of his descendants, of the deeds of righteous men and also their faults, typical of human frailty, and even indeed of the crimes of the wicked. 'And most surprising of all, in the annals of wars and of the victors and vanquished certain hidden things (ἀπόρρητα) are made clear to those who are able to extort the meaning. And yet more wonderful, through a written lawgiving the laws of truth are foretold. . . . For the clothing of spiritual things, I mean the bodily sense (σωματικόν) of Scripture, was put upon them to make something which in many ways was of no little advantage, and able to improve the multitude of ordinary folk as they are able to receive it' (De princ. IV, 2, 8).

It is easy to see how the historical character of Pauline typology has here been replaced by a literary allegorism, operating on three levels. First, it is no longer the historical realities which matter, but the Book which uses these historical events as symbols. Secondly, the events and the institutions of the past are no longer types of other events and other institutions which are to come; instead the visible reality, the 'body', is a symbol of an invisible reality, which can just as easily be past as present or future. Historical typology has been displaced into a vertical symbolism characteristic of hellenised gnosis. Finally, there is no longer any progress in the knowledge of reality; it has always been known to the spiritual man, and hidden from the psychic. A hierarchy of degrees of perfection has been substituted for the succession of stages of revelation.

As a final proof that the Holy Spirit must always have had the allegorical sense primarily in view Origen reverts to an argument which he had used earlier in order to demonstrate the necessity of going beyond the literal meaning. This argument stresses the apparent impossibilities or contradictions which the text of Scripture exhibits, if taken literally, and asserts that they are deliberately included in order to arouse the reader to an awareness of the need to go beyond the literal sense. This new attempt to deal with the problems presented by the plain meaning of Scripture is more fully integrated than Origen's previous efforts into his general conception. Origen is very much alive to the difficulties which his predecessors, both Jewish and Christian, have encountered, and by his highly personal approach seeks both to resolve them, and by resolving to make them support, his own speculative ideas.

Origen stresses, however, that the fact that certain episodes are not to be taken literally, such as, for example, the story of the temptation in the garden of Eden, or that certain precepts are considered to be impossible to observe, does not mean that this is predominantly the case. Almost everywhere in Scripture the historical reality is the one meant (*De princ.* IV, 3, 4), and likewise there are many precepts which must be taken as they stand. This is in keeping with Origen's previous assertion, namely that cases where the literal meaning is impossible are merely pointers intended to warn the reader that there must be a hidden meaning.

One final comment which must be made relates to the very concept of a spiritual (πνευματικόν) meaning. In Saint Paul the phrase κατὰ πνεῦμα is contrasted with κατὰ σάρκα as that which is given life by the Holy Spirit as opposed to that which is left to its own lost and sinful state, whether this be the body or the soul. In Origen, however, the spirit is contrasted with the body (σῶμα) as belonging to the higher intelligible world as opposed to the lower visible world, the latter being the image of the former. This is a Platonist conception which came into exegesis with Philo and the Gnostics, and is the medium whereby gnosis became linked with Scripture, and in the end came to be regarded as its true meaning.

Such are the principles on which Origen based his exegesis, though in practice he often cut loose from them. It has become clear that his writings contain a genuine typology, worked out on the three levels of shadow, image (a complex concept this, with several different aspects), and reality. The theory of the three senses represents a distortion of this in terms of a pattern relevant only in a totally different context. His work thus

181

consists of a curious amalgam of disparate elements of very unequal value. Frequently he is led to adhere to a severely traditional treatment, and bears witness to the standard exegesis of the Church; but on the other hand he never retracts the principles laid down in his early treatises. If at times he prefers to leave the more systematic aspects of his thought in a prudent obscurity, they are nevertheless always present as the background of everything he wrote.

Heinrich Schlier
1900-

Heinrich Schlier was born in 1900 in Neuburg on the Danube. He was raised a Lutheran and studied at the universities of Leipzig, Marburg, and Jena, numbering Karl Barth, Rudolf Bultmann, and Martin Heidegger among his teachers. During the Hitler years he served as a pastor in the anti-Nazi "Confessing Church" movement of Pastor Martin Niemöller. After the war he was appointed to the New Testament chair in the Protestant Faculty of Bonn University.

Schlier announced his conversion to Catholicism in 1953 and thereby set off a theological debate in Germany. "He had contributed the commentary on Galatians to the Meyer Kommentar, *the most prestigious of the Protestant New Testament commentary series. He was acknowledged as an authority on Ephesians, the New Testament book that brings up acutely the problem of the Church. Yet it was precisely his study of that Epistle that had been influential in leading him to Catholicism! . . . Schlier's position . . . has shattered the image of a Catholicism that could not tolerate biblical criticism or hold its own in the exegetical field" (Raymond E. Brown).*

Intervening events have lessened the seemingly incongruity of Schlier's conversion, but at the time, when the ecumenical movement was in a far less advanced state, it seemed anomalous indeed that a leading Bultmannian Form-Critic should find that study of the Bible led him to Rome. But his subsequent studies have made it clear that the central focus of his entire theology is the elaboration of the Biblical relationship between world and Church, resulting from the Incarnation. As he puts it elsewhere: "The Wisdom of God, focused on the Son and the sons in Him, kept the Church in view when it pronounced the word in which the world was created. And so creation is ordered toward the Church, and the Church points back to creation."

The Relevance of the New Testament *consists of 14 essays on various topics. The selection that follows is chapter three, an essay which the author wrote in honor of his old teacher and colleague at Marburg, Rudolf Bultmann, on the occasion of his 80th birthday (1964). It is entitled "What is Meant by the Interpretation of Scripture," and serves as a fine example of the richness that can be brought to such a question by modern studies. The impact of the existentialist approach of Heidegger is obvious, but the resulting overview is a marvel of synthesis, giving one a keen appreciation for the complexity and importance of Biblical interpretation in the Church of our day.*

Schlier's style is sometimes overly dense, but the wealth of insight which he provides repays careful reading. To many a Catholic, only too recently rediscovering the Bible, he stands as a challenge and a model, reminding all of the work that needs to be done to recapture the kind of appreciation of the Bible that is at the root of the Christian tradition.

THE RELEVANCE OF THE
NEW TESTAMENT

CHAPTER III

WHAT IS MEANT BY THE INTERPRETATION OF SCRIPTURE?

In what follows we shall be trying not so much to describe the procedure of scriptural exegesis as to discuss its significance from one or two points of view. Since the meaning, as well as the method, of any interpretation depends on the text which is being expounded, we must first and foremost make clear the special character of our text, sacred scripture. The interpretation of the legal source of legal decision presupposes law as a reality that can be known. The exposition of a literary work opens out the pleasurable domain of the true in its beauty, and makes man "give praise that he is permitted to be". If a statesman interprets an historic document, by the act of exposition itself our history becomes part of past history, though obscurely, as if it were a future possibility. What happens, then, when holy scripture is interpreted? That will become clear when we have determined what holy scripture is.

I

Holy scripture, as itself indicates, is in the widest sense historical testimony to historical events in which God revealed himself in the actual world of history. In its text those events have found written expression in which God made himself and his will known to the world. They are the events, decisive for all history, involving the person of Jesus, in which the repeated promises of God to Israel were fulfilled. The apostle Paul says, at 2 Corinthians 1:20 f., "All the promises of God find their Yes in him" (the Jesus Christ who is preached). This Yes, a concrete historical occurrence in which all God's promises to his people were realized, is preserved in holy scripture.

Those promises of God, which remained promises even in the fact of the refusals of the disobedient nation, were accomplished in the course of actual history and, what is important, *as actual concrete history*. Israel's history, to which, as to all history, both deeds and words belong, conveyed God's promise to Israel. Just think of that course of events, so difficult to determine in terms of historical research, as it confronts us in the Old Testament from the times which, to express it in Greek concepts, had not yet any *logos* and were hidden in *muthos,* down to the days when Israel's history no longer found expression and fell silent. We read that a few nomadic Semitic tribes formed a settlement and, after taking over the land gradually in the midst of overwhelmingly powerful states, formed little oriental principalities with a holy city and a central sanctuary. Those principalities had scarcely arisen and united than they fell apart again. Those tribes and little states were led by charismatic heroes and kings and directed by priests, prophets, wise men and scribes who accompanied them throughout a long, sorrowful history, through deserts and exile, collapse and deliverance. And all that was not merely an historical setting; the actual events, great or small, together with the word that always accompanied them, constituted a divine intervention and relevation. The Old Testament was convinced that Israel's history and, in conjunction with it, all history, takes place in such a way that its course expresses God's will. And this expression is not simply something that supervenes on the event; it occurs in the very event itself. The Old Testament understands the occurrences concerning and in Israel and the world as an "event", if, as M. Heidegger has it, it is proper to an event that in it "saying" is found and "the saying" which is contained in the event, as manifestation, is the most authentic mode of the event. For the Old Testament, history in its occurrence is God's summons, declaration and promise. That is why, though the connection was not always consciously realized, events are called *debarim,* "words". And that is why the great masters of words who to a considerable extent determined Israel's history, the prophets, who fixed, even in advance, the word of Yahweh comprised in his historic deeds and gave it expression, did not really add word to event. That is the basis on which the special relation between Yahweh's action and the word is to be understood. The event in which Yahweh's deliverance or judgment takes place is only the utterance, and in that sense the fulfilment, of his word. When Yahweh causes something to happen he utters his word, and he fulfils it when he pronounces it in the event. If he utters it in the event, it occurs. "Declaring the end from the beginning and from ancient times things not yet done, saying: 'My counsel shall stand, and I will accomplish all my purpose', calling a bird of prey from the east, the man of my counsel from a far country. I have spoken, and I will bring it to pass; I have purposed, and I will do it" (Is. 46: 10f. cf. also Ezek 12:21-8). As long as the word is not fulfilled, it stands threatening or promising before expectant history. If then Israel experiences Yahweh's action as a carrying out of his word—"I watch over my *dabar* (my word) to perform it" (Jer. 1:12)—this action comes as an utterance which aims at an answer from Israel. " 'I gave you cleanness of teeth in all your cities, and lack of bread in all your places, yet you did not return to me . . . I smote you with blight and mildew; I laid waste your gardens and your vineyards; your fig-trees and your olive trees the locust devoured; yet you did not return to me',—says the Lord" (Amos 4:6ff.).

Since the Old Testament regards historical events as a word spoken by Yahweh, it is implied that this word manifests Yahweh's summons to the people of Israel. As Yahweh's events, the historical happenings concern Israel from the first and do so by the very fact that they are addressed to Israel. There is no "neutral" history which, as in our detached contemplation based on research, could be understood as an element in an historical picture. There is only one history, which makes a claim on Israel. History does not lose this character of being a claim even in the course of time and with increasing remoteness. Even when it has occurred, history remains a perpetual summons from Yahweh. "If you say in your heart, 'These nations are greater than I; how can I dispossess them?', you shall not be afraid of them, but you shall remember what the Lord your God did to Pharaoh and to all Egypt . . . You shall not be in dread of them, for the Lord your God is in the midst of you" (Deut 7:17 f., 21). And in the sabbath commandment, the admonition to grant rest even to the slave is given as basis, "You shall remember that you were a servant in the land of Egypt, and the Lord your God brought you out thence with a mighty hand and an outstretched arm;

therefore the Lord your God commanded you to keep the sabbath day" (Deut 5:15). The act of deliverance remains a call here and now. "And you shall remember all the way which the Lord your God has led you . . . to know what was in your heart . . ." (Deut 8:2; cf. Josh 24:1-18). In history which in its unfolding is simultaneously Yahweh's pronouncement, claim and promise, there is no indifferent happening, there are only significant events.

If what happens is a significant event and, as such, a word spoken, it follows that it occurs with the whole ambiguity or multiplicity of meaning that words have. For words both reveal and conceal. History as speech is always history as a question requiring an answer. The deliverance from Egypt can be understood as follows: "Thou hast led in thy steadfast love the people whom thou hast redeemed, thou hast guided them by thy strength to thy holy abode" (Ex 15:13). But it can also be understood as follows: "Would that we had died by the hand of the Lord in the land of Egypt, when we sat by the fleshpots and ate bread to the full" (Ex 16:3). History as a summons keeps the truth which it expresses so open, that it can be heard or misheard, seen or overlooked. The truth of Israel's history is the fidelity of Yahweh, prevailing as hidden yet manifest, in events, in his commandment and in his promise, and known as such in the "quiet" and the "upward gaze" of faith.

If in the Old Testament view God reveals himself in an event which is an intelligible utterance, it follows that this utterance in and by the events opens out a horizon of experience in which it finds a meaningful context. We are thinking here of the domain in which it finds expression, perhaps even before it is spoken about. The world is latent in language. Into this world the event is uttered, and in such a way that there is a response within a domain which it creates for itself. Thus God's revelation took place in such a way that its occurrence "chose" Israel and created its own effective domain in Israel. It can also be said that as an event God's revelation opens out its own historical horizon within which it is historically preserved with the claim it makes, manifested again and again against repeated obscuration through contradiction.

The same structure of an historical event shown in God's revelation of promise in the Old Testament is also displayed in its fulfilment, which is attested in the New Testament. Of course there is a difference deriving from the realities themselves. The revelation-events of the New Testament do not all lie on the same plane. In fact they are only fulfilled and disclosed (and with them the promises of the Old Testament) in the light of a single event as revelation-utterance. This event is the resurrection of Jesus Christ from the dead in its manifestation to the witnesses. In it God's Yes is manifest, and this is no longer only God's promise but also his coming. In the light of this event, this advent of God in the risen Jesus Christ, the person and previous history of Jesus Christ, which culminated on the Cross, are manifested as being in their actual occurrence the word of salvation fulfilling all God's promises. That is noted several times in the gospels, in references of various kinds.

This history of Jesus of Nazareth which in the perspective of the appearance of the risen Christ is significant as God's advent—it is often called "eschatological history"—is, like Old Testament history, a concrete history. Seen from outside it is the out-of-way and rather striking, yet at the same time commonplace affair of a Jew who was more or less like a rabbi but also rather like a prophet and something more than a prophet, and who caused a stir in a corner of the world in Galilee and Judaea and little Jerusalem, among an exhausted nation and a Roman garrison, and who did so by his strangely Jewish yet unJewish talk and charismatic deeds. Like many other prophets and teachers, he gathered disciples and pupils around him, became an object of suspicion to the secular and spiritual authorities, gave offence even to many pious people because he proclaimed God's reign here and now and also for a time soon to come, strictly and frankly, harshly yet humanely. Eventually he encountered bitter resistance, was brought to trial for alleged sedition and probably also for blasphemy, and with the help of the occupying power, was put to death on the Cross as a criminal. The story was soon forgotten in the official world and among historians, though various rumours were still in circulation about him, for example about some slave or other, Chrestus, who had caused disturbances among the Jews of Rome. From the inside, in the eyes of those who had been with him and who in the context and the light of those events in Galilee and Jerusalem after his death which indicated that he was God's future advent understood things which had been quite unintelligible to them, the story looked rather different, very plain in fact, and almost simple, if only it had not always also given the impression of being an extreme case. Seen from the inside, it was the occurrence of a man's total obedience to God's will, complete fulfilment of God's will in mighty words and deeds, as against the disastrous and devastating devilry of men with their own man-made god and his inhuman law and satanic spirit destructive of body and mind. And seen from the inside, this story of Jesus of Nazareth, as the actual realization of unshakable obedience to God, was a total dedication to men, a total self-giving for those who were bowed in body and soul under the burden of self-seeking and fear, vanity and loneliness of sin. Seen from within, the inflexible obedience of Jesus to God's will that he should be inflexibly present for men, culminated in the Passion and ended on the Cross. The Cross, therefore, was at once understood and proclaimed, thanks also to the appearance of the risen Christ, as the decisive event in which this profoundly significant history was fulfilled and revealed. Here God definitively expressed his promise.

Jesus and his history, therefore, a history of real obedience and real love, of extreme obedience and extreme love, are the language of action in which God's last pronouncement is made. That is already implied in statements like Mark 8:38: "For whoever is ashamed of me and of my words in this adulterous and sinful generation, of him will the Son of man also be ashamed when he comes in the glory of his Father with the holy angels" (cf. Mt 11:6 and Lik 12:8f.). The same fact is similarly referred to in the description of Jesus Christ as the Amen contained in God's promises and now uttered (2 Cor 1:19f.). In Acts 10:36f. we hear that God sent "the word" to the children of Israel. What word? The "event that had happened" ($\dot{\rho}\dot{\eta}\mu a$) throughout all Judaea. The Letter to the Hebrews makes even plainer the nature of the event that occurred in the person of Jesus Christ, in which God expresses himself, and at the same time links it with God's speaking to the fathers through the prophets. And it is God's last utterance "in these last days", his final word (Heb 1:1f.). In the Johannine writings these facts found their appropriate terminology. Thus the opening of the first Letter of John proclaims "what we have seen and heard", namely, "concerning the word of life" (1:1f.). According to the prologue of John's gospel, however, "the Word became flesh", i.e. man, and in such a way that man proved himself, by word and sign in his journey to God, to be the Word of God. He "made known" (ἐξηγήσατο) God whom no one has ever seen; one would almost like to translate it "interpreted", "expounded" (1:18).

Moreover, this historical self-expression of God in the historical man Jesus of Nazareth as the "Son", takes place in such a way that the whole significant event of this life and activity in its totality constitutes a claim to be heard. The disciples of John are to go and tell "what you hear and see" (Mt 11:4; cf. 11:13ff.). That, of course, as the Baptist's question shows, is by no means unambiguous. Even Jesus' mighty deeds, and in fact precisely they, share the ambiguity of the language of events. The Jewish scribes, for example, said that Jesus cast out demons by the most powerful demon (Mk 3:22).

But the third characteristic of revelation as an historical event reappears here: when it happens, it creates for itself a domain to exist in, and a perspective within which to be effective, where it is preserved both as understood and yet not understood, and it adapts itself to a community and claims this as its own. In the present case it was the disciples whom Jesus called and the people which attached itself to him and to them.

We see, therefore, that the happenings in which, as the Old and New Testaments are convinced, God revealed himself in the destinies of Israel and, unveiling and fulfilling these, in Jesus and his way, forms an occurrence in the sense of a significant event which, by taking place, constitutes an utterance, and one which is a question and a summons adapted to a certain domain. God reveals himself in the action-language of this history of his, which was definitively accomplished in Jesus, in whom he finally expressed himself. But to express is itself to interpret, or perhaps it would be better to say that it is already to be on the way to an interpretation. With such a significant event, in which God by revealing himself accommodated himself to the world, God already opened up and entered upon the road to interpretation.

II

Self-interpretation of this kind by God occurs in concrete experience and language. It takes shape in words in the oral tradition and writings of the early Church and in scripture. In the latter, fundamentally, it reaches its conclusions. We have said that in the significant event of the history of Jesus Christ, God expressed himself definitively. That is not a figure of speech, but denotes the very fact which that history states by occurring; occurrence and statement coincide. Nor do we mean it in a metaphorical sense, but are describing the course of this history, when we now assert that the language of this "statement" is the language of those who experience it. What this event says is articulated in the interpretative response of those who hear it. That holds good of all human history. It never occurs without occurring in men's understanding, whether this is expressed or not. That is also true of the history in which God speaks to the world. The New Testament is quite aware of this. What is meant by the history in which God reveals himself, becomes fully explicit in the tradition which interprets and states it, and which preserves it. If we may express the matter rather too briefly, the communication of God by Jesus Christ to the world merges into communication of him by the tradition of those who experienced it. God's self-disclosure to the world is disclosed precisely as such in history, in the explanatory speech of those who have opened themselves to it.

According to the New Testament, such speech, where it is an adequate response and so expresses the meaning of the divine event itself, is speech elucidated by the Spirit, and of course is expressed in the midst of all other speech. The Spirit as the revealing might of God, as his power of self-disclosure (cf. 1 Cor 2:10f.), the Spirit of the risen and glorified Christ, authentically unfolds the event constituted by the words, the deeds and the person of Jesus, in the corresponding speech and answer of those who thereby experience it in its truth despite all concealing and distorting untruth. In view of this, it can be said that by the power of the Spirit, God disclosed himself in the Jesus Christ-event which reached completion in the appearance of the risen Christ. But God now discloses by the power of the same Spirit the Jesus Christ-event in the interpretative word of those who experience it in the Spirit. That is to say, in Johannine terms, the event of the Word made man in Jesus, in virtue of his departure and ascent into the *doxa,* the radiance of God's power, is "brought to remembrance" by the Spirit and given expression in such a way that it is possible to perceive it in its truth. That happens, however, in and in the midst of, all other words and human language.

Here too we must not overlook the fact that the event of God's revelation in Jesus Christ manifests itself in concrete human language within the horizon of man's experience. What is preached, as the apostle Paul writes to the Christians in Thessalonica (1 Thess 2:13) is "the word of God". It is not "the word of men". But it is God's word as "the word of preaching from us which you have heard from us", that is, God's word spoken by men in human language. That must be taken with its full implications. For it means that the language of the event took concrete form not only in a particular human tongue, Hebrew, Aramaic, Greek, with its possibilities and limits, but also in the modes of speech and thought of the circle in which the event occurred. We are often naively convinced that the mode of statement of historical events to which we are accustomed, at least in theory—what we call an objective historical account—is the kind of report current at all times, and the one that was also preferred in those days. But that is not the case at all. Other forms were available for conveying history, and were not felt to be inadequate or untrustworthy. Not only popular narrative or rhetorical elaboration, but also the style of legend and of myth supplied a linguistic mould for events, or was authorized by the event to serve as its expression. If we may so phrase it, revelation as an event was not afraid that it might put obstacles to its own truth and certainty thereby. Obviously it considered that such a linguistic and thought-form suited it better in certain circumstances than an "historical" account. It is not only the latter, we might say, that was baptized, but also myth and legend. To deny this on principle as impossible by the very facts of the case, would amount to contesting the historicity and human character of God's revelation and, ultimately, the incarnation of the Logos.

There is a further significance in the fact that the revelation-event expresses itself in the speech of the language area which it has determined for itself. It means that from the start it only finds expression in the interpretation of those whom it encounters. Even the most literal transmission of a saying of Jesus is interpreted by the context in which it comes to us. In other words—and this is one of the findings of historical research which will certainly be welcome to Catholic exegesis—from the start the voice of the Church is also heard. The original community in the broad sense of the term, interpreted what happened, inevitably but not arbitrarily, on the basis of the prior understanding it already had, and in the light of its own interest and its own questions. A. Vögtle has recently said, and rightly, "the transmission of elements contained in the story of Jesus, even in the stage before it was committed to writing, was a tradition with an eye on the present and, to a certain extent, varying from case to case, it linked factors of topical relevance with the transmitted account. Here and there, in other words, features serving to clarify, interpret and point out an application were introduced. These derived from the changing concrete vital necessities and questions of the early Church, its missionary, catechetical, liturgical, apologetic, disciplinary and other purposes." But the advance of the revelation-event into the corresponding speech of the early Church must certainly not be imagined as if in the first place a tradition was current which corresponded more or less to an historical report in our sense, composed with the detachment and impartiality necessary to anyone who intends to trace an historical picture, and that that account was subsequently corrected and supplemented on the basis of certain questions and interests of the early Church. There never was an historical account in that sense. From the beginning, rather, there was only the manifold, dispersed and yet somehow single utterance made by the significant revelation-event of Jesus' history, an utterance expounded in the modes of statement proper to that age in answer to the questions of the community of disciples.

The forms in which the oldest oral tradition is met with, themselves indicate that it bore an interpretative character of that kind. Not only the gospels but their "sources" themselves were familiar, for example, with the story of Jesus told in the style of the miracle stories and with typical, or even characteristically adapted, features of exorcisms, but told with no other purpose than the claim made by the Jesus-event as this was understood in the Church. That holds good even of the story of the healing of the Gerasene demoniac, told at length and, one might almost say, with relish. Mark in fact (5:1-20) had rescued it for the kerygma when in the oral tradition it was already threatening to disappear. Matthew then vigorously condensed it, while Luke with more taste for an entertaining account, gave it the stamp of a short story. But even the short story has to serve God's summons in human language and must not be treated as of no account. Or we may think of the narrative of the Passion, which probably was told as a connected whole even in oral tradition, the oldest connected series of narratives of the story of Jesus that we possess. The decisive event of the Passion, in which the ground and meaning of Jesus' deeds, words and way were manifested and reached earthly fulfilment, perhaps first found linguistic expression in a eucharistic anamnesis of the worshipping community, perhaps also in a baptismal catechesis, and there the events were immediately and almost as a matter of course understood and given form as the fulfilment of Old Testament prophecy. And was such anamnesis not right? Yet it did not, for all that, supply a systematic historical report, and was not in a position to give one, not through incapacity or lack of information, but because an historical report would never have been adequate to the significant event itself, in which, as clearly emerged in the light of Jesus Christ's resurrection, God's action "for us" crystallized in its most concrete reality. An historical report, in fact, would have had to disregard the decisive aim of stating the actual intention of the event, which was to be an utterance fulfilling and manifesting all God's promises and by its truth claiming nothing less than faith. The very earliest tradition, shaped by the event itself as its expression, did not wish to, and could not, disregard that. After all, the tradition aimed simply at responding to and expounding the event.

Of course the oral tradition, of which in any case we have only an inadequate idea, was exposed to all the dangers of historical contingency, and so too as a consequence was the voice of the event. Not only could it have fallen into oblivion but it could have been drowned by talk in innumerable ways. The mythical or legendary form of speech might have unfolded its inherent linguistic tendency and so obscured or falsified the truth of the event's claim, or abandoned the truth of the claim to a mythical gnosis or an historicizing moralism. We can form some idea of such dangers if we consider the surviving apocryphal sayings and stories of Jesus, or the tradition, similar to the synoptic tradition, which John the evangelist saved in his gospel, by his and the Spirit's interpretation, from being deformed by talk. But it is characteristic that in the face of this threat, inherent in the historical nature of tradition, the pronouncement constituted by the revelation-event, endangered in a variety of ways but ultimately preserved, was maintained in the power of the Spirit in its language and interpretation, which were those of the primitive Chruch, through scripture and for scripture.

For this latter was what from the very nature of the case was required for saving, preserving and perfecting tradition. At the same time it represented the critical taking over of the latter by the Church. It is only in scripture that the utterance which the revelation-event constitutes, was fully unfolded in time and for time. In scripture it was inscribed in history for history, reached its provisionally definitive form and so achieved its purpose. For the revelation-event was to be present everywhere and at all times. It was a significant event in the sense that while in itself it aimed at its immediate sphere of influence, it tended towards an unlimited horizon of experience. In scripture, however, it is kept close to the world.

Old Testament prophecy was already aware of this. "And now, go, write it before them on a tablet, and inscribe it in a book, that it may be for the time to come as a witness for ever" (Is 30:8). The word pronounced and past can, when written, become God's call, by which the future of Israel itself is decided. This kind of conception lies behind the various literary versions of the history of Israel, which represent ever new interpretations made on the basis of the present for the present. Yet Israel's future is decided, as all future is, only at the end of the ages. This end has begun with Jesus Christ. And so the history of Israel,

196

for example, the journey through the desert, though it certainly happened at a definite time in the past, was written for today, when God's advent redeemed his promise. Paul expressly points this out in 1 Corinthians 10:1ff. (cf. Rom 15:4). The New Testament views it in the same way. The fact that the apostle Paul wrote down his preaching, in which Jesus Christ speaks (Rom 15:8; 2 Cor 13:3), in letters, serves to bridge distances in place and time and so makes possible his, or rather our Lord Jesus Christ's, presence at all times in every place. When in Mark, in Jesus' apocalyptic discourse issuing a warning against Antichrist (Mk 13:14) we suddenly find, "let the reader understand", it is implied that Jesus' word is written for future readers too. The Revelation to John wants the prophecy of the book to be read aloud and kept as it is written (1:3; 22:7, 18f.), because in it the entire future is regarded as evoked and manifested by the revelation that has taken place in Jesus Christ.

But holy scripture not only represents a consolidation in time and for time of the revelation-event and one appropriate to its purpose; in scripture that event attains its own definitive expression. To the extent that the writings which emerge from oral tradition later find a place in the Canon, the revelation-event expresses itself in a new, definitive interpretation and form. And in those writings, in critical confrontation with oral or even on occasion written tradition, the action-language of the revelation-event puts its definitive stamp on the authoritative written language of scripture. The preservation of tradition which we mentioned above, can be observed here in the form of discrimination.

The new interpretation, which such committing to writing of the meaning of the revelation-event represents, concerns the whole and also certain details. It concerns content and form. Just as the great narrators of the Old Testament or the prophets interpreted again and again and gave contemporary force to the ancient tradition and this process continued until a fixed form was attained in the scriptures, so the New Testament writings represent a last and authentic fundamental interpretation disclosing definitive aspects. In these writings, the Church's decisive realization grew through that of their authors belonging to the circle of the apostles. And so the summons of the revelation-event finally found expression in them as part of the whole body of scriptures. The various scriptures represent in this respect, of course, very different features. The saving-event is expressed in the Gospel according to Mark, for example, as the occurrence of the manifold *exousia* of the hidden Messiah, who after defeating the demons and overcoming the law, and after his revelation in word and deed before the world and before those who were his own, sets off, not understood, on the road to Jerusalem and the Cross. This saving-event is viewed differently from, though it is the same as, the one to which John and his *ecclesia* testify: the passing of God's *doxa*, in Jesus' words and signs, to its eternal manifestation, which occurs by his departure. And again it is expressed quite differently, for example, in the Letter to the Romans of the apostle Paul. Here, in confrontation with Jewish thought, it is expressed as the judicial rule of God's active fidelity to the alliance, which had been shown in decisive saving deeds for Israel and has now been fulfilled in Jesus Christ, and opened to faith as that "righteousness of God" which is one with his "grace". It would be possible to continue characterizing one writing after another, and by doing so to show one past aspect after another in which the saving-event now presents itself in written form. In so many fundamental aspects, it is obvious that the individual details will be different and that they too arose through new questions being put, or were discovered through renewed attentive listening.

Moreover, by fixing in writing the tradition which had been discriminatingly accepted, the expression of the revelation-event attained its definitive form. If we consider the gospels, not only was tradition preserved from disintegration into talk, but Jesus' sayings, and narratives concerning him, and also the historical sources of the Acts of the Apostles, for example, were shaped, in accordance with the tendency inherent in them from the start, in relation to the claim which by their very nature they make. It is not difficult to recognize that in this process the forms springing from the life of the early Church, its worship, catechism, preaching, law, etc. also exercised formative influence. Thus, for example, the farewell discourses of St. John's gospel are perhaps to be taken as agape-discourses. Some sections of Paul's letters are determined by hymns tacitly expounded in them, for exam-

ple Philippians 2:5ff.; Colossians 2:12ff.; Ephesians 2:11ff. But
above all in this consolidation of the event-language of God's
revelation into scripture, there took shape the general form
which corresponded to that event and its language: the *evangelion*
from which our gospels take their name, the *martyria,* the testimony of the so-called Acts of the Apostles, the *Logos parakleseos,*
the word of exhortation as, with Hebrews 13:22, we might call
the letters of the New Testament, and prophecy, of which we
have of course in the New Testament the Revelation to John.
Whatever distinctions have to be made in detail, it is clear that
through these general forms which apply to the whole of the
scriptures, the sense of the claim involved in the revelation-event
was definitively brought out and fixed. That, however, also settled from the start the sense of the truth which the revelation-
event bears within it and seeks to have acknowledged: its truth
is God's summons uttered authoritatively in it and decisively
open only to attentive obedience. Only those come into the presence of this truth who, drawn by it, approach it resolutely
receptive, in order to expose themselves to it.

These writings in which the historic event of God's revelation in Jesus Christ finally expressed itself, now immediately
cooperated in consolidating and extending more and more the
domain of experience traced by the event, i.e. the Church, which
had also been vocal in the formation of tradition and scripture.
But as that happened, something occurred in regard to the various
individual writings also. They entered into dynamic relation to
one another. Their intrinsic unity, which is scarcely perceptible,
or at least difficult to demonstrate from the writings themselves,
drew them together, separating them from others. This occurred
in the course of the experience of interpretation which they imposed on the Church. In the midst of abundant oral and written
tradition and a long process, these writings manifested themselves
to the Church as the authoritative and guiding expression of the
revelation-event. In a long process of clarification of its own
mind, the Church decided that these writings and no others, but
just these as they stand, represent *the* collection of writings in
which the revelation-event, bearing witness to itself, is authen-
ticated as norm and has finally adapted itself to the Church. So
brought fully into the domain which the revelation-utterance

itself assigned, the New Testament, and in conjunction with it the Old Testament, becomes, as the counterpart of that utterance, its product in language and the mode of its continued existence in language. It becomes so with the whole contingent character of its historical nature which is now once again apparent in the peculiar disparate and fragmentary character of this "Canon" of belief. "The whole in the fragment" of which H. Urs von Balthasar speaks in regard to the cosmos and the Church generally, is visible here also.

But did the revelation-event entirely enter scripture? Is there not outside scripture, though of course linked with it, also an authoritative and normative tradition which does not consist simply in the interpretation of scripture? And if it exists, what is its nature? This question cannot be answered here. But it must at least be raised and formulated so as to show its relevance. Is there not in the revelation-event, as according to M. Picard there is in language (and therefore in history) generally "a surplus of truth in language which does not appear as spoken truth" but which is also a way in which truth is present? Or, to put it differently: is there not a domain of langue in which scripture and its spoken language moves, in relation to which scripture is open, and which alone permits the word of scripture to live and prevail? Is there not, to put the question in yet another way, something unexpressed in the word that has been spoken, a silence in which that word dwells, which protects that word as word, but which that word itself takes under its protection too? Something unspoken which is preserved by silence but precisely as what is unspoken in the language of revelation, emerges as a question, and by questioning and being questioned gives answer through scripture and beyond it? We must leave this at this point. After this exhausting approach we must come to the very topic of our inquiry.

III

We have in fact reached it, for we have laid bare the specific character of the text we are interpreting. We have thereby thrown light on the process in which we receive a share if we undertake to interpret this text—that of God's self-utterance in the Christ-event, set forth in the authentic, fundamental, final and authoritative tradition of scripture. The function of exegesis is actually to expound that from scripture for the sake of present understanding. If it does so, exegesis is simply fulfilling the intention of the event, of tradition and of scripture which, because they are all intelligible utterances, words, have themselves already made possible, and communicated, understanding. Exegesis must, therefore, heed the guiding principles indicated by scripture itself.

In the first place these show that scripture is to be interpreted as a document of definite times, places, situations, persons, languages etc. The Bible shows itself to be such at first glance, and when more closely examined presents itself, as a whole and in its various writings, as historical testimony to a distant past. Its form and forms, its languages, ideas, terms, mode of thought and mental presuppositions show that. The problem is to trace these through methodical comparison with contemporary texts from the surrounding world and through careful regard for the context in the narrower and wider sense, and so to determine in the usual philological and historical manner what scripture primarily says. The more discriminatingly that is done, the more readily and altogether impartially what is strange and remote in sacred scripture is accepted, the more carefully the specific character of the particular affirmation there and then, and the manner of its affirmation, are accepted, the more readily the text will open itself to a first understanding. An approach of this kind to the text, taking due account of its historical distance and difference from us in the perspectives of historical investigation, does not imply an arbitrary or resumptuous attitude to it, but shows respect for God's having revealed himself into the course of history and tradition, and demonstrates the will to recognize his revelation for what it is. By that, of course, the interpretation of sacred scripture which takes account of its withdrawal into the domain of what is past, is also involved in the risk which, if we may so express it, God himself incurred by deciding to meet man historically and in language. The interpretation of scripture as an historical document with historical methods inevitably shares all the uncertainty of the scientific historical approach to reality, its actual defectiveness, which can be kept within bounds, and its fundamentally questionable character which is inescapable and which is evident, for example, in the fact that the decisive personal or general experiences of history are met with quite apart from or beyond the way of learned research. But that does not relieve exegesis of its task of methodically presenting the "historic" i.e. universally significant text of holy scripture, which proves to be an historical one, as it is, with its specific historical character, and precisely by so doing to make it cast its first glance at us or address its first words to us. In fact, realization of the limitations of the methods of historical inquiry can only emphasize the conscientiousness with which they must be handled. Certainly the enthusiasm of the historian must not count on a supposed omnicompetence of the historical method. Perhaps it will turn out on some not too distant day that that method was justified and necessary only in the time of what Heidegger called "subjectivity", and even then was not adequate for meeting actual reality. Historical enthusiasm can be of use because God has revealed himself in real and significant events and therefore (for our categories formed on the basis of the course of past events as we represent this to ourselves) in a way that can be the subject of historical investigation. Accordingly he meets us in the historical documents which are sacred scriptures, which we may not, therefore, treat as a mythical heavenly book but must acknowledge in their historicity. Holy scripture as the historical counterpart of an historical revelation-event intrinsically requires an effort of historical, philological comparison and reconstruction in accordance with its historical character, an effort capable of establishing contact with it over the interval of time, and of perceiving its specific character, which means its own mode of statement and its own proper content, persuading it as it were to spell out the alphabet in which its language is written.

But then the second guiding-principle which scripture lays down for exegesis emerges: scripture must fundamentally be understood as documenting a claim expressed in God's self-utterance in Jesus Christ, a claim now expressed in scripture. For when the formal and linguistic structure of scripture has been elucidated by conscientious historical work, as the conscience of the time requires, scripture turns out to be something quite different from a merely contingent historical document. Even the much-reviled form-history school, reviled chiefly by those who understand it least, contributed to this new clarification of scripture, by exhibiting the so-called kerygmatic nature and structure of all its strata. And the history of religions school itself, which was regarded with no less distrust, gradually led to an increased sense of the decisive difference of Christian preaching from any religion contemporary with it. Today exegesis is, generally speaking, aware that holy scripture contains the special call of God revealed in Jesus Christ, a claim which entered into the course of real events and thereby into the object of historical research. Scripture therefore indicates that it must be interpreted in relation to the truth of its claim. This involves two things. In the first place the interpretation of holy scripture cannot ultimately or from the start be guided by an endeavour to build up from it, as though it were an historical source book, a picture of those significant events, a picture which, by representing the orderly and coherent interconnection of causes, would "explain" the events in question and subject them, so to speak, to the scholar's "research"; such a picture would, of course, give him no assurance of salvation but only encourage his self-assurance. If scriptural exegesis is to follow the intention indicated by the form and content of its text, it must rather aim first and last at hearing the claim of the revelation-event of which the expression is fixed in scripture. For this purpose it has also to form ideas about the historical situations and persons and events, but that belongs to the fulfilling of the first requirement mentioned above, and in principle has only a subsidiary and transitional significance. The aim of exegesis must be to hear God's claim, expressed by and in scripture. For this and no other is the truth of scripture. To encounter it and no other, establishes truth. To unfold it from scripture for understanding, means to make truth take place.

The truth of scripture, to put it over-succinctly, is not the correctness of the information it gives on particular historical facts and dates. It does not consist in the fact that everything happened just as it says. For that would presuppose that it was written to guarantee men (of our age!) the course of facts presented, and to make men blessed by putting at their disposal a picture of events in agreement with history as it happened. But the truth of scripture is the peremptory claim of the promise and advent in history of God's fidelity historically fulfilled in the act of judgment and grace in Jesus Christ. And this truth, as we have already said, adopted even a mythical or legendary form of thought and speech, for example in the stories of the Flood or the narratives concerning Elijah and Elisha, or even in some miracle narratives of the New Testament. These have their truth in the purpose for which they address the reader or hearer. They too speak to him of the truth of God's fidelity realized in the history of Israel and its fulfilment in Jesus Christ. They too—viewed from the point of view of historical research—are effects (in the form of mythical or legendary or even deliberately stylized representation) of concrete experiences of God's action and then finally of the person of Jesus Christ and his history. For sufficient can be established about the latter even by historical research. Because they are effects of that history, which of itself demands the scope of myth or legend as a mode of verbal expression, those sections of scripture also are bearers and mediators of the truth of God's claim, which in that way too makes his fidelity heard. But exegesis has to grasp that truth. Its function is to expound it.

Besides, the fact that the truth of an occurrence also finds expression through fantasy—if mythical and legendary forms of verbal expression may be so described—and is not confined solely to historically exact report, is a universal historical phenomenon. Truth certainly does not always come home to us most in an historical report which sets great story by facts and dates and their correctness. That report may offer me a host of such facts and dates and guarantee the historical exactitude of what is narrated. Yet a single anecdote may make me better realize the truth about a human being, an event or a situation. That is not to say that the claim of truth when it is expressed in an historical report, could dispense with agreement with facts and dates, or, in the case of sacred scripture, to the extent that it aims at giving an historical report, that it did dispense with them. But the truth which according to its own intention is addressed to us as the truth of God's revelation, is of such a kind that it is not concerned only with such agreement, but reduces it to merely relative importance and in fact makes it inoperative. If I attend to the truth, to the God who is revealing himself, in the narrative concerning

Jesus in Gethsemane, the question of the precise sequence of events (and of course, most emphatically, the question of the source of the account) becomes as indifferent to me as it was to the evangelist John, who completely passes over the event from the chronological point of view and proclaims the truth of its tradition in quite a different context, in the light of his whole understanding of Jesus and in a decisive dialogue of Jesus with the Father (Jn 12:27f.). Similarly, the very existence of John's gospel side by side with the synoptic gospels unmistakably shows that for the primitive Church the truth of the revelation-event is indeed connected with its historical reality but does not depend on the historiographical or purely factual character of what is reported. The truth lies in the claim of scripture as a document which in the most varied modes of statement preserves and testifies to the occurrence of God's revelation in Jesus Christ. The truth consists in the claim of this scripture as a manifold and multiple authentication of historical revelation. Perhaps in this connection the following must also be considered. What help would it be to man if, for example in the synoptic gospels, he only had historical reports, which in that case would of course harmonize with one another? He would only have an abstract of history. In itself, in the sense of the rational inference of historical inquiry, there is no fact more certain than the death of Jesus on the Cross on Golgotha. But what actually is that fact? What is the truth of that fact? Viewed simply on the basis of the fact itself, the question must remain an absolutely open one. But in that way the very fact as an historically significant fact evaporates. For it is an historic fact, in itself and in its historical influence, only when interpreted. Whose interpretation is to be considered valid? That of historical research, explaining the unknown on a mundane, causal basis, interms of what can be verified, psychologically and sociologically, or the interpretation of the evangelists? The latter at all events were convinced that their interpretation alone brought out the truth of the event. They understood that event, the death of Jesus on the Cross, as —speaking generally—an earthly event and yet one which transcends everything earthly, produced by God for us men, a fulfilment and manifestation of all the suffering of God's Servant and of the just of the Old Testament. They were convinced that the "remembrance of Jesus' death", which is what the Passion narrative essentially is, could appropriately take place only in a form in which report and interpretation, reality and meaning are expressed together in mutual implication. And for that purpose even the legendary mode of expression was available among others. Exegesis today must of course bring to light this state of affairs by a systematic historical method, especially, for example, by that of form-history. But if exegesis is to give expression to the truth of Jesus' death in accordance with the intention of the gospels for the present time, it must cause this event to meet with understanding in its *truth*, that is to say, it must interpret the event as set forth in its truth by its interpretation.

That can only succeed, of course, if exegesis observes the other part of the second principle indicated by the special character of scripture. The claim of the truth can only be laid open to present-day understanding if the distance which separates us from scripture is bridged by philological and historical elucidation, and, in addition, if there is active attention to, and concern with, the truth which is making a claim on us through scripture. And it is simply appropriate if in the interpretation of scripture a kind of understanding is all the time at work which is derived from the subject-matter itself and which motivates the exegesis, an understanding which opens out into candid, living and obedient listening. Naturally that introduces into exegesis a risk which contradicts the ideal of a science safeguarding itself as far as possible against all imponderabilia. But it inescapably belongs to the elucidation of historic texts generally. Significant historical texts, themselves fixed by historic events, seek to beget history. They tend to be texts in the history of the very person reading them. That is most certainly the case as regards sacred scripture, as itself testifies. The history of Jesus for example, as it is consigned in the Gospel according to John, is certainly non-historical in the sense of methodically verified and verifiable scientific history, yet it is certainly historical recollection of the historical words and signs of the Word who came into history in Jesus, and is intended to awaken faith in response to the claim made by the truth of that history. But all the greater success will be had in interpreting intelligibly and bringing home to the understanding precisely that history and its texts if the methodical movement

206

towards what the text meant at that time and place in the past, is accompanied and permeated by a kind of concern for, and indeed implication in, that history, which is non-methodical, imponderable but genuinely historical because duly attentive to the historical claim involved. The process of understanding at work in this kind of historically motivated exegesis, entirely corresponds to the general understanding of a human being and his history. I have not understood a person's life and history when I know many verifiable dates and facts, chronological, psychological about a human life, and set them in order for myself, perhaps with a certain power of sympathetic insight, to form a coherent picture of his personality, but rather when, knowing perhaps little or only vaguely about him, I open myself to the appeal of his life, concern myself with it, abandon myself to it. Only in that way shall I learn to understand the substance and language of his history. Of course, such intangible sensitivity and receptivity to the claim of holy scripture is not a licence for a pious caprice convinced it can replace methodical interpretation by arbitrary fancy. Someone who really is attentive to the claim of the truth of God's revelation unfolded in scripture and who meets it with understanding as he listens, will, because it is a question of the summons of scripture and not of his own heart, do his utmost to make contact by every possible means with scripture in the objectivity of its own specific nature. But he will do that in a way which also exposes him to the claim it makes.

Only because there is also, and in an ultimately decisive sense, this access to scripture through understanding of its historic significance, are three matters of common experience intelligible. There are in the first place the inadequate commentaries, inadequate not because they are lacking in learning or method—though there are of course those that are so lacking—but because they do not penetrate to, or bring out, the essential subject-matter at all, and ultimately do not wish to go as far as that, because that would be "unscientific". Anyone who reads them has the definite impression that he has been cheated of the essential. There is also the phenomenon, of which too little account is taken by what is called specialist exegesis, that for seventeen hundred years there was no question of understanding the text by its methods at all and, what is of even greater importance, that even today there is an exegesis which reaches the substance by a mysterious, abbreviated process of living historical understanding. It cannot be denied that the voice of revelation emphatically makes itself heard in its truth even to an unanalysed but in fact effective procedure of "naive" interpretation. Once again it must be repeated that the fact that this is possible does not mean any moratorium on methodical philological historical work which, respecting the contingent character of revelation, endeavours to elucidate what is actually stated by scripture, and exercises a critical function in regard to anyone interpreting it. But it does amount to a hint to the exegete not to neglect or forget the legitimate and proper process of interpretation. Finally, mention must be made of the phenomenon, notable even from the point of view of exact scholarship, that with the same method and equal ability in handling it, the results of interpretations are nevertheless often very different or, which is another aspect of the same thing, that exegesis is perpetually striving afresh to understand the biblical text. That is only to be explained by the fact that the situation of the interpreter, of his school and of his age, continually varies because it is determined by numerous factors and expresses itself in ever new questions put to the text which provoke ever new answers from the text. But that is precisely what points to the historical factor in the process of interpretation which, like all hermeneutical activity, in the last report is refractory to regulation, however carefully the rules are observed.

A third guiding-principle of the interpretation of holy scripture follows from the specific nature of the text. We have seen that God's revelation as a significant event traces for itself a domain of experience which constitutes a mental perspective within which it is preserved, whether understood or not. The interpretation of that event from scripture also occurs within and under the influence of that domain. Not as though, to put it briefly, there is not exegesis outside the Church, or as though the text did not permit of interpretation on the basis of some general historical, aesthetic or ideological interest, often with a certain amount of success. Otherwise, of course, it would have to be denied that the text is generally intelligible and is itself capable of inspiring faith. But such interpretation is not the regular kind with most prospect of success. Leaving aside the fact that interest in this text was only kept alive through the centuries, and is emphatically so maintained at the present day, by the Church, it is a feature of exegesis as an historical process that it takes place in communication with other interpretation of every kind and in that way realizes the vital urgency of its questions and often receives its actual direction.

The Church, however, is the domain in which the claim of the revelation-event has always been already heard and is ever to be heard anew. Consequently the Church is the domain in which this event is perpetually the topic of mutual discussion, so that one understanding is offered to another and light is generated by mutual understanding. That does not mean that the interpretation which takes place within the Church as the domain where revelation is known, abolishes the role of the individual exegete as critical hearer—critical towards, in the sense of passing judgment on, the interpretation produced by others and by himself, based on their attention to the language and voice of scripture. Exegesis as discussion and through discussion, is only possible if each partner is also and in the first place listening to the subject-matter itself and if he succeeds in making intelligible what he hears. But exegesis with mutual interchange of understanding always means that the question put by the individual, and therefore the answer which he receives, are constituted in part by the questions that precede and follow. In this it must also be borne in mind that the discussion which interpretation pursues, not only with the subject-matter itself but also with the interpretation given to this within the domain in which it is experienced, need not necessarily take place explicitly. That applies not only to the individual commentator but also to the interpretation current in the domain of experience of scripture. The interpreter may refer to the subject-matter all the more intensely by not expressing any argument over such interpretation, although the latter in fact is vigorously enough pursued. And the interpretation which as a matter of fact prevails at a particular time in the Church, is found not only in exegesis but also and often more influentially in ownership, charism and law. It takes place in the life of the Church as a whole. This establishes the general initial understanding, perpetually puts questions to the text and also in fact gives answers to exegesis, perhaps without the latter's being aware of what has happened. This can be dangerous, if the answer which perhaps once was directly relevant has become anachronistic and therefore distorts the text. It can be useful, however, if it has maintained its authenticity and so helps exegesis to inquire in the right direction. Here too, therefore, exegesis must be critical, not out of an itch for originality but in order to serve to elucidate the subject-matter, scripture and the mystery of revelation. This dialogue character of exegesis which ultimately derives from the character of God's revelation in Jesus Christ as a significant event and from the way in which it is encountered in experience, can only be overlooked or felt as a burden by an ideal exegesis which dreams of purely objective interpretation and is not willing to admit the historical character of the process of interpretation in this respect either.

The interpretation of sacred scripture takes place, as we have said, implicitly in the whole life of the Church, but there are, nevertheless, processes which in a certain way can be understood as a prolongation of interpretation actually and explicitly at work and with which exegesis is connected in a special way. For what holy scripture states also finds expression, linked explicitly with interpretation, in the liturgy, in doctrinal reflection and preaching. It is not part of our subject to determine the relation of these activities to exegesis. But a few indications may be given.

The liturgy is permeated by sacred scripture and is therefore determined by its interpretation. Every prayer is based on direct or indirect scriptural interpretation and on direct or indirect understanding of scripture. Liturgy is scripture transposed into prayer and action. But scripture itself figures in the liturgy and is quoted there on principle, so that its very words are present. What scripture states operates in this case as recapitulation. And this presupposes the conviction that the text of holy scripture itself gives expression, in a way that is effective for salvation, to the summons of God's revelation, and does so within the order which, as an order of prayer, is directed towards the Eucharist, because by the nature of the case, and historically, it has its foundation in the Eucharist. But even scripture read aloud is present as interpreted. The interpretation is tacitly shown by

choice and arrangement of the passages of scripture, which everywhere exhibit some particular understanding of scripture, even
if in the extreme case this amounts to no more than the implication that there is no question of understanding the particular
passage from the context and in the context.

The relation of exegesis to dogmatic reflection is of course,
of a different kind. For even when in exegesis the revelation-event
is brought out in all its aspects for present-day understanding in
just the way it is viewed in the books of the Bible, it has not even
then been thought out in its full meaning, but only as it was
originally conceived. The reflective and inquiring elucidation of
the theological content, which has been introduced by biblical
theology as the goal of exegesis, must be carried further. It must
be drawn from the content itself i.e. from actual reflection based
on that content and directed to it. This occurs in doctrinal reflection. Perpetually spurred on by exegesis, this must above all enter
into discussion with what has already been thought in the Church
on the basis of scripture, and must think over what has been
thought, so that this may yield up what has not been thought
and disclose further the mystery of the subject-matter itself. In
such thinking directed towards the very reality that is in question,
the Church's reflection on the faith does not move away from
the truths of revelation but comes nearer to them, for they mirror the one truth of the revelation-event. What exegesis works
out by a methodical process and attentive understanding as being
what holy scripture proposes for our consideration, is committed
to the believing reflection of the Church, so that this meditation
may think over what has to be thought and penetrate the subject-
matter itself. Perhaps at this or that point success will be reached
in thinking something out to a conclusion. Such thinking out to
a conclusion, which is shown by the consensus of the Church
concerning its belief, may, if the hour requires and permits, lead
to its fixing in dogma. This, however, does not mean the end of
reflection, but signifies that what has been thought, reflected on,
thought over, and here and now thought out to a conclusion, is
raised to the rank of what is incontestably and permanently
worthy of thought. For exegesis, that does not mean the sus-
pending of activity within the radius of this or that text, but
sends decided thought back to its beginning, to think it over

afresh. Precisely by dogma (which of course owes its truth to the revelation-event as such, through scripture and through the surplus of truth recalled above which has borne fruit), exegesis can learn that its very nature consists in an ever-new and endless activity within the course of history.

There is, however, a third prolongation of exegesis which is more direct than dogmatic theology and if one may so express it, more concrete and individual than the liturgy—preaching of all kinds. It does not always have to be spiritual preaching though, for a renewal of preaching, it would be well if it were so today. In preaching, the interpretation of the revelation-event from scripture is pursued here and now to the point of addressing the hearers in the particular, individual way appropriate to them in their particular individual situation. The concrete life of the individual in the first place and then that of the congregation, is brought by preaching into the light of the revelation-event and thereby disclosed in its truth. Scripture, therefore, speaks once again. But of course that is not the word which crystallized in scripture, so that every preacher would be more or less an apostle or prophet; it is language which expresses scripture. As such it is at best, and to the extent that it places no obstacle to the voice of scripture but allows its own discourse to be prompted by it, an approach to the word of revelation made possible by scripture. In that, of course, all the factor already mentioned as connected with scripture and its interpretation, play a part too. In *one* respect nevertheless, the intention proper to scripture is apparent in this word of peaching: that of bringing out the claim of God's truth, God's fidelity, in the concrete, here and now, and of making the hearer obedient to it. For, of course, biblically speaking, to preach is to bring to a hearer what the preacher has heard and continues to hear, in such a way that it is given an obedient hearing. In preaching, the arrow of the word reaches its target.

Viewed as a whole, exegesis of scripture undertaken specifically and responsibly in order to promote understanding, proves to be a laborious but important activity. The methodical elucidation and translation of the language of the revelation-event which has assumed written form is laborious in itself. For that language stands remote and alien in the far domain of distant history. No less laborious, and in fact even more laborious, is the attentive concern with the summons addressed by revelation, which the expositor must hear in and behind his methodical procedure, for such hearing is of decisive hermeneutical importance. The dialogue about interpretation which is always in progress within the horizon in which revelation is encountered, can be of general assistance to the particular interpretation, but can also on occasion be a powerful hindrance to understanding. Yet, despite the labour, there must be scriptural exegesis. For even it if represents nothing but a perpetual process of elucidation, a service which never ends, and which is ever new because of its ever-new questions and because of its constantly questioning the old answers, nevertheless precisely as such, if it has a right understanding of its nature and does not waste time on useless matters, exegesis expounds the claim of God's truth which occurred as an event in history and is voiced in scripture for each successive present-day, and it holds open the rule of that truth in the world and for the world. In a world that does not know what it will be like tomorrow, who would not wish to live under that clear call of God which opens out all things and admits all that God's future holds?

Hans Urs von Balthasar
1905-

*Hans Urs von Balthasar was born in Luzern, Switzerland,
and studied in Engelberg, Feldkirch, Zurich, Vienna, and Berlin.
His dissertation in German literature submitted at Zurich in 1929
later grew into a three-volume work called* The Apocalypse of
the German Soul. *That same year he joined the Jesuits and studied
philosophy for three years at Pullach where he was deeply influenced by Erich Przywara. His theological studies from 1934 to
1938 were done in Lyon, France, where Henri de Lubac was the
decisive influence.*

*This unusually diverse background combined with his un-
usually diverse talents has made him one of the most unusually
interesting figures on the modern theological scene. Breadth of
vision is his trademark. He has written on art, literature, philosophy, patristics, and history. His 1951 work on Karl Barth
marked the opening of a new era in Catholic-Protestant dialogue
in German-speaking areas, while his* Martin Buber and Christianity *demonstrated the vital necessity for Catholic-Jewish dialogue.*

*From 1940 to 1948 von Balthasar served as chaplain to the
students of the University of Basel, and in 1950 he left the Jesuits
in order to devote himself to developing the "secular institutes"
that were emerging at the time as a contemporary expression of
Christian spirituality. He has continued to produce an amazing
array of stimulating writings, including a four-volume theological*

synthesis on an aesthetics of the glory of God. Among the bewildering variety of themes to which he has addressed himself, most can be related in one way or another to the three central issues in his thought: Christ, world, and time.

If, as he illustrates so abundantly, one can today write theological syntheses about numerous topics, one can no longer write a synthesis or summa of all theology. The cascading discoveries of our era are too revolutionary and undigested. The best a theologian can hope to do is draw sketches. Word and Revelation *is a collection of six of these efforts. The one we have chosen to include here is the third, "The Implications of the Word." It is meant to serve as a good example of the richness of von Balthasar's approach, his omnipresent Christocentrism, his ability to set familiar items in a new light.*

WORD AND REVELATION

T he relations between natural and supernatural revelation, between that given by the very being of things
and that given by the word, and all the consequences
in the spheres of natural truth (philosophy), natural ethics and
law, etc. is one of the central problems in the controversy between catholic and protestant theologians—though of course the
latter are not in accord (consider the discussion between Barth
and Brunner, and Lackmann's statistical summary of the interpretations of Rom 1:18f); and catholics vary considerably in
their interpretations of the Vatican definitions. It is not our
intention to survey the problem in its entirety but rather to
consider just one limited though essential aspect, one which
may help to reconcile differences and allay prejudices. It is by
no means a new aspect, being simply the application of the
generally accepted christology to the problem of revelation; but
perhaps it has not yet been adequately worked out in. detail.

Once the older apologetic and fundamental theology had
shaken off the imprecise ideas of german idealism, both philo-
sophic and christian, according to which creation was simply
identified with revelation or the manifestation of the divine
being, and the revelation of the word, in all its depth and force,
seemed reduced to a mere stage in the utterance of creation itself, there began a period marked by the emergence of a direct,
and therefore naive, unreflective dualism between the two
forms of revelation: on the one hand an independent revelation
derived from the creation, whose content could be detailed with
some precision, even though uncertainty remained about fallen
man's capacity for attaining knowledge in the religious sphere;
on the other the denial of any such "second" source of revelation alongside that of the word of God in Christ. This second
source seemed merely to tone down, obscure and distort the
clear, definitive and exhaustive word that the father willed to

give to the world through his son, since men then claimed to derive most of what it concerned them to know simply from nature—and to reserve for philosophy and ethics much that derived from the word of God, almost to the point of supplanting it.

Surely this ostensibly catholic misconception, which occasionally *seemed* to be adopted even by authorized exponents, is a clear indication of some defect in basic principles. It is true that catholic theology has endeavored to rise from the second period of simple dualism to a third which would be characterized by a consistent and comprehensive christological outlook; but its consequences have yet to strike our evangelical brothers as sufficiently forceful and practical.

What follows is to be understood as an expression of a christological outlook. It will not however adhere to the usual course which starts from principles drawn from the revelation in creation to arrive at the revelation in the word as the crown and summit—a course many evangelical theologians consider impossible as a method and at the least involving insuperable difficulties. Here we proceed in the reverse direction, from the revelation in the word to that in creation. This we do not on the basis of the well known if sparse texts of scripture, which speak of revelation in creation and whose meaning is the subject of considerable dispute, both philological and theological, but by determining what the word of revelation itself presupposes and implies. It may be that the resources of modern philology and psychology make us more amenable to this method than were our immediate predecessors. These sciences have taught us to discover, in an apparently uniform structure, different superimposed layers: philology by going back to "sources" and to previous redactions or verbal traditions, and thus, especially as regards texts of the old testament, coming upon certain archaic, legendary or mythical foundations; psychology by its parallel attempt to formulate the implications of the conscious spiritual life in the spheres of the instinctive, organic and vegetative life—processes which are at very early ages submerged into the twilight and total darkness of the unconscious. Yet this method did not have to wait for the coming of these two sciences. It was known from the very beginning of philosophical thought, and practiced as the method of "analytics," which is not only the title of Aristotle's book on logic (indicating the results of reflection on direct perceptions of the categories of being), but was the metaphysical method employed by Socrates and Plato, and later by neoplatonism in its ascent to God by way of reflection. Perhaps too it might be possible to read Hegel in this light (the reverse of the usual): to explain the "nothingness" of the pure hic et nunc we must, by analysis, traverse all the stages of reality until we reach the divine ground. But we are not now engaged in philosophy, but in christian theology; and if, whatever its method and system, Christ is for it the summit and crown of all God's work in the world, if he is, as Paul and Irenaeus say he is, the anakephalaiosis of the entire creation, then theology's duty is to portray this in all its sublimity. This is its aim, and its means is an analysis of christology, bringing out the cosmic presuppositions that the incarnation of the word of God implies.

1

Our starting point is the "directness" of God's word as it encounters us in holy scripture. It could reasonably be objected that what comes to us most directly is not the scriptural word but the word in its living proclamation, which is essentially continuous with the word to which scripture is a pointer, the word Jesus Christ who endowed the apostles with the office and charismatic power of preaching. This is true enough; yet the scriptural word has as its function to bear witness, under the inspiration of God, to the word of life, to the total Christ, both head and body. For this reason, and because it is word, in the human and primary sense (whereas that to which it bears witness can only be so described in a deeper and not directly intelligible sense), it is above all methodical and objective. Scripture is one book among many, or rather a collection of books of various kinds; moreover it is one of extreme complexity, posing more scientific problems than any other in world literature—one therefore that must be painstakingly examined philologically. We cannot agree with Origen (himself a great philologist!) when he equates the application of the tools of philology to scripture with a handing over of the incarnate word to the torturer. This implied identification of the scriptural word with the word himself and of the interpretation of scripture with the incarnation of the logos is so absolute as to lead to numerous false conclusions. Insofar as it expresses mistrust of anything to do with natural philology this ingenious theory is really an outcome of the alexandrian tendency toward the doctrine of one nature.

Nonetheless, after allowing due scope for the science of the word, we must acknowledge what is correct in Origen's view. Holy scripture, as the uniquely privileged witness to a unique event, is so intimately bound up with it that, apart from the event—understood in the sense in which it is witnessed in scripture, or witnesses itself in scripture—it cannot be interpreted at all. Philology can help toward this understanding but it can neither compel nor replace it. To understand the scriptural text according to its own defined mission (and to do otherwise would be to mistake its whole tenor) means accepting it on faith as the witness of the Holy Spirit (through the instrumentality of men) to yahweh's dealings with his chosen people of the covenant, and to the fulfilling of this covenant in the person of Jesus, God and man. It is true of course that in every human statement there is a gap between what it conveys and what it means to convey, the word holding them apart as well as conjoining them. Yet we can never postulate a unique word that should correspond with the uniqueness of what is meant, for the very reason that no event in the world can claim absolute uniqueness; there is always some point of comparison with other events, and so there is always something one event shares with another. Consequently, however personal and relatively original a given utterance may be, it always contains an element of generality and formality, bringing it within the purview of linguistics, grammar, syntax, poetics, comparative philology and so forth. What scripture bears witness to is, on the one hand, a section of human history, and thus something which can be expressed quite simply in human words. But scripture is also so unique in kind that there is an absolute limit fixed to its comparability with other events, and thus necessarily a clearly drawn limit to the application of philology to the word thus witnessing. If what it conveys is wholly unique then this uniqueness is the central, dominant factor in the statement designed to convey it. In other words this testifying word necessarily implies this content; and, if scripture is to be understood as essentially the word authorized by the Holy Spirit (since only God can speak adequately of God, only God can say what he means by his revelation), then it must be seen as the Spirit's word about the word that is the son; and this, its sublimest aspect, implies a relation to the trinity. This brings out the partial truth of what Origen says, namely that the distinction between the testifying word and the word testified to is an incomplete one. Large tracts of scripture do not merely relate the revelation made by Yahweh to his people through the intermediation of Moses, the kings, the prophets, even the pagans, and finally in the word that is Christ. They are themselves revelation. In the prayers of the psalmist the Spirit reveals what prayer means for God; the words of the prophets not only indicate a particular historical background, but the core of what God willed to speak is contained in the actual situation through the prophets. The sapiential books do not refer to any historical background but are themselves a tranquil contemplation of the historical revelation, and bring out, in the form of revelation, the goods therein contained. In the new testament the interaction is still more evident. This alone imparts to the words of scripture not only a unique value in themselves but also a peculiar resonance that carries to every generation and causes a great turbulence in the sea of human words. Something of the uniqueness of the object testified to inevitably belongs to the word that testifies, imparting to it its inner trustworthiness as witness. Something of the logic of the object testified to, above all the cross and the resurrection of Christ, colors the logic of the expression. This has been often noticed, but at the same time seems never to have been adequately treated.

2

The word of the Spirit, which is what scripture is, bears reference to the word of the father, which is the son. The word uttered by the church in her preaching, a word we directly encounter, originates in this word of the son, so much so that, in every detail, it refers back to it, represents and expounds it, and impresses it on the hearers. It permits of no independent, definitive sense of its own but, as with the church's liturgical sacrifice, only has meaning in relation to Christ's words, acts and being, a meaning brought about in obedience to him. Thereby an unimpaired vision of the reality scripture means to convey as a living tradition (proclamation), and this reality, together with its implications, is the subject of the present study, namely the incarnate word of God. We may take as our point of departure Christ as word, that is, preacher and "prophet" of the father and of his kingdom. As such he implies straightaway the entire revealed word of history since Abraham, indeed since Noah and Adam, for inasmuch as he satisfies all justice, fulfills all the promises, his word, teaching and truth build up into a single whole all that God has shown forth and effected as truth relating to him. Likewise what is, according to his word, also a part of the revealed word can now only be understood as rounding off the exposition of his depth and height and breadth and length— we refer to the theologies of Paul and John, the Acts as the prototype of church history (to which belong the catholic epistles by way of completion), and the Apocalypse as the recapitulation of the whole old and new testament theologies of history. Further all that belongs to the church's official exegesis and every partial manifestation of the fullness of the word of Christ in individual charismatic missions—all this is a palpable result of the living power of the word exercised over the whole of history.

We only make mention of the historical dimension of the divine utterance in order to see how it centers on the word of Christ. For this indeed is a word spoken by a man to men, understandable by them as a human word, yet, in the opinion of those who heard, a word of one who spoke as no man ever spoke (Jn 7:46), who spoke "as one having power, and not as the scribes" (Mt 7:29). Wherein this power consisted he himself made known: in his being sent by the father, in his obedience to the father, so that what he taught was the echo of his father's teaching, and his whole life, the very flesh and blood that he had assumed, was through his obedience taken up into his word. His word transcended the temporal, reaching up both to God and to his own life; yet it belonged to the general human category, while being at the same time absolutely unique. Had it not come within that category it would not have been human at all, and the word would not have been made flesh. Nor would we be able to understand Christ's word in its special mode of transcendence. But we now see what it means for someone to stake his life for every utterance he dares to make, and to say that he means thereby a truth that surpasses his own relative existence and that is absolute. He may fall short of it either in understanding or conduct; still he means it, and he does not necessarily fail it. Yet the transcendence of Christ's word in reaching out to his own life and to his father has, with all its humanness, something setting it wholly apart, for to it alone the plenitude of authority was given by the father. Let us take as an example the parable of the unmerciful servant. Does the word here give us a similitude that, however, wholly transcends the category of similitudes because it springs from a reality already given and made visible by its means, a reality immanent within it? What gives it that force which attaches to every particular application but which is yet only present for one who assents to the reality signified as the basis of the narrative? What but precisely that fact, present behind it all, that Christ is the price paid for the redemption. Each of the words here spoken is, for its utterance to be made at all possible, covered with a warranty sealed in blood. The utmost justice—to the point of delivering the unmerciful servant to the torturers (consider what this means, when God is king)—is also, since behind it lies Christ's sacrifice of body and blood, the adequate expression of the utmost mercy of God. We cannot interpret this story in merely human terms, merely ethically, nor, despite its severity, merely as "old testament" in tone. It must be accepted as told by Christ making his way toward the cross; in fact the verse that follows speaks of his return to Judea (Mt 19:1). The parable form is preserved and, at the same time, transcended. It is preserved insofar as there is a story with a formal correspondence between it and what it signifies; transcended because here the similitude does not indicate the reality, as is the case with poetic parables, but the reality directly points to itself in the similitude, creates its own breathing space. This transcendence is the despair both of philology and psychology. Both of these, relying on the doctrine of the incarnation, according to which everything belonging to Christ's human activities proceeds in a wholly human fashion, claim the existence of a sphere which, for the time being, is not transcended in favor of what is wholly unique. This sphere however does not exist, therefore both can only propound their judgments while they themselves are, at a deeper level, the objects of judgment. It is not as though they were not allowed to carry out their work to the end and then have to interrupt it at a certain point when the mystery begins. The mystery, for that matter, begins at the outset so that if they want to pursue their objects to the end no one stops them. The question is simply whether, once they realize that they are wholly subject to the judgment of the word, which they proposed to judge, they must begin all over again in faith.

Does this then mean a total collapse of scientific procedure, and imply that it is absurd to include theology as one of the faculties? Apprehending this conclusion theologians take refuge in a theory of "two storeys." On the lower level is the Jesus of history, exhaustively analyzed both philologically and psychologically, while on the upper storey is the word of Christ as son of the father, the object of faith, both communal and individual—as if there were in Christ anything comprehensible in human terms that was not to be interpreted, from the outset, in function of his divine mission. This methodic schizophrenia is the counterpart of the cleavage in the individual inquirer who, though believing, is still a sinner. But even so, it is inadmissible since what determines the method is not the inquirer but the object. This object is Christ whose word, if it is to be at all understood in its content and intention, comprises both the cross and his mission by the father. For the cross guarantees the truth of his words by the sacrifice of his own life, and the mission guarantees that his sacrifice is not that of a fanatic, but an act of obedience to a divine commission. We see that there is a connection between word, cross and commission that is of its very nature wholly unique, a logic thought out ad hoc, or better, ad hunc, and applying to this case alone but with ineluctable necessity. It is especially in John that the uniqueness of the logic of Christ's words comes out, formulated as it is in an almost abstractly scientific way. There we have presented a clear gradation between the primary proof of the truth of the word and a secondary, supplementary process. The former rests on the analytical connection between the truth of the word (for example "I am the light of the world," "I am the resurrection") and the sacrifice of body and blood, both being understood as obedience to the father and as self-revelation of the father—a perception which leads directly to faith and which issues from faith in a mysterious, living identity. But if anyone, through some spiritual weakness, some resistance to the truth arising out of sin, lacks the power to follow this christological logic and to yield to its evidence, another way opens to him, one which is given first place in Christian apologetics—that of miracles and prophecy. This is the argument for belief in the uniqueness of the all fulfilling word in the son from the evidence of the relationship between promise and fulfillment, between the charisma proclaimed (prophecy) and the charisma manifested (miracle) (Lk 4:18). It accords with the logic of the redemptive process where, instead of dwelling on the unique character of the central feature and letting conviction follow from having seen the justness of its structure, we turn to the various factors connected with the preparation, the earlier stages and pointers; these can only be understood, individually as well as collectively, if interpreted as promises of something to come, and this is only possible after the fulfillment has taken place. The overwhelmingly clear proof which God bestows on those of lesser insight is the correspondence between the old testament and the new, a most remarkable thing, so wide and manifold as to be exemplified in countless instances. It is in virtue of the sovereignty of the son of God that he assigns this historical consideration to the second place. It is not his will to be argued to from premises outside himself, for he is the truth which bears all evidence in itself, and which is susceptible to no comparison other than with itself. The whole economy of the two testaments consists in applying the essential truth of the incarnation to the whole range of human history; this is not just something accidental, exterior, made for apologetic purposes, a concession to human need. Consequently the first thing to be made clear is that the father has given all power to the son, and that what he fulfills, namely the promise, derives from him its persuasive force.

It is necessary to insist that, in addition, the perception of the "harmonies of the two testaments" (Charlier) is far superior, as a mode of comprehension, to the methods of philology and psychology, as these themselves show us (unfortunately, we may say) only too plainly. Whatever natural precondition is required for understanding *this* logic of revelation, it does not consist in a fine discrimination of philological minutiae, but rather in a feeling for form, a sense of the proportions of the whole, of the relative importance of detail, not only in regard to sensible but also to spiritual reality. The great spiritual writers who have made this the focal point of their theology— Irenaeus, Origen (with his enormous influence in both the east and the west), Augustine, Rupert, Pascal, Newman—all had this esthetic sense and outlook. Certainly this does not mean that it is possible to prescind from faith in cultivating a biblical esthetic productive of factual results. All it means is that God, for the understanding of the truths of faith, calls upon all the cognitive powers of man, and that the coarse-grained philology to which the old testament makes no appeal, as being "unmodern," is only dumb in its regard because of a want of sensibility.

The argument from Christ as manifested in scripture has, all through history, both ecclesiastical and secular, refuted with a truly divine irony all the insidious suggestions of his enemies. It is so cogent because the recorded facts rule out the alternative: either son of God or else purely man of the highest religious perceptions. It compels this other alternative (as philology and psychology might propose): either son of God or else the hallucinatory invention of enthusiastic followers, God's son or psychopath. Anyone who thinks "religious genius" is a sufficient explanation has certainly not read the new testament objectively. All attempts to bring the unique figure of Christ within general laws miscarry; they fall back for an explanation on deception or mental disorder, as the Jews did once, and have always done (Mt 28:15; Jn 8:48).

3

We only need to contemplate the mystery of the union of the divine and human in Christ from the other aspect in order to perceive its entire implication. In Christ there is nothing human (we speak of course of the actus humani, not of the actus hominis) that is not the utterance and expression of the divine; and likewise there is nothing divine that is not communicated and revealed to us in human terms. This applies not only to all the acts of the public life, his preaching, founding of the church, passion and resurrection, but equally to his hidden acts, his prayer to the father, his obedience, his love for the father unto death. It is precisely this inner aspect that is most essential, definitive, in the whole economy of the redemption. For it is not true that the acts and states of the redeemer, by which he makes for redeemed humanity a new spiritual and heavenly home, are only partially human acts (that is to say, a subordinate part therefore), while those where the human nature as such falls short of the divine call for the intervention of the higher nature, that of the God-man. That would be pure arianism. The acts and states by which Christ redeems us are genuine human acts, from the lowest to the highest; and though they are never solely human they are always human. Scholasticism, for purposes of classification, confines the idea of "religio" to certain bounds; but once we free it from these and set it in the light of the adoration to be given in spirit and truth, self-surrender in faith, hope and charity, everything by which Christ signifies his love to the father and to men is an actus religionis.

These acts then, as we have just emphasized, are not to be exhaustively explained by derivation from the "abstract" nature, man. At the same time it is obvious that, despite the uniqueness of Christ as divine and human, they are still acts of a man who to be man must fall within the range of the "abstract" term man. Consequently there is no question of applying to Christ a definition which would distinguish him as man essentially from other men, setting him apart for instance as "man *for* his fellowmen," as opposed to "us others" who are only "men *with* our fellowmen." In any case such an account of what

Christ and other men are respectively only brings out the specifically social, horizontal function of human nature, prudently omitting its relation to God; and besides, it makes, if we examine the argument closely, Christ and the rest of men share a common nature only analogously, not univocally. The "ordinary," "normal" man is a self-contained person, and this fact confines his relationship with his fellowmen to certain limits. He cannot be their representative before God, still less offer himself as a sacrifice for them, or feed them with his own substance, his flesh and blood. Christ's humanity on the other hand is, from the outset, a function of his divine person and so a fit instrument for all those acts which are required for the redemption of mankind. Because of this, and since in spite of all Christ's humanity must be designated a pure humanity, it could well be maintained that the rest of men become, in Christ, competent as regards acts to which they are not fitted by their own human nature. The above-mentioned theology of man fails, on a decisive point, to take full account of the incarnation. In becoming man Christ falls into the universal category of man, and so Paul's expression "found as a man" (Phil 2:7) implies an identity of nature persisting, regardless of the analogy conveyed by the κένωσις, even in the greatest of his acts as God-man; and in this precisely consists the taking of man's nature into the unity of the God-man in order to redeem it. It certainly follows that the acts of Christ—being acts of his human nature, and therefore insofar as the man Christ manifests his "religio" toward the father in adoration and obedience during his agony in the garden—are truly acts of natural religion. They are not merely natural religion, but this is no reason for denying that they are *also* natural religion; it does mean that we have both the right and the duty to affirm natural religion as necessarily implied in christology. Were this not so then the "religio" of Christ must have seemed supernatural in a way inconsistent with the ordinariness, lowliness and accessibility he showed in his human relations. He must have seemed quite other than those quasi-divine wise men and religious founders in his capacity for acts beyond ordinary human nature. Then his summons could only have involved a misconception, and the twelve, on being asked "Will you also go?" would have had to withdraw—

at any rate after his promise to make his flesh and blood the food of all, a thing absolutely supernatural. Of course they did not dream of "imitating" him in such incomprehensible acts, nor did he demand that they do the exact same thing as he. Nonetheless he did not intend their following of him to be no more than a mirroring of his acts in a different sphere, one appropriate to *their* humanity. He meant it to be a real identification with him, and this despite all the emphasis he laid on the uniqueness of his sonship. This is what we now have to consider.

When we say that Jesus, as man, performs the acts of religion the expression as man means that he does so not only as exemplar but as a model, not only as filius unicus but as primus inter filios pares. This implies that the act of religion is an act of man as such, apart from which it would be impossible to understand either the incarnation or the redemption. It would amount to losing sight of man's elevation through Christ to community with the divine nature, were Christ as exemplar to be emphasized to the detriment of him as model, or the equality of nature stressed to the point of forgetting the uniqueness of his sonship, which predestines him, in an altogether different way from Adam, to be the head of mankind and makes him draw all things (Jn 12:32) in heaven and earth (Eph 1:10) into his unique status (visibly expressed in his being raised up on the cross). The elevating, transforming and creative power of the gratia capitis is so great that, between the religio appropriate to human nature as such and that offered to man through the grace of redemption, the only relation is one of analogy; any relation less than this is inadmissible. And though human nature was impaired by sin still, despite all its disastrous consequences, *this* analogy is not annulled. All it means is the inhibition (seen constantly in the individual) of an ever-present essential function. No other interpretation of the guilt persisting in mankind is possible.

The analogy between natural and revealed religion is conceived correctly and in accordance with what revelation itself tells us only on two conditions. We must neither deny the existence of natural religion nor see it as self-contained and sufficient. It must be taken, according to the intention of the creator of the natural order, as of its very nature an initial stage. This means that God, in the order of creation, truly began what he was to perfect in the order of Christ's redemption; began, that is to say, in the sense of establishing an enduring initial stage wherein what is begun does not imply a reaching beyond itself (*a desiderium naturale visionis, sive efficax sive inefficax*), nor (what comes to the same thing) claim to be understandable only when raised to the order of grace. Neither is its incorporation into the final synthesis to be held dependent on its essence being considered merely as a "promise" of something of a higher order. Such conceptions would impair and even exclude the freedom of grace as God's self-revelation to the creature, God's freedom to enter into a covenant with a people chosen at his discretion. To speak of continuity between the two orders is in fact highly misleading and, sooner or later, involves making grace (even as *medicinalis*) an epiphenomenon of nature.

We can speak of "implication" in this connection only in the sense of nature (that is, human nature) being taken into a mode of being it cannot attain of itself—since this mode is divine and unique and thus only accessible through Christ, God and man—without having to be completed in its own order, its "substantiality," as regards a missing part—namely religion. Nature possesses a predisposition for this superadded mode by reason of its inchoate character. This character however does not consist in a platonist longing after grace and the vision of God, a longing that includes a latent claim to these. Nor is this predisposition a constant attitude of resignation and indifference to what is to come on the ground that no one can see into the divine counsels. What it means is active readiness, the expression of the true essence of creatureliness, for every possible initiative on the part of God's will without at the same time anticipating it. This readiness was taken up and fulfilled by Christ, which shows exactly what analogy here means.

We cannot conclude this line of thought without exhibiting the analogy as one of personality and so of the uniqueness of the individual. Uniqueness enters into the very essence of man, so much so that it must be taken into consideration even when we view him in the abstract. So it was that Hegel was obliged to find room in his metaphysics for history in the concrete;

and only so was it possible for the only-begotten of the father to become a man among men. And in him the uniqueness of each individual rises superior to its precarious situation in time, and so attains to the "father's house" and the co-inheritance.

4

Now at last we can profitably consider another implication, already alluded to in section 2, namely the christian and ecclesiastical existence implied in that of Christ. This subject, like all others broached here, is far too extensive to be treated fully; we must be content to indicate its place in the general ensemble. If the relationship between nature and grace, as seen from the aspect of the incarnation, almost defies expression in rational terms, this is even more the case here. Previously it was a question of seeing one reality being imparted through a higher one in such wise that the latter, in its sovereign freedom, bestows a mode of being, a selfness, to which the self as nature has no claim; yet this self had from the outset been formed in view of this new being. Now we are concerned with how God's word in Christ arranges a participation in himself in such a way that the participator thereby realized himself at the deepest level of his being, attains self-knowledge in the unique relationship of member to head. The similes of head and members, of vine and branches, are taken from the natural, subspiritual order and so are only pointers to the reality, not the reality itself. The members and branches have their own personality and responsibility for their acts, and thus are bound by ethics and religion. Their obligations are by no means superseded by reason of the event represented by the two similes, nor through the supervention of the order of sin and its debilitating effects. We are concerned here not so much with the latter as with the accord between ethical and religious ideals and the soteriological fact: what the christian is obliged to bring about is granted him by Christ as already effected, without however removing the necessity for striving after perfection. What this means is most clearly seen in the special case of the apostles. They were entrusted with the word of God, with proclaiming not the bare word but the word along with its characteristic powers. The authority to speak included the messianic power to work miracles, as if to show that this conjunction of word and deed was not the specific mark of Christ who alone, in virtue of being sent by the father, could equate his existence with the mission received. The disciples received something of this identity by communication from him, and not merely something after the fashion of the credentials given to the prophets of the old testament. The holiness attributed by Paul to the faithful is not that of the synagogue, but a participation of that of Christ, their head. His death and resurrection, as an accomplished fact, was the grace communicated to them, and this primary grace of Christ became the ethical ideal they were called to realize subsequently. Peter received the office of feeding Christ's flock which, because it is Christ's, can only rightly, that is, in Christ's way, be fed by Christ, in whom the priest-shepherd and lamb-victim are one and the same. This is why, immediately after, there followed the prophecy of Peter's following to the death of the cross; an express "follow thou me" is appended to the gift of this conjoined function of Christ (Jn 21:19, 22). This special case of the apostolic office in the church throws light on that of the ordinary believer, also sent to live the life of the word. What differentiates Christ and Peter is not for a moment neglected. In fact the lord of the church stresses it to the utmost, and thus brings out all the more strongly the paradox of the christological unity so entrusted to him. Furthermore the theological paradoxes of the relationships between Peter and John, between authority and charity in the church, brought out at the end of John's gospel, are contrasted (admittedly only in the catholic interpretation) almost to the point of making them at variance. Nonetheless the effect is not one of fragments lying lifeless and apart, as in the paradoxes of Pascal, Kierkegaard and Dostoevsky, but of elements bound together by the head into a formal unity, one of supreme beauty, the beauty of the new testament bridal church, realized in Mary and every true case of sanctity. It is a unity free of the tortured complications of human dialectic, possessing the simplicity and directness of the attitude "Behold the handmaid of the lord." So perfect is its simplicity as to be almost equated with the human ideal, which indeed it is, but only because it is conceived by God and bestowed by the son.

Here it is well to remember that being human cannot be expressed simply in the abstract ethical formula "self-perfection in freedom." This striving is inseparable from man's organic nature, whose laws operate in the direction of freedom, though they must be acknowledged and admitted in the patience befitting a created being. It was not in climbing the steep path to "self-perfection" that Mary became a mother, but in self-surrender to God's direct will and to the disposition intrinsic to her womanly nature and to what took flesh within it. In this way the fruitfulness of her faith was conjoined with that of her womb and of her whole being. This shows us how Luther's conception of the act of faith was somewhat restricted in comparison with the older german and christian accounts wherein the element of surrender and loyal discipleship, the human in other words, was far more prominent than in the protestant dialectic of sin and grace. If this human factor is not seen as implicit in the holiness of the church the "naked" soteriological dialectic only too easily reduces faith to an academic abstraction.

5

The last implication we wish to mention (without trying to reach any systematic conclusion) requires, for complete acceptance, a much more thorough exposition; an abbreviated account is almost inevitably misleading. The history of God's dealings with man is wholly centered in Christ, from whom it radiates into two periods of time; starting from him we gain an understanding of all that is disposed in view of him and all that proceeds from and through him. Christ himself often indicated this implication of all that was ordained in view of salvation (Jn 5:46-47; 8:52-58; Mt 22:41-45) and, having accomplished his own part and risen again, expounded it to the infant church for forty days (Lk 24:44f). For Paul this implication is identical with the mystery whose servant he has become, and for the author of the apocalypse it is once again the dramatic meaning of world history. In fact when we speak here of world history we must include a further, and necessary, implication of the whole history of man in the history of salvation. This implication is only too familiar in one way, and yet when examined closely appears a very strange one. Of course we see Christ as the head elevated above all history who will come again to pass judgment on the living and the dead, and so over the whole course of history. But this hope of ours is wholly eschatological; the gospel admonishes us to watch and persevere in prayer rather than to set about theologizing history. The meaning of history is so dependent on the mind of the creator and judge that we cannot determine it in advance.

Yet, since the word was made flesh, the various histories comprised in that of Christ himself, that of the covenant with Israel, the course followed out by God with his people, all belong, as history, to the content of revelation. The whole patristic and medieval theology of history is based on the idea that the different stages, up to Abraham, from Abraham to Moses, from Moses to the judges and to David, from David to the prophets, from the prophets to post-exilic Israel, and from that time to Christ, were actually a progressive revelation; so much so that these stages were taken, in summary fashion, to pertain not only to sacred history but also world history in general. The ordo et gradus in profectu mundi, spoken of so frequently and in such detail by Bonaventure and other great scholastics, was derived from their view of sacred history, but it was also connected with their philosophical reflection on the possible meaning of the general course and progress of history. They saw this as a processus ab imperfecto ad perfectum consisting of 1) the eliciting of free acceptance from mankind of the salvation freely given (and so the eliciting of Mary's assent from each successive generation); 2) a corresponding inner understanding of and cooperation with God's plan of salvation together with a longing for its fulfillment, which is elicited from the witnesses, both explicit and implicit, and figures of the old testament; 3) an ever deeper embodying of grace in the world in its historical course, so as to penetrate it in its own created being and guide it to its true home, and so to attain to the incarnation of God—Deus cum limo—the integritas universi (see Breviloquium 4, fourth ed, Quar 5, 244).

It may be objected that this theology of history is necessarily confined to the time of the old testament, the one time when the great stages of salvation could coincide with the different epochs of world history, and that, once the fullness and end of the times are reached in Christ, any subsequent interpretation along these lines of the stages of history is impossible and superfluous. It is true that the older theologians made the whole course of world history fit into the chronology of the bible, and saw the eschatological consciousness of the new testament as an awaiting and experiencing of the last, the seventh period of time, the time of Christ, as a brief coda to the preceding. But our consciousness of history extends so much further in both directions that the old idea of world history implied in the history of the incarnation of the word is no longer relevant. So nowadays it is the archeologists (Albright) and culture philosophers studying the near east who assure us that we must not just give up the whole project. Unhampered by the doubts and inhibitions of the theologians, they approach the whole question from the opposite end, from the angle of secular history, and ask what part the bible plays in the two millennia before Christ, so decisive for the spiritual development of mankind. All that precedes them is but a vast, uncoordinate series of events, of hardly more than biological significance, preceding the real history of culture. What follows is hardly more than the logical outcome of the premises laid down in that period; for it was during those two millennia that the spirit broke through and allowed of the formation of higher cultures and their social structures, their political, religious and esthetic myth; and from these essential prerequisites there finally emerged the birth of abstract ideas, and so of liberty of thought and of the universality of spiritual understanding in the Greek world. It was this period, so decisive for the human destiny of mankind (what Jaspers calls the "axis period") that the historical articulation of the divine revelation occurred, on the one hand pursuing its course in sovereign independence, quite apart from the political and religious designs of the great nations all around, and on the other not simply rejecting this world of culture but reckoning with it and adapting it. "Moses was instructed in all the wisdom of the Egyptians" (Acts 7:22); the cultural influence of Mesopotamia and Syria on the thought and categories of the bible need not be emphasized.

The question thus arises, decisive for our subject, whether the historical development that took place in the sphere of the biblical revelation has any sort of inner relationship to the contemporary development in the near eastern culture within which the minute state of Israel was embedded. There is no question here of deriving the "progress" in the religious sphere from that in the secular, or of simply proving them parallel. Yet we have to ask whether the clearly visible steps by which the spirit of biblical revelation—in contrast to the rigid conservatism of the Jews—in its own fashion emerges on the plane of the incarnation, form a process having no real bearing on the steps by which the spirit of the world advances from one level of understanding to another until it reaches the plane of a universal human culture in Greece. The question suggests itself more readily if we do not ascribe the biblical revelation and its gradual development solely or even primarily to God acting from outside and above, but rather to the growth of real understanding among the jewish people of the spiritual consequences arising from a vital religious element present since the time of Abraham and Moses. There is no reason to regard this question and a possibly affirmative answer as an encroachment of liberalism into theology. It is in fact simply the extension, only now made possible, of one of the central aspects of patristic and scholastic theology, and more profoundly a necessary outcome of christology in its fullest sense. For the history of the human race, into which the redeemer inserts himself, is not divided into two clearly separate and distinct histories. There is only one history, that of man from paradise to the last day, and its significance is not exhausted in the fact of Adam's fall and the eschatological redemption through Christ. Nor does the divine seed implanted in world history, there to "die and rise again," wish to establish its own second history alongside the first, but rather to propagate salvation in the one and only history. Let it suffice here only to note this conclusion and its necessity, though it still requires a great deal of elaboration and analysis. We simply propound a thesis without fully exploring the grounds which support it, but we do so in view of the implications of the word which, in their interaction, seem to lead to this conclusion. Theology of course cannot, in hegelian fashion, reach a full clarification of the meaning of world history, which would make Christ's judgment superfluous. But it can reach the decisive conclusion that if secular history in its temporal ramifications is proved to be of real consequence in the biblical sphere, it cannot, in its secular meaning, be indifferent as regards sacred history, for it has *in its totality* been impregnated through and through by the word.

A similar relationship holds good between the categories (we might say the archetypes) of the natural religious reason and the biblical teaching of the living God and the unique redeemer of mankind. This was brought out with increasing force from Justin and the Alexandrians up to Eusebius, from whose time it was never lost to view. A purely passive "hearing reason" is self-contradictory; thus man's thought of God, even when allowance is made for the excessive presumption of reason tainted by original sin, cannot persist without some rudimentary system in which it tries to represent the relations between God and man in the events of history. What happens perforce is that the word of God, in replacing the false gods, condemns and indeed scorns the material content of man's ideas of the Godhead, but nonetheless takes over for its own use the bare framework, and thus, on occasion, even preserves (in the economy of grace) something of the content. Why should the sapiential books and the epistle to the Hebrews not employ the language and modes of thought of platonist cosmology and theology to reveal the truth of what Plato dimly envisaged? Why should Paul not use the language of those whom he addressed in explaining the mystery of Christ to the Ephesians or the Colossians? To his mind it was only necessary to see the myth of these jewish gnostics aright, that is, in the critical light of the actual events of the life of Christ, in order to make clear that it too had some intimation of the truth. At the same time he held that Christ's redemptive acts must be seen in the light of the myth for only then does one aspect of the truth emerge, namely that the law, its enmity, the crushing of this enmity by Christ, all had a cosmic scope, affecting in other words the whole universe of being; that these are not merely moral but ontological phenomena. Such is Schlier's interpretation of the mind of Paul, and he goes on to say: "Formally and basically, what Paul's interpretation of the gnostic ideas amounts to is their adaptation to the apostolic message. This process of continual reinterpretation carried out, consciously, in the apostolic mind, indeed in christian thought generally, is a sign of a consistent essential correspondence in the objective order. For why whould we not be allowed to do as regards the gnostics what is accepted as regards the Jews? Probably we have here a latent dogmatic prejudice. . . ." (*On Eph* 133).

Furthermore why should John not pour out the content of his singular visions into the mold of contemporary apocalyptic speech? This is what the catholic epistles did in large measure, and what Christ himself did not scorn to do. It is not just a matter of literary form, a choice of one rather than another equally good, as a comparison with the texts of the Torah makes clear; but this is no reason to treat the matter shame-facedly. For it should not be too difficult to ascertain the correct mean between a theology which admits the necessity of myth on the grounds that sinful reason cannot do other than construct idols, and so be unable to discard them in its theology, and a liberal theology which fails to attribute to God's word the final judgment in the confrontation. A theology that discards natural judgment cannot escape it, since the bible is about natural religion. Such a theology may attempt to relegate it to the forecourts of philology and archeology, tamen usque redibit. But we may then be thankful for the difficulty of the problem which sends us, when we tire of philosophizing, back again to look at the theology of the bible.

Augustin Bea
1881-1968

Bea was born in Riedböhringen, Baden, Germany. Afflicted with a lung ailment, he nearly died at age eleven. After two years of study at the University of Freiburg, he went to Holland to join the Jesuits in 1902. He studied in Valkenburg and Innsbruck, and was ordained in 1912. During World War I he supervised a convalescent center in Aachen, then in 1917 he began to teach Old Testament in Valkenburg. When the German Jesuit province was revived in 1921, Bea was named first provincial, residing in Munich, but in 1924 he was sent to Rome to begin his career of teaching at the Biblical Institute.

Becoming rector of the Institute in 1930, Bea visited the associated Jesuit Biblical school in Jerusalem each spring, using the opportunity also to take part in some of the archaeological expeditions sponsored by the school. During this period he also edited Biblica, *the review of scriptural studies published by the Institute, and exercised considerable influence in opening the way for the acceptance of modern views and methods in Bible study. He played a large role in the preparation of Pius XII's encyclical* Divino Afflante Spiritu *in 1943.*

Pope John XXIII named Bea a cardinal in 1959 and made him head of the new Secretariat for Promoting Christian Unity in the following year. When Vatican II opened in 1962, many viewed Bea as Pope John's personal spokesman in the debates.

It was one of the strange twists of the Council that this relatively conservative octagenarian became the symbol of the reform movement, paired off against another octagenarian, Cardinal Ottaviani, the symbol of those who saw no need to change.

The work reproduced here originated in the context of the Council. As Bea explained, "During the first session of Vatican II a number of my brother bishops asked me—and very insistently—to compose for them a brief, clear, and easily understandable exposé of the questions raised by Form Criticism."He circulated his thoughts in mimeographed form among the Council Fathers. Two years later, when the April 21, 1964, Instruction of the Biblical Commission on The Historical Truth of the Gospels *appeared, Bea allowed his work to be printed as a kind of commentary on that document. It originally appeared in two installments in* Civiltà Cattolica *in June 1964, then later in book form as* The Study of the Synoptic Gospels: New Approaches and Outlooks.

What follows is the first half of that book. As Bea says in the foreword, "It seeks to show above all how the results of the most modern research and studies on the Gospels are consonant with the age-old principles of Catholic exegesis. Not only may these results be utilized by the Catholic commentator who would live up to the tradition of his forebears in explaining the word of God to the faithful, but he must use them."

The origin of the work must be kept in mind to appreciate its genius. This is not the work of a pioneer researcher at the cutting edge of contemporary investigation. It is rather a patient, conciliatory, elementary effort on the part of a well-informed churchman to open a window on an area which he knew many of his fellow bishops were accustomed to view with suspicion. It was precisely in this role of "promoter of peaceful progress" that Cardinal Bea made his finest contribution in the final decade of his life.

THE STUDY
OF THE SYNOPTIC GOSPELS

CHAPTER I

THE HISTORICITY OF THE SYNOPTIC GOSPELS FROM A HUMAN
POINT OF VIEW

E veryone who is acquainted with the present status of Catholic exegesis, and in particular with that of the Gospels, will recognize the great importance of the recent Instruction of the Pontifical Biblical Commission on the Historical Truth of the Gospels. For there was, and still is, a whole series of important questions about them which can best be summed up under the heading, "the application of the principles of the encyclical of Pope Pius XII, *Divino afflante Spiritu,* to the interpretation of the Gospels". This immediately implies—again after two decades of meditation and study on that encyclical—a fresh consideration of this fundamental document. For its importance and modernity are constantly being revealed to us.

The proximate occasion of the publication of the recent Instruction is the fact that today there is a proliferation of writings which question the truth of the sayings and events contained in the Gospels. The Instruction speaks of this situation in general and does not state that this is happening specifically among Catholics. But the result of it is to create notable bewilderment and perplexity not only in the circle of the specialists, but more widely in the whole Catholic world. Consequently, the need has been felt for some time now of an official document that would clarify the situation.

To understand the nature of the basic problem discussed in the Instruction, some reference must be made to Form Criticism which in the last half century has posed the problem of the historicity of the Gospels in a new and special way. In an effort to explain the genesis of the Gospels, the proponents of this method of criticism have often affirmed that the setting in which the Gospel message originally took shape was the primitive Christian community which resembles the popular setting where legends are born. Such settings are indeed both creative and susceptible to influence from ambient cultures. These two factors give rise to alterations and deformations of the primitive content. Now it is said that the Gospel message, before being fixed in writing, was exposed in this way to alterations, intrusions, and in part at least to serious deformations. Given such a point of view, a problem naturally arises for the Catholic exegete: what is the credibility and the historical value of the Gospels accounts? Do they really give us an authentic picture of the life and the teaching of Jesus?

Now this generic problem can be posed in a twofold way —or in two stages. One can ask, first of all in general, whether the Gospels are documents of historical value, whether they really intend to report faithfully events which historically occurred, and whether they actually do so in a way that makes their testimony trustworthy. Secondly, the problem can be posed by beginning with the presupposition of Catholic teaching that the Gospels are inspired by God. They enjoy an absolute inerrancy because their primary and principal author is God who is truth itself, whereas every work of man, even of the best informed and best motivated, is always subject to the danger of error. If this is so, the question arises: how is one to judge the differences in the various Gospels as they recount the same event or report the same saying of Jesus? For it is well known that even the most crucial words of the Lord, such as the Our Father and the words with which he instituted the Eucharist, are not recorded by the Gospels in a fully uniform manner, but rather with variations. Hence the question: how does one explain these facts and show that the Gospels actually do state what historically occurred and that there is no error in the way in which they state it, but rather that this is perfectly consonant historical truth?

These two ways of considering the Gospels and their historicity find counterparts in the Instruction of the Biblical Commission itself. For it states that one must apply to the Gospels as to any other human composition, the criteria of the historical method (par. IV). At the same time, one must keep in mind that the apostles in their preaching were filled with the Holy Spirit and were guided by him; and furthermore that the Gospels were written under the inspiration of the Holy Spirit who guarded the authors from all error (par. XI). In this first chapter, then, we begin by treating only the first of these two aspects of the problem. The second—that concerned with inspiration and inerrancy—will form the subject of Chapter II.

The first step, then, is to explain and evaluate the essential points of Form Criticism, that is, its main theoretical presuppositions and its methodology. When this has been done, it will be possible to propose an explanation of the salient data and the main problems arising from this method and to draw the proper conclusions bearing on the historicity of the Synoptic Gospels. Our aim is to show that the Gospels, even aside from their divine inspiration and considered solely from a purely human and historical point of view, are worthy of credence; that their testimony fully merits consideration. Since Form Criticism has cast doubt not only on the Catholic doctrine of the divine inspiration of the Gospels, but also on their purely human historical value, there is need to establish, first of all, this very value. It is an essential factor, and constitutes the indispensable foundation for all the rest. As Pope Leo XIII remarked, "Since the divine and infallible magisterium of the Church rests also on the authority of Holy Scripture, the first thing to be done is to vindicate the trustworthiness of the sacred records, at least as human documents.'

1. The methodology of Form Criticism

Form Criticism aims at explaining the origin of our Gospels, by reconstructing the "history", that is, the genesis and the development, of the "forms" in which the Gospel message was presented, preached, and passed on, until it was definitely fixed in the Gospels as we have them today. More precisely, it is a question of the "history of the *formation*" of the Gospels.

To understand Form Criticism, we must take into account the various sources on which it has drawn, especially literary criticism, sociology, and the history of religions. The early proponents of Form Criticism, in interpreting the New Testament and especially the Gospels, were inspired principally by the work of H. Gunkel on literary forms and on the formation of the books of Genesis and the Psalms. The studies of Gunkel and of other Old Testament scholars who furthered his work served as a model for the Form Critics. In applying to the Gospel narratives the findings of all these studies and disciplines, Form Criticism seeks to understand the genesis of the present text of the Synoptic Gospels. Through literary criticism of the present Gospels, it uncovers the smallest units which existed prior to the present Gospel framework and determines the "literary forms" of these smaller elements (for example, "sayings and maxims", "controversies", "miracle stories", etc.). It also seeks to fix the *Sitz im Leben* (or *vital context*) of these smaller elements.

Now this *Sitz im Leben,* the cradle in which the Gospel message was born and grew, is said to have been *the primitive Christian community.* To understand the work of this community with respect to the Gospels, one must first of all understand the community itself. According to the Form Critics, analysis of the New Testament and especially of the Gospels shows that the primitive community from which the Gospels come to us (or better, from which what the Gospels narrate come to us) was quite similar to popular milieux, or anonymous masses, in which legends are born. According to at least one group of Form Critics the primitive community neither had nor was able to have an interest in history since it lived in eager expectation of the imminent end of the world and of the glorious coming of Christ. What would be the point of such a community being interested in history, that is, in past events? Even apart from this view of the eschatological school the question arises: what possible interest in history could be had by common men such as the apostles and the simple folk of the primitive community?

The Form Critics speak of "legends", because the Gospels are a product of "faith", and not of history. Faith and the attitude of an historian are incompatible; faith is nothing more than the taking of a stand in favour of the object, whereas the attitude of an historian must of necessity be absolutely objective and impartial. As the principle phrased by Tacitus has it, the historian must write *sine ira et studio* (without passion and attachment).

Another characteristic of the community, of the popular environment in which the Gospel was born and grew, was that it was "creative". Impressed by some act or word recounted by those who saw it or heard it, the community further developed it—explaining, drawing on its imagination to make additions, borrowing from the religious ideas of its environment to clarify and increase the original data. Thus the original material grew in size and was handed down in ever increasing quantities.

2. *The reasons for such a position*

And in proof? The reply to this question is that literary criticism permits one to pass through diverse strata, as it were, and in the process isolate first the larger groupings of passages and then the small, primary units. These are labelled, according to the literary forms variously assigned by different critics, as "sayings and maxims", "miracle stories", "controversies", and the like. It is also said that the literary forms of these small units as well as the literary presentation employed in them are found in contemporary Rabbinic and Hellenistic literature. There are also similarities in ideas and content. Hence the conclusion: there must have been borrowing by Christian writers from these sources. Further, only on the supposition that there existed a creative activity in the primitive community can one explain the lack of precision, the loose way of narrating, and the undeniable differences among the Gospels. It is up to the historian, then, to excise by patient analytical labour all that little by little accrued, that is, legendary elements or whatever was added by popular fancy. Above all he must remove elements borrowed from neighbouring religions, known Hellenistic myths about earthly apparitions of the gods, their intervention and involvement in earthly events. Only in this way can one gradually uncover the real historical nucleus of the life of Christ and of his message. Thus what we know historically of both the life and the teaching of Christ is really very little.

As can be seen from this last conclusion, we are dealing with a type of criticism no less destructive than that of Strauss or Friedrich Christian Baur of the past century. Only the method is different. Even in cases where such extreme conclusions as these are not reached, it often tends to weaken the historical value of the Gospels. It is thus of the utmost importance to get a clear view of the matter.

3. *Presuppositions or theoretical postulates of Form Criticism*

Let us look, first of all, at the presuppositions or, more exactly, the theoretical postulates of Form Criticism. The first of these postulates is that the material at the source of our Gospels comes from an anonymous primitive community which had no historical interests. This community, precisely because it was carried along by faith, was incapable of taking the position of objectivity which is essential for the historian; history and faith are incompatible. In addition, this community was creative, that is, it elaborated the material it received—expanding, inventing from its imagination, combining borrowings from the religions of its environment.

Now against these gratuitous affirmations stand the following facts:

The primitive Christian community is not an anonymous community but one which is *well known to us, guided by the apostles* as authorized eyewitnesses. So it appears, in fact, at Jerusalem, where Peter repeatedly preaches as the head of an apostolic college (Acts ii. 14-40; iii. 12-26; iv. 8-12; v. 29-32). He has already acted as the head of that group in the election of a substitute to take Judas' place, even before the Pentecostal descent of the Spirit (Acts i. 15-26). Then, when the good news spreads beyond Jerusalem, the leaders Peter and John go to "inspect" the communities, for instance in Samaria (Acts viii. 14-17). Or Peter alone moves about through the different cities of the Palestinian plain (Acts ix. 32-42). Later Barnabas comes for the same reason to Antioch, having been sent from Jerusalem (Acts xi. 22-3). We are not, then, confronted with the preaching of enthusiasts and fanatics, but with preaching that is well organized and directed by the apostles.

Later on, in his own way, Luke reflects this situation in the introduction to his Gospel. "Inasmuch as many have undertaken to compile a narrative of the things which have been accomplished among us, just as they were delivered to us by those who from the beginning were eyewitnesses and ministers of the word, it seemed good to me also, having followed all things closely for some time past, to write an orderly account . . ." (Luke i. 1-3). Neither Luke's predecessors nor the evangelist himself made it a rule to cull everything that was recounted in the community about Jesus, but only that which the authorized eyewitnesses had passed on who had become in time the ministers of the word.

From all this it follows that the apostles had a *genuine interest in history*. Obviously they did not intend to write history after the manner of Greek or Roman historiography, that is to say, a history ordered either chronologically or as a chain of cause and effect—history, that is, as an "end in itself". Nevertheless, their interest contained what is essential for any interest in history—the intention to report and faithfully to transmit past deeds and sayings.

A good proof of this is the very notion of "witness", "testimony", or "bearing witness" which in its diverse forms occurs over one hundred and fifty times in the New Testament. For a witness is a person who is in a position to affirm something officially, as it were, on the basis of his own immediate experience. The apostles refer to themselves repeatedly as witnesses of the events of the life of Jesus (Acts i. 22; ii. 32; iii. 15; v. 32; x. 39, 41; xiii. 31; xxii. 15; xxvi. 16; 1 Pet. v. 1). Jesus indeed had said to them before his ascension, "You shall be my witnesses" (Acts i. 8; cf. Luke xxiv. 48). Then in the Cenacle during the period between the ascension and the descent of the Spirit on Pentecost, when the problem of finding a substitute for Judas arose, certain qualities were explicitly required in him. He would have to be a person who had been an eyewitness of the deeds of Jesus "during all the time that the Lord Jesus went in and out among us from the baptism of John until the day that he was taken up from us" (Acts i. 21-2). When St Paul lists for the Corinthians the official witnesses who had seen the risen Lord, he says, "[Christ] appeared to Cephas, then to the Twelve. Then he appeared to more than five hundred brethren at one time, most of whom are still alive, though some have fallen asleep. Then he appeared to James, then to all the apostles . . ." (1 Cor. xv. 5-7).

Yet even if the main *object* of the apostolic *testimony* was the resurrection of Christ, in consonance with its fundamental importance, it was not its sole and exclusive object. On the contrary, the resurrection itself demanded in a very emphatic way the explanation of all that preceded it. For if it really constitutes the supreme glorification of Jesus of Nazareth, it all the more urgently calls for an explanation of his condemnation and death. Indeed, it is well known that the primitive preaching of the apostles pointed to an historical cause of this condemnation and death, ascribing it to the actions of the Jerusalem leaders (see Acts ii. 23; iii. 13, 15; iv. 27; v. 30; x. 39; xiii. 28). But it also proposed a more profound reason, a supernatural one, the fulfilment of the salvific will of God already made manifest in the Scriptures (Acts ii. 23; iii. 18; iv. 28; xiii. 27; 1 Cor. xv. 3). The two causes are intimately connected. A truncated or defective explanation of the events of the historical order would have run the risk at least of creating doubts about the realization of a specific plan of salvation on God's part. For that reason it was necessary to explain not only the facts connected with the trial and the death of Jesus, but also those which preceded little by little for the final conflict. It was necessary to expose the occasions and the motives which led up to the conflict itself. Jesus had made claims about his person and his messianic, divine dignity. Statements had been made about the responsbilities of the leaders of the Jews and the future destiny of the people. Finally, the genesis, development and climax of the conflict itself had to be explained. In other words, there had to be an exposition of several points of doctrine intimately connected with the account of the basic facts. This was all the more urgent since Jesus had asserted with considerable emphasis that the Kingdom of God had come with him (Luke xi. 20; Mark i. 15). In using that notable formula, "You have heard that it was said to the men of old . . . but I say to you" (Matt. v. 21), he had contrasted his own person and his teaching with the very foundation of the Mosaic tradition. And yet, his teaching was not just another one of the many traditions passed on to the Chosen People, but rather the teaching of the promised teacher of messianic times.

Finally, from all that has been said it is clear how we must regard the alleged *creative activity* of the primitive community. Let us prescind from the value of the philosophico-sociological theory on which this allegation rests. Today this theory no longer finds the favour among scholars it once did. It is sufficient to recall the facts that have been thus far set forth in order to prove its inaccuracy. For the apostles were authorized witnesses of Jesus and of the events of his life—and not only of the most important events, but also of others intimately connected with them. They witnessed his public life and his preaching.

Moreover, a rather characteristic feature of such preaching was its transmission or "tradition". This involves the ability to receive a teaching, to preserve it, and to pass it on faithfully (cf. 2 Thess. ii. 15; 1 Cor. xi. 2, 23; xv. 1-3; 1 Thess. ii. 13; 2 Thess. iii. 6; Rom. vi. 17; Gal. i. 9, 12; Phil. iv. 9; Col. ii. 6, 8). We should recall above all the well-known formulae of St Paul, "I received . . . what I also passed on to you" (1 Cor. xi. 23); "I passed on to you as of prime importance what I myself received" (1 Cor. xv. 3). Again and again he echoed the advice to preserve the teaching as it had been passed down (2 Thess. ii. 14; 1 Cor. xv. 2; xi. 2). Once he even used a very strong expression in this regard: "Even if we, or an angel from heaven, should preach to you a Gospel contrary to that which we preached to you, let him be damned. As we have said before, so now I say again, If anyone is preaching to you a Gospel contrary to what you have received, let him be damned" (Gal. i. 8-9).

In speaking of such preaching, Paul reports that he went up to Jerusalem "as a result of a revelation", and there laid before them the Gospel that he was preaching among the Gentiles. This he did in private before those who were men of repute, in order to be sure that he "was not running or had run in vain" (Gal. ii. 2). Paul thus refers to the "council" of Jerusalem which is so important for the subject we are discussing. For it was concerned with the controversy which arose over Paul's preaching among the pagans and over the obligations to be imposed on Gentile converts. Various communities of Jewish Christians had been disturbed over this matter because of Paul's preaching. But the controversy in itself shows that the communities exercised a control, one over the other, in the matter of fidelity to the transmission of the Gospel message. The controversy between Paul and the Judaizers was brought before the elders and above all settled by the apostles. The profound significance of this recourse to the apostles and of their intervention is seen in the fact that whether an accusation of infidelity was levelled or a defence was made against such an accusation, there was a common, deep conviction that one must faithfully preserve and pass on unadulterated the received teaching, and that the apostles were to guard over it.

4. *Methods and procedures of Form Criticism*

(*a*) Let us note in the first place a *methodological error* which Form Critics frequently commit in using the comparative history of religions. The argument usually runs as follows. In the small units shown to exist in the Gospels we find the same literary forms and the same literary presentation as in Rabbinic and Hellenistic literatures; hence we are dealing with elements borrowed from these literatures. Now it is known that the external form of a literary unit is generally dictated by its subject-matter. This is especially true in the Near East, where the same subject-matter is usually treated in quasi-stereotyped terms. Consequently, similarity in literary presentation does not really prove dependence or borrowing, nor does it argue against the truthfulness of the account. For one must attend not only to form but to content as well. When the Gospels are compared with the religions of neighbouring lands, the point which clamours for explanation is the unique element of originality in the Gospel message. It is something for which there is no counterpart either in parallels taken from the religions of the Gospel environment or in parallels taken from religions of other environments. What is more, against the hypothesis of borrowings stands the incontrovertible fact of the apostles' scrupulous care to hand down the deeds and sayings of Christ with fidelity and to see to it that everything be preserved unaltered.

(*b*) Another methodological procedure used by Form Critics is that of *literary criticism*. Literary criticism has no necessary connection with the gratuitous theoretical postulates discussed above, since it is neither the exclusive patrimony of Form Criticism nor was it invented by it. Form Criticism, it is true, has developed a special way of applying literary criticism to the Gospels, but only after having borrowed this way from various studies of the Old Testament (as was observed earlier) were, moderately, prudently, and soberly employed, it has produced good results. For some time now literary criticism has been widely employed by Catholic exegetes. In their "Introductions" to the individual books of Sacred Scripture they try to illustrate with data *taken from the book in question* the person of the author, his characteristics, his mentality, his style and language, and his purpose. All of these factors are precious data which must be kept in mind by the one who wishes to interpret the book.

The Encyclical *Divino afflante Spiritu* itself deduces the ultimate reason for such a procedure from the fact of inspiration, that is to say from the fact that the human author of a book of the Bible has been employed by the Holy Spirit as a living and intelligent instrument. When an author writes a book under the inspiration of the Holy Spirit, he keeps the full use of his powers and faculties, with the result that all can easily gather from the book produced by his work his distinctive genius and his individual characteristics and features, as Pope Benedict XV indicated in his Encyclical *Spiritus Paraclitus*. For this reason too Pope Pius XII added his exhortation, "Let the interpreter then endeavour with all care and without neglecting any light derived from recent research to determine the distinctive genius of the sacred writer, his condition in life, the age in which he lived, the written or oral sources he may have used, and the literary forms he employed. He will thus be better able to discover who the sacred writer was and what he meant by what he wrote."

(c) A final procedure used by Form Critics is *to determine and to study literary forms*. In this area various proponents of Form Criticism have clearly gone too far in following criteria that were more often than not subjective. It is no wonder, then, that considerable diversity in determining such forms reigns among them. Their classifications, often minutely detailed, seem to correspond more to Hellenistic Greek than to Semitic mentality. It is certainly also an abuse the way some authors have recourse to an alleged literary form in the face of any and every difficulty. Still more objectionable are the tendentious classifications and the use of terms which imply doubt (or worse) about the historical value of the accounts, as, for, example, when they speak of "legends".

And yet neither the excess nor the abuse nor even that degree of uncertainty which inevitably accompanies such study—particularly at the outset—is a reason for condemning the procedure as such.

The existence of definite modes of speaking, narrating, and of teaching which are proper to Sacred Scripture has always been recognized by all who have had any familiarity with the Bible. The meaning of such modes of speaking and of expressing oneself is not always easy to determine. But it becomes progressively more intelligible as the literature of the ancient Near East comes gradually to light—a process that is as yet far from being finished. Every serious student takes account of this difficulty. Recently the Encyclical *Divino afflante Spiritu* recognized it, saying:

> Frequently the literal sense is not as obvious in the words and writings of ancient oriental authors as it is in the writers of our own time. For what they wished to express is not to be determined by the rules of grammar and philology alone, nor solely by the context. It is absolutely necessary for the interpreter to go back in spirit to those remote centuries of the East, and with the aid of history, archæology, ethnology, and other sciences, determine what literary forms the writers of that ancient period intended to use and did in fact employ.

It is important to note that in speaking of literary forms the Encyclical not only refers to poetry and doctrinal statements, but also to the manner of recounting *facts and historical events*. It is precisely in this very context, in fact, that the Encyclical underlines the singular fidelity to historical truth by which Israel excelled the peoples of the ancient Near East. For the Encyclical adds: "At the same time, no one who has a correct idea of biblical inspiration will be surprised to find that the sacred writers, like any other ancient authors, employ certain fixed ways of exposition and narration, certain idioms especially characteristic of the Semitic languages, so-called approximations and certain hyperbolical expressions and even paradoxical expressions designed for the sake of emphasis." The Encyclical insists that the use of these modes of expression is decidedly not against divine inspiration.

With all these reasons as its basis, the Encyclical *Divino afflante Spiritu* directs a serious exhortation to Catholic exegetes. They must make "prudent use of this means" (i. e. of the study of the literary forms of the Bible), in order to "respond fully to the present needs of biblical science". It further says, "And let him [the exegete] be convinced that this part of his task cannot be neglected without great detriment to Catholic exegesis". One should not miss with regard to this exhortation the new and important specification given to it in the Instruction of the Biblical Commission. If anyone had the impression, for one reason or another, that the principles of the Encyclical *Divino afflante Spiritu* concerning the literary genres of the Bible referred only to the Old Testament, he is informed by the Instruction that this impression is not correct. In this respect the Instruction is evidently providing an authentic interpretation of the encyclical. For it states,

> By this piece of advice Pius XII of happy memory enunciated a general rule of hermeneutics by which the books of the Old Testament as well as the New must be explained. For in composing them the sacred writers employed the way of thinking and writing which was in vogue among their contemporaries (par. IV).

This is a matter of a *general* rule of hermeneutics. Indeed, when there is need of an accurate interpretation—especially in theological matters—every exegete knows what valuable help is derived from the determination or discovery of the mode of speaking, of presenting a maxim, of developing a discussion, or of singling out the precise point towards which the whole passage is converging. This concern for the literary form aids him to discover precisely what the author intended to say. And this is, according to St Athanasius and the Encyclical *Divino afflante Spiritu,* the "supreme rule of interpretation" (*summa interpretandi norma*).

5. *Form in which the Gospel message was originally presented and transmitted*

With the theoretical presuppositions and procedures of Form Criticism thus clarified we are in a position—as far as one can be within our restricted compass—to answer the questions, "In what forms was the Gospel message originally presented and then transmitted?"

The Instruction gives a directive on this very point. "The exegete will use all the means available to probe more deeply into the nature of Gospel testimony, into the religious life of the early Churches, and into the sense and the value of apostolic tradition" (par. IV). A little further on it undertakes this very task itself, by indicating the general lines of such probing in a way consonant with its purpose. "To judge properly concerning the reliability of what is transmitted in the Gospels, the interpreter should pay diligent attention to the three stages of tradition by which the doctrine and the life of Jesus have come down to us" (par. VI). The three stages, described in some detail in the rest of the Instruction, are these: (*a*) what Christ the Lord did in proposing his teaching and educating the apostles; (*b*) what the apostles did; (*c*) finally, what the authors of the Gospels did.

The contribution of Jesus, insofar as it pertains to the genesis of the Gospels, is found in his preaching and the instruction given to the apostles that they might be in a position to continue his work. It will be sufficient to cite the short passage of the Instruction itself dealing with this stage of tradition, since different aspects of his work have already been emphasized in the preceding pages, and we can return later to one point or another. The Biblical Commission speaks as follows:

Christ our Lord joined to himself chosen disciples (Mark iii. 14; Luke vi. 13), who followed him from the beginning (Luke i. 2; Acts i. 21-2), saw his deeds, heard his words, and in this way were equipped to be witnesses to his life and doctrine (Luke xxiv. 48; John xv. 27; Acts i. 8; x. 39; xiii. 31). When the Lord was orally explaining his doctrine, he followed the modes of reasoning and of exposition which were in vogue at the time. He accommodated himself to the mentality of his listeners and saw to it that what he taught was firmly impressed on the mind and easily remembered by the disciples. These men understood the miracles and other events of the life of Jesus correctly, as deeds performed or designed that men might believe in Christ through them, and embrace with faith the doctrine of salvation (par. VII).

As for the second stage of the Gospel tradition, *the contribution of the apostles,* our point of departure is the conclusion reached above, that in the final analysis the Gospels come from the preaching of the apostles, the "ministers of the word" (Luke i. 2). For that reason we must make sure to give a clear picture of that preaching, since its distinctive features will necessarily become part of the Gospels.

(*a*) We recall what has been explained above. Preaching does not mean the drawing up of a complete and chronologically ordered "Life of Christ" in the modern sense of the word. This was not the task Christ gave to the apostles. Besides, a very superficial analysis of the Gospels shows at once that this was neither the intention of the authors of the Gospels nor of the apostolic preaching.

And yet, that preaching had an aim which was *fundamentally historico-biographical.* Not that it intended to compose a biography in our sense of the word, but that it tended to preserve facts about the life of a person, Jesus of Nazareth, facts about his existence and his activity in the context of his teaching.

It is true that in this complex of details the events of the death and resurrection hold the first place—as they are emphasized in the Instruction. But these very events demand an explanation. And this was sought in the deeds of Jesus' public life, in his claims to dignity, and in his teaching.

(*b*) This apostolic preaching differed too from ordinary history by the *specific purpose* for which it preserved and handed on the historical facts. It was "preaching", that is to say the proposing and explaining of facts related to *religious instruction* which was to be accepted with faith as man's way to salvation. Now as has already been seen, it is certainly not true that faith and history are incompatible. On the contrary, the faith of the New Testament was precisely of a nature to suppose the historical truth of facts and to base itself upon them. Faith and history do not exclude one another, but the religious aim influenced the *presentation* of the facts, without however changing the facts themselves. This religious purpose required that the facts be explained to one who had not experienced them or who perhaps came from a different environment from that in which the events occurred. The explanation then was given by witnesses who after the descent of the Holy Spirit on the feast of Pentecost were mature in the faith and understood a great many things which they had not understood during the earthly life of Jesus. It was natural for these men to explain things (without altering them) in the light of this more profound understanding of the facts and the doctrine.

(*c*) This practical, religious aim had still another consequence. Since it was a matter of "preaching", the facts were clearly not handed on mechanically but rather *in a vital way which corresponded to the character of each preacher.* The various preachers were in agreement on the facts and the substance of what they reported, as was demanded by the exacting responsibility of fidelity to their charge of bearing witness to Christ—to his life, activity, and teaching. But their preaching necessarily differed from preacher to preacher. This was all the more natural since they were eyewitnesses and earwitnesses who were not interdependent. Each was aware of his own previous experience. And it was made up of varying personal observations and varying personal impressions of the person of Jesus, of his deeds and his sayings. This variety was reflected in the preaching. The very *manner of recounting* or explaining things varied according to the different qualities of the speakers' personalities. (How well these features are revealed in the Gospels!) For that reason, even the living "tradition" which the evangelists inherited necessarily had various forms. The comparative study of the synoptic Gospels, carried out in the last decades and extending to the most minute details, shows that one cannot suppose that a *completely uniform* oral tradition underlies the Gospels. In addition to the main lines and the many details on which the evangelists agree, there are perceptible differences in the sayings or deeds narrated as well as in the manner of recounting them.

(*d*) Another characteristic note of this apostolic preaching was that it remained *on the popular level*. This was true not only because its authors (the apostles) were simple folk who were not especially educated, but also because they found their principal audience among people of humble circumstances. Thus one should not expect them to speak about Christ after the manner of an official record obtained from archives. Even less should one expect from them the sort of thing to which modern man is so accustomed, a stenographer's report, or the accuracy of a photograph or tape recording. It is sufficient to recall in this regard the vague nature of the many chronological indications which are contained in the formulae of transition, such as "and then", "on that day", "at that time", etc.

The Instruction, going still further, illustrates the adaptation of the apostles' preaching to its specific purpose and to the mentality of its listeners by enumerating the different ways of proposing the message of Christ which is observed in the Gospels. Account must be taken of these different ways: "catecheses, stories, testimonia, hymns, doxologies, prayers— and other literary forms of this sort which were in Sacred Scripture and were accustomed to be used by men of that time" (par. VIII).

(*e*) In speaking of the "council" of Jerusalem above, we noted that the faithful preservation and transmission of the teaching of Jesus did not imply a *mechanical* transmission. It was indeed inevitable that in the course of time new cases would be brought up, which had not yet been experienced in precisely that form. In such instances the really faithful preservation of the spirit of the message demanded a more profound meditation on it and an assessment of the circumstances of the case in order that the teaching might be correctly applied to it. Now the religious and didactic purpose of the preaching imme-

diately implied on the part of such a "preacher" a more profound meditation of the message in order to apply it correctly—
without any deformation of its sense or content—*to audiences
in the different environments* in which he found himself. He
did this by applying the teaching to the special needs of the
listeners, that is by emphasizing those aspects of the deeds and
sayings of Jesus which corresponded to the listeners' needs; or
by selecting from the large body of material available to him
precisely those deeds and sayings which would clarify or correct
the previous religious beliefs of his hearers, root out vices, and
encourage them in good and useful tendencies. All this the
preacher did by presenting the deeds and sayings in a manner
best suited to his aim.

Another quality of this apostolic preaching came from the
fact that it was directed to men of the people, to men of little
education, and to an environment where *few knew how to write
and books were rare.* This circumstance made it necessary to
limit the teaching to a restricted number of points, *to the
essentials, in the manner of a catechism.* It demanded that the
explanation be to a certain extent standardized. Mnemonic
devices also had to be used in order to help fix events or sayings
in the memory. We find in the Gospels mnemonic techniques
of composition in the use of the numbers 7, 3, 5, 2. There are
instances where various sayings of Christ are linked together by
means of catch-words (for example, Mark ix. 33-50; Luke vi.
38a-b). We also find compilations of the discourses of Christ
addressed to the people (Matt. v-vii), or to the disciples (Matt.
x), as well as groupings of parables (Matt. xiii; Luke iv. 1-34),
and miracle stories (Matt. viii-ix), etc.

6. *The function of the evangelists*

The third stage through which the teaching and the life of
Jesus passed was that of the commitment of the apostolic
preaching to writing. It cannot be doubted that prior to the
composition of the four Gospels the preaching of the apostles
began to be *fixed in writing.* All this is quite clear; it is deduced
from the previously cited text of St Luke in which he says that
before him "many have undertaken to compile an account of
the events that have happened among us" (Luke i. 1). It follows

that prior to our Gospels more or less extensive literary units were in existence. And these sources reproduced the various differences in the apostolic preaching we listed above.

What precisely was *the function of the evangelists* in compiling their books? It is important to get a clear understanding of this. It should not be conceived as the work of a stenographer recording a speech or a sermon. For even if the venerable tradition of the Church states that Mark wrote his Gospel is dependence on the preaching of Peter, and if Luke manifests an affinity with the ideas and preaching of Paul, none of this should be understood in an exclusive sense. Luke himself speaks in general terms of his own toil. Just as others before him undertook to compile an account of the things that happened "among us, as these were passed on to us by those who were eyewitnesses from the beginning and became ministers of the word" (Luke i. 2), so did he too, "having followed up all things closely from the beginning".

The Instruction too is quite explicit and clear in this respect. The evangelists committed to writing, it tells us, the preaching of the apostles "in four Gospels for the benefit of the Churches, with a method suited to the peculiar purpose which each one set for himself. From the many things handed down they selected some things, reduced others to a synthesis, still others they explicated as they kept in mind the situation of the Churches. With every possible means they sought that their readers might become aware of the reliability of those words by which they had been instructed (Luke i. 4)" (par. IX). The function, then, of the evangelists is stated very summarily in the Instruction with these three terms: selection, synthesis, and explication. The criterion and norm which guided their work was the purpose or goal which each evangelist proposed to himself—either the generic purpose that the readers might learn the basis of the apostolic preaching, or the more specific one motivating each of the Gospel writers. But that norm also included a respect for the situation of the readers for whom each evangelist was writing. In this regard the Instruction says:

> Indeed, from what they had received the sacred
> writers above all selected the things which were

> suited to the various situations of the faithful and to the purpose which they had in mind and adapted their narration of them to the same situations and purpose. Since the meaning of a statement also depends on the sequence, the evangelists, in passing on the words and deeds of our Saviour, explained these now in one context, now in another, depending on (their) usefulness to the readers (par. IX).

The Biblical Commission, with its own topic, the historicity of the Gospels, ever before its eyes, adds this important sentence:

> The truth of the story is not at all affected by the fact that the evangelists relate the words and deeds of the Lord in a different order, and express his sayings not literally but differently, while preserving their sense (par. IX).

This statement is supported by the authority of two of the greatest exegetes of antiquity, St John Chrysostom and St Augustine.

It is true that the evangelists were faithful to the preaching of the apostles, and to previously existing documents in which their preaching had been set down. But they still had a wide field for their own authentic activity as writers. They had to sift the documents at their disposal, collect the preaching and other testimonies of the apostles still alive, order all this material, and from it construct their book according to their own personal conceptions and the needs of their readers. Rightly therefore, even though their dependence on oral and written sources was essential, the evangelists are considered, according to ancient ecclesiastical tradition, *authors* of the Gospels which go by their names.

7. Conclusion

The examination of Form Criticism and of the facts which it has brought to light and on which it is based has revealed to us how complex was the reality in which our Gospels took shape. This reality was the living preaching of the apostles, substantially the same in its wide variety of forms, and the documents in which it was fixed prior to the Gospels.

Realization of this complexity serves at once as a warning against a characteristic tendency of modern man: the desire to solve all problems overnight. He is easily led to forget tradition and, in an impossible effort to solve personally all problems, to ignore what has been achieved and to jettison the most elementary certitudes. What is required then is rather a cautious and patient labour distinguishing what is certain and solid from what really needs further study and re-examination. In his wild haste modern man forgets that things of the spirit cannot be treated like material things; they require time for reflection and mature judgement. Otherwise, hasty and erroneous solutions to problems lead to a terrible loss of time and energy. The serious consequences of such haste are in fact to be seen in Form Criticism and especially in its extreme forms, such as "demythologization". Therefore no one should rush rashly into this type of study if he is not properly trained, especially in sound theology. And even with such training one must proceed with great patience and reflection, never losing sight of the tradition and teaching of the Church.

If, then, the reality in which our Gospels took shape was very complex, it is not for that reason less solid. It is not lost in a vague, hazy, and uncertain obscurity. Quite the contrary. Our explanation has revealed the solid basis of our Gospels, "the truth of the teaching" (Luke i. 4) which we have received. What is reported rests on the solid rock of the testimony of "the ministers of the word"—a testimony which, notwithstanding the variety of presentation, agrees not only in the larger, over-all picture, but even in many details. This testimony is worthy of our acceptance, even when there are divergences, provided that we look at them not with the mentality of today but with the patient effort of one who seeks to transfer himself to the time of the authors, to their mentality, and to their way of speaking.

Thus far we have been considering the Gospels from a purely human and historical point of view. We have not taken into account inspiration and therefore we have not asserted the absolute inerrancy of the Gospels although this is their privilege, because they are not only human works, but also and principally the work and the word of God himself. Whoever considers them in this way, as every Catholic exegete must, is confronted with still further problems. These we shall consider in the following chapter.

George Henri Tavard

1922-

George Tavard was born in Nancy, France, and studied in Paris before being ordained in Metz in 1947 as a member of the Augustinians of the Assumption. He received his doctorate in theology in 1949 from the Catholic University of Lyon, then spent two years teaching in Surrey, England. He came to the United States in 1952 and in due course became a citizen. After five years in New York City and one in Worcester, Massachusetts, he became chairman of the theology department of Mount Mercy College in Pittsburgh in 1959. In 1970 he joined the faculty of the Methodist Theological School in Ohio.

For more than a quarter-century now Fr. Tavard has been a prolific contributor to the American theological scene, especially in the area of ecumenical thought. He was a peritus at the Second Vatican Council and is a member of the Secretariat for the Promotion of Christian Unity. Among his books are: The Catholic Approach to Protestantism (1955), Holy Writ or Holy Church? (1959), Paul Tillich and the Christian Message (1962), The Quest for Catholicity (1964), and The Pilgrim Church (1967).

The excerpt that follows is taken from his commentary on the Constitution on Divine Revelation produced by Vatican II. When that document was promulgated in 1965, there was an audible sigh of relief from Catholic Biblical scholars. In three *short years such dramatic progress had been made that many could hardly believe it. What previously seemed barely tolerated was embraced by the official magisterium.*

Tavard's commentary is divided into six chapters, and we have selected the middle two for inclusion here, discussing first the plan of the Constitution, then touching on six theological problems that the document has a bearing on. In describing the conciliar process by which vast numbers of modifications were made in the original drafts, Tavard summarizes what the overall impact of these changes was: "These revisions made the text eminently pastoral, open to contemporary theology, permissive of theological plurality on controversial matters, and highly encouraging to the researches of exegetes on the interpretation of Scripture and of theologians on the nature of Tradition." In those few words one gets a sense of what made Vatican II so unusual and why it will continue to have an impact comparable to few other Councils in Church history.

That is what is meant by the common observation that the Constitution on Revelation is both progressive and conservative. It does not break new ground or open exciting new avenues of Biblical study. But neither is that what was called for from Church authority at the time. What was needed was a new attitude, putting aside as much of the polemics of the past as possible, and encouraging, even challenging, Catholic scholars to dive into rather than to dodge the difficult work to be done. The keen eye of Fr. Tavard helps one to focus on the highlights achieved by the Council Fathers in this document, and in doing so gives one a sense of the renewed way in which the Bible has been brought back to the center of Catholic life as a result.

COMMENTARY ON THE DOGMATIC CONSTITUTION ON DIVINE REVELATION

CHAPTER III

THE PLAN OF THE CONSTITUTION

The plan of the Constitution is not merely a matter of organization; it is mainly one of doctrine. The Constitution begins with a chapter on revelation and ends with one on Scripture in the life of the Church. Its entire purpose is precisely to show how revelation, given once for all in Jesus Christ to mankind as a whole, becomes life in the Church for all those who, by baptism, have been incorporated into Christ. In other words, revelation is neither essentially a doctrine, although it implies one; nor a set of propositions and formulations to be believed, although it may be partially expressed in such propositions; nor the promulgation of an ethical law of prescriptions and proscriptions, although it also implies judgment of the morality of human behavior. Essentially, revelation is a life. It is the very life of God imparted to man through the incarnation of the Son; it is the communication of God's Word understood by man in the Holy Spirit. Thus the first and the last chapters of the Constitution constitute the general framework of the document and of the doctrine it teaches. The first explains how God reveals himself; the last shows how Christians may develop the life of God in themselves by better following the mind of God as shown in the Holy Scriptures. God comes to us as a spoken Word which has resounded temporally upon earth after resounding eternally in God himself; and he is to be perceived through the words of the Scriptures.

Between revelation and the place and use of Scripture for spiritual life in the Church in general and in Christians in particular, the Council has placed several chapters of a somewhat more technical character. Revelation was given through the Word, speaking to the patriarchs and the prophets of the Old

Testament, and himself made flesh in Jesus the Savior. But this revelation was meant to reach all men, and not only those who, like St. John, were able to testify: "That which was from the beginning, which we have heard, which we have seen with our own eyes, which we have beheld, which our hands have touched of the Word of life—for the life was manifested; we have seen it, we testify to it, and we announce to you this eternal Life which was with the Father and has appeared to us—that which we have seen and heard, we announce to you, that you also may have communion with us." Revelation reached the apostles directly so that they could bear witness to the light they had seen; it has to reach those coming after the apostles through the testimony of the apostles themselves, the only qualified eyewitnesses.

How revelation reaches the believers after the time of the apostles forms the topic of chapter II: it is transmitted in a Tradition (the word "tradition" means "transmission") channeled down the ages and carried to the ends of the earth in a double movement, spread in space by missionary expansion and preserved in time by historical succession. When it is preached by the apostles and their successors, revelation becomes the Gospel, that is, the "good news", the "glad tidings" of salvation. This Good News, orally communicated by the apostles, was also written down in the Scriptures of the New Testament, which embody the apostolic tradition of the Christian covenant, as the Scriptures of the Old Testament embodied the patriarchal and prophetic tradition of the Mosaic covenant. The Holy Spirit is active both in the verbal transmission of the Good News and in the writing, the preservation and the interpretation of the Scriptures. For the Church's indefectibility is at stake in all these actions: she must be able to safeguard fidelity to the doctrine once received, and she must also be in a position to discern the mind of the Spirit when she reads the holy books. Therefore, she is assisted, though in different ways, by the grace of the Holy Spirit, who was sent, as Jesus promised, in order to "guide you into all the truth".

The logic of this line of thought leads naturally to the third chapter, where the inspiration and the interpretation of Scripture are explained. These two concepts go together in theology, as they primarily go together in the experience of those who are familiar with the spiritual reading of the Word of God. Inspiration is the process by which the Spirit took part in the writing down of Scripture, penetrating the minds of its human authors, expressing his purposes through their human conceptions, ideas, hopes, dreams, interpretations of, and reflections upon, the events of their times or of the past. Interpretation is the corresponding process of reading, by which the Church and her members endeavor to read the mind of the Spirit in the writings composed under his inspiration. Since inspiration was granted to individual men for the sake of the Holy People, whose divine calling it was destined to record in the ups and downs of the People's pilgrimage on earth, interpretation must also be made for the sake of the Holy People gathered into the Church under the new covenant. Although it has to be worked out by individual men using the human resources of their talents and scholarship, these men must pursue a purpose that is infinitely larger than they themselves can ever be: the Church's own purpose of communicating with the Father through the real Word understood in the Spirit. They are at the service of the People of God, sensing the mind of the holy community in its permanent encounter with the spoken Word of Tradition and the written Word of Scripture, thereby helping the Church in prophetic anticipations to discover its own faith, and thus contributing their share to the development of doctrine, to the continuation and enlargement of the divine Tradition.

It follows that certain rules must exist for the guidance of experts, exegetes, theologians and preachers in their function of translating the Bible in the language of contemporary men. Exegetes try to discern the meaning of the texts with the scientific tools of history, archaeology, philology, linguistics, comparative religion, hermeneutics; theologians, who need not be different persons, try to interpret the result of exegesis in the context of the analogy of faith and in the continuity of the Church's Tradition; preachers, who of course may also be exegetes and theologians, try to formulate this in the language of the pulpit and to make the written Word which they have understood, a spoken Word through which their hearers may be grasped by the power of the apostolic kerygma.

Accordingly, the third chapter includes several references to the principles of hermeneutics, or interpretation of the Old and New Testaments. The passage explaining these points must be read in the context of contemporary exegetical practice and methods, and in the line of recent pontifical documents regarding problems of exegesis, that is, mainly of Pius XII's encyclical *Divino afflante Spiritu* and of the Instruction *Sancta Mater Ecclesia* of the Biblical Commission on the historical value of the New Testament (May, 1964).

A distinction had always been made between the Old and New Testaments within the Holy Scriptures. The Old Testament, in which the preparation of the coming of the Savior is recorded, is not only a propaedeutic document introducing the New Testament. By showing the roots of the Church and of Christ's doctrine in the People of the old covenant, the Hebrews and the Jews, it reveals something essential to the Christian belief in the unity of God, author of both Testaments and partner in both covenants; and it shows the profound penetration of the Church in the stuff of mankind, through the Holy People from whom she comes and through her relation with all the peoples of the earth, who are called to enter the ark of salvation and to become members of the household of God, where "there is neither Jew nor Gentile . . . but all are one in Christ Jesus". In a century that has seen the worst persecution of the Jews in history—and this in a nation boasting a great Christian past—it was important that Vatican Council II insist on the perennial value of the Old Testament for the life of the faithful of Christ. This is the topic of chapter IV, in which the nature of the Old Testament, its relevance to the history of salvation, its importance for Christians, and its unity with the New Testament are briefly explained.

Chapter V moves to a discussion of the New Testament. It stresses the Gospels and their historical value and the influence of the early Christian community on their formation. The Acts, the Epistles and the Apocalypse are briefly described, rather too briefly in comparison with the Gospels. Why is there an imbalance in treatment between the four Gospels and the rest of the New Testament? It results less from a disregard of the Epistles than from a prevailing concern about possible

inroads of Bultmann's exegetical conceptions in Catholic exegesis of the Gospels. The influence of the "post-Bultmannians"
and their existential hermeneutics tends to cast doubt on the
value of the four Gospels. Are these truly more than God-given
occasions for existential decisions of faith? The existential
exegesis of Bultmann and the "post-Bultmannians" sees no
more than this in the Scriptures. Carried to its extreme, this
tendency would ruin the Catholic conception of the Word of
God as actually present in the reading of the Scriptures, which
not only ask man questions, but also present him with God's
answer as given in revelation.

At the time of the Council, such exegesis focused anxiety
on the four Gospels rather than other New Testament books.
For this reason chapter V appears slightly unbalanced. Yet, it
was never the intention of the responsible Commission to
underrate the Epistles, the Acts or the Apocalypse.

The last chapter has already been explained: it shows how
Christians can and should, by assiduously reading the Scriptures
of the Old and the New Testaments, increase their understanding
of revelation, their fidelity to the Word of God, their communion
with the three divine Persons, and, in a word, develop their
spiritual life. This reading will also help to renovate theology
by bringing it "back to the sources". It will renew catechetics
and preaching. Bishops must promote the reading of Scripture
among the people of their diocese. Priests must place their
reading at the heart of their pastoral concerns.

CHAPTER IV

SOME THEOLOGICAL PROBLEMS

A. Revelation and Faith

The approach to revelation and faith of the Constitution
Dei Filius of Vatican Council I reflected the concerns of the
second half of the 19th century: what mattered was the rationality of faith and the acceptability of revelation by reasonable
beings. While the supernatural elements were not neglected, the
stress lay on the compatibility of faith and reason. The Church
was facing a rationalistic age and had to express her position
adequately in the mentality of the time.

The situation has changed considerably since 1870. Our contemporaries are more interested in existential and personal values than in rationality. In the realm of theological research and elaboration, the climate of the 19th century, which gave apologetics a central place, is all but forgotten today. Theology is now investigating Christian experience rather than the rational aspects of revelation. It restores its mystery to revelation and its mystical dimension to assent. The steps toward faith, which used to be carefully analyzed through the evidences of credibility, rational assent, moral certitude, ecclesiastical faith and divine faith, now appear to be quite secondary. What primarily matters is the revelation itself, rather than the impact of revelation on intellectual knowledge and its importance as a source of ideas. Now we hear God speaking, revealing himself to the heart of men, whether these be the prophets, the apostles, those who, in many places and in different ways, have been selected by God to deliver his message, or even the unknown man who seeks God without knowing if he can ever find him. God revealing himself and man's personal, irreplaceable response to God are at the center of modern theological reflection on revelation.

It follows that revelation is now considered in two related dimensions. In its historical dimension, revelation has been couched in the human language of inspired authors who, in the Old or in the New Testament, have recorded the great acts of God in his dealings with men. In its personal dimension, revelation is inseparable from the act of hearing and of responding by which man acknowledges in his heart and in public that God spoke in the past and that he speaks here and now.

These aspects of the rationale of revelation are naturally emphasized in the *Constitution on Divine Revelation*. Revelation as the communication of "revealed truth" comes only at the end of the first chapter, after a condensed survey of revelation as sacred history, as *Heilsgeschichte*. Historical revelation, as recorded in the Old and New Testaments, first of all communicates realities through gestures and words, through the acted parables of the history of the Chosen People. The God who manifests himself does not speak as a professor or a scholar, but as a person. He evokes not only intellectual acceptance of what he says, but personal commitment to himself; he does not want only students and disciples, but friends attached to him through a personal relationship. This is clear in the Old Testament, where the religious attitude is essentially one of gratitude for God's loving condescension, for the lowliness of God who, without losing his transcendence, made himself friend to our Father Abraham, who spoke to Moses, who was heard by Elijah and who through all the ages speaks to the hearts of those who love him. It is still more patent in the economy of the new covenant, in the person and the life of his Son, the eternal Word made flesh for our salvation. This is the ultimate revelation that will never pass away because the Father has nothing to add once he has spoken his eternal Word and once this Word has manifested himself on earth. But the Spirit's mission is to guide men toward a loving response to Jesus the Savior. Revelation in the context of our document is the appearance of Emmanuel, of God-with-us, in the course of human history and in the texture of our lives.

The faith with which we answer this coming down of God toward us is much more than an intellectual assent. Vatican Council II on this point is neighbor to the Council of Trent and its *Decree on Justification*. Faith, for the Council of Trent, is "the beginning of human salvation, the foundation and root of all justification". As Vatican Council I wrote, it is "the full assent of intellect and will to God revealing". In order to be full, this assent of the will and the intellect must proceed from the whole human personality, and include, besides consent to what is said, trust in Christ, commitment, hope and love. The believer is not placed in a static situation; he is dynamically oriented toward the divine encounter in the person of Jesus the Lord. His eyes are opened, and he passes from blindness to sight in an anticipation of the full vision.

The treatment of revelation by Vatican Council II is radically soteriological. That of faith is personalistic. This may become the starting point for a theology of the human person coming to spiritual maturity in his encounter with God-who-speaks.

B. Scripture and Tradition

The discussions on the schema *De Fontibus Revelationis* in the first session of the Council centered on one major point: Should the Church canonize the "two source" theory of revelation at a time when this theory is under revision in many theological quarters? Whereas the schema (Text I) fully endorsed the "two source" theory, a growing number of theologians had for years completely rejected this theory as inadequate and as unable to do justice to the phenomenon of Tradition and to the fulness of the presence of the Word in the written Scriptures. A short explanation of the historical aspect of this problem will lead us to the theological question itself.

The Council of Trent, as mentioned at the beginning of this introduction, said that the Gospel *i.e.,* the Good News of salvation, "is contained in written books and in unwritten traditions", and stated that it venerated them all "with an equal attitude of piety and an equal reverence". In other words, it placed on a par the Scriptures and the apostolic traditions, insofar as they convey the Gospel. In the course of the Counter-Reformation, theology was divided in the interpretation of this text. The most influential authors, following the conceptions of some pre-Tridentine theologians, interpreted this to mean that a part of the Gospel is contained in the Scriptures and another part in the apostolic traditions. The first author to state this clearly was St. Peter Canisius, whose *Catechism* became influential wherever the Counter-Reformation gained ground in German lands. Meanwhile, many lesser known writers continued to assume, as patristic and scholastic theology until the later Middle Ages had done, that Scripture and the apostolic traditions cannot be quantitatively divided. Far from being two sections of the deposit of revelation or, according to a formula which appeared gradually in the catechisms of the 18th and 19th centuries, two sources of faith, the Scriptures and the traditions or, equivalently, Scripture and Tradition, constitute one single whole, which is the Church's expression and handing down of the Gospel. Scripture cannot be understood apart from Tradition, for it embodies the Tradition of the apostolic Church; and its reading needs to be guided by the Holy Spirit in the Church,

272

as manifested in the ecclesiastical documents which form the post-apostolic Tradition.

The question placed before Vatican Council II by the first form of the schema was this: Since the Council of Trent avoided the problem of the quantitative extension of Scripture and the traditions, and since Vatican Council I also shunned it, should the Council of 1962 follow these precedents or not? The discarding of this first text of the schema in November, 1962, meant that the Council refused to be tied to the recent theory of two sources of faith. It did not imply, however, that it wished to identify itself with the opposite and older view, namely, that in a certain sense all revelation may be held to be contained in Scripture. Like the Council of Trent, it refused to pass judgment on the question of the quantitative extension of Scripture and Tradition. The question is left for theologians to discuss.

In keeping with the vote of November, 1962, the subsequent drafts of the schema and the final text as adopted on October 29 and promulgated on November 18, 1965, prescind entirely from this debated question. The necessary unity of Scripture and Tradition and their value as channels of transmission of the Gospel are stressed rather than the extension of revelation in Scripture and in Tradition.

If Vatican Council II did not wish to decide any theological controversy on the question of Tradition, it nevertheless provided indirect evidence in favor of the historians who have maintained that Trent never taught the "two source" theory. For, had Trent canonized such a theory, Vatican Council II could not ignore it. Since Vatican Council II consciously kept away from the "two source" theory of Tradition, such a theology cannot belong among the questions already settled by the Church's extraordinary magisterium. One may also conclude, by a similar reasoning, that the "two source" theory has no place among the truths unquestionably taught by the ordinary magisterium. If, as has been asserted, the ordinary magisterium, by granting the *nihil obstat* and *imprimatur* to catechisms teaching "two sources of faith" or "two sources of revelation", had fully committed itself to such a concept of Tradition, the ecumenical Council would have included in the deposit of faith preserved and taught by the universality of the bishops. By

273

refusing to recognize this, Vatican Council II indirectly supported the opposite contention, namely, that the ordinary magisterium has never universally taught the two sources of faith, in spite of what a number of catechisms—by no means all—may have said.

The concept of Tradition that has been endorsed by the Council is described in paragraph 8. Briefly, Tradition is identified with the permanence of the apostolic proclamation in the Church. Expressed in a special manner in the Scriptures, the apostles' preaching goes on in the Church and is destined to continue until the end of time. The apostles themselves had received it from Christ; and they handed it on to the faithful in their discourses and their letters. What was thus transmitted cannot be reduced to intellectual truths expressing doctrine; rather it implies all that contributes to the life and faith of the People of God. The idea that Tradition is essentially transmission of truth cast in the form of propositions is thereby ruled out by implication. This transmission is not only a matter of teaching, but, as our text says, of "teaching, life and worship".

Understood in this realistic way, the Church's Tradition is profoundly related to Scripture. This constitutes the topic of Paragraph 9, which clearly teaches what I have called "the mutual inherence" of Scripture and Tradition. This means that Scripture and Tradition are implied in each other. They flow from the same unique source, namely, God speaking through Christ; and they run toward the same fulfillment, which will be the eschatological flowering of the Gospel, when God will be all in all. To Scripture, Tradition only adds—though this is of paramount importance—the experience of its transmission to and through post-apostolic times, under the guidance and illumination of the Holy Scriptures. On the basis of this radical unity of Scripture and Tradition, Vatican Council II is led to endorse the formula of the Council of Trent: "equal pious affection and reverence" (*pari pietatis affectu ac reverentia*) are due to both.

C. Tradition and Magisterium

One of the questions that the 19th century and the subsequent modernist crisis forced upon theology concerns the relations of the magisterium to the process of transmitting and receiving revelation. To some extent this was already raised by the Reformation, since Protestantism questioned and denied the authority of the magisterium, which was dwarfed, in its eyes, by the awesomeness of the mystery of justification by faith alone. Yet, it took time for Catholic thought to cope with this problem. No satisfactory treatment of the magisterium's relevance to Tradition and to the Church's reading of Scripture could be made, as long as ecclesiology remained in its formative stage. By a natural transition, the Counter-Reformation turned out to be the great age of the institutional aspect of ecclesiology. The magisterium gained ground in the consideration of theologians and in the organization of the Church, as it also gained confidence in itself through its political, architectural and polemical triumphs over a slightly receding Protestant wave.

One had to wait for the second half of the 19th century, however, to collect the fruits of this development as regards the theology of Tradition. Among the dominant authors of that time who devoted their thought to this question, the main contribution comes from men of the so-called Roman School, who precisely studied the problem of the place held by the magisterium in the traditional process by which the Church hands down to successive ages what it has received from preceding generations.

Starting with Giovanni Perrone (1794-1876) and reaching its high point with Johann Baptist Franzelin (1816-1886), the Roman theology of Tradition, which was part of a wider Roman theology of the Church, was characterized by the growing importance it gave to the magisterium, especially of the Roman pontiff, in the traditioning process. The other factors of Tradition receded; they became ancillary to the discerning and deciding function of the pope and, under him, the bishops. Scripture, the Fathers and the Doctors contribute to the stream of Tradition, yet the decisive factor, which actually creates Tradition by giving it the ultimate form of doctrine, is the magisterium. Some of the theologians of Vatican Council I like Carlo Passaglia (1812-1887) and Clemens Schrader (1820-1875) understood Tradition to be, in its core, the series of documents officially approved by the Church's authority; accordingly, they saw the present authority of Tradition as centered in the authority of the episcopal body today and singularly in the supreme authority of the Bishop of Rome. In this view, the definition of papal infallibility entailed the identity of Tradition with the decisions of the supreme magisterium.

Admittedly, the 19th-century theologians did not rule out other aspects of Tradition. Franzelin popularized the distinctions that are still familiar, even though they are no longer very meaningful, between active and passive or constitutive and interpretative traditions. All of these, however, draw their sense and their binding force from their connection with the pope's teaching authority.

The modernist crisis brought this movement to its logical extreme: for Louis Billot (1846-1936), reacting against the immanentist notion of doctrine propagated by modernism, the magisterium is the Tradition.

What took place in this progressive identification of magisterium and Tradition was primarily a narrowing down of the formerly very wide concept of Tradition to what was only one of its factors, the *regula fidei* or rule of faith, originally destined to act as the standard by which a tradition would be judged to be authentic. In the Roman theology of the 19th century, the rule of faith was simply identified with Tradition, thus impoverishing the latter considerably. For although the *regula fidei* has always been held to contain the core of faith, it was never meant to be exhaustive. The equation between rule of faith and Tradition was accompanied by a shift of meaning in the very notion of rule of faith. For the Church Fathers, who originally introduced the concept, the rule of faith is the faith accepted and taught in the past. It is known by the teaching of the main Sees and primarily by that of the Roman See. In a derivative and slightly narrower sense, it is the Creed, especially that of the Councils of Nicaea and Constantinople. In the line of thought of the 19th century, this came to mean that faith is not established by turning to the past, but by listening to the voice of the present-day magisterium, which has inherited the rule of faith and now teaches it with authority.

Paragraph 10 is the relevant passage of the *Constitution on Divine Revelation*. Here, the dual unity of Scripture and Tradition becomes a trilogy, of which the Church's magisterium constitutes the third term. However, far from being on a par with either Scripture or Tradition, the magisterium is at their service. Its function consists in "authentically interpreting" the "deposit of God's Word", which is itself made of the unity of Scripture and Tradition. It does not interpret Scripture by itself or Tradition by itself, but their co-inherence in the deposit of the Word. Thus, the magisterium's task cannot be equated with that of exegetes or that of historians of doctrine. It resides in a higher synthesis than those of biblical or of historical theology, at the level of the Symbols of faith, the Creeds and other authentic expressions of the deposit of revelation. In no sense, therefore, may the magisterium lord it over Scripture and Tradition; on the contrary, it waits upon the Word of God, to which it listens, which it keeps and which it explains.

D. The Development of Doctrine

Among the problems that the theology of Tradition brought on the theological scene of the 19th century was the question of the development of doctrine. The older Church had known that doctrine develops or, in other words, that Tradition is not simply a transmission of final truths and of set statements, but a self-enlarging stream of spiritual experience. The whole ground of the defense of orthodoxy against the Arians and semi-Arians after the Council of Nicaea was that the very "rule of faith" required the introduction of *omoousios* into the Creed and the corresponding development of trinitarian thought, as warrants of fidelity to scriptural revelation. The Councils of the early Church implied the legitimacy of development, since they elaborated trinitarian and christological doctrines (Nicaea to Constantinople III, 325-680), and they upheld the cult of ikons (Nicaea II, 787), and since the appearance and acceptance of patriarchates implied developments in the hierarchical structure of the Church. The constant appeal to the Tradition of the Fathers and to the rule of faith did not, therefore, exclude a search for better formulas and for a more adequate penetration into the Christian mystery. On the contrary, this very fidelity made it possible for the Church to progress in understanding and living the renovation of the paschal mystery as the life of the Holy Spirit in her.

Toward the end of the patristic period, St. Vincent of Lerins voiced the consensus of the Fathers when he described the Church's faith as uniting "universality, antiquity and unanimity", and the rule of faith as that which has been taught "everywhere, always and by all". He did not mean to endorse a static view of the Catholic faith, for he also added, in a pregnant summary of patristic thought, that the faith of the Church of Christ increases "in each man as in the whole Church, in the succession of periods and centuries, in understanding, knowledge and wisdom, although it does so according to its own nature, namely, in the same dogma, the same sense and the same doctrine".

Since then, the idea that the Catholic faith unfolds itself in the course of its transmission has been inseparable from the Catholic assent to revelation. Yet, it has seldom been the object of detailed theological reflection or of official pronouncements. This is one of the underlying realities of Catholic life which are rarely analyzed because they are constantly experienced and they therefore dominate the very reflection one can make about them. But the concept of "sacred doctrine", as it was accepted by the medieval Schoolmen, entailed a development of doctrine in the Church's interpretation of Scripture: the sacred doctrine is Holy Scripture as it unfolds itself in the experience, the practice and the reflection of the Church age after age. The interpretation of Scripture does not add anything to Scripture from the outside, yet it presides over a self-development of the revealed mystery, which, after being proclaimed, is heard; after being heard, is accepted; after being accepted, becomes life in the Christian heart. In this way, the revelation, once veiled in the sacrament of Scripture, becomes life and experience in the hearts of the faithful, doctrine and teaching in the minds and mouths of doctors and bishops. It never ceases to be Good News, the announcement of salvation and the preaching of the coming of the kingdom of God; it never stops being experienced in the mystical reenactment of the Last Supper and in the faithful's participation in the mysteries of the death and the resurrection of the Lord; yet, it also becomes a body of doctrine that can be apprehended by the mind in the light of the Spirit. "Depths of understanding vary according as the soul is more intimate with him," wrote Bonaventure.

In the last century John Henry Newman devoted considerable attention to this question in his *Essay on the Development of Christian Doctrine* (1844), in which he concluded that a genuine development of any point of doctrine must respect the following seven principles: preservation of its type; continuity of its principle; power of assimilation; logical sequence; anticipation of its future; conservative action upon its past; chronic vigor. These are studied at length by Newman, the gist of whose ideas in this matter is that development of doctrine, without being illogical, transcends pure logic. Doctrine grows in the fashion of a living organism, which has in its self the principles of its growth, yet whose growth is nurtured by its assimilation of outside elements. A vital process then takes place, by which an interplay between the Gospel and the situation of the world to which it is preached results in new light being thrown on the Gospel, aspects of its unveiling themselves and being perceived in their integrity for the first time.

It was not until the modernist crisis, however, that the importance of doctrinal development was perceived by theologians in general. No less than eight propositions concerning the evolution of doctrine were anathematized by the decree *Lamentabili* (July 3, 1907). The encyclical *Pascendi* (Sept. 8, 1907) condemned what it called the modernist theory concerning the origin of dogma, which distinguished between the primary or essential core of the revelation—ultimately God himself—and secondary symbolical expressions of this core. The dogmas of the Church are, in the modernist mind, provisional canonizations of symbolic formulations, which in the course of time become obsolete and have to be replaced by other symbols. The oath against Modernism (Sept. 1, 1910) also contained the following statement: "I sincerely receive the doctrine of faith which has been transmitted from the apostles to us by the orthodox Fathers always in one same sense and one same doctrine; and I therefore reject the heretical concept of the evolution of dogmas, passing from one sense to another one which differs from what the Church formerly acknowledged."

The dilemma raised by Modernism found its solution, during the modernist crisis itself, in Maurice Blondel's letter on *History and Dogma* (1903), in which Blondel showed the insufficiency of the contradictory positons which he termed "extrinsicism" and "historicism". Extrinsicism removes faith from the realm of history and conceives of the supernatural as having a minimal area of contact with nature. Historicism finds that history not only carries but also creates faith, which accordingly changes and varies according to the successive moods of the times. A truly Catholic theology steers its way between these unsatisfactory philosophies, thanks to a concept and practice of Tradition as that which "anticipates and illuminates the future, and is disposed to do so by the effort which it makes to remain faithful to the past". Blondel concluded that such a Tradition, excluding all "fixism", implies "development" as part of the Church's ongoing experience of the faith which seeks understanding.

More systematic theologians than Blondel also treated this delicate problem with great insight during the modernist controversy, especially Antoine Gardeil, in *Le Donne Révélé et la Théologie* (1909). No thorough study of the question of doctrinal evolution, however, appeared before the book of the Spanish Dominican Marin Sola: *La Evolución Homogenea del Dogma Católico* (1923). But this study was dominated by an excessively rigid Scholastic point of view, for which logical deduction is the only final tool of doctrinal evolution. Marin Sola admitted, at least in the second edition of his book (1924), an "affective way of development", which he understood to be an intuitive anticipation of what reason and logic would later deduce from the deposit of faith. Since the publication of this volume, theologians have been divided between those who recognize logical deduction as the main instrument of doctrinal evolution, and those who admit with Newman and Blondel that doctrinal development proceeds by way of a vital process of growth for which logic alone cannot account.

The controversy launched in 1946 about what was falsely called "the new theology" brought up again the question of the development of dogma. No major work on the question, however, appeared. The encyclical *Humani generis* (August 12,

1950) described in these words what it considered to be an erroneous conception:

> "They"—that is, some unidentified authors—"do not consider it absurd, but altogether necessary, that theology should substitute new concepts in place of the old ones in keeping with the various philosophies which in the course of time it uses as its instruments, so that it should give human expression to divine truths in various ways which are even somewhat opposed, but still equivalent, as they say. They add that the history of dogmas consists in reporting the various forms in which revealed truth has been clothed, forms that have succeeded one another in accordance with the different teachings and opinions that have arisen over the course of the centuries."

Clearly, Pius XII feared the resurgence of a relativistic conception of religious truth which, however, need not be associated at all with a Catholic view of the development of doctrine.

Taking account of this, the *Constitution on Divine Revelation* attempts to bring together the various ways in which Catholic theology, lately and in the past, has conceived the development of doctrine; by so doing, it brings to an end the fear of development which reaction against Modernism had fostered among some. It clears of suspicion the authors who were frowned upon after the publication of *Humani generis,* although their thought was elaborated outside the modernist or anti-modernist frame of reference, within which *Humani generis* was conceived.

The relevant passage of the Constitution is in paragraph 10, where the idea of a development of Tradition is clearly expressed. Several aspects, incentives or causes of such a development are indicated. What increases is not the objective datum of revelation: the *Constitution on Divine Revelation* perfectly agrees with the statement made in the *Constitution on the Church:* "They (*i.e.,* the Roman pontiff and the bishops) do not receive a new public revelation as belonging to the divine deposit of faith" (n. 25). It is the Church's insight into the meaning of the realities and words handed on by Tradition which becomes sharper, thereby enlarging her vision. This progress follows the converging, yet in themselves distinct, ways of contemplative study and of spiritual experience. The former pertains more to the intellectual order; the latter to that of a sense of God beyond and above the intellect. The former opens the door to man's activities at the service of a faith which seeks to understand; the latter is lived in man's passivities under the delicate brush of God's hand in the soul. The former is cataphatic; the latter, apophatic.

These ways of unfolding the mysteries of God orient the Church toward the fullness of saving truth, to which the Spirit guides her. Their final fruition will come in the eschatological encounter between the Church and her Lord, at "the ultimate fulfillment of God's words in herself" (n. 8).

E. Hermeneutical Problems

It is not possible in this short introduction to raise all the exegetical questions connected with chapters III, IV and V of the Constitution. Evidently, these chapters ought to be read together with Pius XII's encyclical *Divino afflante Spiritu* (1943) and with the instruction *Sancta Mater Ecclesia* published by the Biblical Commission on August 21, 1964. The purpose of *Divino afflante Spiritu* was to endorse the renewal of biblical studies which was heralded by M. J. Lagrange in the first decades of this century and which has flourished, since then, in the works of many scholars inspired by the two great centers of Catholic exegesis, the Ecole Biblique de Jérusalem and the *Institutum Biblicum* in Rome. The purpose of the Instruction, prompted partly by recent discussions of the historical life of Jesus, partly by the debates around the Council concerning the interpretation of the New Testament, was to set down norms for the study of the historical character of the four Gospels. It was important to place at the Council fathers' disposal an authoritative compendium of recent research relative to the criticism of the New Testament, as this has been found acceptable to Catholic exegesis. Brief comments on a few points pertinent to exegesis will be appropriate.

The Canon of the Bible

The Constitution provides no list of the canonical books, the decrees of the Councils of Florence (*Bulla unionis Coptorum,* commonly called *Decretum pro Jacobitis,* February 2, 1442, *C.O.D.,* p. 548; *D.S.,* n. 1334-1335) and of Trent (Session IV, April 8, 1546; *C.O.D.,* pp. 639-40; *D.S.,* n. 1502-1503) being sufficiently clear. The Catholic Church admits as equally inspired and canonical both the protocanonical books of the Hebrew Bible of Jerusalem and the deuterocanonical books— usually named "apocrypha" by Protestant authors—contained in the Greek Bible of Alexandria called the *Septuagint.* These are usually not admitted by Protestants, although they were ordinarily printed as an appendix to the Old Testament until the British and Foreign Bible Society decided to do away with this practice in 1826.

Texts and Translations

The Council specifically mentions the Greek *Septuagint* as traditional since the beginning of the Church. Already quoted in the New Testament, this version deserves a privileged place on a par with the available Hebrew texts. The Latin *Vulgate* and other Latin versions, as well as the "other Oriental translations", are said to have "always been honored" in the Church. Other translations, well adapted to the many modern vernaculars, are recommended in general: they should be made mainly on the original texts, and, at the opportune time, in common with scholars of other Churches. This passage, which happily completes the corresponding text of the Council of Trent, should do away with the mistaken, yet still widely spread, notion that the Latin *Vulgate* contains the only official text of the Bible.

Inspiration

As explained in the *Constitution on Divine Revelation* (n. 11), the doctrine of scriptural inspiration holds God to be the author of the books of the Bible: this fact provides the basis for their canonicity, which is simply the Church's recognition of their divine authorship. Yet, the human writers and redactors are also "truly authors", in the ordinary sense of human authorship, of their books. The relations between these two simultaneous authorships are not investigated here, as they belong to a field where several theories may be proposed and debated without threat to the basic doctrine. At any rate, God expressed himself through the literary qualities and methods of men whom he guided through the charism of inspiration which is described in the encyclicals *Providentissimus Deus* of Leo XIII (Nov. 18, 1893; *D.S.*, n. 3291-3294) and *Divino afflante Spiritu* of Pius XII.

Inerrancy is a consequence of, yet cannot be equated with, inspiration. Whereas inspiration implies an active or positive guidance of the human author's mind by the Holy Spirit, inerrancy is simply a preservation from error, which is more passive and negative. The salient fact in this matter is that the Constitution avoids the term "inerrancy" on account of its negative tonality. Instead of presenting Scripture in the negative perspective of its freedom from error, it prefers to stress positively its teaching of the truth "firmly, faithfully and without error". The truth in question is that "which God decided to put down in the sacred writings for our salvation's sake" (n. 11). Attention to the problem of inerrancy is thus oriented in two directions. In the first place, Holy Scripture is free from errors as regards the truth of salvation, but not necessarily in merely philosophical or scientific matters. In the second, God's positive guidance of the author into the truth is more important than its negative consequence of inerrancy, and should become the focus of theological reflection on inspiration.

Interpretation

Scriptural interpretation, or hermeneutics, is approached in a broad way, for the Council need obviously not lay out detailed regulations, or restrict legitimate freedom of research within the framework of Catholic Tradition. The instructions already published by Pius XII and by the Biblical Commission are in no way superseded by the *Constitution on Divine Revelation;* rather, they are solemnly endorsed for the encouragement of Catholic exegetes and the further development of biblical studies both at the scholarly and at the more popular levels.

Especially pertinent to the interpretation of the Bible are the following points:

(a) The Old and the New Testaments belong together. The Church cannot forget or forgo her roots in the People of God from whom the Savior came. The Old Testament, recording the main stages of the preparation of mankind for Christ's advent, is truly the Word of God, just like the New, which reports the fulfillment of salvation-history in Christ and in the apostolic community centered on the faith in his resurrection. They both formulate and foster man's response to God in living and loving faith. Therefore, one should read the Old and the New together for the light which each throws upon the other.

(b) Both Testaments are at the same time historical records of the events of salvation and profoundly spiritual writings in which the Word speaks to man in the Spirit. For this reason the Church maintains that they are sufficiently accurate, as concerns sacred history, and that they are also open to a spiritual understanding reaching beyond the documentary letter to the supernatural depth of what history reports.

(c) In order to assess the historical sense, one should study the literary forms of the various biblical books (n. 12), as *Divino afflante Spiritu* clearly indicated and as exegetes have done for a long time. The genre of the New Testament and especially of the four Gospels implies the true history of what Christ said and did (n. 19), even though, as the instruction *Sancta Mater Ecclesia* explained, this history took the kerygmatic form of a living testimony for the ultimate purpose of preaching and spreading the Good News.

(d) Catholic Tradition has always paid great attention to the spiritual sense, or senses, of the text, concerning the history of which major works have been published by Father Henri de Lubac. Primarily, this means that bibilical interpretation goes further than the discovery of the literal or historical sense reached by scientific exegesis. It also tries to discern the sense intended by the Spirit, not only for the original readers or hearers of the Word, but for those who at all times and in all places will be eager to hear the Word in their reading of the Scriptures and to keep it. Commonly called "spiritual" in the past, and traditionally divided into three senses (allegorical,

285

tropological, anagogical), this dimension of Scripture underwent a partial eclipse during the 18th and 19th centuries. It has reappeared in our times under the influence of historical studies of patristic and medieval exegesis and under the impact of biblical theology, which opened insights into the typology of the Bible (typological sense) and into its *sensus plenior* or fuller sense. Without entering current discussions, in which it does not want to take sides, the Council gives the green light to continued studies along these lines, by insisting on the role of the analogy of faith in interpreting Scripture (n. 12), on the unity of the two Testaments (n. 16), on the everlasting worth of Scripture as, "for the Church, support and vigor, for the Church's children, strength of the faith, food of the soul, source of the spiritual life" (n. 21), on searching for "a day by day deeper understanding" (n. 23), on the place of Scripture as "the soul of sacred theology" (n. 24), on interiorly listening to the Word (n. 25), on Scripture reading as the initiation of a "dialogue between God and man" (n. 25).

F. A Theology of the Word

The Constitution reaches its highest point in the last chapter: "Holy Scripture in the Church's Life." Shortly before the opening of the 3rd session, Pope Paul VI, in a radio speech to the 80th *Katholikentag* meeting at Stuttgart, said: "The Word of God is a light that gives strength and consolation to our life. The Word of God, which, for the Council fathers, constitutes the supreme authority and the symbolic center, is also the soul of your deliberations." In these few words, Paul VI expressed his interest in what should be the ultimate fruit of the *Constitution on Divine Revelation,* namely, that the Word of God may become the heart of both doctrine and life in the Church. In order to grasp this potential value of the Constitution, one ought to remember that, during the preparatory phase of the Council, the Secretariat for Promoting Christian Unity had written a project for a constitution or decree on "the Word of God". This project was never formally presented to the Council for discussion, although the Archbishop of Durban (South Africa), Denis Hurley, in his conciliar speech of November 19, 1962, asked for an immediate debate on "the excellent schema *De Verbo Dei*". However, the reporter of this chapter in the Council, the Bishop of Haarlem (Holland), Johannes van Dodewaard, noted in his report that the last chapter of the Constitution had been composed with the help of the schema *De Verbo Dei* prepared by the Secretariat for Promoting Christian Unity.

This last chapter should be read, not only as a fitting conclusion for the *Constitution on Divine Revelation,* but also as a starting point for an opening of the Catholic concern for Scripture, for Tradition and for a pastoral reading and preaching of Scripture, to a broader interest in a theology of the Word. Since the 16th century, Catholicism in general has shied away from placing the Word at the center of its theology, mainly through a fear of Protestant interpretations of the centrality of the Word in doctrine and preaching. Although the great Catholic preachers of the 17th century, Bossuet, Mabillon, Massillon and their lesser colleagues, understood their function as "sacred orators" to be that of instruments of God's Word, the theological synthesis of the Counter-Reformation, by and large, included no like insight. In the course of time, knowledge of the text of the Bible by both clergy and laity waned. Fewer and fewer priests preached on biblical themes, and fewer and fewer laymen used the Bible for the daily food and expression of their piety. Of late, however, a reaction has started, and reflections on the Word of God have become more frequent in theological literature.

The ultimate purpose of the *Constitution on Divine Revelation* is to invite all Catholics to restore the written and preached Word to its centrality in theology and in worship. The Constitution insists that, in the Scriptures, God the Father himself addresses his children so that the very strength and vigor of the Church comes from his Word. There must follow a diligent scanning of Scripture by those who enjoy gifts of scholarship. Their purpose should not be to satisfy intellectual curiosity, but to enrich spiritual life and theology. For theological reflection cannot be severed from the live font of divine wisdom in which God speaks to us. "The study of the sacred page" should be "like the soul of sacred theology" (n. 24). By the same token, it should be the soul of preaching and catechesis, so that it may eventually become the daily food of the faithful.

Both clergy and laity are encouraged to read Scripture. Yet, reading will not help much unless it contributes to transform our mind in the light of biblical thought. Since the Scriptures constitute the very form of revelation and embody the human language in which God couched his self-manifestation to men, the mentality of the biblical authors and the characteristics of the Semitic way of thinking and praying should be felt throughout the Christian approach to worship, to faith and to the application of faith to world problems. A theology of the Word should start here. It could solve the pastoral problems formerly raised by the advocates of "kerygmatic theology", and it would help Catholic thought to unloose its ties to Western culture and civilization, thereby making itself more ready to encounter world cultures and world religions. The biblical forms of thought came from a Semitic, near-Eastern environment, at the crossroad of the great civilizations of Europe in the West, of Asia in the East and of Africa in the South and Southwest. The historical circumstances, which directed the spread of Christianity to the West by way of the Roman Empire and of Hellenistic culture, have now run their appointed course. The time has come for a re-orientation of Christain ways of thought and forms of worship toward the other corners of the earth. This has already been anticipated by the geographic spread of revelation over all continents. Nevertheless, the missionary expansion of the Church cannot bear its fruits as long as it is not accompanied by a translation of Christian revelation in the categories of non-Western minds.

By helping us to rediscover the Gospel in its pristine form, a theology of the Word will be the means by which the Church's Tradition will expand beyond the limits of the Greco-Roman world. In this way alone can we become fully Catholic.

Rudolf Schnackenburg
1914-

Schnackenburg was born in Kattowitz, Germany, and received his doctorate in theology from the University of Breslau in 1937. He did post-doctoral work at the University of Munich, receiving his Habilitation for New Testament Exegesis in 1947. He taught at the University of Dillingen, then of Bamberg, until his appointment to the University of Würzburg in 1957 as Professor of New Testament exegesis and Biblical theology. He lectured at the University of Notre Dame, Indiana, for the fall semester of 1965, and received an honorary doctorate from Innsbruck University in 1970.

Schnackenburg's The Moral Teaching of the New Testament *(1954) and* God's Rule and Kingdom *(1959) received much attention, especially when English translations came out in the 1960s. Between 1965 and 1975 he produced two major commentaries; a two-volume work on the Gospel of Mark and a massive three-volume work on the Gospel of John. From the very timing of his work it was inevitable that he would be among those scholars whose rich Biblical studies paved the way for Vatican II, and followed up by presenting more and more substance for those who were turning for help in the search for a more Biblical theology.*

One of the problems in an era like the 1960s was the availability of a superabundance of new information as a result of the "boom" in Biblical studies among Catholics, but the absence of any kind of synthesis. Such a period is inevitable in a time of rapid growth when new doors are opened faster than one can explore behind them. In this type of situation a scholar like Schnackenburg can make his greatest contribution. As a specialist he has a firm grasp on all the tools, but his great power of analysis is complemented by an unusual ability to synthesize, to keep the whole picture in view.

His two-volume work on Christian Existence in the New Testament is a good example of this kind of work. The first volume, in seven chapters, deals with such basic themes as the Biblical view of man, the meaning of conversion, the kinds of faith in the Bible, the imitation of Christ in conduct, the relevance of the Sermon on the Mount today, what Christian perfection means in Matthew, and the concept of the world in the New Testament. We have selected chapter six for inclusion here.

To appreciate "Christian Perfection according to Matthew" it is best to keep in mind the way in which it was interpreted throughout much of Western history. The clergy-laity distinction, the religious vs. secular outlook, led to a dualism that in practice reserved perfection for an elite minority of Christians. The Church in our century has tried mightily to overcome that dichotomy. There is a radical difference in practical Christian ministry depending on whether one views the call to perfection as addressed to all or directed to a few. Schnackenburg demonstrates here the way in which modern Biblical studies contribute toward the solution of such a dilemma, and the consequent manner in which they alter the whole style and thrust of Christian life and ministry.

CHRISTIAN EXISTENCE
IN THE NEW TESTAMENT

CHAPTER VI

CHRISTIAN PERFECTION ACCORDING TO MATTHEW

Perfection is often called the highest goal of Christian endeavor, "the highest religious and moral achievement attainable for the individual man on this earth." It is often mentioned in connection with the evangelic counsels—voluntary poverty, virginity, and perfect obedience. If these counsels are adopted as a permanent form of life, by a solemn vow, we speak of a "state of perfection"; and this has given rise to many misunderstandings. Moral theology has long since established that the "counsels of perfection" with the orders are by no means perfection itself, but only ways and means to attain perfection. The expression "state of perfection" does not mean "that all those who have taken this road are thereby more perfect, or will become more perfect—and even less that they are better merely for taking this road—than are those who remain in the world." Each man, in this view, can and ought to become perfect in his walk of life, and this goal would be more readily within his reach in proportion as he performed the duties of his walk of life with loyalty and devotion. The essence of Christian perfection, further, is love of God and neighbor.

Christian perfection so understood does certainly correspond to the spirit of the New Testament, and thus may express the Christian endeavor. But the question remains whether we are not here choosing a concept that plays no part in Jesus' message, but rather derives from Greek ethical doctrine. Since this kind of perfection can never be attained completely on earth, it seems to be an ideal that is not attainable in practice; and modern man, realistic and factual as he is, may find such an ideal discouraging.

It is worth our while, therefore, to trace the Biblical concept of perfection. It has its roots in the Old Testament, and stems from Hebraic-Semitic thought. This thought follows other roads than does Greek ethics; in many respect it is closer to today's "existential" thought than to the Greeks. We encounter the word "perfect" only twice in the gospels. The first time is in the general summons in the Sermon on the Mount: "You, therefore, must be perfect, as your heavenly Father is perfect" (Mt 5:48); the other is in Jesus' answer to the rich young ruler: "If you would be perfect, go, sell what you possess . . . " (Mt 19:21). We are justified to see it as the expression of the evangelist's own special views; and since he betrays a strong interest in Jesus' moral teachings, we may also regard him as a competent early Christian interpreter of Jesus' message. But we must keep in mind that he comes from a background of Jewish thought, as we now try to determine what he understands by "perfect."

The Hebrew term for "perfect" (*tamim*) probably comes from the language of the sacrifice. In the cultic instruction of Leviticus, and elsewhere as well, sacrificial animals without blemish are prescribed. This is precisely what the Hebrew means to convey: that something be untouched, complete, undiminished in its constitution and its value. While the Greek conceives of "perfection" as an ideal which reality can at best approach, the Hebrew by contrast starts out from reality which he considers in its original integrity. It is no longer perfect when it is in any way damaged or spoiled (cf. Jos 10:13; Ez 15:5). Here, too, the Hebrew idea of wholeness prevails: the individual things are parts of the whole, and if they drop out of the whole there is destruction of the order, and decay. To a world of thought which takes this view of integrity, the striving for perfection means something else than it does to idealistic Greek thought: it means to hold on to, or regain, an originally given unity and reality, and not the gradual approximation of an ideal goal. This is the world of thought in which the first evangelist, too, has his roots; and for this reason we shall trace the Old Testament concept of perfection somewhat more fully.

THE OLD TESTAMENT FOUNDATION OF THE CONCEPT OF PERFECTION

Let us examine more closely the concept *tamim* insofar as it applies to religious and moral concerns. To be "blameless" before the Lord (Deut 18:13) means to belong to him wholeheartedly, without practicing idolatry, sorcery, and other abominations (cf. 18:9-12). Such total surrender must be constant: "Fear the Lord, and serve him in sincerity and in faithfulness. . . ." (Jos 24:14). To give one's whole heart to God in its purity, unblemished by alien thoughts and inclinations: this is what the substantive *tom* expresses, and what we might translate with "innocence, simplicity." This is how the Lord speaks to Solomon: "If you will walk before me, as David your father walked, with integrity of heart (*b'tom-l'bab*) and uprightness (*b'-joscher*), doing according to all that I have commanded you . . . then I shall establish your royal throne over Israel forever . . ." (1 Kg 9:4f). Guileless and sincere talk, too, is described with this word. Integrity (*tom*) and uprightness (*joscher*), according to Psalm 25:21, protect the faithful who is waiting for the Lord. The Old Testament term for just conduct, *saddik*, also implies this exclusive and total surrender of the *tamim* to God. Of Noah we read: "Noah was a righteous man, blameless in his generation; Noah walked with God" (Gen 6:9; cf. Sir 44:17). Exemplary conduct could be described in these terms: righteousness before God and a life united with God.

The passage quoted last shows that the Israelites considered such "perfect" conduct a human possibility. God exhorts Abraham: "Walk before me, and be blameless" (Gen 17:1); and the father of Israel did as he was told. Many rabbis interpret the passage to mean that there was nothing objectionable about Abraham, except his foreskin, and when he had been circumcised he was called "perfect." David, too, can say of himself: "I was blameless before him" (2 Sam 22:24); "For I have kept the ways of the Lord, and have not wickedly departed from my God. For all his ordinances were before me, and from his statutes I did not turn aside." What is decisive, then, is always God's will and judgment; man must live up to the image that God has of him. "To walk blamelessly" and "to do what is right" is the same thing (Ps 15:2; cf. Prov 2:21). Job calls himself a just and blameless man (Job 12:4). In the same way the substantives "blamelessness" and "righteousness" occupy parallel positions.

The more the Torah, the Jewish Law, becomes the expression of God's will and the standard of conduct, the more is "blamelessness" identified with irreproachable obedience to the law. To be blameless is the same as to keep the law of the Lord (Ps 119:1). "Walking" and "way" are the most usual Old Testament images for human conduct, and we encounter such expressions as "those of blameless ways" (Prov 11:20), "a righteous man walks in integrity" (Prov 20:7, cf. 28:18), and "the way that is blameless" (Ps 101:2, 6). In the rabbinical tradition, a "perfect just man" is one who has kept the entire Torah; patriarchs especially were thought to belong in that category.

The Qumran texts, too, speak frequently of "perfection" or "righteousness" and perfect or righteous men, and once again in connection with the images of "walking" and "way." Here too we find the expressions "ways of the righteous," "those who walk in blamelessness," or "in perfection (of the way)." This distinctive vocabulary is in Qumran applied only to members of the community of God; the community has "a house of perfection and truth in Israel" (1 QS 8:9). The references in Dam 20:2, 5, 7 to the "perfect men of holiness" sound as if they meant the community itself (see also 7:4f., "in holy perfection"); the same holds for 1 QS 8:15. Such walking in perfection is possible only if these elect know God's way, that is, have the right understanding of the law; but such true knowledge is revealed to them by God.

Even more significant is the fact that the members of the Qumran community are convinced, despite their heroic efforts, that man is by himself incapable of walking in perfection; God has to justify him and to grant him grace. Accordingly, the final psalm of the community rule says: "As concerns me, my justification is in God's hands, and in his hands is the perfection of my ways" (1 QS 11:2); "from his hands comes the perfection of the way" (ibid., 10 f.); and there is a similar passage in the Hodajoth (songs of praise): "And I have understood that there is no justice with men, and no man walks in righteousness. All the works of justice are with the highest God, but the way of man is uncertain, except by the spirit which God created for him, to make the way of man righteous, so that men may know

all his works in the strength of his power, and the fullness of
his mercy upon all the sons in whom he is pleased" (1 HS 4:30-
33). Here the morality of the Torah is made richer by a deeply
religious thought which did not emerge with like force in the
Old Testament. Just as true knowledge becomes possible only
through revelatory grace, just so the way of perfect righteousness
is possible only by the mercy and with the help of God.

We must ask ourselves another question also: Do the Old
Testament and the late Jewish texts speak also of the perfection
of *God?* God himself is never given this attribute directly, no
doubt for the intrinsic reason that with God no defect in his
nature is possible, so that the predicate "perfect" becomes for
him superfluous and hardly meaningful. But as concerns God's
acts, their perfection can be stressed (cf. Deut 32:4). The Lord's
precepts are right (Ps 19:8), and to the pious and the just the
perfection of God's works stands revealed. In Psalm 18, in
which David looks back upon his life (an almost exact parallel
to 2 Samuel 22), the psalmist says: "With the loyal thou dost
show thyself loyal; with the blameless man thou dost show
thyself blameless" (v. 25). The context shows that he is thinking
of God's loyal, unfailing help: "This God—his way is perfect;
the promise of the Lord proves true; he is a shield for all those
who take refuge in him" (v. 30). We hear a faint echo of the
thought in the Qumran texts: "The God who girded me with
strength and made my way safe" (v. 32). The Qumran community rule, too, speaks of the righteousness of God's ways (1 QS
1:13). And it is further significant that another divine attribute,
holiness, is in many passages coupled with "perfect." It might
be that the "men of perfect holiness" were thinking of the
ordinance in Leviticus (19:2): "You shall be holy; for I the
Lord your God am holy."

After these preliminary investigations we now turn to the
two passages in Matthew's gospel.

PERFECTION ACCORDING TO THE SERMON ON THE MOUNT

The exhortation that man must be perfect as the heavenly
Father is perfect (Mt 5:48) stands at the end of the explanations
concerning the duty to love one's enemies. The reference to
God's works in verse 45 serves to give natural man a reason for

the otherwise incomprehensible and exacting demand. Since God makes his sun to rise on the evil and on the good and sends rain on the just and on the unjust, we, too, ought to love our enemies and pray for those who persecute us if we want to become sons of our heavenly Father. The concluding exhortation in verse 48 falls into place; it lays still greater stress on the need to imitate God. In Luke's version, the connection is even closer and clearer (6:35f.). Matthew inserts several sentences on human conduct (5:46 f.). Even the tax collectors love those who love them, even the Gentiles salute their "brethren"—Jesus' disciples must do *more* than that. In Luke, the sequence of the verses is reversed: the reference to God's works is followed immediately by the final exhortation. Most likely this is the original sequence.

But the exhortation is also phrased differently in Luke: "Be merciful, even as your Father is merciful!" (Lk 6:36). This is likely to represent the original wording, although the exegetes are not united on the matter. J. Dupont rightly points out that Luke's "merciful" is far more in harmony with the language of the Bible, since the Old Testament frequently applies *this* attribute to God himself. The word "merciful," further, follows naturally from the description of God's works that has gone before (even though Luke abridges that description), and is in harmony with what Jesus himself says about God; we need think only of the parable of the prodigal son, the unmerciful servant, or the laborers in the vineyard. Matthew has changed "merciful" intentionally to "perfect." What may have been his motives? First of all, probably the intention to stress more strongly the attitude expected of a *disciple;* for, as we have seen, "perfect" is a quality for which man must strive, while it can hardly be applied to God.

There is further observation. There is a good reason why Matthew has inserted those sentences—on the love and kindness which all men, even tax collectors and Gentiles, show to their likes—between the statements about God's works and his exhortation to perfection. "If you love those who love you—do not even the tax collectors do the same?" This turn of phrase, found only in Matthew, reminds us of the programmatic sentence with which all the antitheses of the Sermon on the Mount are introduced: "Unless your righteousness exceeds that of the scribes and Pharisees, you will never enter the kingdom of heaven" (Mt 5:20). In Matthew's version, the Preacher on the Mount demands a greater justice, one that exceeds the Jewish aspiration. This moral endeavor expected from the aspirants to God's kingdom, which goes far beyond prevailing standards, is the subject of all the antitheses and reaches its climax in the commandment to love one's enemies. Here, the "excess" over the legally oriented morality of the Pharisees is to be highlighted once more—in the light of God's paradoxical behavior. This attitude, which is focused on God's own holiness, Matthew sums up at the climactic end of the antitheses in the concept of "perfection." Matthew does not intend that perfection shall consist *only* in love of one's enemies; he merely uses this extreme case to reach the all-encompassing conclusion: "You therefore must be perfect, as your heavenly Father is perfect!" That man is perfect who belongs exclusively and completely to God, and who desires nothing else than to do God's will totally, so that he may enter into God's kingdom.

And finally, there is one more reason for Matthew's formulation of the sentence. We have noted repeatedly that the first evangelist, of Judeo-Christian background, was probably influenced by Leviticus 19:2, which reads: "You shall be holy; for I the Lord your God am holy." It can be shown that Matthew (probably following a Jewish tradition) combines the decalogue and the law of holiness, and weaves both into his paraenesis which is designed for the instruction of the members of the early Church. In Matthew 19:18 f., too, the prescriptions of the decalogue are followed by the commandment to love one's neighbor, in accordance with Leviticus 19:18. The antithesis of the Sermon on the Mount not only include statements from the Ten Commandments (cf. Mt 5:21 and 27), but also other instructions from the Pentateuch (Leviticus and Deuteronomy)—e. g., 5:31, 33, and 38—including finally the law of love according to Leviticus 19:18 (Mt 4:43). It seems likely, then, that the evangelist in the final exhortation of Mt 5:48 had in mind that fundamental demand for holiness of Leviticus 19:2. He did not mean merely to repeat that demand, he meant also to exceed it: the holiness demanded in the Old Testament, as the Lord God of Israel is holy, must now prove itself as perfection as the Father in heaven is perfect. This may be no more than a shift in language—but it is not unimportant to the evangelist who is forever intent on underlining what is new, insuperable, definitive in the message and summons of Jesus.

This insight brings us closer to determining the meaning of perfection as Matthew sees it. For him, perfection is an all-embracing term for man's duty—which grows out of Jesus' message of God's kingdom—to show himself worthy of the salvation offered to him, to love God with all his heart, and above all "to seek first his kingdom" (cf. Mt 6:33). This is not the place to explicate Jesus' entire ethic concerning God's kingship. But we may present a few points which throw light on the specific nature of that perfection which the Sermon on the Mount demands of the Christian.

We must first call to mind that Jesus' message is eschatological. Because he proclaims God's kingdom as imminent, indeed as present, palpable, and effective in his own person and works, he therefore demands also a new morality which is in keeping with the time of salvation and thus must also completely "fulfill" the old law (Mt 5:17). Of course this does not yet mean sinlessness, that incorrupt and incorruptible union with God which the saved will possess in the kingdom of God, that change of heart by God's spirit of which even the prophets spoke; but it is that state of belonging to God, and that brotherhood, which are focused on that vision and motivated by it and which are made possible by the measure of salvation that has already been granted—possible as far as can be on this earth, in this eon. Jesus expects and demands that such a conduct, pointing toward eschatological consummation, be realized in thought and deed. Thus it is justified to define Christian "perfection" as the "way of life reflecting the salvific reality of the eschaton." But we must emphasize that the call to "perfection" is addressed to every Christian; every Christian ought to reflect in his individual and social way of life something of the glory of the eschatological union with God. The demands of the Sermon on the Mount deal after all with life in this world. Jesus addresses the married when he demands married faithfulness down into the recesses of the heart (Mt 5:28), or forbids divorce which until then had been allowed (5:32). It was his intention that the expected eschatological consummation should cast its radiance ahead upon the conditions of the present world and time. Dissension, revenge, and enmity among men were to be extinguished even now; the paralyzing worries of earthly life were to be conquered; and that love of wealth which separates man from God was to be overcome.

But Jesus' message may also be regarded as a restoration of the original order. Such a view does not conflict with the eschatological aspect, since the eschaton is at the same time a *restitutio in integrum* (cf. Acts 3:21, *apokatastasis*). It is true that the antitheses of the Sermon on the Mount are eschatologically motivated in the introductory statement (Mt 5:20): to enter into God's kingdom requires a greater righteousness; but the individual statements are presented as a new interpretation of the divine will, as Jesus' authoritative proclamations ("But I say to you . . ."); and that presupposes that Jesus has knowledge of God's original, uncurtailed, pure, and holy will. There is a telling example of the way in which Jesus understands and justifies his new interpretation of the old divine law, and that is the exchange concerning divorce, which is reported elsewhere than in the Sermon on the Mount (Mk 10:2-9; Mt 19:3-9). In contradiction to the permission granted by Moses, which allowed a letter of divorce, Jesus refers back to Genesis (1:27; 2:24) and demands that the union of man and wife which God created in the beginning must not be dissolved. He thus reduces Moses' command—which after all was also given in God's name!—to a relative status, to a concession limited in time and made "for your hardness of heart"; but now he demands that God's original will be obeyed completely. The reasons given for the love of one's enemies go in a slightly different direction, but come down to the same: because God is kind and merciful to all men without exception, including the evil and the unjust, therefore Jesus' disciples are to follow God's example and imitate his absolute and holy nature, without regard to their human emotions and inner reluctance. This thought is combined with the eschatological motivation; in this way, the disciples are to become the sons of the heavenly Father (Mt 5:45a; Lk 6:35c). What is meant is not that they are to become like God here and now; rather, the promise that men "shall be called sons of God" speaks of a gift to be bestowed in the kingdom of God to come, and Luke's version adds further: "Your reward will be great" (Lk 6:35b). The primary and closest motivation for love of one's enemies, however, is the example of the heavenly Father, who acts in just that way and thus points the way to the disciples. We might also say: Jesus leads men once again back to an immediate relation to God, in which they experience God's will in its purity, complete, and are to become "perfect" by doing God's will. "To be perfect as your heavenly Father is perfect" also means: "because your heavenly Father is perfect" and demands such an attitude from you.

Here we must not overlook an aspect which is inherent in Jesus' whole message of salvation, and also underlies the demands of the Sermon on the Mount. It is: The new eschatological and primally pure morality of Jesus' disciples, the undivided surrender to God, and the unlimited love of brother become possible only by God's anticipatory love and by his present work of salvation. Perfection is not only a requirement, it is a gift as well: it is man's answer to God's work which makes man capable of perfection. God's anticipatory love is best illustrated by the parable of the unmerciful servant (Mt 18:23-35). That servant had experienced unmatched forbearance from his master, who had expected him to show forbearance to his fellow servant in turn; when he fails, the master rightly reproves him: "Should not you have had mercy on your fellow servant, as I had mercy on you?" (v. 33). Overwhelmed by God's love, we are to return supreme love. God asks nothing from us which he has not first given to us in incomparably richer measure. The capacity for perfection is not stated directly in the Sermon on the Mount, but it is given, proclaimed implicitly, simply in the manner in which Jesus speaks to his disciples of the Father. In the "Our Father" (Mt 6:9-13) he teaches them to talk to God like his children, and in the discourse on needless anxiousness (6:25-32) he teaches them to trust in him as children do. The important exhortation to prayer of petition (7:711) encourages them to lay before God everything that concerns their discipleship, their efforts, and their tasks in behalf of God's kingdom: God, in the love and power of his nature, is even more eager and more capable than our fathers on earth to do "good" (Luke has "give the Holy Spirit") to those who pray for it. This is at least an allusion that all strength for his work, and for his moral endeavor, comes to Jesus' disciple from the Father.

Now we are in a position to distinguish the "perfection" called for in the Sermon on the Mount from that idea of perfection which dominates us all as heirs of Greek thought. That perfection is not an ideal which we are to approach step by step, without ever reaching it; rather, it is a total surrender to God which we as Christ's disciples must perform, and by which we are to structure our life in the world, each according to his vocation. It is the love of God with all our heart and all our strength, the love from which grows also our love of neighbor and of our most distant brothers, of friend and enemy, in the image of God's love. Nor is this perfection inspired by a humanism which is striving for a fully rounded humanity, with all its powers developed to perfection—it is a life in the sight and in the company of God, so that we may pass muster before him, however miserable our humanity may still remain. Finally, that perfection is not an ethical blueprint but a religious demand: the demand to submit and surrender to the eternally superior God in obedience to his call, in the resolve to be pure in heart and radical in deed, and also in reliance on his mercy, help, and salvation.

Matthew described this inner attitude in conscious contrast to the legal-minded piety of Pharisees and scribes which fails to realize the will of God, and closes rather than opens the kingdom of God to mankind (cf. Mt 23:13). He employed the Jewish terminology which is found already in the Old Testament, and tried to show what is the true "justice" and "perfection" demanded by Jesus. Luke, addressing a formerly pagan audience, interprets Jesus' eschatological message and demand differently, and yet he teaches the same thing. Immediately after the blessings and the cries of woe, he leads off with the challenging demand to love one's enemies—and never allows his audience to escape again from this grasp with which God grips the whole man. For him, there was no reason to depart from the original wording. On the contrary, he would welcome the demand: "Be merciful, even as your Father is merciful!"

The second passage in which Matthew (and only he) uses the expression "perfect" leads us still more deeply into our complex of questions. Differing from the Sermon on the Mount, Jesus' demand is addressed this time not to all men, but only to the "rich young man" (Mt 19:21). Further, Jesus' twofold answer seems to imply also a twofold demand: the keeping of the commandments is (seemingly) just a preliminary step, and only the surrender of all possessions constitutes real perfection. Finally, and this is the most important point, perfection is tied very closely to the imitation of Jesus. We shall for the moment leave aside the problem of the "evangelic counsels" which have long troubled the treatment of this pericope.

We shall start again by trying to throw some light on the procedure and intentions of the first evangelist in giving to his account a special structure and formulation differing from Mark (and from Luke who here follows Mark very closely). According to Mark 10:17-22, Jesus replies to the man's question, "What must I do to inherit eternal life?" with the reminder ("You know . . .") of the Ten Commandments, and enumerates the second tablet, in an unusual sequence. To the man's answer, "Teacher, all these I have observed from my youth," Jesus says: "You lack one thing; go, sell what you have, and give to the poor, and you will have treasure in heaven; and come, follow me!" Numerous observations prove that Matthew had Mark's report before him and consciously altered it. The divergences significant for our purpose are these: *1.* Jesus' first answer is expanded: "If you would enter life, keep the commandments!" And only after the man asks "Which?" in return, does Jesus enumerate them. *2.* The law of love from Leviticus 19:18 is added to the selection from the decalogue. *3.* The "young man" asks of his own accord: "What do I still lack?" *4.* Jesus' further answer runs: "If you would be perfect, go, sell what you possess. . . ."

302

Rudolf Schnackenburg

The fact that our starting point is the Sermon on the Mount will facilitate our understanding of the evangelist's intention with this pericope. We have pointed out above that in both instances the examples from the decalogue are followed by the law of love (cf. the second alteration). Matthew did not at all wish to see the Old Testament law abrogated, even after the Sermon on the Mount; on the contrary, he underlined its validity and binding force (cf. 5:17-19); this is why he now lays stress also on Jesus' first reply to the young man (cf. the first alteration). But he also interprets Jesus' Sermon on the Mount in the sense that the law has to be fulfilled and exceeded in a new way; this is why he ended the antitheses with the formulation: "Therefore be perfect . . .!"; this is also why he now includes the same summons to perfection in Jesus' further answer to young man (cf. the fourth alteration).

To gain a still fuller understanding, let us try to imagine what practical catechetical purpose Matthew had in mind with the pericope of the rich young man. We shall make no mistake when we assume that he wanted Judeo-Christians (or Jewish catechumens) to learn from the example of the rich young man what demands Christ made on them in excess of their traditional Jewish law. The fact that the young man is intended as the type of the Jewish aspirant for baptism is possibly revealed in the third alteration, where the young man himself is made to ask: "What do I still lack?" And Jesus, without retracting his first instruction that the young man must keep the commandments, now adds a further demand: In total self-surrender, in complete submission to God (which here takes the concrete expression of giving away his fortune), the young man must enter *Jesus' followership*. This demand explains the peculiar parallelism and dialectic of Jesus' double answer (the first and the fourth alterations): In order to enter into life it is necessary to fulfill God's commandments—in the sense in which Jesus understands fulfillment (cf. the Sermon on the Mount). And yet, considered in a different light, that is not enough, because it could be done in a purely legalistic way (as the young man has perhaps done so far). If he wishes to be "perfect," which means blameless before the law, as God wills him

303

to be, then he must take radical action, here give up his wealth, and follow Jesus.

A few points need to be clarified to substantiate our interpretation. Jesus' double answer cannot refer to two different degrees of moral endeavor to which the inquirer may or may not rise as he wishes, and even less to two different degrees of blessedness he might thereby attain. The matter has been clearly stated by J. Herkenrath. "To enter eternal life" is synonymous with "to enter the kingdom of God," and this is the sole and also the supreme promise which Jesus has to give. " 'Treasure is in heaven' is here not intended as a special reward (no more than it is in Mark), but as the recompense for the surrender of worldly wealth: it thus coincides with 'eternal life' in Matthew 6:20." The expression "If you *would* be perfect" leaves it up to the young man whether to seek perfection or to forego this "higher" resolve; for Jesus' first answer to him uses the same expression, "If you would enter life . . . ," and confronts him, as is generally recognized, with an urgent necessity. In Mark's gospel, all doubt is removed by Jesus' answer: "You lack one thing!" while in Matthew the same expression is ascribed to the young man. Thus J. Schmid is right in saying "that the thought in Matthew is the same as in Mark. Jesus' demand of 'perfection' cannot be regarded as a mere counsel, since the surrender of one's possessions to the poor is part of the followership of Jesus (cf. Lk 14:33), that is, is not left to the decision of the disciple."

We may then draw this conclusion: *For this man,* Jesus interprets the surrender of his fortune as the fulfillment of God's commandments the way he understands them, as the expression of abandonment to God, of radical obedience—altogether in the sense of the Sermon on the Mount (cf. Mt 6:24). The same thing is suggested perhaps by the manner in which Jesus right at the start recites God's commandments to the young man. In Mark, Jesus follows "Do not bear false witness!" with "Do not defraud!" According to Jewish parallels, this may also mean "Do not withhold just wages!" It is thus possible that Jesus makes this demand in view of the inquirer's wealth. Matthew omits the expression, but after the decalogue adds the law of love, which may here also intend to remind the young man of his particular duties arising from his wealth. While it may be doubtful that Jesus' intent can be immediately gathered from his first answer, his second reply makes it quite clear that he regards it God's inexorable call for this man to separate himself completely from his possessions, and to follow Jesus in poverty. Jesus' demand is of one piece, although it is *revealed* gradually. He who would enter life must be perfect. He must obey God's commandments, but in the way in which Jesus interprets them; in case of the rich young man, it means he must renounce his earthly goods and follow Jesus.

We may now ask how the *Imitation of Jesus* is related to *perfection.* We must remind ourselves that "imitation" or "followership," and "discipleship" have undergone a change of meaning. Originally, "to follow (or imitate) Jesus" meant to follow Jesus' call and become his personal disciple. However, in the early Church the concept of "disciple" acquired a wider meaning, clearly shown in the Acts (Chapters 6-11); in the gospel of John, too, all those are "disciples" who join in the faith (cf. 8:12, 31; 12:35 f.). In the evangelist's own comments, the distinction between Jesus' words to his "disciples" in the narrower sense, and his words to the people, is often blurred. There can be no doubt that those demands which stemmed from his message of God's kingdom were addressed by Jesus to all men; but neither can it be doubted that he called only a small number to become his special disciples and give up house and home, family, and profession.

Does this mean that the idea of perfection remains limited to that small number of disciples? The answer is an emphatic "no"; Matthew makes it sufficiently clear in the Sermon on the Mount that every aspirant to God's kingdom ought to be "perfect" (5:48). Accordingly, we may not interpret the second passage in the pericope of the rich young man to mean that "perfection" consisted generally in the surrender of earthly wealth. Jesus' final words to the young man are of course an invitation to him to follow as a "disciple" in the fullest sense: but we must understand it to mean that, *for this man,* the perfection that is demanded of all men—complete surrender to God—took the specific form of a life in poverty such as it was lived in the community of Jesus' constant followers. Our earlier

305

interpretation is thus confirmed; but we must inquire further. How did the early Church understand Jesus' demand when it extended the "followership of Jesus" to all believers? Doubtless in this way, that the demand for perfection takes concrete form for each and every Christian in and through the imitation of the Lord. If formerly, in the presence and by the decision of Jesus, God's call took on a concrete form for every man, should that not apply in a similar way for later believers? In this light, the "common property" of the Jerusalem community (Acts 2:44 f.; 4:32) becomes more intelligible. It represented the realization of the idea of poverty in the specific circumstances of the original community. Assuming the believers who came after Easter transposed the idea of "followership" into their own situation, applied it to their conditions of life—did they not have to ask themselves what concrete demands the Lord was making on them and on each individual? (cf. Acts 4:36 f.; 5:1-11).

In this light the "evangelic counsels" assume a new complexion. They have a biblical basis, although they have not always been properly based on the Bible. They are God's call to the individual man to enter into Christ's service more firmly than other men who do not hear the call; they are addressed to men who are to be directly and exclusively available for Christ and his work. We cannot here analyze in detail the three classic counsels; we shall show only briefly how poverty, chastity, and obedience fit into this perspective.

The decision of individual men to make themselves eunuchs for the sake of the kingdom of heaven has been accepted by Jesus in Matthew 19:11 f., and obviously been defended against unfriendly critics. They were followers who were moved by Jesus' preachings of God's kingdom to renounce marriage, either from the start or by giving up their existing marriage. The matter has the character of a counsel, since Jesus did not demand it of everybody, not even of all the disciples in the narrower sense; the majority of the "apostles" themselves after Easter do not seem to have given up marriage (cf. 1 Cor 9:5). Jesus approved of that condition, even while he himself led a virginal life. He regarded it as a form of total surrender to God to which such men had been inspired—indeed he regarded it as a special grace of God (cf. v. 11). He seems to have demanded surrender of all property from all those who wanted to share permanently his wandering life (cf. Mk 10:28-30; Lk 14: 33). In this respect, the counsel of poverty is far more compelling.

The counsel of obedience is least clearly expressed in the gospels, because it was added later and became the principal mark of the monastic life. Its biblical foundation would seem to be Jesus' repeated call to service. "Whoever would be great among you must be your servant, and whoever would be first among you must be slave of all!" (Mk 10:43). When Luke shifts the disciples' quarrel over their rank to the scene of the Last Supper, and emphasizes Jesus' service at the table (22:26 f.), he surely had the conditions of the later communities in mind. John underlines still more the example of Jesus in his description of the footwashing (13:1-5). The disciples' obedience to Jesus and to God lies as such on a different plane. But if we consider that the group of disciples around Jesus, with its distinctive ways of life, could become a paradigm for later believers, we can also understand as an extension of the biblical example St. Benedict's thought that in the monastic family the abbot represents Christ himself, and that obedience shown to him is as good as obedience to Christ himself.

The insight that every Christian has the duty to be perfect, and is called to realize his perfection concretely in the imitation of Jesus, yields an important consequence for the believers living in the world. Although they have not heard the call to lead a life apart, in the manner of the original disciples, they have been called nonetheless to seek for concrete ways in which they may attain perfection. For them, too, Jesus' demands in the Sermon on the Mount are not just a distant and unattainable ideal, nor are they of concern only to the priesthood, but are demands addressed to them as well. In their earthly station and profession they, too, are called to attempt total surrender and the radical striving for God's kingdom. And here again, the primary commandment of love points the way: by loving their brothers, their neighbors, and their enemies, they must strive to meet Jesus' demand: "You, therefore, must be perfect, as your heavenly Father is perfect!"

Raymond Edward Brown
1928-

Born in New York, Raymond Brown studied at Catholic University, St. Mary's Seminary, and Johns Hopkins University. He entered the Sulpicians in 1951, was ordained a priest in 1953, completed his Scripture degrees before the Biblical Commission in Rome, and taught at St. Mary's Seminary in Baltimore from 1959 to 1971. At that time he joined the faculty of Union Theological Seminary in New York City where he has been teaching ever since.

Brown is probably the most highly respected of Catholic Biblical scholars in America today. His consistent ability to produce both quantity and quality, to attend to minute detail and keep a balanced overview, and to appreciate the past while pointing out the demands of the future has resulted in his well-deserved reputation. Three prestigious universities in different European countries with different Christian traditions—Edinburgh, Uppsala, and Louvain—honored him with doctoral degrees in the 1970s.

Well known for his monumental two volumes on The Gospel according to John in the Anchor Bible series (1966/1970), his central role in the preparation and production of the Jerome Biblical Commentary (1967), (along with Joseph Fitzmyer and Roland Murphy) assures him of a lasting place in the annals of American Catholic Biblical scholarship. It is one of the chapters *from this highly-acclaimed work that we have chosen to present here, chapter 71 on "Hermeneutics."*

The possession of sacred writings entails an inherent problem: written words do not automatically convey the sense intended by the ones who composed them. Understanding a text always involves interpretation, a selection from among possible meanings. This is at once an extremely important and an extremely difficult business. It has been the central concern throughout Christian history. How is the Bible to be understood? We have seen the question confronted from the time of Origen to our own day. In the treatment that follows we have an example of Brown's synthesizing clarity, his ability to provide a helpful perspective and orientation in a labyrinthine realm where most lose their bearings.

Hermeneutics, it is safe to say, will continue to be an area of lively discussion, perhaps especially because of its ecumenical implications. Actually, it is a sphere where philosophy, literary criticism, psychology, and theology all meet and have relevant insights to contribute to each other. With the assistance of men like Raymond Brown, American Catholics have been able to leave the "precritical theology" of the past behind and join fruitfully in the contemporary debate.

In 1976, in accepting the honorary doctorate conferred on him by the University of Louvain, Brown concluded his address with a glance toward the future: "American Catholic New Testament criticism, as it begins to be more trenchant than was possible in the period of the Council, must draw out honestly the implications of its observations for theology and ecclesiology and ecumenism. It has the power to serve as the conscience of the Church by reminding us what it was like when men and women first began to follow the Lord Jesus Christ." The recovery of such a vision is obviously the ideal toward which every hermeneutical effort must strive.

HERMENEUTICS

INTRODUCTION

(I) MEANING OF HERMENEUTICS

T he Greek word *hermēneia* was used to cover a broad scope in the process of clarification. First, it could refer to interpretation by *speech* itself, inasmuch as language interprets what is in a man's mind; this usage of the word was especially significant when there was an instance of human language used to interpret the divine will. Second, the word *hermēneia* could refer to the process of *translation* from an unintelligible language to an intelligible one, e.g., the *hermēneia* of tongues in I Corinthians 12:10, which was a charismatic gift with a revelatory character. Perhaps we should stress that "translation" here should also be taken in a sense that is no longer common except in ecclesiastical jargon, namely that of moving things from one place to another (e.g., translating a body to a new burial ground). Part of the clarifying task of *hermēneia* was to translate past meaning to the present. Third, the word *hermēneia* was used for *interpretation by commentary and explanation.*

The understanding that *hermēneia* covered speech, translation, and commentary as part of the process of clarification was lost sight of in the subsequent evolution of the use of the word, and now modern scholars are trying to recapture the fullness of the concept in their study of the hermeneutical task. We shall confine the word "hermeneutic," in the singular, to this larger modern understanding of the task of interpretation; and we shall use "hermeneutics," reflecting the Latin plural *hermeneutica*, for the science of meaning (in this case, the meaning of Scripture). Whereas in the more ancient and fuller understanding, *hermēneia* involved exegesis or interpretation, in the standard biblical manuals hermeneutics is distinguished from exegesis, as the theoretical from the practical. Exegesis is looked upon as the practical application of the theoretical rules supplied by hermeneutics. Cf. J. M. Robinson, *New Hermeneutic*, ix-x, I-II.

In discussing hermeneutics as the science of biblical meaning, biblical manuals have customarily divided it into three treatises: (I) noematics, which deals with the various senses of Scripture; (2) heuristics, which explains how to discover the sense of a passage; (3) prophoristics, which gives the rules for expounding the sense of a Scripture passage to others. These formal divisions are unwieldy; below, in treating the senses of Scripture (literal, more-than-literal), we shall cover both noematics and heuristics, and under the titles of "Preaching" and "Communication" we shall treat certain aspects of prophoristics. Moreover, since the overspeculative treatments of hermeneutics in the manuals often have an aspect of unreality, we shall concentrate on the practical consequences of what we discuss.

(II) GENERAL OBSERVATIONS

To determine the sense of any written work is largely to determine what its author meant when he wrote it. As we shall see in the treatment of the more-than-literal senses of Scripture, it is true that sometimes the written word takes on a life of its own, and the words may convey more than what their author meant them to say. Modern literary criticism seems to be moving away from an exclusive emphasis on what the author intended to a broader emphasis on what his words actually convey to the individual reader. Nevertheless, allowing and, indeed, insisting on this broader emphasis, we still maintain that the principal task of interpretation centers around the author's intended meaning.

In the Bible this task is especially complicated because, as with other ancient books, the author's period of time, manner of expression, and (Semitic) cast of thought are so far removed from our own. Even to specify what or who an "author" is, is difficult because the ancient concept of author is wider than our modern concept. In reference to the biblical books, the word "author" covers at least five different relationships between the man whose name is attached to a book and the work attributed to him. And so, when we speak of the sense intended by the author, obviously we must narrow down the broad conception of authorship.

The long process of editing that the biblical books have undergone also complicates the task of determining the sense the author intended. We refer here to editing that took place within the period of the composition of the biblical books (up to *ca.* 100 BC for the books of the OT; up to *ca.* AD 125 for the books of the NT), not to subsequent scribal changes in the copying and translating of the completed biblical books. For instance, the composition of the Book of Isaiah covered a span of at least 200 years; not only were new sections added to the original parts that came from Isaiah's lifetime, but also some of the additions had the specific purpose of modifying and changing the meaning of the original. The last verses of Amos may be an addition; they supply an optimistic conclusion to an otherwise pessimistic book. In instances like this, one must determine both the sense of the book after editing and the sense that the parts originally had before editing.

Perhaps the greatest complication in biblical hermeneutics stems not so much from the multiplicity of human authors and editors but from the unique status of the biblical books, which had both a divine and a human author. In the traditional understanding of inspiration, there stands behind each verse of Scripture not only the mind of the man or men who contributed to its writing but also the guidance of God. We recall the formulation of *Providentissimus Deus,* which states that God so moved the human authors to write and so assisted them in that writing that they faithfully committed to apt words the things that he ordered. Thus, we have a twofold problem: What did the divine author intend and did that intention exceed the intention of the human author? With this general survey of the difficulties, we shall begin our discussion of the senses of Scripture with the literal sense—the sense that by definition is the one intended by the human author.

THE LITERAL SENSE OF SCRIPTURE

(I) DEFINITION

The term "literal" is used today to designate the most basic sense of Scripture, a sense that in the past has been designated as "carnal," "historical," or "philological." As the name itself indicates and as the term was used in the Middle Ages (Thomas Aq., *Quodl.* 7, q.6, a.14), the *sensus litteralis* was the sense conveyed by the words (*litterae* or *verba*) of Scripture, as distinct from the sense contained in the "things" of Scripture (the *sensus spiritualis* or typical sense flowing from the *res*). The early writers on the subject were little concerned with the awareness of the human author, and they designated as "literal" any sense the words conveyed, whether or not that sense was intended by the human author (Thomas Aq., *De pot.* q.4., a.I). Some modern theorists, like A. Fernández and P. Benoit, would still maintain this broad definition of the literal sense, subdistinguishing a primary literal sense intended by the human author, and a secondary literal sense intended by God unbeknown to the human author. It is more common, however, for modern writers to confine the designation "literal sense" to that meaning of the words of Scripture intended by the human author. The encyclical *Divino Afflante Spiritu* seems to imply this when it speaks of the task: "to discern and define that sense of the biblical words which is called literal . . . so that the mind of the author may be made clear." Recently, P. Grelot has suggested that in French the older, broader connotation of *sensus litteralis* might come under the heading of *sens littéraire*, whereas the more recent and narrower connotation might come under the heading *sens littéral.*

In any case, we shall define the literal sense thus: *The sense which the human author directly intended and which his words convey.* First, we note that it is a question of the *direct intention* of the human author. This qualification confines the literal sense to the meaning that was in the consciousness of the human author and excludes ramifications that his words may have taken on in the larger context of the Bible but of which he was unaware (such ramifications belong to the *sensus plenior*).

Second, the literal sense is a sense *conveyed by the author's words.* The author's intention does not become a sense of Scripture until it is effectively conveyed by his words. The principle that we are not concerned with the author's thought alone but with the message he conveys is important in discussing the limitations of biblical inerrancy. In particular, concerning the words of Jesus, it must be noted that what Jesus intended by his words is in itself not strictly a sense of *Scripture,* for Jesus was not the

314

writer of the Gospels. The inspired literal sense of a Gospel passage is the meaning attributed to Jesus' words by the individual Evangelist. Often the various Evangelists attribute different meanings to the same words of Jesus, as we can see from the different contexts in which the Evangelists have set these words; and sometimes, since we do not know the context in which Jesus actually spoke the words, it may be impossible for us to tell exactly what the words originally meant when Jesus first uttered them. Nevertheless, in the Evangelists' interpretations we have an understanding (or several understandings) of Jesus' words that the Holy Spirit has inspired for the Church, and our faith in the working of the Spirit gives us assurance that this understanding is not a distortion of Jesus' historical teaching, although it may go beyond his teaching.

Third, the two parts of our definition of the literal sense, the intention of the author and the sense conveyed by the words, cannot be separated. Such a separation has been responsible for what historically has been one of the great confusions about the literal sense. Often the biblical authors wrote in poetic and figurative language. Many of the Church Fathers, e.g., Origen, thought that the literal sense was what the words said, independently of the author's intent. Thus were Christ spoken of as "the lion of Judah," the literal sense for these Fathers would be that he was an animal. This is why some of them rejected the literal sense of Scripture. To avoid this confusion, many manuals have distinguished between the *proper* (nonmetaphorical) literal sense and the *improper* (metaphorical, figurative) literal sense. There is no real danger of confusion when we insist that the literal sense is what the author *intended* whether he used plain or figurative language.

There is another confusion in the history of the literal sense that we should mention. For a while it was thought that a single passage of Scripture could have several literal senses. Both Augustine and Thomas seem to have been of this view; and the view is still defended by modern writers like Desnoyers and Sertillanges. Our judgment on this is that no text of Scripture can have two heterogeneous, independent literal senses, for quite obviously no author intends to have his words convey two totally unrelated meanings. Most of the other aspects of the problem of two literal senses would come under the heading of double meanings or subordinate meanings that are perfectly possible. See also the discussion of the *sensus plenior,* which envisages the possibility that God may have intended a meaning of the words of Scripture deeper than the meaning intended by the human author.

(II) PROBLEMS IN DETERMINING THE LITERAL SENSE

We shall not emphasize here the usual rules for determining the sense of any author and book (correct translation of his words; attention to phrase and sentence structure; context; peculiar style and usage; etc.). We shall concern ourselves with special difficulties to be faced in reading the Bible.

(A) Common Fallacies

It is easy to become romantically enthusiastic about the reading of Scripture and the obligation that all should know Scripture. Such enthusiasm quickly runs against the hard fact that to interpret Scripture and determine its literal sense is no simple task. And so, throughout the ages, there has been a consistent attempt to get around or minimize the obstacle of the hard work involved, and this attempt has left us with a number of fallacies.

(a) Simplicity of Scripture

Because Scripture is inspired and presumably this inspiration was for the good of all, there has arisen the fallacy that everyone should be able to pick up the Bible and read it profitably. If this implies that everyone should be able to find out what the sacred author is saying without preparation or study, it really demands of God in each instance a miraculous dispensation from the limitations imposed by differences of time and circumstance. Of course it is true that considerable portions of Scripture are easily intelligible to all because they voice universal sentiments, e.g., some of the Psalms and some of the simple stories of Jesus. It is also true that spiritual solace and insight may be drawn from the Bible by those who have no technical knowledge and indeed do not understand its literal sense. (Conversely, those who have technical knowledge have at times overlooked the religious depths of the Bible.) Nevertheless, when it is a question of finding out what the human author meant to say, and therefore what God inspired, there is no substitute for educated effort. The inspired author wrote in a language and culture far removed from our own; his primary duty was to be intelligible for his own times. That what he said also has meaning for us today is certainly true; but he did not express himself primarily for us in our terms, and so it requires training on our part to decipher what he meant.

This problem is not met adequately by saying that we must reinterpret Scripture into a language that is intelligible without effort to the man of today. We shall mention below the quest to demythologize and the legitimate desire so to interpret Scripture that its phrasing is not an obstacle. For instance, translations of the Bible into truly modern English can, to a certain extent, give us the equivalents of biblical ideas and facilitate understanding. But much of the biblical imagery cannot be modernized; and if it can be interpreted, it cannot simply be dispensed with, for it is too integral a part of the biblical message, e.g., the symbolism of the Apocalypse. A full answer to the problem of unintelligibility caused by the difference between the world view of the biblical author and our own must involve educating the modern reader to understand the ancient mentality so that he can grasp both the message and the modality which that mentality gives to the message.

The problem of the scripturally uneducated reader is often brought forward as an objection to the thesis that we have been proposing here. If the literate but simple folk of times past could read and love Scripture, why cannot the scripturally uneducated do the same today? Yet there is a difference between the man of past generations who had little education in any field and the man of today who has general education in other fields but not in religion or in Scripture and its auxiliaries. From his general education the man of today asks complicated questions about Scripture, the answers for which require training. No one with a grammar-school education can read the first chapters of Genesis without wondering if the world was really created in six days; yet considerable training is required to be able to distinguish between the religious teaching of Genesis about creation and the naive prescientific outlook of the author. To supply a standard, we may say that in order to read the Bible with intelligent appreciation a man's biblical education should be proportionate to his general education. Only thus will he be able to answer the questions suggested by his general education.

Part of the fallacy about the simplicity of the Bible is the idea that all one needs to understand the Bible is the Bible itself. On the contrary, to uncover the literal sense of Scripture there is real need for auxiliary knowledge, e.g., geography, archaeology, textual criticism. But above all a *knowledge of history* is required. The Bible is, for the most part, the story of God's action in the history of a particular people, an action that is largely unintelligible without a knowledge of Near Eastern history. To seek to divorce God's action from the history of the ancient Near East and to make it timeless is to distort a fundamental message of the Bible, namely that God acts only in concrete circumstances and times (such as yours and mine). What we say here is particularly applicable to the historical and prophetic books of the OT, easily two-thirds of the Bible. Many students, loathe to familiarize themselves with the dates and events of long-dead civilizations, lose through their lack of interest in ancient history the wealth of some of the richest sections of the Bible.

Another important auxiliary for reading the Bible is the *knowledge of the biblical languages.* Only a small percentage of those who study the Bible can be experts in Hebrew, Aramaic, and Greek; yet some familiarity with the structure and thought-pattern of these languages is essential for the type of biblical knowledge that a theology student should have. Such a demand is again part of the recognition that God has acted in particular times and places—his message would have taken a different form and nuance had it been expressed in other languages. Unless one has some idea of the latitude of the "tenses" in Hebrew, one has difficulty in understanding the undefined time designations in the words of the prophets, i.e., a lack of temporal precision that opened these prophecies to future as well as present fulfillment. Some of the basic words of biblical theological vocabulary defy adequate translation into English, e.g., *hesed* (covenant kindness, mercy) in the OT, and *alētheia* (truth) in the NT; modern translations catch only part of a wider connotation. The frequent plays on similar-sounding words in OT poetry and on words of similar root in NT Greek are lost to the student who takes no interest in

318

the biblical languages. With English as one's only linguistic tool, it is possible to have a good knowledge of the Scriptures but scarcely a professional one.

(b) Quest for Relevance

Another fallacy is the thesis that only some parts of Scripture are important, namely those most relevant to our life today. There is a legitimate quest for relevancy in biblical studies, as we shall insist. It is quite true that, at times, strict historico-critical exegesis produces knowledge primarily of antiquarian value; it is also true that the intensive study of some areas of Scripture belongs more to an advanced stage of research than, for example, to the training of the average theological student. For instance, the description of the geographical boundaries of the tribes in the latter part of Joshua is fascinating for the professional biblical historian and geographer; but to give more than summary attention to this section in a survey course of the OT would be bad pedagogy. Thus "relevance" sets legitimate guidelines in both study and teaching.

The abuse with which we are concerned is the tendency to allow a quest for relevance to give an orientation to basic biblical studies that is not true to the Bible itself, e.g., the desire to study only those parts of the Bible that have easily convertible theological value, or preaching value, or value for the spiritual life. Such interests can supply a secondary emphasis in the study of Scripture, but to make them primary reflects a basic misunderstanding of what the Bible is. As Barr has eloquently stated, on the student level or on the scholarly level this form of the quest for relevance is theologically doubtful and basically anti-intellectual. The books of Scripture were not inspired or written primarily for the dogmatic theologian, nor for the preacher, nor for the ascetic. They deal on a much wider scale with God's action for man, and with man's understanding of God and of his own existence and history. The scale of biblical action and thought is the scale of life itself. In particular, the value of the OT is precisely related to the broadness of its scope that includes, not only the spiritual and theological aspects of life, but also the secular and the sordid (war, depravity). The Bible shows how men learned to fit the *whole* of life into their relationship to God.

To select from this totality only those portions of the biblical narrative that meet the narrow requirements of a modern understanding of what is religious or spiritual is disastrous. Indeed, the failure to appreciate the importance of the OT often springs from the false concept that what God has inspired should be consistently noble, beautiful, and uplifting—a concept that implicitly reflects the thesis that religion has nothing to do with the secular and the profane. What strikes such a mentality as irrelevant in the Bible (e.g., the chain of history, the humdrum causality of human events, the careers of bad men and indifferent men) is in a deeper sense precisely what is relevant, i.e., relevant to a man's life that is part of humdrum history and full of encounters with evil and indifference. In short, this artificial quest for relevance reflects the failure to understand the basic biblical truth that God has acted in *history*.

In its consequences for theology such a selectivity on the basis of relevance is truly frightening. We accuse a past generation of turning the Bible into a mine for proof-texts, so that a student's knowledge of the Bible was often confined to parts useful for apologetics or for a scholastic propositional theology. But is not the same mistake being made today when some would tell us to concentrate on the portions of Scripture that enable man to understand himself existentially, or on parts that favor personalism, or community spirit, or an "I-thou" relationship? A future generation will condemn such selectivity just as harshly as we have condemned the apologetic selectivity of our ancestors. To pass on to the next generation only what we find relevant in Scripture is to censor Scripture, for precisely what we do not find relevant to our times may be God's principal word in Scripture to another generation.

A particular aspect of the unbalanced quest for relevance is centered on biblical theology. The sterility of 19th-century critical exegesis has produced by way of salutary reaction a very valid 20th-century interest in biblical theology. This is an attempt to preserve the wholeness of the scriptural message where theology is a major (but not exclusive) dimension. However, a great desire for biblical theology on the part of beginning students *can* be another example of the tendency to turn Scripture studies from the hard path of exegesis into easier fields. Students frequently prefer a course on biblical themes or "biblical theology" to a course in exegesis. Yet a real knowledge of biblical themes can be built up only by analyzing the texts of the Bible that pertain to the themes and then by synthesizing the results. To feed the beginner a steady diet of synthesized results without first leading him to the biblical text itself is both to blind the student to the difficulties of Scripture and to substitute the study of compendia for the reading of God's word. An earlier generation of Catholic theological students complained that they never studied the Scriptures themselves but spent all their time on introductions to the biblical books; a contemporary generation may in retrospect voice the same complaint about an exaggerated stress on biblical theology. Once again, we insist that we do not wish to undervalue the study of biblical theology, but rather to emphasize that such study can be effectively pursued only after the student has worked through the exegesis of the Bible.

In the history of biblical interpretation in the Catholic Church, each time there has been a movement that put emphasis on the primacy of literal exegesis (e.g., Jerome, the school of St. Victor in the Middle Ages, Richard Simon), this movement has been quickly swallowed up in a more attractive movement that stressed the theological or the spiritual aspects of Scripture almost to the exclusion of literal exegesis. And so Origen's spiritual exegesis conquered Jerome's literal exegesis through the efforts of Augustine; the exegesis practiced at St. Victor was swallowed up in the theological and philosophical use of Scripture in later Scholasticism; Bossuet and Pascal outshone R. Simon in popular influence. The encyclical *Divino Afflante Spiritu*, confirmed by Vatican II, has made a thoroughgoing quest for the literal sense by historico-critical exegesis a real possibility for Catholics for the first time in centuries. This quest is the primary duty of those who teach and study Scripture, and we should not allow ourselves to be misled into easier paths which, in the long run, will take us away from the Bible.

(B) Need for Establishing Literary Form

Having pointed out the fallacies that might distract from the quest for the literal sense, we now turn to the problem of the basic steps in that quest. The *first step* in finding out what the author intended is to determine the literary form the author is employing. If we walk into a modern library, books are classified according to the type of literature: fiction, poetry, history, biography, drama, etc. Often the classification for individual books is indicated by the dust jacket. The knowledge of the type of literature to which a book belongs causes us to make adjustments in our approach to the book, e.g., if we have two books treating of the same event, and one book is fiction, the other serious history, we do not place the same credence in the narratives of each.

The Bible is what remains of the library of ancient Israel and of the Ist-century Christian Church. This library has all the diversity we would expect in the literary output of an articulate culture that spanned nearly 2000 years. In the Bible the books of this library have been bound together into one, without the advantage of dust jackets. It is the task of the student of the Bible to classify the biblical books or their parts according to the type of literature they represent. This is what is meant by determining the literary form (*genus litterarium*) the author has employed. (This emphasis on literary form is an offshoot of the German development of Form Criticism). The encyclical *Divino Afflante Spiritu* and Vatican II have made this approach imperative on all serious Catholic students of the Bible, so that the first question we must ask in opening any part of the Bible is: What type of literature do we have here?

In a broad sense, of course, the determination of literary form has been a principle implicitly recognized from a very early period. From the time of Rabbi Gamaliel II (late Ist century AD) the Jews have classified the books of the OT as Torah, Prophets, and Writings; but the Christian division of these books into Historical, Prophetical, and Sapiential is even closer to a distinction of literary types. Only in modern times, however, with the discovery of the literatures of people contemporary with Israel, have we realized just how many types of literature were current in antiquity. Let us illustrate this from the OT since it is a more varied library than the NT. There are many varieties of poetry in the OT: Epic poetry underlies some of the narratives in the Pentateuch and Joshua; lyric poetry is found in Psalms and Canticle; didactic poetry is found in Proverbs, Sirach, and Wisdom; elements of drama are found in Job. Within the prophetic books there are both prophecy and apocalyptic. There is not one type of history in the OT but many types: a factual penetrating analysis, seemingly by an eyewitness, in the court history of David (2 Samuel II-I, Kings 2); stylized, abbreviated court records in Kings and Chronicles; romanticized and simplified epic history of the national saga in Exodus; tales of tribal heroes in Judges; stories of the great men of yore in the patriarchal accounts. There is even pre-history in the Genesis narratives of the origin of man and of evil, narratives that borrow legends from the lore of other nations and make them the vehicles of a monotheistic theology. The instances we have given by no means exhaust the literary richness of the OT library; there are fictional tales, parables, allegories, proverbs, maxims, love stories, etc.

As with other literature, once the reader has determined what type of literature he is dealing with in the section of the Bible that he is reading, he applies the standards of that type of literature to determine what the author meant to say, i.e., the literal sense. If the reader knows that Jonah is a fictional parable, he knows that the author is *not* giving a history of the relations of Israel and Assyria and is *not* presenting the story of Jonah in the whale's belly as a serious account of a true happening. If the reader understands that the statement about the sun standing still in Joshua 10:13 comes from a fragment of highly poetic description in a victory song, he will judge it in the light of poetic license rather than according to the rules of strict history. If the reader understands that the Samson narratives are folk tales, he will not give to them the same historical credence that he gives to the history of David's court. Many of the past difficulties about the Bible have stemmed from the failure to recognize the diversity of the literary forms that it contains and from the tendency to misinterpret as scientific history pieces of the Bible that are not historical or are historical only in a more popular sense. We have taken our examples from the OT; but we must caution that the same problem exists in the NT. The Gospels are not scientifically historical biographies of Jesus but written accounts of the preaching and teaching of the early Church about Jesus, and their accuracy must be judged according to the standards of preaching and teaching.

The approach to exegesis that we have just discussed, based on determining the type of literature that one is dealing with, is subject to two common misconceptions. First, some conservative spokesmen regard the quest for literary form as an attempt to circumvent the historicity of biblical passages, and therefore they think it dangerous to apply the theory of literary forms to the more sacred sections of the Bible. This misconception is vocalized in statements like the following: "That is *just* a literary form" or "It is permissible to apply the theory of literary forms to the OT but not to the NT." But every piece of writing can be classified as belonging to one type of literature or another. Factual history is a type of literature; fiction is another; both exist in the Bible, as do almost all the intermediary literary types between these two extremes. If one correctly classifies a certain part of the Bible as fiction, one is not destroying the historicity of that section, for it never was history; one is simply recognizing the author's intention in writing that section. If this is understood, the statements quoted above are nonsense. The second misconception concerns the relation of inspiration to the diversity of biblical literary forms. There is a feeling that somehow the recognition that certain parts of the Bible were written as fiction weakens or challenges their inspiration. The encyclical *Divino Afflante Spiritu (EB* 559) gives an answer: God could inspire any type of literature that was not unworthy or deceitful, i.e., not contrary to his holiness and truth (e.g., pornography, lies). Biblical fiction is just as inspired as biblical history.

(C) Need for Knowing Literary History and Aims of Composition

After one has determined the type of literature involved, the *second main step* in the quest for the literal sense is to find out the literary history of the biblical book or section that one is studying. This is a special problem in biblical study because of the long history of editing. One must unravel the individual traditions of the Pentateuch, the collections that compose Isaiah, the chronological order of Jeremiah's prophecies (different from the present order of the biblical book). In the Gospels it is important to know that a particular saying of Jesus has come from Mark or from Q or from one of the sources peculiar to Luke or Matthew, and to know by means of comparison how it present phrasing in the Gospel differs from its more original form—thus one discovers the author's theological intent made evident by his adaptation of the material that has come down to him.

Here we touch on the approach to the Bible known as *Redaktionsgechichte*. If *Formgeschichte* is concerned with the different forms or types of literature in the Bible and the rules germane to them, *Redaktionsgeschichte* is concerned with the way in which these literary pieces are made to serve the general purpose of the writer. For instance, in the Gospels an exeget has done only part of his work when he has classified a story as a particular type of parable and has determined to what extent it conforms to the general rules for the parable-type. Why is the parable included in this Gospel; Why is it set in this particular context within the Gospel? What meaning does the Evangelist attach to it? To answer these questions is to take our second main step in determining the literal sense of Scripture.

After the two steps that we have described (determining the literary form; determining the literary history and the aims of composition), the exegete is then in a position to seek the literal meaning of individual passages and verses. Here the process is the same as for any other ancient work. The literal meaning of some 90-95 per cent of the Bible can be determined by a reasonable application of the ordinary rules of interpretation. There are some passages whose meaning eludes us because their text has been corrupted in transmission, because they use rare words, because their author expressed himself obscurely, or because we do not have sufficient knowledge about the context in which they were composed. Continued study is constantly giving enlightenment even on passages such as these.

MORE-THAN-LITERAL SENSES

We now turn to the sense of Scripture that go beyond the literal, i.e., senses that by definition go beyond what the human author intended. The theoretical possibility of such senses is based on the presupposition that Scripture had a divine author who at the time that Scripture was written foresaw the future in a way the human author did not and who took cognizance of this future in the writing of Scripture. The quest for a more-than-literal sense—a quest as old as Scripture itself—is based on the contention that in the scriptural record of the past, God speaks to the present and intends the reader to find therein a depth of meaning that goes beyond the local and limited circumstances in which the original was written. Such presuppositions and contentions have been questioned, and certainly they leave themselves open to reckless application. Yet the fact that they have been invoked in exegesis from the time of the biblical authors until the present day and that they attract the attention of the most scientific biblical exegets suggests that the idea of a more-than-literal sense cannot be dismissed lightly.

(I) HISTORY OF MORE-THAN-LITERAL EXEGESIS

Perhaps the best introduction to the problem of more-than-literal senses is to trace briefly the history of this tendency in exegesis.

(A) To the End of the New Testament Era

Within the Bible itself we find the author of Wisdom (11-19) taking the older narratives of the plagues and the deliverance from Egypt and reading out of (or into) them a theme of deliverance for his own time. A parallelism between past and present is seen in this type of exegesis; another example would be the connection that Deuteronomy-Isaiah draws between the Exodus from Egypt and the return from Babylon. Such parallelism is based on the thesis that God's actions on behalf of his people follow a pattern of fidelity: He is the same yesterday, today, and forever. It is not based on a cyclic approach to history.

In the intertestamental period (last two centureis BC) there was a development that had profound effects on both Jewish and Christian exegesis. Whereas in more ancient times the prophets had been understood primarily as the spokesmen of God to their own times with a divinely given foreknowledge of God's plan for the immediate and relevant future, now the prophets of old were thought to have predicted the distant future. Apocalyptic was an important factor in this change of emphasis, following the pattern of Daniel wherein purportedly a prophet of the 6th century had visions of what would happen in the 2nd century. Such an understanding of the prophets, and indeed of other biblical writers like the psalmists, gave birth to the pesher exegesis of Qumran where evey line of the ancient books was interpreted in terms of what was happening to the Qumran sect hundreds of years later.

Moreover, this understanding of the OT prophets and psalmists explains to some extent the principles according to which the NT authors interpreted the OT. Isaiah (7:14) could be pictured by Matthew (1:23) as foretelling the virgin birth of Jesus; Deuteronomy-Isaiah in the Suffering Servant passages could be pictured as foretelling the sufferings and death of the Messiah (Luke 24:26); the author Psalm 22 could be pictured as foreseeing in detail the passion of Jesus (Matthew 27:35, 39, 43, 46). Some would compare this exegesis to the pesher exegesis of Qumran, but there are important differences. The Qumran interpreters set out to explain God's plan in the OT in terms of what was happening to the Qumran sect. The novelty of Jesus changes the direction of the current in NT exegesis: The necessity was not to explain the OT in terms of the Christian community, but to explain Jesus in terms of the OT, the only theological language available to Jews. There were no systematic Christian commentaries on the OT in NT times (and indeed not until the late 2nd century, e.g., Hippolytus commenting on Canticle and Daniel), and so we have no evidence that the NT writers felt that every line of the OT applied to Jesus or had a Christian meaning— a theory that became popular in patristic times. The NT exegesis of the OT was extraordinarily varied, and any attempt to classify it as one type of exegesis is doomed to failure. It had elements of *sensus plenior*, typology, allegory, and accommodation. A particular feature of this NT exegesis was to read the presence of Jesus back into OT scenes (I Corinthians 10:4).

While we shall be concerned in the rest of our brief history with Christian exegesis of the OT, we should note that in Pharisaic and rabbinic circles the quest for a more-than-literal exegesis was just as common as in Christian circles. The targums really supply an exegesis of what they translate and are free in reading messianic elements into the OT. The midrashim are also very free in interpreting previous Scripture in application to current problems. The Jewish nonliteral exegesis that had the greatest influence on Christian exegesis was the allegorizing of Philo.

(B) Patristic Era

In the early Christian writings of the 2nd century we find evidence both of a very free spiritual exegesis (pseudo-Barnabas) and of a rather sober exegesis. Yet even the sober exegetes, like Justin and Tertullian, ransacked the OT for proof-texts referring to Christ, and they interpreted these passages in a way that went far beyond the literal sense. It was *Alexandria* that produced the first great Christian school of exegesis; and through men like Clement and Origen, Philo's allegorizing achieved a dominant place in the Christian exegesis of the OT. Clement based his exegesis on the existence of a Christian gnosis, i.e., the secret knowledge of the profoundest truths of the Christian faith to which the elite were initiated. The key to the gnosis was an allegorical exegesis of the Bible, an exegesis that ran the gamut from authentic typology through arbitrary accommodation to the Philonic concept of the Bible as a lesson in psychology and cosmology.

Origen probably had more influence on patristic exegesis than any other single feature, although later his theological orthodoxy became suspect. Almost every manual states that Origen's exegesis was unrestrainedly allegorical, and he is usually blamed for denying the literal sense of scripture. A. von Harnack spoke of Origen's "biblical alchemy." Recently there have been serious attempts by H. de Lubac, J. Daniélou, and others to modify this picture and to re-evaluate Origen's exegesis. Origen did not simply disregard the literal sense (although he did not understand that the metaphorical sense was literal), but he was interested greatly in a sense of Scripture that could make the Christian see the OT as his book. A good part of his allegorical exegesis was based on the theory that the OT was Christological in many passages. Granting that we should judge Origen more appreciatively and that there is a restrained element in his exegesis (which De Lubac calls spiritual sense, and Daniélou calls typology), this writers does not share the view that Origen's exegesis can really be revived for our time.

Just as oversimplification did not do justice to Origen's exegetical stance, so also the exegetical school of *Antioch*, Alexandria's rival as a great Christian center, has been too naively

heoricized as the champion of critical exegesis, in contradistinc-
tion to Alexandria's allegorical exegesis. At the end of the 3rd
century Lucian of Samosata laid the foundations of this school;
and some of its representatives were Diodorus of Tarsus (d. 390),
Theodore of Mopsuestia (d. 428), and, to some extent, John
Chrysostom (d. 407). In the West, Julian, the Pelagian bishop
of Aeclanum (d. 454), was the leading adherent to Antiochene
principles. The great Antiochenes, then, were not contemporaries
of Origen but of the later Alexandrians like Athanasius (d. 373)
and Didymus the Blind (d. 398). In many ways, Cyril of Alexandria (d. 444) showed a perceptivity in literal exegesis that
placed him between the Alexandrian and Antiochene schools.

Little Antiochene exegesis has been preserved. In theory,
and to some extent in practice, Antioch did give more attention
to the literal sense (with all the limitations of exegesis in the 4th
century). But Antioch also proposed a more-than-literal exegesis
that involved *theōria*, for all practical purposes a close equivalent
of Alexandrian *allēgōria*. *Theōria* was an intuition or vision by
which the prophet could see the future through the medium of
his present circumstances. After such a vison it was possible for
him to phrase his writing in such a way as to describe both the
contemporary meaning of the events as well as their future fulfillment. The task of the Antiochene exegetes was to find both
meanings in the words of the prophets; and in their search for
the future meaning of the prophets' words (the product of
Theoria), the Antiochenes took into account the problem of the
awareness of the human author more often than did the Alexandrians, who tended to see the future in symbols and events,
as well as in the prophetic word.

Meanwhile in the West some of the Latin exegetes (e.g.,
Ambrosiaster, *ca.* 375) showed sobriety in exegesis. However,
with Hilary (d. 367), Ambrose (d. 397), and especially Augustine
(d. 430), the waves of Alexandrian allegorical exegesis swept into
the West. In Hilary's *Tractatus mysteriorum* we find the principle
that the OT *in its entirety* is prefigurative of the NT. Tyconius,
a Donatist exegete of the late 4th century laid down the rule in
his *Liber regularum* that every verse in the OT could be interpreted in a Christian way. Augustine epitomized this approach

in his principle: "The New Testament lies hidden in the Old; the Old Testament is enlightened through the New."

In his early days Jerome (d. 419) followed Origen's principles, but the commentaries written at the end of Jerome's life betray greater interest in the literal sense. Yet, after Jerome's time and the close of the 4th century, the style of Alexandrian exegesis dominated in the West, and Antiochene exegesis had little lasting influence. Indeed, once the Council of Constantinople II (553) blackened the name of Theodore of Mopsuestia, the Antiochene heritage was looked on with suspicion. In the works of some of the great figures of Western exegesis, e.g., Gregory the Great (d. 604) and Bede (d. 735), allegorical exegesis ran riot.

(C) Middle Ages

The guiding theoretical principle of medieval exegesis may be said to stem from John Cassian's (d. *ca.* 435) distinction of the four senses of Scripture: (1) the historical or literal, (2) the allegorical or Christological, (3) the tropological or moral or anthropological, (4) the anagogical or eschatological. Eventually this division gave rise to the famous couplet:

Littera gesta docet; quid credas allegoria
moralis quid agas; quo tendas anagogia.

The four senses of Jerusalem, an example supplied by Cassian, illustrates the theory. When Jerusalem is mentioned in the Bible, in its literal sense it is a Jewish city; allegorically, however, it refers to the Church of Christ; tropologically Jerusalem stands for the soul of man; anagogically it stands for the heavenly city. In such an exegetical climate, the literal sense was considered to have historical importance, while the other senses were essential for belief and behavior. Monastic mysticism, the preaching to the faithful, the search for theological material in the schools—these depended more heavily on the more-than-literal senses and gave a dominant nonliteral cast to medieval exegesis. Perhaps we should note that the same love for allegory appears also in the secular literature toward the end of the Middle Ages (e.g., *The Romance of the Rose, The Faerie Queene*).

However, there were moments when the recognition of the importance of the literal sense shone through. Especially influential in this respect was the school at the Abbey of St. Victor in Paris founded in 1110. Hugh of St. Victor attacked the tradition of Gregory and Bede; Andrew of St. Victor revived interest in Hebrew and in the technical tools of exegesis. Since the time of Jerome the Western church had had a few men capable of studying the OT in its original languages; and Herbert of Bosham, Andrew's pupil, was the most competent Hebraist in the Christian West in the 1000 years between Jerome and the Renaissance. Moreover, the development of theology as a discipline separate from strict exegesis enabled scholars to consider Christological truths in themselves without basing their discussion on Scripture interpreted allegorically. Thomas Aquinas made it clear that metaphor belonged to the literal sense and argued that doctrine should not be based solely on the spiritual sense. His principle was: "Nothing necessary to faith is contained in that spiritual sense [i.e., typical sense or sense of things] that Scripture does not put forward elsewhere in the literal sense" (*Summa* 1.1., 10 ad 1). Men like the English Dominican Nicholas Trevet and the Franciscan Nicholas of Lyra (d. 1349) recognized that not all the Psalms were messianic and gave rules for determining which of them were. Roger Bacon, although theoretically supporting the Alexandrian views on exegesis, showed a fascination for textual criticism and philological apparatus. During the 12, 13th, and early 14th centuries, these tendencies rose to the surface like islands in the sea, but they did not survive; and the Middle Ages drew to a close with allegory once more dominant in writers like Meister Eckhart (d. 1328), John Gerson (d. 1429), and Denis the Carthusian (d. 1471). The movement to translate the Bible into the vernacular, which, like most efforts at translation, made people think about the literal sense, was often unfortunately tainted with heresy and thus backfired as a possible corrective to the exaggeration of the spiritual sense.

(D) Sixteenth and Seventeenth Centuries

Turning now to the context of the Reformation and its immediate aftermath, we find that, with Cajetan on the Catholic side and with Luther and Calvin on the Protestant side, there was a reaction against allegorizing and a stress on the historical background of the biblical works. However, we must not forget that while Luther attacked blatant allegorizing, he remained firmly convinced of the Christological character of the OT and, therefore, continued to indulge in a typological exegesis that would be questioned by many today. Calvin was even less in favor of allegorizing than Luther; yet he too was often more-than-literal. (In his work *The Bible and the Church* [N.Y., 1948] 111-14, R. M. Grant justly recognizes the good points and the limits in the Reformers' return to the literal sense.) It is interesting to note that the dissenting sects of the Reform movement, the Anabaptists and the Antitrinitarians, supported spiritual exegesis, often because OT passages were used literally by the more conservative branch of the Reform as scriptural justification for persecuting the sects.

The Catholic counterreform had to answer arguments flowing from Protestant literal exegesis by also calling on the literal sense of Scripture. The Jesuit Maldonatus (d. 1583) produced exegetical commentary of substance. However, when the immediacy of the danger from the Reform was over, spiritual exegesis returned, especially under the banners of Jansenism, e.g., Pascal. The Catholic emphasis on the Church Fathers was another strong magnet toward spiritual exegesis; for, if the Fathers were pointed out as the prime example of how to interpret Scripture, their exegesis was more-than-literal. Cornelius a Lapide (d. 1637) filled his commentaries with spiritual exegesis culled from the Fathers. In Protestantism, too, in the Pietism of the 17th century, typology and accommodation made a comeback as the Scriptures were tapped for ascetic wealth. Cocceius (1603-69) presented an exegesis impregnated with typology.

But the revival of spiritual exegesis was not to hold the field forever. This same 17th century saw the career of Richard Simon (d. 1712), a prophet before his time and the first of the modern biblical critics. Rejected by his contemporaries and even by his Church, Simon inaugurated a movement that would make literal exegesis supreme.

(E) The Situation Today

The 19th and 20th centuries have seen the triumph of the critical and literal exegesis to which R. Simon gave the impetus so long ago. In his method of exegesis the scholar of today finds himself in another world of thought from the exegesis of the past. Looking back on that past, he finds an exegesis where imagination ran riot and where the literal meaning of the Scriptures, even when it was recognized, was constantly submerged beneath a strong tide of symbolism. The great difference between modern exegesis and that of the past became apparent more quickly in OT studies—a Christological approach that found Christ in every line of the OT was patently out of step with the modern source-criticism of the Pentateuch, the emphasis on the limited perspective of the prophets, and the recognition of contemporary pagan parallels for much of what was found in Israel's sacred books. The limitations of past exegesis of the NT became apparent more slowly, at least in Catholic circles. Only a research that had become historically conscious could detect the distinction between the theology of the NT and the theology of the subsequent ·Church; this distinction made it clear that the Fathers and the Scholastics had found in the NT theological insights of which the original authors were innocent.

In the light of the modern emphasis on literal exegesis, what happens to the whole idea of more-than-literal exegesis? Does it have any possibilities for our time? We find three basic reactions to this question.

(a) Attempt to Preserve Past Symbolic Exegesis

Among those who maintain that more-than-literal exegesis is still important, some seek to hold on to the exegesis of the past. In its *extreme form* this attitude is accompanied by a frantic rejection of literal exegesis as sterile and anti-Christian. Such a rejection of historical criticism occurs in Protestant Fundamentalism without a return to patristic or medieval symbolism; here the nostalgia is for a precritical theology, i.e., "What the Bible says." A similar fundamentalistic attitude in Catholicism is superficially more subtle, for Catholic precritical theology was not so tightly wedded to the Bible. The last major Catholic attempt to revive spiritual and symbolic exegesis at the expense of the literal sense, that of Dolindo Ruotolo, was condemned by the Pontifical Biblical Commission. The fact that Vatican II gave its approval to biblical criticism militates against any wholesale spread of these extremist ideas, but undoubtedly they will recur from time to time.

More serious is the *moderate approach* of respectable scholars who appreciate modern literal exegesis but contend that the spiritual exegesis of the past is still valid for today. Some of the studies of Origen mentioned above, written by men like De Lubac, Daniélou, and Hanson, not only defend the sobriety of much of the Alexandrian exegesis but also implicitly or explicitly plead for the continuing relevance of some of this exegesis. We have in A. G. Hebert, *The Throne of David* (London, 1943) and W. Vischer, *The Witness of the Old Testament to Christ* (London, 1949) two prominent contemporary advocates of symbolic exegesis. While the opinion of these scholars deserves a hearing, most others remain convinced that such symbolic exegesis has little to offer modern man. The symbolic has a role today in art, poetry, and drama; but consistent symbolic interpretation of what seems to be a straightforward biblical narrative meets opposition, for it smacks more of ingenuity and inventiveness than of interpretation. In the time of the Fathers spiritual exegesis was an attempt to let the Scriptures speak to a contemporary situation; to revive it today would seem to sidestep the obligation to make Scripture relevant in a truly modern way. A symbolism that was once meaningful becomes another barrier today.

In this attempted revival of patristic symbolic exegesis of the OT in particular, one cannot but suspect that part of the motivation lies in an inadequate appreciation of the OT in its literal sense without conscious Christian orientation. Perhaps we may cite a paradoxical warning of D. Bonhoeffer, "He who desires to think and feel in terms of the New Testament too quickly and too directly is in my opinion no Christian."

(b) Acceptance of a "Modern" More-Than-Literal Exegesis

Although the majority of critical scholars have firmly turned their backs on the symbolic exegetical methods of the past, many still express interest in a more-than-literal exegesis that is related to the results of modern criticism. They recognize the validity of the instinct to find a greater message in Scripture than historical criticism directly uncovers. If the 19th century has made us uneasy about the symbolic and imaginative interpretation characteristic of the Fathers and the Scholastics, the pretensions of historical criticism to be the only key to the word of God has, in turn, met with a challenge in the 20th century. It is interesting that in our era when the art of biblical criticism is practiced with great finess, some of the most prominent practitioners have expressed dissatisfaction with presenting the literal sense as the whole message of Scripture. Their attempts to solve the problem have taken many directions.

The development of biblical theology has been a partial attempt to find a fuller message in Scripture. (We speak here of biblical theology that is solidly built upon critical exegesis and not a substitute for it.) Other attempts concern more directly the senses of Scripture, e.g., the Catholic interest in the *sensus plenior* on the part of competent exegetes like P. Benoit and J. Coppens, and the interest of both Catholics and Protestants in a form of typology as seen in the writings of W. Eichrodt and G. von Rad. Later we shall study in detail the *sensus plenior* and typical sense of Scripture; here we wish to discuss the two larger movements that imply a more-than-literal sense, that of the new hermeneutic and that of the Christian interpretation of the OT.

(i) The New Hermeneutic

(For what follows see J. M. Robinson, "Hermeneutic since Barth," *The New Hermeneutic* 1-77.) In this movement "Hermeneutic," in the singular, is not a science of rules for interpretation (= hermeneutics, in the plural) but is more closely related to the original meaning of *hermēneia*. It concerns the way in which God's word becomes clear to men.

In an important discussion of biblical theology (*IDB* 1, 418-32), K. Stendahl has isolated the core of the hermeneutical problem today, namely the contrast between "What *did* Scripture mean when it was written?" (the goal of literal interpretation) and "What *does* it mean to me?" W. Dilthey first pointed out the problem when he made the fundamental distinction between explanation and understanding. Historical criticism can *explain* what a text of Scripture once meant, but how does a reader come to an *understanding* of that text? In his commen-

335

tary on Romans, K. Barth insisted on the proclamation of Paul's message in the language of today. Attacking A. von Harnack's thesis that theological scholarship's sole task was the pure knowledge of its object, Barth stressed that theology must remember that its object was first subject and must become subject again.

A similar desire to make Scripture speak today lies behind the development of *Sachkritik,* a criticism that recognizes the applicability of the subject matter even when the language in which the matter was objectivized is inappropriate. R. Bultmann's demythologizing is also directed to this positive goal: It is the decoding rather than the elimination of myth, and only inadequate mythical conceptualization is eliminated for the sake of stating more adequately the myth's meaning.

In the later philosophical writings of M. Heidegger, hermeneutic means the process of interpreting being, especially in terms of an appreciation of the role of language. This philosophy of interpretation does not give exclusive attention to the author's perspective (literal sense) but rather to what finds expression in the language of the text itself even independently of the author's intention. Drawing on the later Heidegger but modifying his ideas, E. Fuchs' programmatic work *Hermeneutik* (1954) goes beyond Bultmann's hermeneutical principles. For Bultmann the self-interpretation of the reader is on the level of preunderstanding, subordinate to interpreting the text itself; for Fuchs the text interprets the reader by criticizing his self-understanding. The "hermeneutical principle" is where the text is placed in order to speak to the reader, and for theological exegesis the basic hermeneutical principle is human need—a need that reveals what we mean by God. "Translation" involves finding the place where the biblical text can strike home. G. Ebeling, a close friend of Fuchs, has also carried forward the development of hermeneutic in the direction indicated by the later Heidegger (cf. the article "Hermeneutik," *RGG* 3 [1959] 242-62). The role he attributes to historical criticism is not so much the role of essential interpretation as the role of removing all distortions so that the text can effectively speak to man. H.-G. Gadamer has written on hermeneutic from a philosophical viewpoint, and he insists that one *always* understands the text differently from the way in which the author himself understood it, and hence interpretation is always a translation from one situation to another.

Whether or not one accepts the heavy philosophical substratum, the new hermeneutic is a modern tendency in favor of a more-than-literal exegesis. The literal sense of Scripture, in this approach, is not necessarily the real meaning of the text at another period. A full exegesis not only discovers the literal sense but also translates that sense into the present situation. (For more detailed explanation, see R. E. Brown, "After Bultmann What?—An Introduction to the Post-Bultmannians," *CBQ* 26 [1964] 1-30.)

(ii) Christian Interpretation of the Old Testament

Since Marcion's time the problem of what the OT means for a Christian has been with us, and neither Marcion's solution of rejecting the OT nor the orthodox patristic solution of finding Christ in every line of the OT seems realistic. And the 19th-century solution has not been much better, namely that of so concentrating on historico-critical exegesis that one forgets that the Bible consists of two Testaments that have a unity. Two recent volumes of essays on the subject show the concern of critical scholars for the Christian dimension of the OT, and the German commentary series *Biblische Kommentar* has stressed that NT relationship is not a goal to be lost sight of.

Not all the authors who write on the subject are in agreement, but in general they distrust any emphasis on OT prediction of Christ as the means of relating the two Testaments. This distrust of prediction is more prominent among Protestant than among Catholic writers; and J. Barr has rightly objected that, whether modern scholars like it or not, prediction was the way the NT writers themselves related the Testaments and that in the intertestamental period the concept of the prophets as foretellers of the future had greatly developed. Be this as it may, the tendency of the authors in the Westermann volume of essays is to seek correspondence between the Testaments, not on the verbal level, but on the level of a typological relation between the events of the OT and those of the NT or on the level of promise/fulfillment in salvation history (typology and promise/fulfillment are not mutually exclusive approaches). W. Eichrodt (Westermann vol., 224-45) and G. von Rad (*ibid.*, 17-39) have been interested in reviving typology (as distinct from allegory) whereby OT realities are divinely established models of NT realities, and both authors stress that history is the matrix in which these realities find their connection. It is this stress on history that separates their typology from much of patristic exegesis, which did not have the tools to discover the flow of Israel's history in any detail. W. Zimmerli (*ibid.*, 89-122) and C. Westermann (*ibid.*, 40-49) work with the concept of promise/fulfillment, seen both within the OT itself (e.g., the convenantal promise) and between the Testaments. The NT fulfills not so much isolated promises but an entire history of promise.

Turning to individual books on the subject, we find that S. Amsler, a Protestant scholar, in *L'Ancien Testament dans l'Eglise* (Neuchatel, 1960), seeks out the NT authors in their use of the OT as a possible guide to how the OT should be read in the Church. He rejects many of the proposed instances of prediction/fulfillment but thinks that the abuses of the method are found more in the Fathers than in the NT (an oversimplification—the NT has much exegesis of the OT that cannot be accepted today as valid exegesis, e.g., Matthew 2:15, 18; 1 Corinthians 10:4). He defends typology, but rejects the *sensus plenior.* A corresponding Catholic work, C. Larcher's *L'actualité chrétienne de l'Ancien Testament* (Paris, 1962), finds that the NT use of the OT does depend heavily on some form of prediction and not only on a broader basis of promise/fulfillment or on prefiguration (typology). Both Larcher and P. Grelot (*Sens chrétien de l'Ancien Testament* [Tournai, 1962]) are favorable to the concept of a *sensus plenior,* although Grelot's views on prediction are not the same as Larcher's.

Beneath all this diversity in approach, the various authors are very committed to the interrelationship of the two Testaments. All recognize abuses in past Christian exegesis of the OT and seek to avoid them by emphasizing a broader historical relationship (as opposed to the minute details on which the Fathers capitalized) and by stressing the element of discontinuity that accompanies continuity—the flow from the OT to the NT was not a smooth one. All recognize that interrelationship is a much larger question than messianism. One must confess, however that these authors do not seem able to find a truly modern way to relate the two Testaments, and in their solutions there are always elements of the very exegesis about which they express suspicion, e.g., typology. The rejection of prediction is really a rejection of a crude concept wherein the human authors were thought to foresee the distant future; a more sophisticated concept where, unbeknown to the human author, God uses Scripture to prepare for the future deserves much more attention than is given to it by many proponents of a Christian interpretation of the OT.

(c) Rejection of More-Than-Literal Exegesis

Not all exegetes share the convictions illustrated in the above-mentioned movements; many specifically reject one or the other approach to a more-than-literal exegesis. In Catholic circles, for instance, some adamantly reject the *sensus plenior* because they fear such exegesis will endanger the hard-fought-for primacy of the literal sense (B. Vawter, *CBQ* 26 [1964] 87-88). That such a fear is not unwarranted may be seen in the cautions that we gave above about the primacy of the literal sense. In Protestant circles, O. Cullmann is most distrustful of the Bultmannian and post-Bultmannian hermeneutical trend. He believes that the literal exegesis of NT texts, limited though they may be, is the exegete's primary theological duty, while the reader's duty is simply to be obedient to what the authors of the NT wanted to communicate as revelation, even if it is quite foreign to the modern mentality (cited in J. M. Robinson, *New Hermeneutic*, 41). Even E. Käsemann, a Bultmannian disciple, expresses reservations about the new hermeneutic of Fuchs and Ebeling. He fears that interpretation may cease to serve historiography which is in need of clarification, and that it may become an arbitrary builder of new constructions. For a critique of Fuchs' position, see P. J. Achtemeier, *TTod* 23 (1966) 101-19.

Nor has the movement for a Christian interpretation of the OT been accepted by all. Although J. D. Smart (*op. cit.,* 23-30) is sympathetic to a unity between the central concern of the OT and that of the Gospels, he is most unhappy about typology. F. Baumgärtel (Westermann vol., 135) objects: "The Old Testament is a witness out of a non-Christian religion; its self-understanding is not identical with evangelical prior understanding." Bultmann (Anderson vol., 31) insists on the discontinuity of the two Testaments to the point of stating: "To Christian faith the Old Testament is no longer revelation." J. Barr (*op. cit.*, 110) has questioned the tendency of Von Rad and Noth to center parallelism between the two Testaments on events, and indeed questions the whole modern Christological exegesis of the OT (p. 152). Many insist that the picture of progressive development in the OT leading to the NT is not true to the evidence. For instance, it is true that personal messianism developed after the Exile in a way that did prepare for the NT. Yet the bifurcation in messianism that led to the expectation of a messianic High Priest and the apocalyptic overtones that came to surround the Davidic Messiah were developments that made it more difficult for Jews to see Jesus as the Messiah.

If below in discussing the *sensus plenior* and the typical sense, we show ourselves sympathetic to the validity of a carefully delineated more-than-literal exegesis, we insist that one must be familiar with the many abuses evident in the past history of this exegesis and that the objections of those who oppose it reflect real dangers against which one must take precautions.

(II) THE SENSUS PLENIOR

The term *sensus plenior* (henceforth SPlen) was coined by A. Fernández in 1925 and has passed into English translation as the "fuller sense." The terminology is related to the NT idea of "fulfilling" the OT and, although recent, is not objectionable, unless one wishes to quibble that logically "full" has no comparative. The proponents of the SPlen contend that by this new term they are drawing attention to a valid aspect of more-than-literal exegesis that is as old as the Bible itself. In modern times Newman, Lagrange (*sens supra-littéral*), Pesch (*altior sensus*), and Prat seem to have been forerunners of the idea (on Lagrange, see *CBQ* 17 [1955] 451-55; 18

Raymond Edward Brown

[1956] 49-53; on the others, see *SPSS* 88-92). Since Fernández' initial suggestion, J. Coppens and P. Benoit have been among the more famous exponents; R. Bierberg, G. Courtade, B. Vawter, and J. L. McKenzie have opposed the idea.

(A) Definition

The SPlen is the deeper meaning, intended by God but not clearly intended by the human author, that is seen to exist in the words of Scripture when they are studied in the light of further revelation or of development in the understanding of revelation. First, the SPlen is, like the literal sense, a meaning of the *words* of Scripture; and in this it differs from the typical sense. As distinct from the literal sense, the SPlen was *not within the clear intention of the human author.* For those who prefer the broad definition of the literal sense in which the intention of the human author is not made part of the definition, the SPlen is only a subdivision of the literal sense (so Benoit). It seems better, however, to keep the two senses distinct.

In saying that the SPlen was not *clearly* intended by the human author, we have hedged on one of the disputed points about the SPlen. All who accept the SPlen would agree that it was not clearly intended; but some would suppose that the human author must have had a vague awareness of the SPlen, while others would require no awareness at all. The latter view seems preferable, since there is a formidable difficulty in explaining what this vague awareness would have consisted in and how it would have been obtained. See *SPSS* 105-14; Brown, *CBQ* 25 [1963] 263-69.

Once we affirm that the SPlen was not clearly intended by the human author but was intended by God, we have to find a way of determining the presence of such a deeper meaning; for the ordinary principles of exegesis will tell us only what the human author meant. This special way of determining the presence of a SPlen is through *further divine revelation or development in the understanding of revelation.* Since it is God who reveals and who inspires, God can tell man through revelation what he intended in inspiring earlier passages of Scripture. When we speak of *further revelation,* the chief instance of such revelation would be through a later passage in the Bible itself, for in-

341

stance the NT may point out the SPlen of an OT text. Actually, since there was a constantly developing revelation within the OT period, later passages of the OT may reveal the SPlen of earlier passages of the OT, although strangely Benoit refuses to admit this and confines the SPlen to an OT-NT relationship.

When we speak of *development within the understanding of revelation,* we mean that, even after the end of the biblical era and the close of public revelation, it may have been possible to uncover a SPlen as the contents of revelation came to be more clearly understood. Benoit would reject this possibility too, but a priori there seems no reason to reject it. God guides the Church and Christians in the understanding of revelation; and he can thus make clear the full purpose, not hitherto recognized, that he had in inspiring a particular section of Scripture.

(B) Justification

The general basis for positing the SPlen would be the fact that in the long history of exegesis given above, texts of Scripture have been interpreted in a way that goes beyond their literal sense, and this fuller interpretation has been sponsored by writings to which Christians give authority, e.g., the NT, the Fathers, Church pronouncements. For example, Matthew 1:23 says that the virginal conception of Jesus by Mary took place in order to fulfill what was spoken by the Lord through the prophet (Isaiah 7:14): "Behold, a virgin shall conceive and bear a son, and his name shall be called Emmanuel." A critical examination of Isaiah 7:14, however, gives no evidence that Isaiah was thinking of Jesus' conception. Isaiah does not speak about a virgin; it is not clear that he is referring to a future conception; and the whole import of the scene in ch. 7 of Isaiah implies that this birth will take place *ca.* 734 BC. Clearly Matthew's interpretation of Isaiah is more-than-literal. Another example would involve the frequent theological use of Genesis 3:15 in reference to Mary's participation in Jesus' victory over evil. This interpretation goes beyond the literal import of the text; for Genesis refers in general to womankind and her offspring, and there is no clear reference to victory, only to struggle.

Now, and this is extremely important, scholars do *not* suggest that every more-than-literal use of the words of Scripture advocated by the NT, the Fathers, the liturgy, or Church documents is a SPlen. Much of it is accommodation, catechetical application, or loose association. But there seem to be cases where, after a rigorous application of the restrictive criteria listed below, we are being told, not that Scripture can be applied in this way, but that this fuller meaning is what God intended when he inspired Scripture. These alone would be instances of a SPlen.

(C) Different Forms

In particular, two types of SPlen have been suggested as especially important. *First,* there is a series of OT passages, principally in Psalms and the Prophets, which have been classically identified as prophecies pertaining to Jesus and to the Christian dispensation. In an older exegesis it was often thought that the human author foresaw specific details about the career of Jesus. Today we recognize that the authors of the OT were concerned with their own times and not with the distant future, and the details of the future of God's plan were hidden from them. The descriptions of the Suffering Servant in Deuteronomy-Isaiah, of the suffering figure in Psalm 22, and of the anointed (messiah) king in Psalms 2 and 110 all seem to have had contemporary meaning rather than intended reference to a distant future. Yet, as Christians have understood God's plan, these passages were to have their full significance unfolded when they were reread in the light of the career of Jesus of Nazareth. The advocates of the theory of a SPlen think that through it they preserve what is valid in the traditional argument from prophecy while still acknowledging the limitations of the human author. This theory permits a Christian to find the literal sense in an OT passage that a Jew would find.

A *second* important form of the SPlen, sometimes called the General SPlen, pertains to the field of biblical theology. Individual passages of a biblical book have deeper meaning when seen in the context of the whole book. Individual books of the Bible have greater meaning when seen in the context of the whole Bible. Themes like faith, sin, and justice have profundity when seen in the context of the whole biblical teaching on the respective subjects. The fuller meaning uncovered in a text which has been placed in a larger biblical context would be a SPlen.

(D) Criteria

How can one distinguish the SPlen of a text from an accommodation that attributes to a text a meaning that goes beyond even God's intention? The *first criterion* is implicit in what we said above about our knowedge of the SPlen coming from further revelation or from a development in the under-standing of revelation. The surest guide to a SPlen is an authori-tative interpretation of the words of Scripture in a more-than-literal way—authoritative in the sense that it comes from one of the guides to revelation, e.g., the NT, the Church Fathers, Church pronouncements, etc. This criterion is aimed against oversubjectivity on the part of the individual exegete. If there are real meanings of Scripture that cannot be detected by the strict rules of critical exegesis and yet are of importance to the divine plan for man's salvation, the most likely matrix for their emergence to clarity and acceptance is the context of Church life.

This does not mean that when the Church proclaims a doctrine like the Immaculate Conception or the Assumption, the Catholic exegete can assume that now the Church has un-veiled the SPlen of some text that it has cited in discussing the doctrine. As the Protestant exegete J. M. Robinson rightly ob-jects, such an approach would make the theory of the SPlen a tool of partisan apologetics and a peg to hang new doctrines on. In relation to the SPlen, Church authority is not looked upon as an agent of exegetical revelation; rather Church life, doctrine, and prayer supply a context in which Scripture is read, com-mented on, and allowed to "speak," so that the meaning emerges which God wished to convey. Robinson is correct in seeing an analogy for this in the Bultmannian theory that the implicit Christology of Jesus becomes explicit in the Church's kerygma, and in relating the question of the SPlen to the whole question of the role of Scripture and tradition in the development of dogma (see E. Schillebeeckx, "Exegesis, Dogmatics and the Development of Dogma," in H. Vorgrimler, *Dogmatic vs. Biblical Theology* [Baltimore, 1964] 115-45, esp. 133ff.).

The *second criterion* is even more effective in avoiding misunderstanding about the role of the SPlen. This criterion is that the SPlen of a text must be homogeneous with the literal sense, i.e., it must be a development of what the human author wanted to say. Jeremiah 31:15 deals with the figurative lament of Rachel (the "mother" of the northern tribes) over the fact that these tribes were taken captive by the Assyrians in the 8th century. When Matthew 2:18 uses this text to describe the lamentation over the slaughter of the Innocents because of a popular but incorrect localization of Rachel's tomb near Bethlehem, there is little homogeneity with the literal sense of the passage in Jeremiah; and in our judgment Matthew is not developing the SPlen of Jeremiah but simply accommodating the OT passage. Wisdom 18:14-15 concerns the nocturnal descent of the destroying angel of the Exodus upon the firstborn of the Egyptians. When the liturgy (Sunday after Christmas) applies this text of Jesus' birth at Bethlehem, there is little homogeneity with the literal sense. When Augustine turns the parable of the Good Samaritan into an allegory of the fall of man, there is little homogeneity with the literal sense. These then, are not examples of the SPlen.

However, the usage of Isaiah 7:14 by Matthew 1:23 may fit this criterion of homogeneity. The original reference seems to have concerned the birth of a child to the royal family, a child who would be a sign of the continuance of the Davidic line and thus of God's continued presence with his people. Even if Isaiah did not think of a virgin birth, this interpretation developed subsequently in Judaism, as we see in the LXX of the Isaian passage, where the girl who is to conceive is identified as a virgin. When Jesus was born of a virgin in the city of David, he was a sign of the continuance of the Davidic line and represented God's presence with his people. Thus, the example has homogeneity.

The critierion of homogeneity seems applicable to the messianic interpretation of Psalms 2 and 110 where the anointed king is thought of as lord and as God's begotten son. Although the original reference seems to have been to the reigning king, once the monarchy ceased after the Exile, the words of these Psalms were reapplied to a glorious future king who was to come. In the Christian interpretation of these Psalms, Jesus, God's begotten in a way much deeper than that intended by the psalmist, seems to be the "Lord." And so when Hebrews 1:5, 13 and Matthew 22:44 apply these Psalms to Jesus, there is a homogeneity with their literal sense.

These two criteria are not always easy to apply, and those who accept the theory of the SPlen do not always agree in practice on what is a good example of the SPlen. For further examples, good and bad, see those listed in *SPSS* 140-45. Benoit thinks that the SPlen is present in many passages of Scripture; others think that only rarely can we detect a SPlen that fits the strict criteria proposed above. It would seem best to exercise caution; certainly the majority of the NT citations of the OT in a more-than-literal sense and the overwhelming majority of the liturgical and patristic citations of Scripture do not meet the criteria for a valid SPlen.

(E) Problems

Some important scholars have denied the possibility of a SPlen on several grounds. Among Spanish writers, S. de Ausejo and A. Ibañez Arana believe that such a sense cannot be reconciled with the instrumental theory of inspiration. Detailed discussion of the arguments on both sides is given in *SPSS* 134-37. If we do not spend time on it here, it is because we find the whole objection too a priori. To decide from a philosophical theory of instrumentality what God could and could not have done in inspiring Scripture is risky, especially since all acknowledge that the instrumentality in the process of inspiration is unique. It is far better to work a posteriori: to see what God has done and then to formulate a theory that can account for it. It is also too a priori to argue that the human agent would cease to be a true author of Scripture if there were present in his words a sense that he did not understand.

A much stronger argument against the SPlen is the contention that when a deeper meaning of a biblical text is recognizable only in the light of further revelation, the meaning is not contained in the text itself but is acquired at the moment of the further revelation. In other words, one should speak of a fuller understanding on the part of the exegete rather than of a fuller sense of the Scripture. Actually God could have chosen to act in either way. In inspiring the words of Isaiah 7:14 God may have withheld any reference to the future virgin birth of Jesus which was part of the divine plan, and in this case he would have made the applicability of Isaiah 7:14 to the virgin birth part of the new revelation underlying Matthew 1:23. Or through a SPlen, God may have included in Isaiah 7:14 a reference to the virgin birth, even though the prophet was not aware of this reference and it would not be discovered for hundreds of years. The first suggestion seems to posit a certain dichotomy in God's plan of action; moreoever, it does not do justice to the fact that Matthew seems to think that the reference to the virgin birth was already in the OT. (On the Isaiah 7:14 question see *EB* 74 where Pius VI insists that in some sense, literal or typical, this verse refers to the virgin birth.) The NT concept of fulfilling the OT is closer to an idea of a fuller sense than to that of a fuller understanding.

Robinson points out that the claim that there is an addition of meaning and thus fuller understanding rather than a fuller sense involves a rather artificial distinction, since it neglects the dynamic factor in the literal sense. The literal sense is what leads to a fuller understanding; the SPlen is part of the organic growth of the literal sense, not a mere addition.

The theory of the SPlen is dependent on a scholastic, instrumental understanding of inspiration. It is no accident that P. Benoit, one of the great champions of the SPlen, is also the leading modern exponent of the scholastic theory of inspiration. There are those who find difficulty with such a theory in which God intimately guides every step from thought to word, and they prefer to approach inspiration as a social charism or from the aspect of the post-factum role of Scripture in the community. These new approaches do not favor the idea of a SPlen whose very definition is phrased in terms of God's intention and man's intention. The future of the non-scholastic approaches to inspiration is difficult to predict; but it would seem that if the theory of the SPlen is to survive in Catholic circles and to find sympathetic understanding in non-Catholic circles, it should not be so dependent on the scholastic, instrumental theory of inspiration. Perhaps the solution is to take the emphasis off the mechanics of the divine and human intentions and to concentrate rather on the close relationship between the idea of the SPlen and the modern interest in the hermeneutical value of language. The language of Scripture may have had one meaning in the human author's situation; yet in a different situation (e.g., that of the Church today) it may make its point in a different way and to this extent mean something different. See Robinson, *art. cit.*, 19; also pp. 23-27 where he responds to Vawter's oversimplified correlation of the sense of words with the author's formal intent.

Another realistic objection against the theory of the SPlen is that this sense is seldom verified and so is of little use in justifying or explaining NT, patristic, liturgical, or ecclesiastical exegesis. It is interesting to note that the proponents of the SPlen tend to confine their discussion of this sense to the theoretical plane, seldom appealing to it in their works of exegesis.

In summary, if one surveys the writing on the SPlen, it seems that the majority of exegetes are willing to accept it as a theory. This is a good indication of its value in preserving an important truth about Scripture, namely that one has not exhausted the real meaning of a text when one has determined by historico-critical exegesis what it meant to the man who wrote it. Yet the difficulties that many have found in the idea of the SPlen suggest that it is only a partial solution to a much wider problem.

(III) THE TYPICAL SENSE

The term *typos* is found in Romans 5:14, where we are told that Adam was a type of Christ, and in 1 Corinthians 10:6, where we are told that the things that happened in the desert to Israel during the Exodus are types for Christians. Nevertheless, the sense of Scripture involving types was not known as the typical sense until late in the history of exegesis. The Fathers spoke of it as "allegory" or as the "Mystical sense"; Thomas Aquinas knew of it as the "spiritual sense." Some modern authors distinguish sharply between typology and allegory, e.g., typology is based on historical connections whereas allegory is imaginative. It is quite necessary from our point of view to distinguish valid from invalid typology; but we should remember that there was no consciousness among the Fathers that allegory was invalid typology. The Fathers received with equal enthusiasm examples of typology that today we consider invalid and examples that we consider valid.

(A) Definition

The typical sense is the deeper meaning that the things (persons, places, and events) of Scripture possess because, according to the intention of the divine author, they foreshadow future things. The typical sense differs from the literal sense and from the SPlen in that it is not a sense of the words of Scripture but is attached to things described in Scripture. Like the SPlen it can be discerned only through further revelation or through development in the understanding of revelation. Let us analyze the definition.

First, the typical sense concerns *things*—these realities are designated as types, while the future realities they foreshadow are antitypes. "Things" must be taken in a wide sense. Not only what we would ordinarily consider things serve as types (e.g., manna as a type of the Eucharist); but also persons (Adam, Melchizedek, Moses, David, and Jeremiah are types of Christ; Eve is a type of Mary) and animals (the paschal lamb is a type of Christ [cf. John 19:36]; the bronze serpent raised on a pole on the desert is a type of the crucified Christ [John 3:14]). Events may also serve as types (the Exodus is a type of baptism [1 Corinthians 10:2]). It is generally conceded that the type may even be a fictional event (Jonah in the whale as a type of Christ in the grave [Mathhew 12:40]). However, some modern authors, like G. von Rad and M. Noth, would confine all valid typology to historical events. For a penetrating criticism of this trend see Barr, *op. cit.,* 110-15.

Second, the things that are types must be written of *in Scripture*. In God's plan David was a type of Christ before a word was written about him, but the figure of David acquired a typical sense only when a human author was inspired by God to write about David. The importance of this qualification is seen most clearly when the factor that makes a thing a type is not its historical reality but the literary description of it.

Melchizedek undoubtedly had parents; but what turns him into a type of Christ according to Hebrews 7:3 is that his lineage is not recorded in Scripture. Some have failed to appreciate this distinction between the extrabiblical existence of the "things" that are types and the typical sense that they acquire when they are described in Scripture, and consequently have denied that the typical sense is a sense of Scripture. Such a denial has no support in the Fathers or in Church tradition; the encyclical *Divino Afflante Spiritu* (*EB* 552) treats the "spiritual sense" as a real sense of Scripture. The objection that the typical sense cannot be a sense of Scripture because the human author was not aware of it is the same objection that is raised against the SPlen.

Third, types *foreshadow the future*. The type and antitype are on two different levels of time, and only when the antitype appears does the typical sense become apparent. The type is always imperfect; it is a silhouette, not a portrait, of the antitype; and therefore realization is bound to bring surprises. This limitation in typology is important because much of the criticism of any more-than-literal exegesis is centered on a failure to appreciate the limited character of the OT and on an exaggeration of the continuity between the Testaments at the expense of their real diversity. Emphasis on the imperfection of the relationship between type and antitype safeguards the typical sense against such an objection.

(B) Criteria

The ordination of type to antitype is of divine origin, and so the criteria for recognizing the typical sense are much like those for recognizing the SPlen. *First,* revelation or development in the understanding of revelation is the safest guide to the presence of a typical sense; without such a guide human ingenuity tends to run riot in detecting types. Thus, most of the types accepted by exegetes are types that have been pointed out by the NT or by a *consensus* of the Fathers, of liturgical usages, and of Church documents. For example, the NT (Hebrews) saw Melchizedek as a type of Christ; later on, liturgy and patristic exegesis specified that Melchizedek's presentation of bread and wine (Genesis 14:18) was a type of the Christian Eucharistic sacrifice.

The *second* criterion for determining the presence of a typical sense is that the type be related to the antitype through an organic development in revelation. We cannot classify as a type every OT foreshadowing that is mentioned in the NT or the Fathers (witnesses who made little distinction between sober exegesis of scriptural senses and purely imaginative accomodation). We should seek evidence that God really planned the relationship between type and antitype. Modern authors implicitly recognize the need of such a criterion by their stress on the relationship of real typology to salvation history and also by a stress on promise/fulfillment. For instance, the whole parallel between the Old Covenant and the New Covenant, between Moses and Jesus, which is basic to much of the NT, guarantees the main lines of Exodus typology. The relation of Jesus to the Davidic line guarantees much of the David typology. It is when typology is attached to isolated things and persons that we must be more skeptical, e.g., is Rahab (Joshua 2) really a type of the Church?

(C) Problem

Is typology too closely associated with the symbolic interpretation of the past to be relevant to modern exegesis? Many scholars who theoretically accept the typical sense and acknowledge some of the principal examples of typology in the NT and in the Fathers are not at all sympathetic to any renewal of typical exegesis. Above we distinguished between the attempt to refurbish patristic and medieval exegesis (De Lubac, Daniélou, *et al.*) and the attempt to construct a more-than-literal exegesis on more modern grounds. But how does typology fit into the latter movement? It is not enough to state with Eichrodt that it is impossible to confuse typology and allegory if one examines them closely, for some scholars regard as imaginative allegory the typology that Eichrodt accepts. Coppens, *Les Harmonies,* 93-94, proposes some interesting examples of a new typology based on the better modern understanding of Jewish history; but one can be skeptical about how much success these new examples will achieve. Probably, as with the SPlen, the typical sense will survive as a truly useful hermeneutical category if it is somehow revamped and treated as part of a much larger more-than-literal sense.

By way of summary we may schematize what we have seen about the three basic senses of Scripture. If we divide them according to the intention of the human author, they fall into two main categories:

1. Meaning intended by the human author = the *literal sense*
2. Meaning intended by God that goes beyond what the human author intended:
   (a) flowing from the words of Scripture = *sensus plenior*
   (b) flowing from "things" described in Scripture = the *typical sense*

RELATED TOPICS

(I) IS ACCOMMODATION JUSTIFIED?

In addition to the senses of Scripture intended by the human and/or the divine author, there are applications of Scripture on the part of the reader or interpreter that we call accommodation. This is not a sense of Scripture but a sense given to Scripture; it is not a product of exegesis but of eisegesis. The range of accommodation is immense, running from catechetical application to literary embelishment. Much of the more-than-literal exegesis in the Fathers and in the liturgy is accommodation—a fact that is quite intelligible when we remember that Scripture was looked upon as the basic text from which a wide span of Christian knowledge was taught. When Gregory the Great told his audience that the Gospel parable of the five talents referred to the five senses, he was accommodating. The liturgy accommodates to the lives of Christian confessor pontiffs the praise that Sirach 44-45 heaps upon the patriarchs. A very frequent use of accommodation is in sermons, e.g., when preachers eulogized Pope John XXIII by citing John. 1:6, "There was a man sent by God whose name was John." Books on the spiritual life accommodate Scripture by applying passages to new spiritual problems.

Accommodation is inevitable with a book that is as familiar and as respected as the Bible. And in truth, a certain tolerance can be extended to accommodation when it is done with intelligence, sobriety, and taste. In matters of taste, for instance, it is not unbecoming to apply John 1:6 in euology of a beloved and saintly Pope; its application to other well-known men named John, not particularly noted for sanctity, is more dubious. Too often scriptural passages, e.g., "The truth will make you free" (John 8:32), are applied to political or social situations with which they have nothing to do.

But, even when accommodation is handled with a certain sobriety, we must insist that it should be only an occasional use of Scripture and not the principal use. Preachers may find accommodations easy and may resort to it rather than taking the trouble to investigate the literal sense of Scripture. Occasional use of the imagination in accommodating Scripture can be attractive, but to substitute it for the literal sense is to substitute man's ingenuity for God's inspired word. If the writer or speaker makes clear to his audience that he is accommodating and not really giving an exegesis of Scripture, some of the danger is removed. But in general it must be said that in this age, when we have come to recognize the tremendous wealth of the literal sense of Scripture, a sound exposition of that sense will render far more service than ingenious accommodation.

(II) AUTHORITATIVE INTERPRETATIONS BY THE CHURCH

When we discuss the literal sense, we explain the rules of form criticism and literary criticism as the best guidelines to the meaning of Scripture. But as Catholics do we not say that the authentic interpretation of Scripture belongs to the Church? In the popular understanding there remains a certain confusion about the Church's role in exegesis as opposed to "private interpretation." The latter phrase is often an oversimplification of what is regarded as a Protestant position. First of all, it should be stated that in the more traditional Protestant groups there is no suggestion that each individual can authoritatively interpret Scripture. There is church tradition among Protestants, even as there is among Catholics. Moreover, since the correct interpretation of Scripture requires education and effort, the average Protestant is no more capable of picking up the Bible and determining at a glance what the author meant than is the average Catholic.

A Protestant's understanding of Scripture comes through Sunday schools, sermons, and church authority, even as the average Catholic's understanding comes from those who taught him. A true difference between Protestant and Catholic opinions is not centered on the existence of a traditional interpretation of Scripture but on the binding value given to that tradition.

Even in the question of the binding Church interpretation of Scripture, however, we must be careful not to oversimplify the Catholic position. The first caution is to distinguish between the *dogmatic statements* of the Catholic Church about Scripture and *prudential decisions* made for the common good. The latter are not infallible guides to truth. For instance, between 1905 and 1915 the Pontificial Biblical Commission issued a series of directives about Scripture; today, with the approval of the same commission, most of these directives are regarded as passé by Catholic scholars. One criterion of whether or not the Church is speaking dogmatically is related to the matter about which the Church is speaking. Since the Church is the custodian of revelation and since Scripture is a mirror of revelation, the Church has the power to determine infallibly the meaning of Scripture *in matters of faith and morals (DS* 1507, 3007). The Church claims no absolute or direct authority over matters of biblical authorship, geography, chronology, and other scientific aspects; and so the Church has not made any *dogmatic* pronouncements about authorship, dating of books, unity of composition, etc.

And when we come to the actual exegesis of Scripture—something that could be a matter of faith and morals—in regard to 99 per cent of the Bible, the Church has not commented officially on what a passage does or does not mean. That task is left to the knowledge, intelligence, and hard work of individual exegetes who claim no more than reasonable conviction for their conclusions. When the Church has spoken on a particular verse, most often it has done so in a negative manner, i.e., by rejecting certain interpretations as false because they constitute a threat to faith and morals. The Council of Trent, for instance, condemned the Calvinist interpretation that would reduce the reference to water in John 3:5 (baptismal passage: "Unless a man be begotten from above [born again] of water and Spirit") to a mere metaphor (*DS* 1615). Again it condemned those who would dissociate the power of forgiving sins exercised in the Sacrament of Penance from the power accorded in John 20:23 (*DS* 1703).

When Church documents cite Scripture positively, we must distinguish as to whether the document is giving an authoritative exegesis of Scripture or simply using Scripture to illustrate its argument. The bull *Ineffabilis Deus* on the Immaculate Conception recalls Genesis 3:15, and the bull *Munificentissimus Deus* on the Assumption recalls Apocalypse 12. Are the respective Popes dogmatically affirming that these texts of Scripture refer in their literal sense to the Marian doctrines? Or perhaps in a more-than-literal sense, like the SPlen? Or do the citations imply no more than that reflection on these scriptural verses aided theologians in understanding the Marian doctrines and thus guided the Church to take a dogmatic position? In the view of many scholars the last possibility is the correct one. In particular, Pius XII seems to claim no more than that the dogma of the Assumption receives support from Scripture.

If we leave aside the instances where the Church has used Scripture to illustrate a dogmatic position, we find really few instances where the Church has spoken affirmatively and authoritatively about the meaning of a passage. And even here it is very difficult to be certain that it is speaking about the literal sense of Scripture. We must remember that the concept of a literal sense established by historico-critical method is very much a modern phenomenon. Modern too is the emphasis on the distinction between what a text meant to its author and what it came to mean in subsequent ecclesiastical or theological usage. In the instance cited above where the Council of Trent condemned a wrong interpretation of John 20:23, did the Council Fathers wish to imply that the author of John had the Sacrament of Penance in mind, or did they not rather wish to insist on the relation of Penance to the forgiveness of sins attested in that verse? If Trent cited James 5:14-15 in relation to the Sacrament of Extreme Unction, did the Council wish to affirm that the author of James knew that the healing of the sick was a sacrament, or rather did it not affirm simply that the power of healing described in James was an instance of a power that later was understood to be exercised in the sacrament? In both instances a knowledge of the history of the development of sacramental theology and belief suggests the second alternative. In other words, in such statements about Scripture the Church does not seem to be settling a historical question (what was in the mind of the author when he wrote the text), but a religious question, namely the implications of Scripture for the life of the faithful. (We do not pretend that the Council Fathers at Trent were necessarily conscious of this distinction; we are merely concerned with the *de facto* import of their decisions.)

Are there any instances where the Church has spoken authoritatively about the literal sense of Scripture? Trent seems to have spoken thus about Jesus' words of Eucharistic institution: "After he had blessed bread and wine, he said in plain, unmistakable words that he was giving them his own body and his own blood. . . . These words have their proper and obvious meaning and were so understood by the Fathers" (*DS* 1637). Vatican I seems to have been speaking about the literal sense of Matthew 16:17-19 and John 21:15-17 when it insisted Christ gave Peter real primacy among the apostles (*DS* 3053-55).

Experts in dogmatic theology, however, are not in agreement about whether even in these instances the Church was defining the literal sense of Scripture. A. C. Cotter (*Theologia fundamentalis* [2nd ed.; Weston, Massachusetts, 1947] 681) thinks that Vatican I did directly define the meaning of the Matthean text. Yet V. Betti (*La costituzione dommatica 'Pastor aeternus' del Concilio Vaticano I* [Rome, 1961] 592) states: "The interpretation of these two texts [Matthew 16:17-19; John 21:15-17] as proof of the two dogmas mentioned does not fall *per se* under dogmatic definition—not only because no mention is made of them in the canon, but because there is no trace of a desire in the Council to give an authentic interpretation of them in this sense."

These few instances of possible Church definition (there may be others) and the instances where the Church has condemned a particular interpretation of Scripture cause much difficulty for Protestants. J. M. Robinson, *CBQ* 27 (1965) 8-11, protests that if an exegete by careful use of method comes to a conclusion about a particular verse of Scripture and then the Magisterium steps in and says his conclusion is wrong, it is a denial of intellect. He observes, "The invalidation of the conclusion resulting from the proper application of method necessarily invalidates the method," and thus in principle the freedom and scientific quality of Catholic exegesis are imperiled.

In response, three observations should be made. *First,* Catholic exegetes would honestly hold that in the instances where the Church has spoken authoritatively about the literal sense of Scripture, negatively or positively, a plausible exegetical case can be made for the Church's position. The meaning that the Church finds in the verse may not be the only meaning that one could derive by critical method, but it is a possible meaning. Therefore, the Church's position does not imply a rejection of proper exegetical method; for the Catholic exegete is simply accepting an interpretation on the surety of his faith where historical criticism alone could lead only to probability or possibility.

Second, in interpreting Scripture the Magisterium does not operate in independence of and isolation from reliable scriptural scholarship. The Magisterium does not come to its conclusion about what a biblical passage does or does not mean by some sort of mystical instinct or by direct revelation from on high. Traditional faith, theological implications, and long usage all enter into the Magisterial decision, but so also does responsible and scholarly exegesis. Both Trent and Vatican I consulted the best Catholic exegetes of the time. We are close enough to Vatican II to know that when exegetes pointed out that Scripture was being misused, such misinterpretation was dropped from the conciliar documents. In fact, Vatican II affirmed that the work done by exegetes is a factor in bringing the judgment of the Church to maturity (*De Revelatione* 3:12). It may be asked if the Church has ever spoken (or ever will speak) against the scholarly opinion of the majority of Catholic exegetes. R. E. Murphy, *Commonweal* 80 (June 26, 1964) 419-20, has correctly insisted, "The Church is hearing the Word ever anew through the work of its theologians and exegetes—and this work must go on *freely.*"

Third, the role of the Church in interpreting Scripture must not be seen only in terms of a possible curtailment of scientific freedom; the Church makes a positive hermeneutic contribution. If the drive of the "New Hermeneutic" is to let Scripture speak to the man of today, the Catholic feels very strongly that the liturgical and doctrinal life of the Church is the "hermeneutical place" where Scripture speaks most truly. The instinctive negative reaction to the Church to rationalism, liberalism, and modernism was not a rejection of the scientific method (although unfortunately and accidentally that method was thus brought into temporary disrepute), but a reflection of the Church's good sense that in such "isms" Scripture was not speaking truly. One may acknowledge that at times, because of the weaknesses of the men who constitute it, the Church does not immediately or adequately respond to a meaning of Scripture that is patent to exegetes—whence the constant need of renewal and reform from within. But despite that, the Church remains par excellence the place where Scripture is heard in its truest and fullest meaning.

(III) EXEGETICAL AUTHORITY OF THE FATHERS

In almost every Roman document pertaining to scriptural studies there has been a statement about interpreting Scripture in loyalty to the mind of the Fathers and Doctors of the Church. Until recently, as a result of the Modernist crisis, Catholic exegetes teaching in seminaries were annually sworn to interpret Scripture according to the unanimous consent of the Fathers. The 1964 Instruction of the Biblical Commission continues the insistence: "Let the Catholic exegete, following the guidance of the Church, derive profit from all the earlier interpreters, especially the holy Fathers and Doctors of the Church."

Yet when one reads the actual exegesis of the Fathers as we described it above, it really has little in common with the methods and results of modern Catholic exegesis. We have recorded a reluctance to return to the more-than-literal exegesis of the Fathers. What then is the practical import of patristic exegesis as a guide?

First of all, the area in which patristic authority is strongest is that of the dogmatic implications of Scripture, not that of literal exegesis. For example, Athanasius was quite aware that no text of Scripture fully answered the Arian heresy; no single text in its literal sense irrefutably showed that Jesus was "true God of true God." But he insisted that in the 4th century problematic the only answer that Scripture could give to the question that Arius was raising was the answer of Nicaea ("Letter Concerning the Decrees of the Council of Nicaea," 5.19-21). Obviously, thus understood, loyalty to patristic authority is no restriction on the liberty or scientific equality of modern Catholic exegesis.

Moreover, when it is taken as an absolute norm, the unanimous consent of the Fathers (morally unanimous consent, not necessarily numerically unanimous) does not affect many disputed passages. In a passage where one might hope for unanimity, e.g., the Petrine application of Matthew 16:18, one finds, for instance, that neither Augustine nor Chrysostom took the foundation rock to be Peter!

In summary, the Church's insistence on the exegetical authority of the Fathers reflects her desire that the Catholic exegete should not forget the dogmatic heritage that comes to him from tradition. But in terms of practical guidance in modern literal exegesis, patristic authority is of restricted importance, especially for the OT.

(IV) BIBLICAL PREACHING

As we mentioned above, prophoristics, which gives the rules for expounding Scripture to others, is a part of hermeneutics. Because space does not allow a discussion of Bible classes, scriptural catechetics, Bible vigils, and many of the other ways of presenting Scripture, we shall concentrate here on preaching. In trying to describe a biblical sermon, we are not denying the possibility, the desirability, and even the necessity of other types of sermons; we are simply trying to make clear what is and what is not a biblical sermon.

We may begin negatively. A biblical sermon is not a tissue of Scripture quotes. Nor is one giving a biblical sermon when he picks a topic from dogmatic or moral theology and cites a few biblical passages to illustrate or prove his thesis. The oratical technique whereby one begins with the Scripture pericope assigned by the liturgy (e.g., the Sunday Gospel) and then proceeds to talk about something that is really not related to that passage is not the procedure of a biblical sermon (and, indeed, is of dubious value). It would be preferable to say that one is going to speak on Vatican II, or on Purgatory, or on interracial issues, or on a charity collection, than to use the Scripture pericope as a springboard for launching into such a topic. If the liturgical setting gives to a Scripture pericope an orientation that is not faithful to its literal sense, e.g., the Christmas use of Wisdom 18:14-15, a sermon employing this orientation is more liturgical than biblical.

A true biblical sermon is: (I) either an explanation centered around the literal sense of a biblical passage, its setting, thought, and import; (2) or an explanation and development of a biblical theme that runs through many passages.

A sermon of the *first type* demands that the preacher possess a certain amount of technical background knowledge, e.g., as to whether there are textual or critical problems in the passage, and whether there are parallels and what light they cast on the passage. Our contention that the preacher should possess or acquire this knowledge does not mean that such information should necessarily be part of his sermon. The preacher should resist the tendency to transfer to the pulpit a digest of what was learned in the classroom; he must select and rethink such matter according to the purpose of a sermon, which is different from that of a lecture. Often technical knowledge can best be put to use in helping one to determine what *not* to say and where *not* to put the emphasis. For instance, if one knows that most scholars do not accept the historicity of a scene, then in drawing a theological lesson from that scene, one avoids statements that would stress its historicity.

Yet, and this is important, questions of historicity are really not in themselves sermon material. Too often, impressed with the novel character of what they have recently learned (correctly?), preachers enter the pulpit with an itch to shock: "There was no Garden of Eden. There were no magi. Etc." Leaving aside the question of the oversimplified and sometimes incorrect tendency of such statements, we must insist that they serve no purpose in sermons whose aim is to bring the wealth of Scripture to the spiritual and salvific aid of the people. One can preach on a topic like Genesis I-3 in such a way that one respects the historical problems involved but nevertheless concentrates on the theological message. See below for a more detailed discussion on the communication of modern critical approaches to Scripture.

As for supplying historical, geographical, and other factual background for a biblical passage, a little bit of technical material in a sermon goes a long way. In some sermons it may be truly useful to set a scene historically and geographically because that is required for understanding the message. One can scarcely understand what Jesus says to the Samaritan woman in John 4 without knowing a little of the Samaritans and Jacob's well; one needs to know something of the problems at Corinth to understand Paul's remarks in the Corinthian letters. But too often valuable preaching time is wasted by displaying erudition that really does nothing for the central message, e.g., sermons on Jesus' passion that go into detail about different methods of crucifixion and types of crosses. The sense of the goal of the sermon should also regulate how much exegesis of individual verses is included. Concentration on only the significant lines is generally more effective than an atomistic dissection of line after line.

Because preaching on the literal sense of a passage requires knowledge and, therefore, effort, the greatest danger in biblical preaching is a tendency to substitute one's personal impressions of Scripture as the subject of the sermon. "What I thought of when I read this passage" replaces what God's inspired author meant when he wrote the passage. Although personal impressions may occasionally be of interest, they frequently descend to the level of moralizing and homespun philosophizing. When parishioners complain about lack of content in sermons, they are often protesting against the impressionistic approach to Scripture.

When the preacher has explained the literal meaning of a biblical passage, he should then point out the relevance of this to the lives of the people. Often the relevance is quite evident from the subject matter, and there is probably more danger of unduly prolonged and irrelevant application than of insufficient application. The burden of the sermon is so to explain the Scripture that the Scripture itself can speak to the needs and lives of the audience, without interposing an elaborate and often individually inapplicable exhortation. If we stress the explanatory rather than the hortatory side of the sermon, it is because it is easier to be hortatory than to explain, and more abuse has come from overexhortation than from overexplanation. The explanation of a theologically relevant portion of Scripture may not change a person's life immediately after he hears it; but like the seed mentioned in Mark 4:26ff., scriptural understanding sinks into fertile soil and bears fruit without overanxious attempts to hasten the process.

Many of the cautions just given are applicable as well to biblical sermons of the *second type*, i.e., preaching on biblical themes or personages. In addition, however, with this type of preaching one should insist that only when a biblical theme is developed in a *biblical way* is the sermon truly biblical. The Eucharist is a NT theme; but if the sermon concentrates on the matter and form of the sacrament, on transubstantiation, etc., it is not a biblical sermon. Yet at times it will be necessary in a predominantly biblical treatment to bring in the more formal and developed theology of later Christianity. Biblical thought is frequently symbolic, imprecise, and inchoative; and in a sermon one should not so compartmentalize the different stages of theology that one leaves the audience without an adequate picture. For instance, a biblical treatment of the Trinitarian (or better "triadic") passages in the NT would reflect the imprecision of Ist century thought on that subject; but a preacher should clarify this imprecision, as historically the later Church did. A biblical sermon on a subject like the Trinity should reflect the biblical aspect of a *larger truth*.

(V) POPULAR COMMUNICATION OF MODERN CRITICAL VIEWS

One other aspect of prophoristics may be treated. The 1961 Monitum of the Holy Office and the 1964 Instruction of the Pontifical Biblical Commission—two documents from Rome, one restrictive in tendency, the other liberalizing—both insist on the dangers of scandalizing the faithful by communicating in the biblical field "vain or insufficiently established novelties." The PBC Instruction forbids those who publish for the faithful "led on by some pernicious itch for newness, to disseminate any trial solutions for difficulties without a prudent selection and serious discrimination; for thus they perturb the faith of many."

Such warnings are realistic. We cautioned above about making historical criticism the subject of sermons. Not only is this dangerous for the faithful, but damage has been done to reputable biblical scholars by enthusiasts who popularize the scholars' views without necessary qualifications and in a context where they were not meant to be presented. The general principle is that one should not leave the audience with problems that the audience is not capable of solving. If one has to bring in elements of historical criticism, then one should take cognizance of possible implications and head off wrong conclusions.

But if we acknowledge the danger of rash popularization, we must firmly accentuate the danger on the other side as well— a danger that unfortunately has not received sufficient attention in Church documents. This is the danger that an exaggerated fear of scandal will prevent popularizers from communicating to educated Catholics the more sophisticated understanding of the Bible that they should have. So often we hear about the few that are scandalized, and no voice is raised about the much greater crime of leaving the many in ignorance of modern biblical criticism. Fear of scandal must never lead to a double standard whereby the simple or the young are taught things about the Bible that are false just so that they will not be shocked. Common sense dictates that all education be scaled to the ability of the audience, but this does not mean that elementary biblical instruction should be noncritical, it means that elementary instruction should be critical in an elementary way. From the very first time the story of Genesis I-3 is told to kindergarten children, they should be taught to think of it as a popular story and not as history, even though the teacher may not wish at that level to raise formally the question of historicity. Even beginners can be taught to think of the Gospels as recorded preaching and teaching rather than as biographies of Jesus.

Unfortunately, too, an exaggerated fear of scandal can hamper scientific research. There are a host of delicate biblical questions that need scientific study and discussion, e.g., the historicity of the infancy narratives, and the human knowledge of Christ. Yet scholars know that if they write on these subjects even in professional and technical magazines, an account, often confused, will soon appear in the popular press. In other words, while competent Catholic scholars are urged to keep these matters away from public notice, whether they like it or not others will popularize their work. The result is that frequently the scholar is accused of being responsible for the scandal and is made the target of recriminations by would-be protectors of the faith. The whole distinction between discussion on a scholarly level and popularization—a distinction presupposed in the warnings from Rome—is rapidly dying out, and we should face this problem more frankly. In the long run more damage has been done to the Church by the fact that her scholars have not always been free to discuss delicate problems than by the fact that some of the faithful are scandalized by the dissemination of new ideas. Imprudence and occasional scandal are the almost inevitable price that one must pay for the right of free discussion. And indeed such free academic discussion has its own way of crushing errors—a devastating book review in a biblical magazine may be more effective in eradicating nonsense than a warning from Church authority.

James Tunstead Burtchaell

1934-

Burtchaell was born in Portland, Oregon, and graduated from the University of Notre Dame. He studied theology at the Gregorian University in Rome (S.T.B., 1958) and the Catholic University in Washington, D.C. (S.T.L., 1960). He then went to the Ecole Biblique *in Jerusalem for Biblical studies, receiving the S.S.B. (1961) and the S.S.L. (1964) from the Biblical Commission in Rome. He received the Ph.D., from Cambridge University in 1966, and since then has been involved in teaching and/or administration at Notre Dame.*

Burtchaell's book is devoted to a particular issue, that of inspiration, but in narrating the story the broader scene must be painted. The selection included here is his sixth chapter, focusing on "The Last Half-Century." In it he has brought together a wealth of information about the events and personalities involved in the struggle since the days of Pius X.

One realization that emerges from his treatment is the communal character of the theological enterprise. On the credit side it keeps the individual aware that the role of the Bible, of tradition, of theology, of the Church as inseparable from the lives of people. Salvation, in God's plan, is corporate, and so are the instruments thereof. But on the debit side it must also be acknowledged that there is a danger in allowing oneself to be locked into the myopia of the past. Just because a question was formu-

lated in a particular way and addressed by generations of scholars does not automatically mean that it was a good question, or that it was posed in the most fruitful way. That is why the community must also be open to the pioneer, the innovator, the one who takes a different stance and points at things from a new angle.

It is especially when one is under attack that the danger of adopting too narrow a base is maximized. In his closing chapter Burtchaell makes the point well: "The Catholic stance . . . was one of resistance and caution. In reply to the Reformers, Catholics first played down Scripture and highlighted the Church as supreme interpreter of religious truth, equipped to preach a correct understanding of the written text, and to supplement it with a further, unwritten tradition. The reversed direction of the Protestants in the 19th century, with the New Criticism and the Modernist dispute, sent Catholic scholars flying with new allegiance to the defense of the Bible so cherished by the Reformers. . . . Thus from the 16th century to our time the thrust of the Protestant argument has undergone a noticeable reversal . . . And Catholics correspondingly assumed contrary positions of defense: vindicating now the Church, now the Bible."

One of the great merits of the ecumenical atmosphere is that it does away with the necessity of this kind of special pleading and encourages Christian theologians to step back and take a fuller horizon into account. In doing so the understanding of both the Bible and the Church stand to benefit greatly.

CATHOLIC THEORIES OF BIBLICAL INTERPRETATION SINCE 1810

CHAPTER 6

THE LAST HALF-CENTURY

L a question biblique had made the threshold years of this century lively with controversy. Much of what was being written in those days of bold expression was careless, much was nasty and simply vindictive. But any close observer of the argument's give and take should have noticed promising signs. For one thing, ancient party oppositions were dissolving: Jesuits like Prat in France and Billot in Rome were making common cause against the Franzelin theory with—of all people—the Friars Preachers. Ecumenical collaboration was on the increase. In Palestine, Catholic and Protestant archeologists worked the same trenches. In England, Catholic credits were appearing in friendly publications like the *Hibbert Journal* and the *Contemporary Review*. In fact, the more competent Catholic biblical journals were reviewing as much non-Catholic literature as Catholic. Relations between Evangelical and Catholic faculties in the German universities, once frosty, were a-warming. Theology through the Church, which during the entire period we have so far surveyed had been dominated by the Roman seminaries, was emancipating itself, even in Italty, and reaching out for a new scholarly professionalism. *La question biblique* was far from resolved to everyone's satisfaction, but there was some hope that in such an atmosphere men might learn better from one another and criticize more usefully, and somehow arrive at a broadly received consensus.

But all this change was rancorous and reckless. It had been held off too long, and Rome at the time had no minds subtle or nervy enough to maneuver the Church through discussions that might end nobody knew where. And so the government of Pius X decided to put an end to it. By 1910, after only three years of papal exertion, it was all over. And as the bickering fell silent, so too did practically all creative biblical scholarship.

Looking backwards over those years when Modernism was overcome in the Catholic Church, and biblical scholarship fell a casualty in the hostilities, the change in scene appears enormous. The list of condemned propositions in the Inquisition's decree *Lamentabili* of July 1907 was so long and, some felt, ambiguous, that many divines with no guilty conscience might still find themselves delated to Rome because of an interpretation put on their students' classnotes by suspicious colleagues. Pius himself had issued his encyclical letter *Pascendi* two months later, and it openly invited authorities to dismiss ruthlessly any churchmen found tainted with these new and proscribed ideas. In November he issued another instruction, *Praestantia*, to emphasize that Catholics were bound in conscience to assent in mind and heart to the decrees of the Biblical Commission. Since then, great men had fallen. Lagrange, called in from Jerusalem, was forbidden to publish on touchy subjects, and for a while was removed from his post at the Ecole Biblique. In France, Loisy and Houtin had both had their publications put on the *Index*, and had been unfrocked and excommunicated. Even old Pierre Batiffol fell afoul of the authorities and was dismissed from the rectorship of the Institut Catholique de Toulouse. Franz von Hummelauer lost his teaching position. Giovanni Semeria was sent into exile by his Italian superiors, and Salvatore Minocchi was suspended. David Fleming had been eased out of Rome back to Britain, and Giovanni Genocchi had been dismissed from his chair at the Apollinare in that city. George Tyrrell died excommunicate without a Catholic funeral, and Friedrich von Hügel found that he was more welcome in non-Catholic circles than amidst his own folk. Henry Poels was expelled from the Catholic University of America and sent home to Holland. And a number of new periodicals that had recently displayed remarkable erudition and promise now perished in the general fright. Among the missing were *Studi Religiosi*, founded by Minocchi in Florence, the *New York Review*, published by St Joseph's seminary faculty in that city, and Robert Dell's *New Era*.

The Biblical Commission began to publish official replies to queries about the mosaic authorship of the Pentateuch, the possibility of non-historical narratives such as midrash, and the theory of implicity citations. All the replies were rigorously negative, and although their small print carried qualifications enough to allow of further investigation into most issues, their tone was so discouraging that Catholic scholars got the message that new ideas, especially if imported from Protestant critics, were unwanted by Rome. Finally in 1910 a loyalty oath against Modernism was imposed on all clerics whenever they received holy orders, applied for confessional faculties, took papal degrees, began office as religious superiors, or taught in a seminary or pontifically approved faculty. It was refused by very few clerics, but it required some arrangement of consciences on the part of many.

By 1910 the issue had been decided, and all that remained was the business of delating individual scholars to Rome. Unfortunately too little discrimination was made between petulant unbelievers such as Loisy, and open-faced researchers like Lagrange. It was generally understood that if men wished to continue teaching and publishing, they must not hazard any hypotheses that could not be comprehended by the consultors of the Inquisition.

Benedict XV replaced Pius X in 1914, and the Great War soon overshadowed domestic theological strife. Those who may have looked to a revival of the recent learning were advised otherwise by the encyclical issued on the 1500th anniversary of the death of St Jerome, *Spiritus Paraclitus*. The letter was drawn up by Leopold Fonck, Jesuit rector of the Pontifical Biblical Institute, who took the occasion to condemn two theories that were still proving difficult to eradicate. The first was the theory of plenary inspiration but limited inerrancy:

> For while conceding that inspiration extends to every phrase—and, indeed, to every single word of Scripture —yet, by endeavoring to distinguish between what they style the primary or religious and the secondary or profane element in the Bible, they claim that the effects of inspiration—namely, absolute truth and

immunity from error—are to be restricted to that primary or religious element. Their notion is that only what concerns religion is intended and taught by God in Scripture, and that all the rest—things concerning 'profane knowledge', the garments in which Divine truth is presented—God merely permits, and even leaves to the individual author's greater or less knowledge. Small wonder, then, that in their view a considerable number of things occur in the Bible touching physical science, history and the like, which cannot be reconciled with modern progress in science!

That had been one of the very common views before 1907, and in fact it is difficult to find evidence that it was still being put about with enough frequency to disturb Fonck. The second theory he attacks is Hummelauer's hypothesis of 'historical appearances':

Those, too, who hold that the historical portions of Scripture do not rest on the absolute truth of the facts but merely upon what they are pleased to term their relative truth, namely, what people then commonly thought, are—no less than are the aforementioned critics—out of harmony with the Church's teaching, which is endorsed by the testimony of Jerome and other Fathers. Yet they are not afraid to deduce such views from the words of Leo XIII on the ground that he allowed that the principles he had laid down touching the things of nature could be applied to historical things as well. Hence they maintain that precisely as the sacred writers spoke of physical things according to appearance, so, too, while ignorant of the facts, they narrated them in accordance with general opinion or even on baseless evidence; neither do they tell us the sources whence they derived their knowledge, nor do they make other people's narrative their own. Such views are false, and constitute a calumny on our predecessor. After all, what analogy is there between physics and history? For whereas physics is concerned with 'sensible appearances' and must consequently square with phenomena, history, on the contrary, must square with facts, since history is the written account of events as they actually occurred. If we were to accept such views, how could we maintain the truth insisted on throughout Leo XIII's encyclical—viz. that the sacred narrative is absolutely free from error.

Pius XI succeeded Benedict in 1923, and the very next year he gave notice that things were not altered. The most venerable of all Scripture textbooks, the *Manuel Biblique,* first published by Sulpicians Louis Bacuez and Fulcran Vigouroux in 1878, had been re-appearing in numerous editions, and was widely used because of its clear presentation and the fact that the Sulpicians directed so many seminaries. In 1923 the latest edition, by Brassac and Ducher, both highly respected exegetes, was put on the *Index* for paying little heed to the decrees of the Biblical Commission and setting forth liberal views in too sympathetic a manner.

It had been supposed back in 1864 that the *Syllabus of Errors* would put the wilt on Catholic scholarship, but this was not to be the case. The fifty years that followed produced an acceleration of inquiry and academic excellence unmatched since the Reformation. By contrast, the events of 1907 and their aftermath did succeed in suppressing almost all Catholic inquiry into the unresolved problem of biblical inspiration and inerrancy. More than ever before, the only manuals admitted to theological schools were those that issued from the Roman seminaries. Those classical views which had gained acceptance before the purge were still being expounded, but in a desultory fashion that shunned further exploration. Things were dull. For example, the Dominicans continued to tender St Thomas' theory of verbal inspiration. In 1913 Merkelbach was claiming that the Jesuit theory was really a result of Protestant influence. As for those who claim that there is no error whatsoever in Scripture, however, he throws up his hands and asks if human stupidity has any limits. In a milder way, Paul Synave continued to explain instrumental causality according to Aquinas. A young Dominican name Jácome, professor of theology at the Angelico in pre-war Rome, and later in Austria, was also offering publicity, if not improvement, to the now well-worn theory of the order. At Salamanca, another enclave of the Blackfriars, Alberto Colunga was putting forth the same theory. And in Rome the secretary of the Biblical Commission, Dominican Jacques Vosté, produced a bitterly anti-Jesuit treatise on inspiration.. He derides Eugène Mangenot, Henri Lusseau, and Lucien Méchineau (none of them Jesuits) for producing nothing but warmed-over Pesch, instead of adopting the more creative theory of the Neo-Thomists. His own study of literary forms is not determinedly creative. He will admit an occasional 'implicit citation', but suspects that unhistorical types of narrative, such as midrash, are incompatible with the veracity of divine truth. One of the newly produced standard manuals, by Hildebrand Höpfl (later re-edited by Benedictine confrères Gut and Leloir), tries to make peace with both Jesuits and Dominicans, but is clearly on the side of the latter. It does suggest that though there are not grades of inspiration, there might be grades of truth in Scripture. Affirmations by Christ, angels, apostles, and other authoritative personages are absolutely inerrant, but other materials presented with lesser endorsement are faithfully reported, though not guaranteed true in themselves. On interpretation, Höpfl is mostly concerned to square himself with the decrees of the Biblical Commission.

Divines of the Society of Jesus were also writing on the subject, with remarkable tenacity. In 1926 Christian Pesch got in his last word by publishing a thoroughly documented review of the Modernist turmoil (*re* the biblical question) and its aftermath. Pesch, very much on the side of the righteous, infers that all opponents of the Franzelin theory of content inspiration were, wittingly or unwittingly, duped by rationalism. He discloses in detail the censure and objections directed against Lagrange years earlier by the Holy See. In 1930 a Dutch Jesuit just beginning a teaching career in Rome, Sebastian Tromp, produced a treatise on inspiration that is all Franzelin. He offers an elaborate study of the meaning of the term *auctor,* insists that God may provide ideas and even words within the author's mind, but that the words on the page are not divinely determined. On the side of hermeneutics he is more cautious than many of his predecessors. He admits that at times the sacred authors quote earlier writers unauthoritatively, but there are many literary forms which he refuses to accept as worthy of divine use. For instance, he would be very reluctant to admit the existence in the Bible of edifying fiction, such as some describe Esther, Tobit, and Judith. Prophecy, he says, is almost entirely predictive of distant future events. And when the historical writers ran out of information they required, the light of inspiration supplied the need. Also, it was being argued by some that, in biblical history, facts were sometimes shaped, filled out, and elaborated in function of some religious point they were meant to convey. This Tromp denies, since the words of Scripture are so authoritative that the authors would have advised their readers if ever they intended to present facts inaccurately. In a word, though accurate and scientific writing was perhaps not always customary among the ancients, divine help could be counted on to make up for this shortcoming.

Just across the square from the Gregorian, at the Biblical Institute, another Jesuit was publishing his own treatise on the same subject in the same year. The views of Augustin Bea were not strikingly different from those of Tromp. He claims that since the turn of the century the Thomists have come round to the Jesuit way of looking at inspiration, by analyzing the notion of *auctor*. Two of the interesting points he makes concern instrumental causality and literary forms. The former, he suggests, is a tricky analogy to use in this context, since it is drawn from irrational instruments and can only awkwardly be transferred to active, human authors. As for literary forms, he feels that too many exegetes, delighted that better literary criticism resolves quite a few of the objections to inerrancy, forget that the narrative forms requires of its very nature historical truthfulness. Thus he is down on these two theological tools that had become so popular, especially among the Thomist scholars.

It is interesting to compare this Bea with the Bea of 1943. In that year Pius XII published an encyclical drawn up mostly by Bea, then rector of the Biblical Institute, that represents some broadening of perspective on the part of its author, and would incite Catholic scholars everywhere to follow suit. Here he urges a study of literary forms:

The interpreter must, as it were, go back wholly in spirit to those remote centuries of the East and with the aid of history, archeology, ethnology, and other sciences, accurately determine what modes of writing, so to speak, the authors of that ancient period would be likely to use, and in fact did use . . . No one who has a correct idea of biblical inspiration will be surprised to find, even in the Sacred Writers, as in other ancient authors, certain fixed ways of expounding and narrating, certain definite idioms, especially of a kind peculiar to the Semitic tongues, so-called approximations, and certain hyperbolic modes of expression, even at times paradoxical, which even help to impress the ideas more deeply on the mind.

As for the notion of instrumentality, Bea explains in his independently published comments on the encyclical that it is one of the pivotal terms used by the pope. Further articles the German scholar was to publish would study the vicissitudes of the instrument-notion in biblical studies. Part of the trouble began, he avers, with the earliest Christian apologists. True, they may not have adopted the Greek idea (from Plato through Philo) of ecstatic prophecy, wherein the human instrument would be passively unconscious, rather than personally creative. But they did adopt the Greek technical vocabulary and thus introduced considerable ambiguity into much of what they said about inspiration. Later, in the middle ages, the Scholastics were similarly influenced by both Arab scholars (Avicenna, Al Gazzali, Averroes) and Jewish (Maimonides) to think of instrumentality as impersonal. Aquinas did make it a more supple analogy, with full respect for freedom on the part of the human writer, but the post-Tridentine divines transferred their attention from the psychology of inspiration (Aquinas' viewpoint) to the authority of the Bible. Thus the question came to be treated, no longer in the treatise on prophecy, but in the treatise on theological authorities, *De locis theologicis.* In this context the concept of instrumentality was largely disused, until its recent revival (for which Bea thanks Kleutgen, not the Dominicans).

Now Bea's importance lies not in the freshness of his scholarship. There is nothing in either his articles or the encyclical he drafted that would not have been conservative and commonplace to the more thoughtful savants back in 1900. What he did do was help the reigning pontiff to smile upon biblical scholars for the first time in four decades. It is the change of climate, the Roman thaw of 1943, that marks the end of incomparably sterile years and invites a second spring of biblical studies. And ever so slowly, after a break of several generations, writers come again to discover that there are problems involving inspiration and inerrancy that must still be resolved, and they set about coping with them.

As things turned out, it was the first scholar to return to the problem that was to attract the largest following. By 1947 Pierre Benoit had been teaching New Testament at the Ecole Biblique in Jerusalem for a decade and a half. That year a translation and commentary on Aquinas' treatise on prophecy appeared, jointly produced by Benoit and his deceased confrère, Paul Synave. Benoit contributed an appendix that was to be the first of a series of studies on biblical inspiration. This initial essay is a fairly staid piece of work, a classic Dominican treatment with somewhat less flair than Lagrange in his better moments. He accepts, as do other Neo-Thomists, that one must distinguish between the charism of the prophet (disclosure of revealed information plus an infallible enlightenment of the understanding) and that of the biblical writer (infallible enlightenment only). A further difference he notes is in the order of judgment. Man's speculative judgment affirms whether or not something is true, whereas his practical judgment concerns itself with whether or not it is good to do something. As Benoit reads his Thomas, the gift of prophecy touches the seer's speculative judgment primarily, causing him to receive and transmit divine truths. But the business of the sacred author is before all else to work up a book. His overriding pre-occupation is the selection and presentation of materials for publication. This is largely a practical problem. His speculative judgment will also be charismatically endowed, but only in the measure in which he personally undertakes to guarantee the truth of what he publishes.

It can happen that the sacred writer categorically asserts some doctrinal truth that he has thought out; his inspiration in this case will entail as thorough an enlightenment of his knowledge as if he were a prophet. On the other hand it can happen that he makes no affirmation at all, but only speaks or quotes others without proposing his own views, in which case inspiration will affect only his practical judgment. Finally it can happen—and this is most often the case—that he does express a knowledge judgment, but one qualified by his formal object, his degree of affirmation, and the general requirements of his over-all purpose; here the light of inspiration will illumine his judgment, not absolutely, but to the exact extent to which the author is speaking his mind.

Benoit then supplements his philosophical position with a hermeneutic. Inerrancy, he explains, follows upon inspiration only insofar as the author's speculative judgment comes into play. How tell this? He offers these criteria: (1) the formal object (everything in Scripture is recounted from a single standpoint, supernatural salvation); (2) the force of any given statement (it may be vehemently underscored, or it may simply be passed on as hearsay); and (3) the literary forms employed. Benoit is confident that an inerrancy thus circumscribed will be possible to defend. He insists that the Bible is totally inspired, but his restrictions on inerrancy, while cautious and infinitely obsequious of Roman pronouncements, do not always escape a certain uneasiness.

Inerrancy, then, is not as often in play as inspiration. There is no doubt that when God teaches, and to the extent that he teaches, he can neither deceive nor be deceived: his word is necessarily free from all error, and this is what we mean by the privilege of 'inerrancy'. But God is not always teaching, and when he has his spokesman make statements that do not involve truth or falsehood, then there is inspiration without inerrancy. Briefly, inerrancy is not a distinct charism; it is a corollary of inspiration, and it is involved only when inspiration guarantees some speculative judgment, insofar as that judgment is enlightened by it.

Another monograph which the French friar issued seven years later pursues his differentiation of prophecy, meant to communicate knowledge of divine revelation, and Scripture, which often speaks without any purpose of formal teaching. All thought content in the latter case may be organized toward some practical effect: to evoke a certain mood or impression, to move readers to adopt a way of life, or even to comfort them. A certain amount of objective truth may be blended into the text, but often only for the sake of other, non-assertive purposes.

Benoit's hermeneutic has by this time grown somewhat more bold:

It must not be thought, indeed, that everything an author writes, even by way of affirmation, constitutes by that very fact a truth which he means to be believed: not all of his thoughts belong in the same way to the purpose of his work. Some are close to his heart and represent the essential element of his teaching—he writes precisely in order to teach them. Others are of less significance in his eyes. In his own mind he may perhaps be quite convinced of their truth, but they do not matter directly to that work and he introduces them only as a means of conveying his central thought. On secondary points he will not insist on being accepted so long as the major teachings which he means to give are accepted.

The distinction between the private person of a writer and his public personality as an 'author' is of peculiar importance in the case of the sacred writer. It is only in the latter capacity that he is 'inspired', not in the former . . . There may be in the Sacred Book many true affirmations which do not fall under the privilege of inerrancy because they are not taught. They are inspired because they play their part in the work as a whole which God causes to be written; but they are not inerrant, because that part is subordinate and is not necessarily bound up with the essential message which is the proper object of the teaching of the book. It would be useless to deny that the sacred writer affirms that the sun turns around the earth, or that Baltasar 'son of Nabucho-donosor' was defeated by 'Darius the Mede', and it would be just as naïve to claim that he was not convinced of these two points. He certainly did believe them as he presents them, and accordingly he affirms them. But he does not teach them as an inspired writer, because they are not of importance to the purpose for which he is writing and about which only he commits the truth of God.

From Louvain, Old Testament scholar Joseph Coppens objected that this sounded like double-talk, with authors affirming yet not teaching what they affirm. And, he warned, it falls into Newman's old theory of sorting out *obiter dicta* and denying them the privilege of inerrancy. Benoit had anticipated this objection, and replied that whereas the earlier, condemned theories had declared a priori that God could teach only religious matters, he, Benoit, had come to this conclusion a posteriori. To Coppens he insists that he is not establishing a material distinction between religious and profane contents in the Bible. He is arguing for a formal one between what is or is not taught by the writer—and he observes that what is taught is taught because of its religious significance.

At the International Catholic Biblical Congress held in Brussels in 1958, Benoit again takes up the problem, but this time in novel terms. Now, instead of placing a divider between prophecy and inspiration, revelation and Bible, he would speak of the one Spirit at work everywhere in the Church: of a single, versatile charism that in an analogous way elevates all activities that contribute to the Christian endeavor. Within a man's personal make-up it will touch his thinking, his speaking, and his writing, and hence Benoit speaks of cognitive, oratorical, and scriptural inspiration. Viewed as contributory to the Church's social mission, the inspiration which produces the Bible directs men as they act (Moses exiting from Egypt would act by dramatic inspiration), as they preach (Isaiah and Peter would enjoy prophetic and apostolic inspiration respectively), and as they actually set down the sacred books in writing (Mark at his inkpot would exemplify hagiographical inspiration). Amid this proliferation of terminology the same point is being made: that the practical judgment of the biblical writer holds his speculative judgment carefully in check, and that the privilege of inerrancy is similarly restrained except where he intends to teach something as true.

What renders Benoit's position tricky is the dilemma he finds himself in regarding inerrancy. He feels bound by the convention that whatever the Bible teaches is God's infallible teaching. This is perhaps most typically expressed in the 1915 dictum of the Biblical Commission: 'All that the sacred writer asserts, enunciates, suggests, must be held to be asserted, enunciated, suggested by the Holy Spirit.' To make this acceptable he devises a reductivist procedure that will minimalize formal biblical teaching to within believable limits. To this end, it has been observed, both his philosophy and his hermeneutic are designed. He is tied to a dogma that no sacred writer can teach *ex persona propria* without also teaching *ex persona Dei*, yet that is exactly what he wants to deny.

> Quite a few of the things an author puts into his book are not included for any interest of their own, or taught as absolute truths. They serve rather as adjuncts to the main point he seeks to teach. Or sometimes they are there just because he wants to put them on record.
>
> The Bible is not composed entirely of revelations. Most often the pure crystal of divine truth is imbedded in a lode that is needed to protect and transmit it. Or to use another image: the precious healing drug of a medicine is mixed with a larger quantity of pharmaceutical 'excipient' that allows it to be absorbed by the spiritual organism of the readers. A lode or an excipient—unlike the crystal or drug—are simply additives with no value in themselves. In this they resemble everything that is in the Bible to help along the substance of its message. The

> truth of divine revelation is really the soul of the
> sacred Book, the heart that sets every phrase throb-
> bing with its pulse. But it reaches out differently into
> the different areas: here in a major artery, there in a
> tiny capillary. The Book as a whole teaches divine
> truth, but it does not do this at every instant.

He is at pains somehow to disengage the substance from
the detail, and thus to minimalize what is inerrant. 'This teaching will not be expressed in every sentence the sacred author
writes. Indeed, the greater part of what he writes will not be
revelation in the strict sense at all. But the idea, the judgment,
the doctrine that God wishes to convey will emerge from a
thousand phrases of minimal importance.'

Benoit's theory and its painstaking defense is not likely to
draw support except from those committed to a 13th-century
system of psychology. But, since almost the entire Catholic
clergy has been educated, until very recently, to regard the
13th-century view of things as classic, his theory has enjoyed
a period of unchallenged popularity similar to that accorded
Franzelin's from 1870 until 1890. It adds little to the position
worked out by Lagrange and his school before the turn of the
century, and in fact never comes unequivocally to endorse the
very liberal position published by Lagrange in 1905 that the
purpose of Scripture is to record, rather than to teach. Though
contrived by a distinguished exegete, it is thoroughly *a priori*.
But as the first even faintly creative theory to emerge after so
long a failure to theorize, it is respectable and can be found in
every popular exposition of the subject by a Catholic writer
since 1947.

Some of the criticism put up against Benoit's scheme is
strictly intra-Thomistic, and concerned largely with issues of
detail. But at least one of his confrères does take him to task on
his reductivist method. P. Zerafa, writing in the journal of the
Dominicans' Roman academy, denies that the limits of inerrancy
can be established by pre-determining the 'formal object' of
inspired writing; God can manifest any kind of truth whatsoever to his charismatics. Nor does it do to distinguish prophecy
and inspiration, speculative and practical judgments. Benoit
himself admits that the sacred writer's speculative and practical

judgments coincide except where he is unwilling to vouch for the truth of what he writes, and this is rare. The overall purpose of the Bible is to propagate a message, and the only valid limitation on inerrancy is the recognition of literary forms. Bruce Vawter, the American Old Testament scholar, is skeptical about Benoit's heavy reliance on the analogy of instrument, an analogy which he considers not always to have been governed by the facts. Often, he says, it leaves as much unexplained as it illustrates. But by and large, the Benoit position rises as the classic theory of the years immediately after *Divino Afflante Spiritu*.

Of the many who follow in his footsteps, some make rather interesting statements of their own, especially when grappling with inerrancy. John Weisengoff considers that throughout the Old Testament period God tolerated faulty ideas until he could gradually eliminate them. The Bible, then, is a record of this progressive sloughing-off of error. Although the individual writers may have had it in mind to teach, the eminent purpose of the whole collection of books is to record. Thus God is not teaching such error as is presented in the Old Testament; he is merely abiding it as a springboard to the New Testament. The exegete may be sure that whatever in the Bible conforms to the Church's definitive teaching is God's message, and is formally taught by the Bible. Whatever fails to conform is accordingly not taught.

Pierre Grelot would likewise attach inerrancy, not to individual affirmations of Holy Writ, but to the Book as an entriety:

> To decompose the Old Testament books into formal propositions, and then assign them the same truth-value you would find, say, in Romans or the Fourth Gospel, would mean forgetting that Christ, by word and action, has *fulfilled* the Old Testament, and unveiled the deep meaning of its Law, its history, and its Scriptures. There is a truth enclosed within those texts that is released precisely by this *fulfilment*. It escaped the grasp of the inspired writers themselves, but if we refuse to go beyond what they understood, we disfigure the *real* burden of their witness.

To allow for this non-guaranteed sort of presentation, he must acknowledge that not everything the hagiographers put onto paper was the Word of God:

> Even in the prophetic books, St Thomas states that in principle one must differentiate between the personal opinions that men advanced on their own responsibility, and the message transmitted in virtue of the prophetic charism. A concrete example may serve to illustrate this. Nathan's two instructions to David contradict one another (2 Sam. vii, 3. 5ff.): one is given as his own view, while the other follows upon a communication from the Lord. This should serve to warn us against granting some sort of universal infallibility to the sacred writers. We cannot track down a revealed teaching lurking beneath the least hint of any idea they happened to have in their heads.

Manuel de Tuya, a Dominican from Salamanca, coins the phrase *disociación psicologica* to describe the manner in which semitic writers tend to use their historical sources. Judging that many of these narratives were useful as teaching vehicles, they often prescinded entirely from this factual value in order to further their non-historical purpose:

> It may well be that the sacred writer *prescinds* from the historical minutiae of a primitive story or amusing anecdote, and *intends only* to convey the religious content or the story. For any one of many reasons this sort of 'disassociation' is possible, for the religious content is not essentially bound up with any one particular account or its details.

One has the feeling that as the years wear on, partisans of this theory are constrained to squirm about to make all facts fit the theory. This would be likely to continue, were it not for other, newer standpoints on the inspiration problem that in most recent years have begun to attract attention away from the venerable Neo-Thomist formula.

In his presidential address to the 1957 convention of the Catholic Biblical Association of America, Canadian Jesuit Roderick MacKenzie, who would later be appointed rector of the Pontifical Biblical Institute, drew attention to the brittleness with which many classic theories treat the concepts of *author* and *book*. In the field of biblical literature, he observes, the production of a book is a collective venture. An example is the book of Judges:

> Its raw material began, in the 12th century B.C., as oral traditions of particular exploits and victories, circulating in different *milieux* before eventually and at different times being committed to writing. In the regnal period, two collections of this material were formed—by two different editors, naturally—one in the north, one in the south. The two were combined after the Fall of Samaria, by another editor who added a moralizing introduction. During the Exile, a Deuteronomic editor produced an enlarged second edition of this work, with the doctrinal lessons made more explicit. Probably in the 5th century, the work was further enlarged by the insertion of the Minor Judges and the addition of the two appendices. Thus the book was 800 years in the making.

As with Judges, so with most of the other books: they are not individual monographs by distinct writers. They are the accumulation of a people, the archives of a family, a deposit that was constantly used, reinterpreted, brought up to date, commented, and expanded. How widely then is the charism of inspiration shared out? To all who had a hand in the collective production of the book? Then why not also to the heathen authors and editors who gave some of the materials their earliest existence?

MacKenzie makes clear that he is not pleading for some sort of authorship by committee. What he does discern is a continuity preserved by various schools of divines, such as the school of Isaiah and that of Matthew: successive generations of men who preserve a recognizable theological tradition, and produce a catena of compositions under the pseudonymous authorship of the school's patron.

John McKenzie, the American scholar, later took up the question posed by his colleague. He is all agreement on the issue of authorship: in biblical literature it is generally impossible to find a single responsible author, even an anonymous one, for any single book. Yet McKenzie feels that allowance by theologians for a distribution of the inspirational charism to the various unknown authors and editors has been mechanical and contrived—and too ungenerous. They have been willing enough to share out the credit to anyone who edited, glossed, compiled, revised, or otherwise altered the text after it left the hands of the original creative writers. But they have hesitated to trace the process backwards into the unrecoverable, primitive, but also creative period when the tradition was being shaped and conveyed, not by what we could call books and authors, but by ballads, oral anecdotes, and scattered folk stories.

McKenzie declines to think of revelation in terms of inner utterance or infused species, the traditional Jesuits and Dominican formulas, but prefers to describe it as a direct, mystical insight and an awareness of divine reality, which provokes a man to respond by trying to articulate his experience to others. He admittedly departs from longstanding convention to identify revelation and inspiration on a single experience:

> I do not wish to conceive revelation as an inarticulate proposition which can be formulated indifferently one way or another, and I scarcely think that the direct insight and awareness of God is an inarticulate proposition. It is an experience, I would suggest, like pleasure or pain which has no definition except that which the sentient gives it. We know one person from another, certainly, but we rarely feel the necessity of defining our knowledge; and if we attempt to tell one person what another is like we often find that we cannot describe with satisfaction a person we have known for many years. Nor would I say that the experience of the Word of God has no effect on the formulation of the word by man. No one who has sat at his desk and writhed in pain searching for the one word which will release the pressure of his thought within him will say that the choice of words is an unimportant and accessory feature of authorship; he is more likely to say that authorship is best defined as the selection of words.

The almost total anonymity of the biblical books is no haphazard result of ancient custom. As McKenzie explains it, the creators did not think of affixing their own names to their compositions because they saw themselves as merely transmitting a heritage not of their own making:

> I suggest that the ancient author was anonymous because he did not think of himself as an individual speaker, as the modern author does. He was anonymous because in writing he fulfilled a social function; through him the society of which he was a member wrote its thoughts. He was its spokesman, and the society was the real author of the literature. What he wrote was the traditions of his people, or the record of the deeds of his people, or the beliefs and cult of his people. And so likewise the oral reciter was the spokesman of the group he addressed; he fostered their solidarity as a group in peace and in war by reciting the deeds and singing the songs of their common heritage. The men who wrote the recitals of the deeds of the kings of Assyria and of Egypt are as anonymous as the artists who illustrated these deeds in sculpture. How could they be anything else? The king was the speaker of the recital of these victories, as he was the agent of the victories; and the king was the people, the visible incorporation of the society.

The experience to which the individual gives voice is a personal experience, yet it occurs within the faith and tradition of a society. So he tends to conceal his individuality as he speaks or writes of the insight he has had. His very artistry is his ability not to memorialize himself as an individual, but to recite the history of his people as the story of God at work saving them with whatever lights his membership in that people has allowed him to see with. Some seers will naturally have a deeper vision than others, a more intense charism of inspiration and revelation than their fellows, which is why we have always considered some of the books more forceful and clear than others.

Not all theologians have been content to let the personal creativity of charismatic individuals be lost to view within their social context. A third Jesuit, Dennis McCarthy, cautions that although no biblical author writes except in terms of the on-going tradition, he is nevertheless conscious of having a hand in shaping the beliefs that would outlive him. Disagreeing with the Scandinavian school, which has argued that the Old Testament literature was consigned to writing only in the very last centuries before Christ, McCarthy submits that writing was used in very primitive times to preserve the prophetic oracles. And the purpose of writing, as distinct from speaking, is width of distribution and permanence of preservation through time. The effort and expense of ancient writing imply an intent that the message endure, and a will to affect a society and its tradition. The most obscure chancery clerk, whose reactions to Israel's historical experience seem lost in featureless anonymity, was quite conscious that as he marked the traditional documents with his own reflections, he was writing to a public: he not only spoke for a society; he spoke to it.

Karl Rahner had been saying that the sacral society was capable of producing authoritative books only at the moment when it was finally invested with definitive stability. Thus only at the end of the apostolic period could the Church draw the Old Testament into her canon of inspired writings. Not so, counters McCarthy. Scripture is the output, not of a finally fixed community, but of the community during the period when it is growing by stages and finding its way haltingly towards the divine purpose. The end of the apostolic period is not the moment when the Church produces Scripture; it is the moment when she ceases to produce it.

> Why does the divinely chosen community produce inspired writing? Is it not precisely because it is relatively unformed and unstructured? Not yet equipped with definitive norms and definitive authorities, its own life, its own utility had to be the criterion which guided the production and recognition of the inspired, and utility is defined in terms of end.

McKenzie seems to have had something similar in mind when he remarked that inspiration was a resource of the Church's infancy that passed away as she crossed the threshold of maturity. He then makes the comment that sounds rather extraordinary for an exegete: 'She [the Church] does not write the word of God because she is the living word which needs no written record.'

A somewhat different slant on the Scripture's communitarian origins is offered by Karl Rahner, in a very brief but remarkably influential monograph. Directing his attention to the Apostolic Church, the Munich divine observes that it differs sharply from what went before it and what was to go after. The Old Dispensation had been in constant jeopardy, and at no time had there been any guarantee that the entire project would not collapse into definitive apostasy. With the eschatological event of Christ and the founding of the Church, however, the possibility of frustration and revocation is removed, and grace is established within the Church for all times. Compared to all subsequent generations, on the other hand, the first generation of the Church is seen to be unique: it is the permanent ground and norm for everything that is to follow. This first age is a determinating origin from which all later ages must derive.

One of the unique, non-transferrable capacities of this paradigmatic generation is the gift of clear self-expression. 'The beginning must therefore enjoy an originality, an irreducibility and a purity in the expression of its own essence which, necessary as subsequent evolution must be, are proper only to the first phase.' The apostolic Church in a special measure could set herself off from all pseudo-Christian contaminants in such decisive fashion as to produce a tangible and unambiguous canon for the Church of all times to come. All other generations will measure themselves by this norm: this generation alone can produce it.

It is the Scriptures which are this self-expression of the apostolic Church's faith, the written embodiment of what she was preaching and believing. They are not simply a record of revelation; they are a testimony to belief. Thus this embodied faith is one of those permanent institutions—like the juridical succession and the sacramental economy—which are supplied by the founding Church to all successive eras of the Church.

'The Bible is *the* Book of the Church; it is inspired precisely as the book of the Church, and it contains a full and adequate concretization of the Church's primal memory of the days of her birth, when she first heard the revelation of God in Christ.'

This, of course, accounts for only the New Testament. Rahner goes on to plead that, in a way, inspiration is incomplete without canonicity: the whole purpose of a divinely-originated book is that it be presented to its readership. But in the Old Covenant there was not the definitive authority necessary to grant full canonical approval to the sacred writings. 'Inasmuch as it remained possible for the Synagogue to fall away from God, it could not have the same power as the Church of distinguishing infallibly between what is foreign to her nature and what is in accord with it.' Further, there was no teaching office that could give infallible attestation of inspiration. Thus, even the Old Testament writings only achieved final canonicity and had their inspiration consummated when they were accepted by the apostolic Church as the crystallization of her prehistory—and precisely of those elements of her prehistory and prefaith that endured and were not abrogated along the way.

Since, then, the Scriptures are a determinant element of the primal Church, God constitutes himself their originator and author in the same formal predefinition whereby he founded the Church. Rahner has nothing to say about the effects of inspiration upon the interior faculties of the writers, but then his Molinist proclivities make it preferable to speak of God influencing from without rather than from within.

He rejects most suggestions of how the biblical books came to be acknowledged as canonical. It was not, as some would have it, that there were indications in the books themselves, nor that they were of apostolic authorship, nor that any list was revealed or drawn up by an apostle. 'Was it not rather that the Church recognized, in the case of certain books dating from the period of the Apostolic Church, that they belonged to that period in the proper sense and as such—in other words, that they were written by an apostle and (or) represented the faith of the Church?'

Lastly, because Rahner presents the Bible as the objective embodiment of the archetypal Church, he rejects the somewhat notorious Two-Source Theory, and asserts that, except for the canon itself, all belief of the Church is to be sought in the Church's Book.

Commenting on this thesis, Yves Congar praises it for showing how Scripture and the Church are in function of one another: Scripture was written for the Church alone, and the Church is its only interpreter. The Reformation had mistakenly subordinated the Church to Scripture. Yet, he complains, Rahner should ascribe the Bible, not simply to the *Urkirche,* but specifically to the apostles and prophets. It is they personally who were normative for the Church, who while part of it yet shaped it. They had received a unique, charismatic mission from Christ as had he from the Father. It is because they were *over* the Church that their authorship was normative and authoritative.

> Simply to say that Scripture is the written formu-
> lation of the faith of the Church, albeit the primordial
> Church, fails to appreciate how conscious that Church
> was that she did not merely *possess* Scriptures as a
> faith formula permanentized in writing, but that she
> had *received* them from men chosen by God, spiri-
> tually gifted by him, and given a mission and authority
> by him for this purpose.

A.-M. Dubarle takes issue with the German *Dogmatiker* on his remarks about the Old Testament books. Rahner says that there was no real Old Testament canon until the early Church added these books to its own writings. Yet the facts argue in exactly the opposite direction. The old books, long before the twelve apostles were anything more than fellow-travellers, were received as inspired and authoritative. It was to this already established canon that the apostolic writings were eventually added. Further, he feels that Rahner overstresses the point that Scripture is an expression of the community's faith. How then explain books like Jeremiah and Job, which fly in the face of common opinion?

Rahner later returns to his subject from another angle. How, he asks, is the truth most loudly proclaimed by Christianity? Not by doctrines or ideas, but by events—and principally that event wherein God sent his Son to take on our flesh. The deepest sense of *paradosis,* of a handing on, refers not to propositions, but to the death and resurrection grace that is communicated in the Church from one generation to the next. The greatest gift which the apostolic Church has to transmit is Jesus Christ himself. But a necessary feature of this transmission is verbal communication. Reality cannot be handed on without speech. The Scriptures are the normative objectivication, he says, of the normative faith of the apostolic Church.

> Now we know . . . that this apostolic Church, this permanent, changeless, normative magnificence that travels in reality and word down across the centuries, has objectified herself, has reproduced, represented, and expressed herself in what we call Holy Scripture. When anyone asks where we can lay hold of the apostolic Church just as it existed, just as it believed— though such appropriation presumes much by way of human capacity and achievement—we can and should give this positive answer, perhaps the only answer: it is to be found in Holy Scripture. There it is that the apostolic Church explains herself to the ages to come. There her words, her beliefs, her life lie open to us to be possessed and read.

Rahner has never seriously dealt with the side-problem of inerrancy. His one treatment of that subject was so maladroit that his critics have generally withheld comment upon it. Another German Jesuit, as experienced in exegesis as Rahner is not, Norbert Lohfink, has undertaken the task quite recently. For centuries, he regrets, the theories devised to explain inerrancy have been forced and abstract. Even Benoit's reinterpretation he finds wanting: a negative inerrancy, which tries to combine thematic error with an unthematic openness to fuller truth. If we are to consider God as author of the Bible, he counters, then inerrancy must be construed as a positive guarantee.

Inerrancy can be predicated of the Bible, of the biblical books or of the biblical writers. The nineteenth century tended to follow the third course, for the authors were then thought of as individual men who sat to their compositions all by themselves. Later criticism discovered meanwhile that many, or even most of the books were, on the contrary, written and re-edited over periods as long as 700 years. Thus there are far more writers to account for, and a far wider variety of outlook and purpose within their books. Each book conceals many strata of expression. Thus, if one insists on retaining the notion of 'inerrant writers', it would become terribly important that we be able to recover from each book, not just the message of the final edition, but all the messages of the diverse preparatory stages—an awesome task. Two escapes from this dilemma have been proposed. Some have attached inspiration to the last writer to rework the material. Thus the final editor would be the charismatic, and all previous writers would be his source-suppliers. Exegetes hesitate to accept this solution, which would deprive the prophet Ezekiel of inspiration, and make him a lesser instrument in God's hands than the anonymous editor who brought his prophecies together into one book. Likewise, it is implausible that the author of the messianic psalms, who wrote them about the king of Jerusalem for use in royal ceremonial, would not be inspired, whereas the later editor who included them in his post-exilic hymnal as referring to an eschatological messiah would be the inspired writer, even though he may not have added a single word to the compositions. A second solution would be this: the individual writers are all inspired, but only insofar as they contribute to the final state of the books. This really only brings one back to the alternative that inerrancy belongs, not to the writers as such, but to the finished books in their canonical form.

Yet even the notion of 'biblical book' is not quite as controllable as it was thought to be in the last century. One conceived of a single person writing a composition with a single, coherent message, which was then added to the canon much as a book is added to a bookcase. This view ignores the unity and wholeness of the Bible, except for a divine control that would keep the books from contradicting one another. Today critics tend to view the process that evolved the canon as a direct prolongation of the process that evolved the books themselves.

There is really no significant difference between the way Yahwist, Elohist, and Priestly documents are alternated and blended within a single 'book', and the way the Deuteronomic and Chronicler's narratives are placed side-by-side within the 'canon'. In either case, diverse historical accounts are bound together, to explain and correct one another, to form together a new, higher unity of statement. The same holds for the addition of the wisdom books to the canon. They explain and correct each other, and cluster into a higher unity that in turn forms a yet higher, contrapuntal unity with the Torah and the prophets.

The books are set into such interdependence that really only the entire canon can be considered an integral book in the strict sense. 'The ancient covenant idea, for example, which infuses the entire Pentateuch, is itself altered by the last additions to the book of Deuteronomy (Deut. iv, 25-31; xxx, 1-10), in light of the prophetic proclamation of a new covenant yet to come. As a result, books like Isaiah, Jeremiah, and Ezekiel, which come much later on in the canon, provide the critical clues for understanding the message of the Pentateuch. This means that the Torah and the prophets can be treated as having a unified texture running throughout.' Every book added to the Bible modifies the meaning of all the former books. Thus, to add a book to the canon is clearly a 'hagiographical' act, which must share in the charisma of inspiration. As long as the Old Testament canon was growing, no single book therein had yet been touched by its final editor, or had grown to its full completion of meaning. The moment when the Old Testament was brought to a close and consummated was when it was accepted and joined to the New Testament: that is, when the Church of the New Testament received it as the foretelling and pre-history of the new covenant arrived in Jesus Christ. In this sense, the New Testament is a hagiographer of the Old—indeed, it is the ultimate one. Having rejected the notions of inerrant writers and inerrant books, then Lohfink ends by affirming an inerrant Bible.

Most earlier treatises had felt it necessary to turn hermeneutical somersaults to explain away the cursing psalms, the holy wars of extermination, the retribution-theology of Coheleth, etc. Lohfink feels that his theory need do none of this. Many Old Testament assertions in themselves can only be labeled as errors. But any Old Testament sentence or book, once isolated from its context of the entirety of the Bible, loses its guarantee of inerrancy. Any part is guaranteed only insofar as it contributes to the total message. The patristic and medieval hankering after a spiritual, non-literal sense of the sacred text, now so discredited, Lohfink recognizes as enlightened. The ancients appreciated that no passage can release its full meaning if examined simply by itself. Also, commenting upon the much-discussed *sensus plenior,* he observes that it is not necessary to make God the sole author of this plus-meaning; it was intended by the ultimate authors of the Old Testament, the editors of the New Testament.

He is unconvinced by the great majority of contemporary commentators who feel that a study of literary forms is the detergent that will dissolve all spots and stains of error.

> Nowadays the real difficulties of the hermeneutical problem are evaded by much talk about literary forms. One is sometimes given the impression that all the dilemmas raised by biblical inerrancy will be resolved by a more precise analysis of the literary form of any given passage. But such is not the case. The study of literary forms is exceptionally important for the recovery of a text's original sense. A large number of apparent problems—especially in statements touching on natural science or history—can be cleared away by use of this tool which is, in any case, indispensable. It is one of the methodological essentials of literary criticism, quite necessary for modern exegesis. Pius XII ingratiated himself with all exegetes by making this so clear in *Divino Afflante Spiritu.* Here and there some will always refuse to get the point, but it is reassuring to hear that the Council intends to emphasize the legitimacy of form criticism. But all this should not blind us to its limitations. It is no cure-all. Among Catholics you occasionally hear extravagant claims made. The creation account in

Gen. i can serve as an example. It is said that the literary form of this text issues in one single assertion: that God created everything. A really competent form critic would surely be alarmed by this kind of talk. Does the form not also intend to assert a good deal more about the sequence and circumstances of creation? It is only from an overview of the Bible in its entirety that we can rightly say that all Gen. i means to assert is creation. There are all manner of cosmic views to be found in the Bible, and they balance one another off. It is the emphatic stress supplied by the New Testament that singles out creation as the operative assertion, so that we are justified in acknowledging this to be inerrant, and not the accompanying cosmogony described in Gen. i.

Joseph Coppens, the venerable old man in Louvain, who had grumbled at Benoit for the most picayune flaws in his theory, seems to have taken warmly to Lohfink's formulation. After a review almost as long as Lohfink's original article, he concludes:

Each Old Testament book contains only a rough draft, subject to revision, because in the divine plan each is designed as part of an ensemble. In most cases, therefore, the partial and provisional sketch usually contains only inadequate and provisional judgments that need to be supplemented. Thus, inerrancy guarantees the sacred writer's affirmations only in the measure in which they lie open to further developments.

Some interesting ideas are added by J. A. M. Weterman. He notes that what precisely sets the Christian movement off from rabbinic Judaism is the fixation of the latter on the Torah by itself, rather than an acceptance of the open field of historical development. Even the Septuagint remains more faithful to the fundamental onward drive of the Old Testament than this, for it recognizes the possibility of reinterpretation within the confines of Scripture itself. Weterman further insists that the

business of canon-making was more a second-century achievement than one of apostolic times:

> In opposition to the secret traditions and writings
> of the Gnostics, the Church drew up a list of both the
> succession of bishops of the Holy See and the canon
> of those writings it used in its public worship and
> which it 'felt' reflected its origin and foundations in
> the right way. And with that, it admitted these
> writings to be part of God's action in founding the
> Church, and therefore inspired, so that it would
> continue to draw its standards from them.

There has been noticeably wide sympathy for the view
that inspiration is a gift distributed as widely as is the responsibility for producing the biblical books. In 1956 Luis Alonso-
Schökel, then professor at the University of Comillas, but
later called to teach in the Biblical Institute in Rome, chided
Célestin Charlier for allowing that only the last redactor possessed the charism. Even Benoit, who had not then yet come
out for the more liberal view, comes in for criticism. Alonso-
Schökel speaks of a 'successive inspiration', and makes much
of the fact that although the various units within the Bible
may appear as so many distinct compositions, they may well
be, on a higher overview, fragments of a larger unity, successive
stages in an ongoing controversy or debate in which a multiplicity of individuals has a say. 'Any notable writer progresses,
and in his later works he enriches or clarifies ideas of preceding
works. The same holds true with writers in a literary school,
as likewise with those of a definite epoch or region . . . God
inspires the author, not simply as an individual, but also as a
member of a literary school.'

Most of the standard treatises on inspiration, he charges
with some vexation, could never have been produced by men
who had made a serious study of language and communication.
Accepted theories he finds overly intellectualized, unhealthily
preoccupied with truth as the exclusive purpose of words, and
neglectful of their semi-conscious, emotive force. 'We are used
to saying that in Sacred Scripture God, analogically speaking,
shares his ideas and thoughts. But why just his thoughts? Is

there nothing else in the divine life that has analogical correspondence to human life?' The second failure of the manuals
is that they have not conceived of the Bible as literature. In
1966 Alonso-Schökel had reduced their approach to a single
false deduction: God has spoken; therefore he has produced
a series of propositions. No, he retorts. God has rather assumed
all the dimensions of human language.

He compares the mystery of inspiration to that of the
incarnation. The heresies of Docetism and Monophysitism,
which hesitated to admit that the Son of God really took on
human flesh, have their counterparts in theories of inspiration
that hesitate to admit that God has taken to himself the full
flesh of human language. They immediately set out to purify
and intellectualize the language until it resembles what they
fancy may have been the speech of angels. It is because the
manuals have considered the Bible as a mere fund of propositions that they have also developed this fixation on inerrancy.
'This one aspect is considered so important that it occupies
half the tract; so fundamental that it dominates the whole
treatment of hermeneutics to such a degree that hermeneutics
become the art of saving the Bible from error.'

What the manuals fail to appreciate is that the basic
medium of Scripture is literary language, which he distinguishes
from technical, or propositional, language.

> Since this language is literary, it cannot simply be
> translated to the level of technical language. It must
> retain its images, its symbols, and its concretization,
> which reveal and yet veil the mystery without ratio-
> nalizing it, as theology does . . . Since this language is
> literary its interpretation cannot consist formally of
> a conceptual categorization and propositional presen-
> tation of its contents. We must proceed from the
> first, elementary understanding of the literary text to
> one that is deeper and more explicit, and thence to
> the content of the message . . . Since this language
> is literary, it obliges us to the greatest respect and
> discretion in applying the principle of 'what the
> author wished to say'. A literary man ordinarily
> says what he wishes to say.

Propositional knowledge can also be contrasted with knowledge by acquaintance, which is usually knowledge of another person, and is often shared through literature. This is knowledge at its most human, and can be arrived at only bit by bit. Knowledge of a person through familiarity is a single, organic insight, yet we express it by speaking of so many little things we know about him: his opinions, plans, looks, character, tastes, ideals. No person manifests himself to us in a single disclosure, but we can gradually get to know him in the steady increment of small observations and insights. Behind them all we catch a glimpse of the person in his radical unity. Alonso-Schökel then suggests that the Bible's inerrancy must be related to this incremental process: that no fragment or portion be forced to carry a burden of truth which only the total impression was intended to provide.

Indeed, the quest for this sort of familiarity with truth is progressive, and revelation takes the form of such a quest. Scripture, rather than presenting truth in finished form, draws the reader into the dialectic of its own search after truth, challenging and stimulating him the further it proceeds, for none of our truths is the whole truth. Scripture hopefully stimulates the reader's appetite enough to entice him into dialogue, thus ensuring that the revelation will continue. 'If one of the functions of language—that of monologue—is to sustain the process of thought, and if another function—that of dialogue—is the contrast of opinions as a means of finding and possessing the truth in common, then there does not seem to be any reason why this dimension of language must be a stranger to inspiration.'

According to Karl Bühler, upon whom Alonso-Schökel draws heavily, language has three functions: statement, expression, and address (*Darstellung, Kundgabe, Auslösung*). It can symbolize, by representing something that is or that has happened. It can express, by disclosing what the speaker feels. And it can beckon, by calling to the listener. In other words, it can move in the third, first, and second persons.

Inspired language utilizes all three of language's functions. These three functions can be related to the three fundamental aspects of divine revelation. For revelation is objective, personal, and dynamic. This means that from now on we must always regard the inspired text under these three aspects: it is objective, in that it reveals facts and events; it is personal, in that it shows us God as personal in the act of revealing himself; and it is dynamic, calling forth and making possible a response on the part of man.

Thus, in the view of this very impressively documented Spanish litterateur-cum-exegete, it is the traditional theories that have been downgrading the Bible, by taking account of only one of the multiple powers and purposes of human language to propositions, and degrading inerrancy to formal logic within propositions, they have ignored the far deeper issues of truth and error that escape so narrow a view. He would hold that there is no error in the Bible, provided one speaks in the broader sense of literary truth, not of logical truth expressed in formal propositions.

Alexander Jones, who played Jerome to the English version of the *Jerusalem Bible*, seems to have similar feelings. Reviewing the various Protestant positions, he notes that the orthodox Protestant belief (shared, he hints, by some Catholics) would see the Bible as a set of absolutely inerrant propositions about God. An alternative view, put out by Barth, Brunner, Reid, and others, sees the Bible as offering a personal encounter that elicits an existential response. Jones does not align himself clearly with this second theorem, but shows much sympathy for it, and evinces considerable hope for an eventual meeting of minds between Catholics and Protestants.

Werner Bulst is another theologian who is critical of the conventional definition of revelation as *locutio Dei attestans*. It is rather, he alleges, 'an act of grace, the personal, salvific self-manifestation of God to man in the realm of his history; it takes place in supernatural divine activity, in visible appearances, and above all, as interpreting and embracing the others, in his attesting word: first of all in Israel, then definitively in Christ Jesus, and present to us in the word and work of the Church; here below remaining in considerable obscurity (therefore to be received by man in faith), but ordered towards the immediate vision of God in eternity'.

In 1963 René Latourelle, French-Canadian dean of theology at the Gregorian University, published a ponderous monograph on revelation, with strong endorsement of the increasingly accepted view that Scripture involves word, testimony, and encounter (like Alonso-Schökel, he is in Karl Bühler's debt), and that biblical expression is rather more interpersonal than propositional. In his review of Latourelle's book, Avery Dulles goes on to insist that the Church enjoys a preconceptual knowledge of the salvation mystery through vital contact with the divine persons—a knowledge that must underpin all articulation. This preconceptual grasp of mystery, he pleads, often finds its most congenial expression in symbolic language.

> As is evident, figurative speech and imagery hold a place of prime importance in Scripture, in the liturgy, and in many creeds. Rationalistically oriented theologians may look on this as a merely pragmatic or rhetorical device designed to impress on untutored minds and wayward hearts the 'straight' truths of revelation. Spinoza held this view, but St. Thomas takes a more nuanced position (*Summa Theol.* 1, 1, 9). Recent language theory finds riches in the 'latent meaning' of metaphorical expression that defy transposition into the 'manifest content' of scientific cognition. Hence we must ask whether the supernaturally given images in Scripture and tradition may not have an irreplaceable role in the communication of God's word to man. Austin Farrer, among others, vigorously contends that we cannot grasp the biblical message apart from the images in which it is clothed; that 'we cannot by-pass the images to seize an imageless truth'. The mutual disclosure of persons is normally accomplished more through symbolism than through propositional speech, more through gestures and accents than through formal statements.

Luis Alonso-Schökel is not the only observer to diagnose the weakness of conventional Catholic inspiration theory as latent Docetism. German scholar Oswald Loretz traces the mistake to Augustine, whose christology suffered from the same fixation upon divinity and ignoring of humanity. From the bishop of Hippo the infection spread to Aquinas, Duns Scotus, Cano, Suarez, and other progentiors of the theology taught in the Catholic academies. Worse yet, according to Loretz, Catholic thought on inspiration has suffered from various alien contaminants. Pagan, rabbinical, and Islamic sources shared their ecstatic notion of prophecy. From Avicenna came a deceptively inflexible definition of truth: *Adaequatio rei et intellectus.* Another impersonal definition later came from Descartes: *Illud omne quod valde clare et distincte percipitur.* It is such views, he alleges, that have led Catholic scholars to demand simple, propositional assertions from the Bible.

Recently, according to Loretz, three ploys have been attempted to rescue the Scriptures from any indictment of error. First it was argued that the Bible does not intend to teach natural science; then, that it teaches history in rude and popular fashion; and lastly, that most apparent errors arise from a misunderstanding of literary forms. But all of these defense measures have ultimately proven unsuccessful. The Bible's own claim to truthfulness is rather different. The Old Testament, speaking of God's truth, or *emeth,* intends not so much that his word is true, as that he is true to his word.

> For the Old Testament, God's 'truth' is primarily given through his faithfulness. Yahweh is the covenant God, who not only demands loyalty from his people, but promises it himself. While the idea is never absent that God's words are true, this never has reference to the Scriptures, as if to imply that they contain no historical error. Any such interpretation would be desperately foreign to the Hebrew tradition that spoke before all else of God's covenant loyalty.

As with the Old Testament *emeth,* so with the New Testament *alētheia.* God is true: that is, loyal to his covenant. The Bible, being nothing other than the by-product and record of the people's covenants with God, must of course reflect this truthfulness and loyalty, as indeed it also reflects the fickleness and disloyalty of that people. Scripture would fail in its truthfulness and contain error only if it presented a God who was unfaithful to his promises, and did not stand by his covenant-people.

It would betray a false notion of what truth is, to expect that the human presentation of God's saving acts must be a scrupulously accurate report of facts, free from error in the least detail. This attitude confuses the truth of Scripture with faultless historical chronicle. It applies to the Bible a standard of truth derived from Greek, western notions of history which, for all their insights and deficiencies, cannot be squared with the Semitic, biblical way of looking at things. As we have explained inerrancy, then, when could Scripture be said to have fallen into error? Since God's truth is established in his people's sight by the way he stands by his covenant, the Bible could be convicted of error only if God were to forsake his pledge to Israel.

In any case, the Bible is as incapable of conveying the full content of God's revealed truth as ink is incapable of capturing the fullness of life. Yahweh's revelation was never intended to be identified with a system of doctrine. The whole point of all the to-and-fro of ideas and teachings in the canonical writings is that God has made a pact with his people. He is not to be made content simply by their being well instructed. What he claims and craves is their total 'yes', their full fellowship.

Meanwhile, in surprisingly high quarters some surprising things were being said along these same lines. At the third session of the late Vatican Council, during debate on the revised schema on revelation, the subject of inerrancy was inevitably broached. *Herder Correspondence* offers the following account of part of that discussion:

Cardinal Meyer [Chicago] objected that the schema treated of inspiration too exclusively from the point of view of inerrancy, whereas a broader and deeper concept of inspiration was required. Revelation was really a personal appeal. Inspiration, therefore, must not be thought of in purely negative terms, a simple guaranteeing of truth uncontaminated by error, but

401

positively in the sense that revelation addresses the whole man and that in inspiring the biblical author God expresses and communicates himself. Nor must we forget that divine inspiration makes use of human instruments.

Inerrancy, then, must be primarily considered in connexion with inspiration, not as something isolated. As to the inerrancy of Scripture itself, Cardinal König [Vienna] and Bishop Simons [Indore] thought that the schema ought not to declare that inspiration preserves the human author from error. The problem was not what he meant to say but what God meant to say; but God was able to use the author, despite his errors, even to use those errors themselves in order to reveal himself and his design for human salvation.

Cardinal König and a number of other Fathers (Léger [Montreal], Jäger [Paderborn], Weber [Strasbourg], etc.) doubted whether it should be said without qualification that Scripture contains no error. This was not true in every respect, for much that Scripture says is scientifically and historically erroneous. The sacred authors had only the limited knowledge which was then available. But God used them as they were. We should be in a better position to defend God's word in the words of men if we bore in mind the condescension whereby the divine word became in all things like the human word. For the sake of the good name of Holy Scripture the text should not read' free of all error' but 'all the books of Scripture and all their parts teach revealed truth in its purity'. Revelation itself must be free of error, but it is not necessary that every affirmation in Scripture should be so.

Over the course of the last decade, the thrust of this debate has swerved from direct consideration of inspiration and its correlative, inerrancy, to interest in revelation. Probably the most perceptive and persuasive work done in this direction is

402

owed to Gabriel Moran, the Christian Brother from Manhattan College. The most valuable sort of human knowledge, Moran explains, is the acceptance of personal self-disclosure. It requires a dialogue between one person who freely manifests his inner self and another who freely accepts the familiarity. Personal knowledge is well called revelation, then: a reciprocal giving and receiving of knowledge in a living exchange. And it is never exhaustive. Such knowledge can grow, but only through those countless embodiments of the self that are its conveyance: gestures, actions, and those best of all symbols, words.

> It is a strange limitation to suggest, as do many theology manuals, that divine revelation, strictly speaking, takes place through speech, through a 'formal utterance on God's part'. Personal exchange of knowledge never takes place by words isolated from the rest of human life; and between God and man this would seem to be most strikingly so. Fully human communication includes the verbal, but the verbal can never do more than point to the non-verbal and interpret other activities which form man's living experience.

Contemporary theology, Protestant and Catholic, has strongly turned away from a propositional notion of revelation towards a disclosure seen in God's saving acts; there is talk everywhere of event and encounter. But Moran warns against misunderstanding. Revelation does not consist in statements, but neither does it consist in history. It exists in the consciousness of man; no matter what its vehicle, it must involve self-disclosure *and* free acceptance. 'Man does not believe in statements or truths, nor does he believe in events; he believes in God revealed in human experience and consciousness.'

Revelation is an organic fusion of word and event—it is a sacrament. A prophet, for example, does not simply have ideas and truths infused into his mind; he is one who gives a total life-response to the experience of his people. 'Prophecy is not only the effect of revelation. Within the continuing intercourse of God and man, prophecy is the cause of a clearer revelation, just as all verbal expression brings to fulfillment the experience which causes it while at the same time it effects a deepening of the original experience. Human discourse is always a process of active response in which each word is both cause and effect within the continuing conversation.' Moran then concludes 'that revelation in its most basic sense is neither a word coming down from heaven to which man assents nor an historical event manifesting a truth. It would be better to begin by conceiving of revelation as an historical and continuing intersubjective communion in which man's answer is part of the revelation.'

If revelation is an intercommunion between God and man, then there is no higher revelation than that which existed within the consciousness of Jesus Christ. The closest contact man has had with God is not the acquaintance the apostles had of Jesus, but the acquaintance Jesus as man had of himself as God. 'He is man receiving as well as God bestowing.' Or, as Moran puts it elsewhere: 'Christ's affirmation of himself includes the awareness of the hypostatic union; the knowledge present to his mind is the transposition into the cognitive order of what the hypostatic union is in the ontological order.' Throughout his life Christ came gradually to an ever deeper insight into who he was—never an exhaustive knowledge, but such knowledge of God as a human is capable of. Through his teaching, healing, comforting, he hinted to men who he was. But the supreme act of revelation, which recapitulated all that has ever been disclosed, took place upon the cross, when God showed forth most forcefully his love, and man opened himself most utterly to full knowledge, as Jesus came through agony to a sight of his own glory.

Jesus could never communicate, even through the cross, the full burden of his self-consciousness. Like other men, and more than them, he was more than he could grasp, and he knew more than he could say. Yet his disciples did receive an outburst of revelation, so much that they, too, were at a loss for words. But just as their exposure to revelation had not been simply a matter of words, but an experience as full as life can be full, so they strove to hand it on in every way that lay open: through witness, sacraments, and the testimony of their personal lives. 'What is true of every person and everything profound in human experience was pre-eminently true of apostolic experience: one could not state it; one could only bear witness to it, testify to it, point to it, expose it in action. All of the human statements that are made concerning any deep experience are an attempt to point out various aspects of it and to awaken in the consciousness of another his own personal experience; such an attempt is always "an infinite search which approaches its goal only asymptotically (Rahner)". This was the problem of the apostles when they tried to state the revelation: the insufficiency of language itself to bear the weight of what they knew and wished to share.'

Yet, ever aware of the inadequacy of what they did, the apostles could not help objectifying their lived experience in what words they could. Moran notes the contemporary distrust of propositional knowledge, but warns against any attempt to remove revelation from the order of knowledge. Knowledge is, indeed, a unitive experience between him who knows and him who is known, but words and concepts are intrinsic elements in this experience. Knowledge is not too narrow a field to allow revelation full play; it has been our inadequate notion of knowledge that has caused the trouble. 'Although words and concepts must live from something deeper than themselves and although they constantly threaten to become a veiling rather than a revealing instrument, experience cannot avoid objectivication as part of the process of becoming fully human.' And he adds a remark seemingly directed at those who would follow Bultmann into the belief that revelation is merely an existential encounter, and nothing to do with the transmission of knowledge:

> While we may applaud the reaction against the notion of faith as a 'holding of true doctrines', there is serious danger of replacing it with something no better or even something worse unless the full depths of the revelation question are reached. In particular, I have asserted that so long as knowledge is equated with the explicit judgments of the mind there will be an inorganic and external relation between revelation and life. When this is followed by a reaction which attempts to place revelation in a realm other than

knowledge or beyond knowledge, the problem is only exacerbated. The only solution lies in overcoming the superficial understanding of knowledge that is the cause of the problem.

The apostolic community, then, undertook to pass on what it knew. One of the media was that of words, in which they sought to objectify their experience. Nor was this simply for the sake of those who were to come after.

Revelation is not only recorded in the Bible; to some degree the oral and written expression of it helped to create and to form the community experience. The Old Testament was not intended to be preserved only as a recounting of past events. The texts existed to be read by the community of the present; they conveyed an understanding of the present by recalling the past and holding out an ideal for the future. The Old Testament, first as oral tradition and then as national literary symbol, was both the effect and the cause of revelation. It originated from the community and was in turn formative of the community.

And since the word is only one of a complex of media chosen to transmit the revelation experience, biblical inspiration is only one of the impulses from the Spirit by which the early Christian community objectified what it knew. Inspiration in a broader sense, infers Moran, has produced a whole medley of expressions. Revelation cannot be put into the Bible; it cannot be put into any book, for it cannot be fully stated. It can only be witnessed to, suggested. 'It is true that the Bible is an intelligible summary of the revelation, the objectivication of the apostolic teaching and the objectivity of the consciousness of the early Church.' Still, full knowledge of revelation comes only through the full efflorescence of Church life, which is the total product of inspiration.

In the apostolic experience, as in all human experience, there was a jumble of impressions, a shifting of attitudes, a convergence of evidence. What man knows always goes beyond what he can bring to full, objective awareness; in the moment of truth he always knows more than he can express. Man cannot avoid representing his knowledge in concepts and words, but the least reflection makes him realize that his concepts are rooted in a more primordial consciousness not completely expressible. But it is senseless to berate conceptual expressions because they are not exhaustive of human knowledge. Words, ideas, and propositions are indeed limited and defective instruments, but they are so because they are human and are the means by which men communicate their experience and bring to full awareness their own experience.

The global experience of the apostles took place at these several levels of pre-conceptual knowledge and its refraction and reflexive objectivication in conceptual judgments. In the case of the apostles there was the additional factor of the Spirit's post-resurrectional assistance in their reflection. This special guidance of the Holy Spirit continued throughout the time of the Church's foundation. The conceptual expression of the apostles' experience became progressively more accurate, or perhaps we should say that their concepts, formulas, and teaching became progressively 'less inaccurate'. This is not to say that their first statements were false. All their words which were spoken from within the mystery were true to the extent that they gave some insight into the reality that went beyond them. Of any experience there can be many true statements which vary in their capacity to convey the truth to another. It is a false assumption to presume that the more primitive a statement is and the closer in time to the original experience it is, the truer and more accurate it is. By striving to translate their global experience into a communicable form, the apostles heightened their understanding of their own experience . . . There is no pure word of God contaminated in varying degrees by human distortion. Instead, the human reception, understanding, and interpretation are intrinsic to the revelation itself.

And because revelation is this interpersonal experience, Moran makes the somewhat unusual but brilliantly defended claim that revelation has by no means ceased within the Church; that it continues whenever and wherever any man accepts God disclosing himself through the sacraments, Scripture, or Christian witness.

It has been the temptation of both Judaism and Christianity to claim to have a revelation. The danger in this is that God will no longer be sought, and religion will be made to serve as a substitute for the living, revealing Lord. Further, community leaders assume the role of dispensers of revealed truths, and force their followers into conformity. Human formulations and objectivications of past, crucial revelation experiences are themselves paid divine honors, and believers settle back into the delusion that they have a mortgage on all truth.

In a similar vein Rosemary Ruether, professor at Howard University in Washington, objects to the persistent search by both Catholics and Protestants for some ultimate, objective norm of belief. Really the ultimate norm is not a material one. It is formal: the personal charism and guidance of the Spirit, which cannot be exhaustively identified with any objective norm or combination of norms. Scripture, she makes clear, is a limited norm, though it enjoys a privileged position among other limited norms, for it is the original expression of tradition, the first laying down of the *depositum fidei.*

> However, Scripture, along with all other expressions of church tradition all occupy the category of human words about God's Word. They attempt to express God's Word within their finite cultural contexts, but they remain finite and historical. Their authority is relativized in relation to the divine Word which is manifest in them, but not exhaustively expressed by them. This inner or divine word finds its primary communication in the living personal relationship of man to God. This is revelation, the inner word, and all outer words, whether of Scripture, tradition, theology or law are as tracks left in the sand by the passing of the living personal relationship of the community to God.

James Tunstead Burtchaell

Across Washington at Georgetown University, philosopher Louis Dupré has somewhat the same to say. Everyone is quick to admit, he points out, that Christianity is an historical religion, but then they all flinch at accepting the inference that every expression of the divine message must necessarily be historically relativized. There is no purely passive reception of truth among humans, for man must make truth, and upon his powers of creativity depends the value of his symbolic expression. Those expressions produced under inspiration are no less circumscribed culturally—indeed, even the thoughts and words of Jesus do not exhaust or absolutize God's Word.

> The words of Christ and the basic directions of his Church guide man authoritatively in his relations with God. To question their way of viewing this relation would be tantamount to rejecting the entire message of Christ. But the symbols in which this view or, in phenomenological terms, this *intentionality* is expressed are, as all human symbols, determined by a cultural tradition. This is not to say that they are false or even inadequate. If a revelation is to take place at all, the symbols in which it is expressed must have at least that minimum adequacy which enables them to transmit the message effectively to later generations. But beyond that, every generation has the task of capturing the message anew.
>
> The difficulty, however, is to distinguish intentionality from expression. A symbolic expression is not a disposable form wrapped indifferently around a content. Man *thinks in* symbols and, as Cassirer and his followers have shown, the content of his conscious activity does not pre-exist its symbolic expression. Without expression there is no intentionality at all. It is, therefore, insufficient to assume that the intentionality of revelation and of authentic magisterium is divinely determined, whereas the expression is not. This over-simplification seems to be inherent to the concept of *demythologization*. If symbolic form and content are so intimately united, it is impossible to separate the 'mythical' form of

Scripture from its content. The concept also seems to suffer under a latent rationalism by presupposing that the demythologized expression will be religiously more adequate than the 'mythical' one.

Thus Scripture, according to Dupré, is indispensable, since it is the authoritative expression of the faith of the original Christian community. But it is not absolute, for no human expression can be. And it serves the present community as a stimulant to further exploration of the mystery, to further creation of forms. Yet there is always the sobering discovery that the mystery can never find forms that are satisfying.

It seems well at this point to draw our review of a century and a half of theorizing to a close. We do so with full consciousness that there is rich promise of continuance for the debate. The present chapter set itself the task of reviewing the past 60 years. The work was simplified by the total absence of discussion during the first, unhappy 40 of those years. At the present time we seem hopefully to be approaching the brilliant noon of a new heyday of creative speculation on our problem of biblical inspiration. One is inevitably drawn to make comparisons between the present day, over which the sun has been two decades in the rising, and that other 20-year heyday of wrangling, 1890-1910.

Most constructive theology is wrung out of divines by pressure, and the pressures brought to bear in this debate have shifted. At the turn of the century the Scriptures lay under accusation of error, mostly by disillusioned evangelicals turned bitterly against the fundamentalist education of their childhood. Numerous emancipated scholars labored on impressively long volumes documenting the numerous errors foisted on the Christian public by their Bible. Today no one would go to the trouble. No one bothers to complain that the Bible is erroneous; it is simply ignored as irrelevant.

With this shift in pressures has come an interesting shift in theological leadership. In the earlier period the argument was conducted almost exclusively by trained exegetes. Biblical scholars like Lagrange, von Hummelauer and Loisy grumbled that the dogmaticians had created many of their current difficulties, and would do them a favor by remaining out of the debate. This was largely the case when Pius XII, using the good services of Augustin Bea, reopened the discussion in the 1940's. It was the exegetes who quickly took the cue, and revived the Neo-Thomist theory of verbal inspiration through instrumental causality. But through the course of this period attention among Catholic philosophers has been preponderantly transferred from Neo-Thomism to variants of phenomenology. Interest in the biblical problem has been aroused once again among speculative theologians, anxious to apply their new tools to the well-worn controversy. The irony is that the exegetes, who today are as amateur about systematics as the dogmaticians were in that earlier time ignorant of biblical criticism, have clung to the Neo-Thomist theory long after it had become clear that there were questions it was not answering. Biblical critics still write articles and books that torturously and awkwardly try to apply remedial surgery to an ideology that is generally considered to have lost what life it had.

As the theologians assume the lead from the exegetes, the focus of debate moves from inspiration to revelation (and will soon, I anticipate, center upon canonicity). Seventy years ago it was *de rigueur* to divide off revelation from inspiration, but the contemporary trend is to see them as correlatives. There is little concern with divine intervention in the psychological processes of the inspired authors, but much concern to calculate just how there is any transcendence in the Christian consciousness that progresses through time, as do all ideologies.

There is a growing consensus that the bugbear of the problem, for exegetes as well as for theologians, was an implicit presupposition that truth was dealt with exclusively in propositional assertions, and that revelation and Scripture must either present such propositions or allow itself to be shrunk down into them. Two insights have caused general abandonment of this view. On the one hand, some Catholic scholars have achieved more sophistication in studies of literature, and realize that it is a medium able to convey far more than can be reduced to dogmatic propositions. Secondly, epistemology has learned lately that there are significant differences between the knowledge we have of things and the acquaintance we have with persons. Revelation has been relocated in this context of personal self-disclosure, and the attempt is being made to appreciate its enhanced relevance. The crucial point at issue now is this: what privilege can Scripture enjoy if it is neither absolute nor exhaustive in its presentation of Christian insight into the mystery of salvation?

No one should gainsay that Rudolf Bultmann's existential, noncontentual understanding of revelation has been one of the chief stimuli to Catholic thought on our subject. Yet there are numerous cautionary passages in the recent literature which make it clear that his theory, in its pure strain, is too virulent to be acceptable. The theologians seem generally optimistic that they will be able to vindicate Scripture as God's Word without somehow sacrificing their commitment to dogma. They will probably succeed. But it ill becomes a chronicler to play the prophet.

Francis Bruce Vawter
1921-

Bruce Vawter was born in Fort Worth, Texas, attended St. Thomas Seminary College in Denver and St. Mary's in Perryville, Missouri, before being ordained a Vincential priest in 1947. He received his S.T.L. from the Anglicum University in Rome in 1950 and his S.S.L. from the Biblical Institute in 1952. For the next four years he taught Scripture at Kenrick Seminary in St. Louis. In 1957 he returned to Rome to receive his Doctorate in Sacred Scripture from the Biblical Institute. Since then he has taught at St. Thomas in Denver, Kenrick in St. Louis, and DePaul University in Chicago. Summer teaching has taken him to Australia, England, San Francisco, and Catholic University in Washington, D.C.

Vawter's first book, A Path Through Genesis, *appeared in 1956 to instant acclaim. He was one of the most effective pioneers in popularizing the results of modern Biblical scholarship for the Catholic community in a most palatable and relevant manner. His 1961 work on the Prophets,* The Conscience of Israel, *continued this important task.*

Vawter's 1972 work on Biblical Inspiration *consists of six chapters. He starts out with an analysis of the concept itself, then surveys the history, first among the Fathers, then the Scholastic synthesis, followed by Protestant thinking on the subject, and concluding with contemporary outlooks. After laying the groundwork in these five chapters, he presents elements that any synthesis ought to include; it is this sixth chapter which we have selected for inclusion here.*

A reading of this presentation makes one eminently aware of how differently a central issue like that of Biblical inspiration is viewed today as a result of the progress made in Biblical studies at large. The rigid, near mechanical notions that sometimes found expression in textbooks were, ironically, "unbiblical." As Vawter says in his first chapter: "The Prophets could never think of the word of God as an oracle delivered polished and finished through a passive mouthpiece; they could not even think of it ordinarily as the result of a divine monologue, for such was not their usual prophetic experience. Rather . . . they tend to represent it as a dialogue between prophet and God, with give and take on both sides, during which each has had his own contribution to make."

But his treatment also makes it clear that further progress is yet to be made, that the very wealth of new data and methods calls for reflection, discussion, and experimentation. If there is one quality absent from the current core of Catholic Biblical scholars, it is complacency with advances made. Their mood is rather one of pushing on, anxious to consolidate what has been achieved in order to attain yet further understanding of God's word.

BIBLICAL INSPIRATION

CHAPTER SIX

TOWARD A SYNTHESIS

I t is hoped that by now enough of the history of the doctrine of inspiration has been brought out to afford a sufficiently clear view of the various issues that it involves. One large omission, perhaps, has been our neglect of relevant theological opinion expressed in the post-patristic period in the Churches of the east. (It may be, too, that some postchristian Jewish thinking could have been investigated with profit.) The elusiveness and the sparseness of such material, however, has persuaded the present author that, for all practical purposes, it is for the Western Church, whether Catholic or Protestant, that inspiration has been a theological problem.

It remains for us now to try to draw together the various threads of thought and suggestion that we have exposed to see whether and to what extent they combine to form any consistent pattern. While the function of a work like this in a series of its kind is undoubtedly expository rather than *bahnbrechend*, still it cannot ignore altogether the perennial theolgical task, which is to examine the past and present status of the question with an eye toward the responses that ought to be made to recognize needs.

A preliminary, negative observation. From what we have had reviewed before us, it seems proper to ask whether by now the traditional theology of inspiration has not rung all the possible changes on the analogy of instrumental causality. Its continued usefulness may certainly be questioned. Despite all the patchwork and modifications, the analogy today probably creates more difficulties than it solves, associated, as it invariably seems to be, with a concept of the Biblical word that does not correspond with the literary realities and demanding a needlessly anthropomorphized idea of divine authorship. This must may be said without even prejudicing the question as to whether the analogy retains a philosophical validity. Surely the present stage of theology indicates that new directions are required.

Furthermore, one may without denigration of the values that the traditional theology has upheld still inquire about its contemporary relevance on other grounds. Sacred Scripture is a unique literature—and, when all is said and done, that is the essential point that the doctrine of inspiration has tried to register. However, for some time the burning question for theology has not been an exclusive contemplation of a once-for-all writing process but an understanding of the relation of Scripture to a continuing and living word of God. Both Protestant and Catholic thinking have conspired to a growing recognition that Biblical inspiration in the narrow sense, the sense in which it has generally been subjected to ecclesiastical pronouncements and examination of theologians, is but one stage in the unfolding of a mystery of communication that encompasses earlier and later stages as well. Is not this entire mystery of a communication identifiable with the spiritual experience that we have traditionally called inspiration? If it is, then a new theological synthesis is obviously needed. As T. H. L. Parker once said of preaching: 'We cannot be content with regarding [it] in a simple and direct way as the human declaration of God's work in Christ, the narrating and explaining of that reconciling activity. This would empty preaching of its character as the Word of God and leave it man's word about God.' It seems a quite parallel thought to expect that any notion of the Christian community's testimony to the word of God as epitomized in Scripture should take into account how that word is transmitted by it and how its further proclamation remains the word of God.

With these preliminaries in mind we can offer several suggestions regarding a desirable theology of inspiration.

1. Inspiration should be thought of primarily as one of the qualities bestowed upon the community of faith by the Spirit of God that has called it into being. This is not to acquiesce to the view that the eventual inspired writer or speaker is merely an outlet for the spirit of the community in the Schleiermacherian sense. To hold such a view would be to reduce the Scripture to nothing more than a culture literature. It is that, to be sure, but

it is also something far greater. To anyone who believes that by definition a people of God has received a call from without its culture that both created it and must continue to sustain it, it should not be hard to accept that people's formative scriptures as, in some real sense, the work of the Spirit of God. This is the new perspective indicated by Rahner, McKenzie, and others, in which we ought to view the reality asserted by the older theology when it defined inspiration as a *gratia gratis data*, that is, a divine action that has had for its object the good of the community rather than that of a specified individual. To denominate this concept of inspiration 'social' is simply to shift one's psychological viewpoint, not to change it radically. Rather than to conceive of God as acting upon an individual directly in favor of the community, we are now persuaded to think of Him as working through the community by affecting the individual. Such, in fact, is the mode of the divine activity as it is otherwise presented to us both in the Scripture and in tradition. In the OT and the NT as well the individual finds his identification as a person in confrontation with God not as an isolated individual but as a member of the community of faith, of Israel, of the Church.

Considered in this way the venerable question of the sacred writer's consciousness of acting 'under inspiration' or not seems to need rephrasing. If, in the spirit of 1 Cor 12, scriptural inspiration was primarily a community charism even though exercised through individuals, what does seem required is that the writers (and those who other than by writing also conserved and developed the tradition) should have been functioning consciously as agents for the inspired community. And whereas it was always difficult if not impossible to verify a given writer's conviction of then-and-there divine impulse to write, it is not at all difficult to show that those who authored the materials and finished works of the OT and NT were indeed conscious of their community function and responsibility. The matter is not always equally clear, of course. Problems are afforded by some books, especially those that lie on the periphery of the canon and were troublesome for the compilers of the canon, works in which some have found it hard to discern the relation in which they stand to a community of *faith*. Among these would be ranged the Song of Songs, undoubtedly, and the book of Esther which

417

in its initial Hebrew form appears to be culture-literature pure and simple untouched by the dominant currents of OT religious thought. In the NT the epistle of James might qualify in a similar capacity, if indeed Luther and contemporary Lutheran exegetes have been correct in their view of it as a polemic directed against the mainstream of NT faith expressed in the key Pauline doctrine of justification through faith.

Even such problems, however, are more apparent than real, more challenges and stimuli to further historical inquiry than settled dogmas. If the purpose, or one of the purposes, of the Song of Songs can be recognized as fulfilled in the assimilation of its healthy eroticism into the Biblical tradition just as the wisdom writers had earlier assimilated into it another equally profane stream of thought, its acceptance into the canon can easily presuppose exactly that kind of community design and function of which we have just been speaking. The book of Esther, like various other parts of the OT including many of its Psalms, invites us to reassess—perhaps with great profit—the somewhat uncompromising wall that we have erected between the sacred and the profane, and to consider seriously what may be involved when the divine condescends to the human condition. (This is to leave aside the question of the amplified book of Esther, the form in which it has been accepted into the Greek and Latin Christian canons.) Finally, it is only by an arbitrary decision imposed on the NT materials, not deduced from them, that we could declare one part of the NT normative for the measure of all the rest.

2. Continuing this line of thought, Rahner's conception of the Scripture, that is, the NT, as a constituent of the nascent Church, and of inspiration as an exercise of the divine constitution by which the Church came into definitive form, is most helpful and instructive. But it is not necessary to relate the OT to this formation as he does only at its terminal period, namely in view of its having been accepted by the Church as part of its normative Scripture. ('Accepted' is perhaps not the word we need in this context. The Bible of the very earliest Church was exclusively the OT, which gave to Christianity the idea of an inspired Scripture.) To make such a restriction is to give the

impression—though unwarrantedly—that inspiration once again has been equated with subsequent approbation.

Rather, the OT was constitutive of the Church from its beginning, as having been produced by a community of the Spirit that was also the people of God. While the Christian does accept the inspired character of the OT (and the NT as well) on the basis of the Church's word concerning it, still it is not that word or teaching that constitutes its sacred but merely discerns it. There has been one history of salvation known to the Bible; and the Bible, OT and NT together, is the record and testimonial of it.

In adopting such a position one must recognize that it carries with it certain attendant difficulties not directly related to our subject. It may be objected that if the NT presupposes the OT, the converse is not true, not merely to the self-evident extent that the OT knows nothing of the NT temporally but even on the score that, when viewed objectively, it did not anticipate it. The response to this objection must be that in matters like this an objective viewpoint, by which is meant a detached viewpoint, is scarcely possible: one either accepts, in faith, the Church as the realization of Israel's aspirations, or he does not. (And in accepting it, he does not necessarily reject as wholly unjustified Judaism's alternative understanding of OT fulfillment.) The early Church had this faith and recognized the inspiration of the OT before there was a NT to assimilate to it. Another objection that has been raised, deriving essentially from the same set of premises, is that from the standpoint of NT faith the OT may be considered an irrelevancy. This seemingly Marcion-like attitude has been assumed by quite serious scholars. It is doubtless even more common as unarticulated, evidenced in the mistrust that is often shown for the literal sense of the OT from the standpoint of Christian relevance, in the practical neglect of it in preaching and teaching, and in the occasional attempt to rehabilitate patristic allegorism as a means of dealing with it. For our purposes, let it suffice to say that we regard the attitude as misguided and out of touch with the view of the OT that is entertained by the great majority of Christian scholars who are engaged with it professionally.

Anyone who is prepared to affirm the unity of the Bible as the record and witness of a continuous *Heilsgeschichte* should have as little hesitation as did the early Church about acknowledging the inspiration of the OT. Vatican II said that God 'chose the race of Israel as a people unto Himself' (*Lumen Gentium*, art. 9) and that 'to this people which He had acquired for Himself He so manifested Himself through words and deeds as the one true and living God that Israel came to know by experience the ways of God with men' (*Dei Verbum*, art. 14). If we accept this, that is, if we accept both the fact of Israel's history and the truth of Israel's understanding of its history, then we should have no difficulty in recognizing that the Spirit was every bit as active in the composition of its sacred literature as in the constitutive literature of the Church. Christian relevance is not here really the prime determinant. Christian relevance we must certainly vindicate for the OT as such—a vindication that may include a genuinely historical typological understanding of the OT—but the OT was and remains, first and foremost, the sacred literature of an existing community of faith that was (and is) of quite as much concern to the divine purposes as was (and is) the Church of the NT or of today. If there is that part of the OT that has no apparent Christian relevance, it is nevertheless relevant to it as part of history of which Christianity is the end-product. In much the same way a medieval theologian may have no apparent relevance to present Christian needs, and yet he may be an indispensable antecedent to a theology of today that can respond to those needs. Looked at from this perspective even the shortcomings (from a Christian or later point of view) of the OT can be readily seen as a proper object of inspiration: they too were necessarily involved in a divine condescension to man's history and evolution.

3. Suppose that inspiration is to be thought of as primarily a community charism. If we now ask what it was specifically as regards the thought and action of those who conspired to write and edit this community's sacred literature, we shall doubtless have to content ourselves with the conclusion that it was many things. It is, and has long been, time that for clarity's sake we separate scriptural inspiration from the prophetic model that has confused the issue as much as it elucidated it. While there is

no doubt that some of the inspired writings may have been accompanied by an experience identical with or closely resembling the type of prophetic inspiration that was envisaged by Aquinas and that underlay Leo XIII's descriptive definition, it is equally clear that most of them were not. To attempt to perpetuate a monolithic concept of inspiration in the face of the complexity and variety of the Bible's literary history is simply to court confusion. We need to accept and develop Benoit's insight into scriptural inspiration as an analogous reality.

The Bible, a collection of works spanning centuries and cultures, is the product of countless inspired prophets, anthologists, lyric and epic poets, Apostles, disciples of Prophets and Apostles, sages, rabbis, scribes Jewish and Christian, apocalyptists, eye and ear witnesses of the revealed word, conservers and shapers of tradition, synthesizers and adapters as well as any number of other categories whose functions we cannot adequately describe. To suppose that we can or should reduce all these separate labors to a single classification of human action or of divine *concursus* would require a *simplisme* that is no longer tolerable. In the concrete, scriptural inspiration must have been as diverse as the human efforts that conspired to produce the Scripture.

Something of this was recognized even by the earliest speculation on the nature and origins of the Bible, though many factors rose to obscure it. Jewish tradition, as we know, from ancient times distinguished in the Bible the three divisions of Law, Prophets, and Writings, to each of which a different kind of inspiration was assigned. The distinction was hardly based on critical grounds, but it did acknowledge in the language of its time that what was taken to be inspired Scripture ought to be differentiated as it already had been on the score of its literary qualities. In much the same way, Jewish hesitations about the canonical status of certain books of the OT were usually raised quite as much by their literary character and contents as by a lack of confidence in their authorship, whether it had been inspired or not.

Early Christian Biblists took this Jewish distinction to mean (as it was doubtless intended to mean) that some parts of the Bible were less inspired than others, in the sense that they were less the word of God and possessed less authority, and for this reason they rejected the distinction. Undoubtedly it was this kind of thought that lay behind the condemnation of Theodore of Mopsuestia by the Second Council of Constantinople in 553— we have had occasion above to refer repeatedly to Theodore's opinion. According to the Council, he ascribed to Job and to the other wisdom books of the OT a purely human origin:

> Among these books which have been written for the instruction of men are also to be listed Solomon's, that is, Proverbs and Ecclesiastes, which he composed from his own experience (*ex sua persona*) for the benefit of others, since he had not received the grace of prophecy but rather that of prudence, which is evidently something quite different, as blessed Paul has said. (Mansi 9:223.)

Today, because of the studies of R. Devreese and others, Theodore of Mopsuestia has been considerably rehabilitated as a man not without his faults but also as one much put upon by his enemies and much misunderstood. When we read the above passage we may wonder what the Council found at fault with it. Obviously, it was then feared that the separation of any scriptural inspiration from prophecy was to render it *ipso facto* something less than inspiration. But Theodore's intention had been neither to deny the inspiration of the books in question nor to introduce degrees of inspiration. Rather, on the now recognizable criterion of literary forms he had attempted to determine kinds of inspiration. It is a pity that his point could not have been grasped at the time, and that what might otherwise have been a distinct and far-reaching contribution to the theology of inspiration and a solvent for many of its confusions became instead a condemned opinion attached to one who for quite other reasons was regarded as a heresiarch.

To think of one Biblical work as less inspired than another, and less the word of God, is to engage in a false problematic: it is to assume what we have just insisted can hardly be, namely that inspiration is something univocal that admits only of degrees. Rather, we must learn to think of one book as inspired differently from another, as therefore being, or mediating, the word of God in its own proper fashion. This surely should not be a difficult conclusion to accept, for it simply acknowledges the laws of human communication of which the Spirit has made use in bringing the Bible into being. No one would seriously try to pretend that Isaiah or Jeremiah is quite the same kind of literature found in 1 or 2 Maccabees. They sprang from entirely different human inspirations which were in turn subject to divine inspiration. Within the same book, even, the same kind of variety is to be expected. The inspiration of Genesis, chapters 1-11, for example, is hardly that of Genesis, chapter 36, for their literary motivation and character are distinct. In the NT the gospels obviously have a character that the epistles do not, and among the epistles the Pauline corpus possesses qualities which all the rest cannot, and should not, try to imitate. This kind of discrimination could be protracted endlessly, for every work and every part of every work has its own distinctive character and quality. For some scholars the apex of NT thinking on Jesus was achieved in the traditional and redactional process that led us to the gospel of John. For others the focus of all interest must remain earlier, on the gospel of Mark. The preferences that are expressed merely follow the lead of these work's separate inspirations and show that the literary term *gospel* is not univocal.

The Church itself, wisely, has never ruled on the relative values of the various parts of canonical Scripture. It is not that the question has not been repeatedly raised or that 'the canon within the canon' has only recently come into discussion. At the Council of Trent the decision was eventually taken to adopt the Florentine canon of 1442 (Denz 1334-36) including the so-called OT apocrypha; discussion of the question of different kinds of authority in this canon was precluded, but the conciliar acts show that Fathers were divided on the issue. The final decree defined the entire books as inspired in all their parts (Denz 1504) but did not necessarily envisage them as identical in any respect except that of their divine origin. (Equally, as we saw before, the purport of the Council of Florence's decree had been to affirm, originally against the Manichees, that both Testaments as dispensations came from the one God.)

The insinuation of value judgments based on the variety of the Biblical literature is not, as we have made clear, simply a reopening of the question of proto- as opposed to deuterocanonical books. As most everyone would agree today, the canon that was the result of early community decision cannot and ought not be reformed by us today on our assessment of relative values, even though by that foresworn criterion some deuterocanonical— or even noncanonical—books might be thought more deserving of inclusion than some of the protocanonical ones. The thing about intrinsic values is that they are both time-conditioned and subject-conditioned. This fact, which should always discourage us from hasty judgments, itself constitutes a major argument in favor of a rigorous critico-historical approach to the inspired word and against patristic-style allegorizing and accommodation to the mood of the moment. The genealogy of Keturah's children (Gen. 25. 1-4) may, when investigated by the right person, advance Biblical religion quite as much as a prayerful meditation on Ps 23. The apocalyptic that J. W. Parkes dismissed as a useless form 'which Judaism was right to reject and Christianity to forget' may, in a new generation of Biblical research, be recognized as holding a key to the true meaning of history and of the presence of God (e.g., W. Pannenberg, J. Moltmann). Such considerations forbid us from comparing one inspired text, of whatever nature, pejoratively with another, while they invite us to recognize and account for the differences in the texts, the differences which, concretely expressed, are their distinct literary characters. We return to the view of literary content as the determinant of inspiration, no longer as excluding it or limiting its exercise, even in respect to what Newman called *obiter dicta*, but as qualifying it, distinctive, somewhat that is not the inspiration of anything else.

4. In refusing to reduce the manifold phenomenon of scriptural inspiration to a single model, however, we should also want to insist that in every case it was *some*thing. We would agree with Lace that 'at some point in the process of conceiving and writing his book the scriptural writer had some unique *experience*, whether or not he was conscious of its uniqueness.' By the same token we would have to dissociate ourselves from what Martin Kähler has expressed with great eloquence:

> The great reality of the Bible has always prevented
> me from simply relegating it to the list of other prod-

ucts of literature. . . . [But] never have I been able to persuade myself of the validity of the claims out of which was spun the fabric of the ancient teaching on the "affections of Sacred Scripture,' the often treated 'ancient doctrine of inspiration.' Here again it was the reality of the Bible that stood in the way, that reality which Hamann comprehended so clearly and described in such a masterful way: its undeniable and complete accord with the nature and qualities of human literature. As far as our eye reaches—and in the NT it reaches in the part at least to the very origins—everything concerned with these writing has been entirely human. Why should it be otherwise where we lack sources of information? And if I trust that in the Bible I have God's revelation, is it not appropriate that I learn from the same Bible *how* God gives his revelation and provides for its transmission and preservation? Rather than do this, the old orthodox doctrine derived its conclusions on what must be held about the Bible not from the Bible in its factual existence but from the requirements which it itself considered it must and therefore could lay down according to its idea of what was necessary for a reliable communication of revelation. . . . It was thought that only an inerrancy in respect to every single detail would safeguard reliability in the one essential. What was forgotten in that essential itself makes up the one great exception, that it alone will not sacrifice God's grace to human error.

Similar statements could be easily gathered from other sources. On the one hand there is high, even exaggerated praise lavished on the word of the Bible, and on the other there is adamant refusal to theorize about its other than obvious human origins. An insistence on the Bible as the vehicle of God's word, and an equal insistence that it is, when all is said and done, human words, and human words only.

There is, of course, much truth in what Kähler has written, as has been brought out in the pursuit of this study. We do not have to repeat what has been said above about the apriorism involved in much of the thinking that has gone on over inspiration, drawn not from the Bible as it is but from other and often alien concepts of revelation and prophecy. The notion of inerrancy has, indeed, often been a false issue that obscured rather than revealed the truth of the Bible. God's word does come through the Bible in the words of men, indistinguishable from any other human words, clothed with all the literary characteristics proper to the time and place of origin. Nevertheless, Kähler also appears to have said something that is logically meaningless to seek a divine 'how' in what has already been defined as strictly human? If there is no more to the composition of the Scripture than he has made it out to be, then we must conclude that the Spirit has been less concerned with the Bible as such than with the use made of it. Put another way, God freely reveals Himself to the devout reader or hearer of the Biblical word, but He had no part in the literary enterprise that made the Biblical word possible as the indispensable medium of revelation. God has truly spoken and does speak through human speech, yet manifested no predisposition so to do. This supposition seems to be an absurdity. To refuse to contemplate any kind of divine intent in the writing of the Bible, through whatever laudable desire to avoid the anthropomorphisms and mythologies of the past, appears to end up by making the Bible unaccountable as an object of faith.

It may be rejoined that merely to insist that in any and every case inspiration was something, a variety of somethings, in fact, is to say very little. Nevertheless, it seems that this is what it is both necessary and adequate to say. To analyze every last line, every particle even, of the Bible and to attempt to specify the kind of divine causality that is responsible for its presence there, is an obvious impossibility. If the reduction of all inspiration to the single prophetic model proved to be unrealizable, so too did the effort to distinguish one, two, or three kinds of inspiration, which was usually the result achieved by those who were in revolt against the inadequacies of the prophetic model. It was unrealizable for the same reason, namely that it imposed on its subject arbitrary categories rather than deriving them from it, despite the fact that such a derivation was precisely what it was attempting to make. The difficulty was then, and is now, the extreme complexity of the literary situation against which the Scripture must be measured.

Some Biblical literature reflects the closely written language of immediate access to revelation and its initial assertion in theology. It abounds in what semanticists call full words, that is, words that are intended to have a meaning in themselves, even apart from context. This is the kind of literature in which the writer or his school may have been at work at language-molding (*pace* James Barr), consciously trying to put into human speech for the first time an original or continuing revelatory experience that has accounted for and identified the community. It would not be too hard to assign to the verbal inspiration of the Thomists. Not much different in nature, perhaps, might be the impulse required in the great Pauline epistles where the Apostles was at pains to elucidate and explicate what were the peculiarities of his own gospel (Gal 1.12). None of the writings in which this kind of literature is found is totally this kind of literature, to be sure. They run the gamut of every literary type that has been incorporated into the canonical writings. Perhaps at the opposite end of the spectrum we would want to place the compilations of wise saws that make up much of the book of Proverbs, or the condensation of the historical work of Jason of Cyrene which became 2 Maccabees. These writings, too, have played a part in the history of God's commerce with man and have therefore been the object of a special divine predilection, for which reason they cannot be excluded from the scope of inspiration. But it is equally clear that any divine activity in their regard has been something rather different as having accompanied a different psychology of literary composition. Between these possible extremes there may have been any number of intermediate variations.

As we have already indicated, we would not wish to classify any type of inspiration as minimal, measuring it against another, but simply insist that it is different. Neither would we allow any room for the old idea of a merely negative divine assistance, an idea that was at home only in the conception of inspiration as a means to guarantee the word's credentials as God's through its inerrancy. Instead, we should think of inspiration as always a positive divine and human interaction in which the principle of condescension has taken at face value. To conceive of an absolute inerrancy as the effect of inspiration was not really to believe that God had condescended to the human sphere but rather that He had transmuted it into something else. A human literature containing no error would indeed be a contradiction in terms, since nothing is more human than to err. Put in more vital terms, if the Scripture is a record of revelation, the acts of a history of salvation in which God has disclosed Himself by entering into the ways of man, it must be a record of trial and error as well as of achievement, for it is in this way that man learns and comes to the truth. The attempt to set up a parity between written word and Incarnate Word whereby the sinlessness of the latter seemed to require the inerrancy of the former was never really valid. Sin is in man a disorder that error is not. Lying and deceit are the proper correlatives in the equation, just as the correlative of an inerrant written word would have been an Incarnate Word who could neither suffer nor die.

When properly understood, this ancient comparison of written word with Incarnate Word can be fruitful and suggestive, as is the concept of divine condescension. But both ideas must be taken seriously, not used as the mythological language of apriori and docetic concepts of revelation. God has inspired a literature: He has infused into it His word, not by depriving it of anything human but rather by utilizing all of its many and diverse human qualities. He has accommodated Himself to the ways of man: not an ideal, unhistorical man, but man in his only historical condition, precisely the man who needs to hear the saving word of God. This is the man we find in the Bible, and thus the word has come to him.

5. The same principles may serve to justify the final quality that we would like to ascribe to inspiration, that is, what we have termed its permanent and dynamic character, responsible for the continued power that the word has to evoke response in the believer. Without denying the obvious once-for-allness involved in the literary fixation of the Bible, we must at the same time acknowledge that it is the continuous reinterpretation of the Biblical word in the life of the believing community that constitutes it effectively God's word to man. By inspiration we

should understand not only the spiritual influence responsible for the Bible's origins but also that which sustains it as a medium of speech.

Surely we can conceive of such a comprehensive inspiration as following the very rules of human communication itself; there is no need to have recourse to a mythified *verbum ex machina* or to a forced exegesis. In producing the Bible the divine condescension was not to individual authors in their singularity, but to them as members of a society, possessing not only the common traits of humanity but also those of the cultures of which they are part. In some sense, as we have seen, they were incapable even had they wished it—and the divine condescension did not wish it—of the use of words in isolation from the communities they represented. And while they wrote at one time only, those communities have endured. Without intending to oversimplify complicated histories, we must nevertheless recognize the genuine organic bonds that connect, over languages and lands, the Israel of the OT with postexilic Judaism, and those with the NT Church and with ourselves. Is it not proper to think of Biblical inspiration in this way, as continuing to reside in the belief and understanding of the communities of faith, perpetuated by the same spiritual life by which they live and following the natural laws and structures which the Spirit has assumed? If we may so think, then perhaps we have a final enunciation of what is meant by divine condescension and adoption of the words of man, in the full context of the people of God.